HILMA AF KLINT

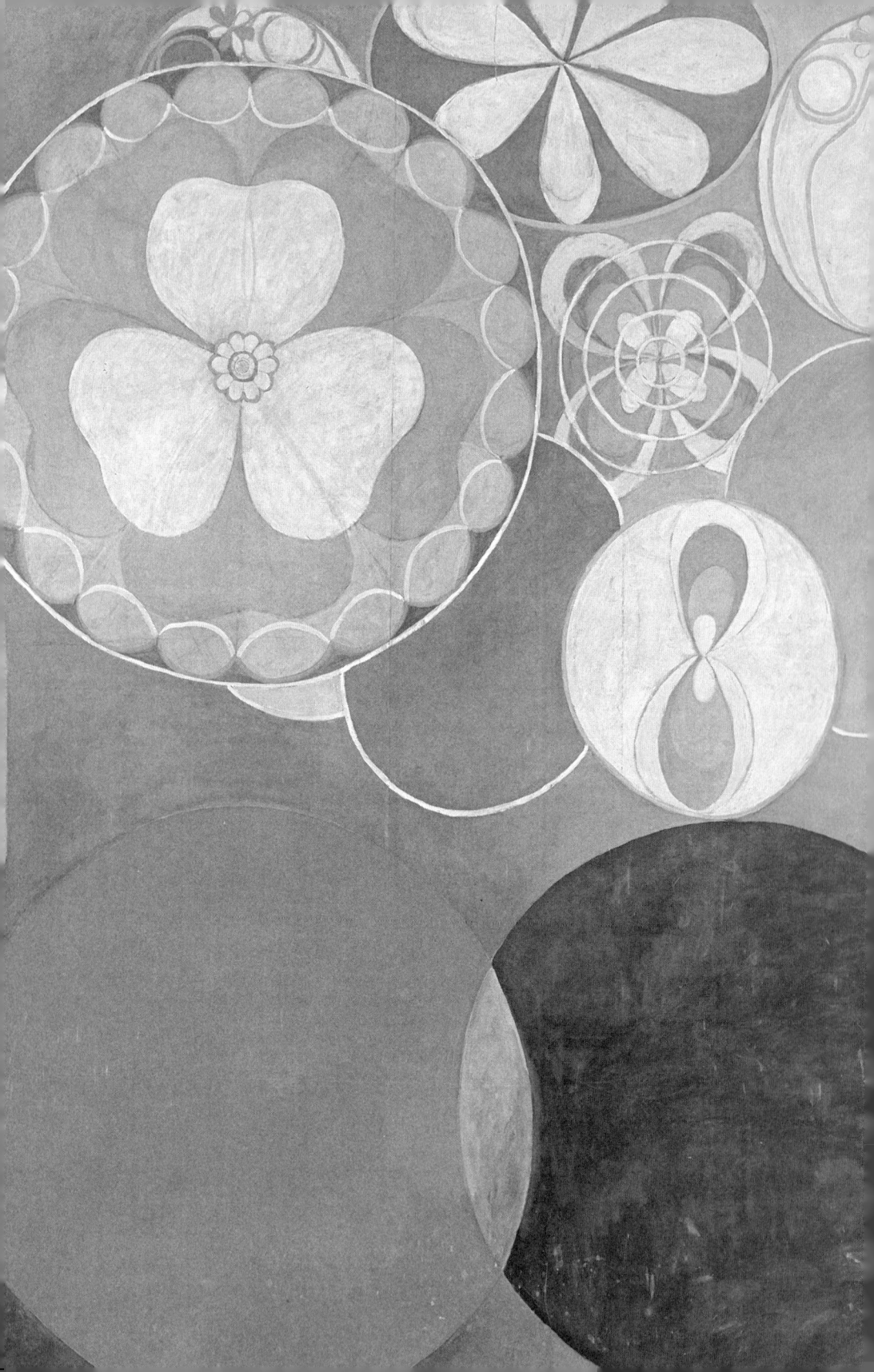

Julia Voss

TRANSLATED BY ANNE POSTEN

Hilma af Klint

A BIOGRAPHY

THE UNIVERSITY OF CHICAGO PRESS

CHICAGO AND LONDON

The University of Chicago Press, Chicago 60637
The University of Chicago Press, Ltd., London
© 2022 by The University of Chicago
Published 2022
Printed in the United States of America

31 30 29 28 27 26 25   5

ISBN-13: 978-0-226-68976-0 (cloth)
ISBN-13: 978-0-226-68993-7 (e-book)
DOI: https://doi.org/10.7208/chicago/9780226689937.001.0001

Originally published as: *Hilma af Klint. Die Menschheit in Erstaunen
versetzen* © S. Fischer Verlag GmbH, Frankfurt am Main, 2020

Published with the assistance of the Getty Grant Program.

Library of Congress Cataloging-in-Publication Data

Names: Voss, Julia, 1974– author. | Posten, Anne, translator.
Title: Hilma af Klint : a biography / Julia Voss ; translated by Anne
    Posten.
Other titles: Hilma af Klint. English (Posten)
Description: Chicago : University of Chicago Press, 2022. | Includes
    bibliographical references and index.
Identifiers: LCCN 2022020200 | ISBN 9780226689760 (cloth) |
    ISBN 9780226689937 (ebook)
Subjects: LCSH: Klint, Hilma af, 1862–1944. | Painters—Sweden—
    Biography. | Women painters—Sweden—Biography. | BISAC:
    BIOGRAPHY & AUTOBIOGRAPHY / Artists, Architects,
    Photographers | ART / European
Classification: LCC ND793.K63 V6713 2022 | DDC 759.85 [B]—dc23/
    eng/20220605
LC record available at https://lccn.loc.gov/2022020200

♾ This paper meets the requirements of ANSI/NISO Z39.48-1992
(Permanence of Paper).

Contents

A Note from the Translator, ix

Chronology, xi

Introduction / 1

PART ONE

Family, Childhood, and Youth in Stockholm

1. Mary Wollstonecraft Visits Sweden and Is Upset / 13
2. Birth / 15
3. School and Religion / 18
4. An Exhibition in London / 26
5. Bertha Valerius and the Dead / 33
6. Kerstin Cardon's Painting School / 41
7. Hermina's Death / 45

PART TWO

Study at the Academy and Independent Work

1. The Academy / 51
2. Guardian Spirit / 55
3. The Prize / 60
4. Anna Cassel / 63
5. "My First Experience with Mediumship" / 69
6. The Young Artist / 70
7. Dr. Helleday and Love / 77
8. The Five / 84

9. Art from the Orient / 94
10. Rose and Cross / 99
11. At the Veterinary Institute / 102
12. Children's Books and Decorative Art / 109
13. Italy / 113
14. Genius / 118

PART THREE

Paintings for the Temple

1. Old Images / 123
2. Revolution / 127
3. Primordial Chaos / 133
4. Eros / 137
5. Medium / 138
6. The Ten Largest / 142
7. "I Was the Instrument of Ecstasy" / 148
8. Rudolf Steiner Visits Sweden / 154
9. The Young Ones / 161
10. Sigrid Lancén / 162
11. The Association of Swedish Women Artists / 166
12. Frank Heyman / 171
13. Island Kingdom in Mälaren / 175
14. First Exhibition with the Theosophists / 182
15. Tree of Knowledge / 187
16. The Kiss / 189
17. Singoalla / 192
18. The Baltic Exhibition / 194
19. War / 197
20. Saint George / 200
21. Kandinsky in Stockholm / 203
22. Parsifal and Atom / 207
23. The Studio on Munsö / 212
24. Thomasine Anderson / 214

PART FOUR

Dornach, Amsterdam, and London

1. The Suitcase Museum / 223
2. Flowers, Mosses, and Lichens / 225
3. First Visit to the Goetheanum / 228
4. "Belongs to the Astral World According to Doctor Steiner" / 232
5. The Fire and the Letter / 236
6. Amsterdam / 240
7. London / 244

PART FIVE

Temple and Later Years

1. The Temple and the Spiral / 255
2. +x / 262
3. A Temple in New York / 264
4. The London Blitz / 268
5. Future Woman / 272
6. National Socialism / 278
7. Lecture in Stockholm / 284
8. "Degenerate" Art in Germany and Abstract Art in New York / 286
9. Tyra Kleen and the Plan for a Museum / 290
10 Last Months / 299
11. Conclusion / 303

Afterword by Johan af Klint, 309
Afterword by Ulrika af Klint, 311
Appendix 1. Hilma af Klint's Travels and Places of Residence, 313
Appendix 2. The Library of Hilma af Klint, 315
Acknowledgments, 324   Illustration Sources, 328
Notes, 329   Bibliography, 379   Index, 401

COLOR GALLERIES FOLLOW PAGES 120 AND 280.

A Note from the Translator

Hilma af Klint: A Biography was originally published in German (*Hilma af Klint: Die Menschheit in Erstaunen versetzen*) in 2020 by S. Fischer Verlag. Since then, more information about the artist's life and work has come to light. This English-language version reflects the new research. The text has also been modestly revised in collaboration with the author to address the needs of Anglophone readers.

Voss draws extensively on Hilma af Klint's personal notebooks, most of which were written in Swedish. Where quotes appear in the German edition, the translations are Voss's own. I have translated these quotes from Voss's translations, often in consultation with her. Af Klint's writing is usually grammatically simple and direct, but since her notebooks are primarily a record of her spiritual experiences, the content and references are sometimes obscure. Many of the messages af Klint received from the spiritual world were unclear even to her and were simply recorded as received. For this reason I have endeavored to translate the primary sources as lightly and directly as possible. On a practical level, most Swedish proper nouns have been translated after an initial mention of the original. Where the author has quoted the German translation of works originally written in English, the original has been drawn from and added to the bibliography. Likewise when she quotes from German works where an English version already exists, the existing translation has been used and added to the bibliography.

Chronology

1862. Hilma af Klint is born on October 26 at the Karlberg Palace in Solna outside Stockholm.

1879. Participates in her first séances, probably in the circle of painter, photographer, and medium Bertha Valerius. Studies at the Technical School and meets Anna Cassel, who also studies art. Af Klint also takes courses at Kerstin Cardon's private art school.

1880. Her sister Hermina dies at the age of ten.

1882–1888. Studies at the Royal Academy of Fine Arts in Stockholm.

1886–1914. Shows conventional paintings in more than two dozen exhibitions, most organized by the Swedish General Art Association (Sveriges Allmänna Konstförening).

1888. Awarded a prize by the Academy for painting from the human model, probably for her oil painting *Andromeda at the Sea*, which she submitted to the Academy's competition on that mythological topic.

1888–1908. Participates regularly in group exhibitions and travels to Germany, Norway, Holland, Belgium, and Italy.

1891. Receives messages from spiritual beings for the first time herself.

1896. Becomes a member of the Edelweiss Society (Edelweiss-förbundet). During a séance, the spiritualist group The Five (De Fem) is founded, comprising Sigrid Hedman, Cornelia Cederberg, Mathilda Nilsson, Anna Cassel, and af Klint. Their meetings are recorded in notebooks with texts and automatic drawings.

1898. Her father, Victor af Klint, dies.

1899. Moves with her mother, Mathilda af Klint, to Brahegatan 52 in Stockholm.

1900–1901. Together with Anna Cassel, draws illustrations for a book on horse surgery written by John Vennerholm, director of the Veterinary Institute in Stockholm.

1902–1908. Rents a studio at Hamngatan 9.

1903. Travels to Germany with Anna Cassel and most likely to Italy on the same trip.

1904. First receives predictions from the spiritual being Ananda about the execution of "astral paintings." Joins the Theosophical Society in May.

1906. In January the spiritual being Amaliel offers her a commission, which she accepts immediately. After a period of preparation, in November she commences the cycle *Paintings for the Temple* with its first series, *Primordial Chaos*.

1907. Paints the series *Eros*, *The Large Figure Paintings*, and *The Ten Largest*. Works also in a shared large studio at Hamngatan 5, above Blanch's Café. The Five undergoes a crisis and dissolves in early 1908. A group of thirteen emerges over the years.

1908. Paints three more series, including *Evolution*. By April the first section of *Paintings for the Temple* comprises 111 pictures. Her mother goes blind, and af Klint gives up her studio. Meets Rudolf Steiner in Sweden for the first time at his lecture about his new Rosicrucian teachings in March 1908. Starts to develop a lifelong interest in Rudolf Steiner's teachings.

1908–1912. Takes a four-year break from the commission *Paintings for the Temple*.

1910. Probably in January 1910 shows Rudolf Steiner works belonging to *Paintings for the Temple*. Steiner lectures in Stockholm January 3–15, including on the Gospel of John. Af Klint joins the Association of Swedish Women Artists (Föreningen Svenska Konstnärinnor) and is the secretary until April 22, 1911. She paints portraits of physicist Knut Ångström and linguist Johan August Lundell and exhibits a conventional painting in the Norrköping Exhibition of 1910.

1912. Resumes work on *Paintings for the Temple* with preparatory studies and on *A Female Series*. Attends the Pentecost

conference of the Theosophical Society in Norrköping May
28–30, where Rudolf Steiner lectures. By the end of the year
Steiner is expelled from the Theosophical Society and in early
1913 founds the Anthroposophical Society.

1913. Buys the lake house Furuheim on the island of Munsö.
Paints the series *US* and starts the series *Tree of Knowledge*.
Exhibits seventeen spiritual pictures in an art exhibition
organized by the Theosophical Society in Stockholm in June,
in which Anna Cassel also participates.

1914. Exhibits an academic painting in the Baltic Exhibition in
Malmö. The First World War breaks out, and af Klint starts
her series *The Swan*. Rents various studios in Stockholm,
including at Eriksbergsgatan (1914–15) and at Ynglingagatan
(1915–16).

1915. Finishes *Tree of Knowledge* and *The Swan*. Her series *The
Dove* follows, then *Altarpieces*, completing the cycle *Paintings
for the Temple*, which now comprises 193 paintings.

1916. Wassily Kandinsky comes to Stockholm and exhibits. Af
Klint creates the series *Parsifal*.

1917. Construction of the studio house on Munsö is completed.
Af Klint paints the series *The Atom*. In a two-thousand-page
volume, *Studies of the Life of the Soul* (*Studier över Själslivet*),
she dictates her thoughts about the spiritual life.

1918. Moves to Munsö together with her mother and the nurse
Thomasine Anderson, who becomes her lifelong friend and
partner.

1919. Starts the creation of "Flowers, Mosses, and Lichen" in collaboration with Thomasine Anderson in German.

1920. Her mother dies. She creates *Series II*, a group of works on
different world religions. In October she takes her first trip
to Dornach, Switzerland, together with Thomasine Anderson—by 1930 they will have made eight more such journeys.
Af Klint becomes a lifelong member of the Anthroposophical
Society on October 20. During one stay in Dornach, she shows
the ten "Blue books" to Rudolf Steiner and notes down his

comments. The books contain watercolor miniatures of all her works from *Paintings for the Temple*, each paired in most books with a black-and-white photograph of the painting.

1922. From now on, paints almost exclusively in watercolor using the wet-on-wet technique, creating more than four hundred works by 1941. On New Year's Eve the Goetheanum in Dornach burns down.

1924. Writes to Rudolf Steiner on April 24, requesting advice on where her paintings could be of use. According to her notes for a lecture at the Anthroposophical Society in Stockholm on December 9, 1924, Steiner advises her not to destroy the paintings, that they could be of use. Steiner dies in spring 1925.

1926. Moves to Uppsala with Thomasine Anderson. Starts editing and revising her old notebooks, partly in collaboration with Anna Cassel.

1927. Travels to Amsterdam in November. Donates her notebook "Flowers, Mosses, and Lichen" and the series *Tree of Knowledge* to the Goetheanum in Dornach.

1928. Travels to London in July and exhibits pictures from *Paintings for the Temple* at the World Conference on Spiritual Science, organized by the English Anthroposophical Society.

1931. Develops sketches for a spiral-shaped temple building intended for the island of Ven in Öresund. Over the years many more sketches and notes follow for the project. Moves to Helsingborg in southern Sweden with Thomasine Anderson.

1932. Marks many notebooks, including the "Blue Books" that contain miniatures of *Paintings for the Temple*, with the symbol "+x," indicating these may not be viewed until twenty years after her death. Writes about her plan to construct "a museum to show what lies behind the forces of matter" and paints the watercolors *A Map—Great Britain/The Blitz* and *The Outbreak of War in Spain and the Naval Battles in the Mediterranean*.

1934. Paints the thought-forms of spiritual beings Ananda, Gregor, Georg, and Amaliel. Moves to Lund with Thomasine Anderson.

1937. Lectures at the Anthroposophical Society in Stockholm on April 16. Argues for the legitimacy of her mediumistic method and insists that it is compatible with Steiner's teaching. Anna Cassel dies.

1938. Erik af Klint (1901–81) visits her on August 20. She shows him *Paintings for the Temple* and her other works in the studio on Munsö and explains their meaning to him.

1940. Thomasine Anderson dies.

1943. Declines an offer by artist Tyra Kleen to keep *Paintings for the Temple* in a new building of the Protestant Sigtuna Foundation. "To put it into hands of people not Anthroposophically inclined" would not be possible, she writes to Kleen. Af Klint is called a "mystic" by her spiritual ambassadors.

1944. In August moves in with her cousin Hedvig af Klint in Djursholm-Ösby, a suburb of Stockholm. Dies on October 21 after a streetcar accident. Her nephew Erik af Klint inherits her paintings, notebooks, and papers, around 1,300 pictures and 124 notebooks of more than 26,000 handwritten and typed pages.

Introduction

Around the age of seventy, Hilma af Klint began to separate the documents and artworks she would preserve from those she would destroy. In this she was no different from many artists, but in other ways she was, and she knew it. Af Klint was not just an artist. She was also a mystic who said that her most powerful, abstract works were painted under the direction of higher spirits communicating from the astral plane. Since the late nineteenth century, an array of spiritualist teachings had been revolutionizing religious understanding the world over. For example, Theosophy, among the most popular, sought to reconcile the spirit with the natural and scientific worlds, and many artists embraced it: Kandinsky, Mondrian, Kupka, and Arthur Dove all studied Theosophy; none of them, however, ever publicly suggested their canvases were the expressions of any consciousness other than their own. Realizing the world was not yet ready for what she had created and what motivated it, in 1932 af Klint wrote that none of her paintings or drawings should be shown until twenty years after her death.[1]

Thus she catapulted her life's work into the future, out of the first half of the twentieth century into the second, safe from the judgment of her contemporaries. They were not to have the last word.

Who was this woman who sent her work to the future in a time capsule, putting her faith in generations to come? When she died, af Klint left behind more than 26,000 pages of text and 1,300 paintings, a formidable legacy. One can see from this material how, over and over again, she broke every rule society set for her—as an art student at the Royal Academy in Stockholm, as a woman at the turn of the twentieth century, and as a modern artist. It is widely accepted now that well before painters like Wassily Kandinsky or Kazimir Malevich claimed to have invented abstraction, she had been painting in that mode for several years—first in small formats and then on an enormous scale. When she began to paint this way, she was forty-four years old. It was November 1906. "The experiments I have undertaken," she wrote as she set off on this new path, "will astound humanity."[2]

Any memory of these works faded after she died, and it took decades to bring them back to light. Why so long? The fact is that profound changes in the fine arts often meet with vehement rejection, and the resistance to af Klint's reappraisal was evident the first time her work was presented to a wide audience. In 1986, more than forty years after her death, the Los Angeles County Museum of Art organized an exhibition titled *The Spiritual in Art: Abstract Painting, 1890–1985*, which offered a new perspective on the history of nonrepresentational art. In the catalogue and exhibition, a relationship was suggested between abstraction and the various spiritual movements that spread through the Western world around the turn of the twentieth century. It was a major show, and landmark works of abstraction were loaned by museums in Munich, Paris, Moscow, and New York.

Af Klint's paintings came crashing into this venerable canon like a meteor. Suddenly her huge canvases were hanging next to those of recognized modernist masters. The unknown Swedish woman seemed to come out of nowhere, and the reception was largely negative.[3] The American critic Hilton Kramer wrote: "Hilma af Klint's paintings are essentially colored diagrams. To accord them a place of honor alongside the work of Kandinsky, Mondrian, Malevich, and Kupka... is absurd. Af Klint is simply not an artist in their class and—dare one say it?—would never have been given this inflated treatment if she had not been a woman."[4] Kramer wasn't the only person who thought so. Silence fell again on the subject of Hilma af Klint.

It took two more decades before the Moderna Museet in Stockholm mounted a large-scale offensive meant to secure a place for af Klint in the modernist canon. In 2013 the institution sponsored *Pioneer of Abstraction*, the largest exhibition of her work to that point, and sent the show on tour through Europe.[5] Excitement began to gather around the artist, and yet again the paintings met with resistance. The objections were phrased more carefully this time, but they came from prominent quarters. Curator Leah Dickerman of the Museum of Modern Art in New York wrote: "[Af Klint] painted in isolation and did not exhibit her works, nor did she participate in public discussions of that time. I find what she did absolutely fascinating, but am not even sure she saw her paintings as art works."[6] It took a third try for the story to take a new turn. The 2018 show at the Solomon R. Guggenheim Museum in New York, *Hilma af Klint: Paintings for the Future*, broke all attendance records, attracting more than 600,000 visitors—more than any exhibition since the museum's founding. The catalogue became a best seller. The *New York Times* ran a piece called "Hilma Who? No More!"[7] Since October 2019, the Guggenheim has continued to show several of her paintings. The art history outsider has become a star.

It is possible that af Klint would have remained a footnote to the history of modern art, at least a while longer, if the Guggenheim had not devoted their entire building to the show, thereby creating a blockbuster—or if the Axel and Margaret Ax:son Johnson Foundation had not advocated tirelessly for the academic reappraisal of the artist's work, organizing scholarly conferences to accompany exhibitions.[8]

It would have pleased the artist to know how excited visitors were to view her work at the Guggenheim, sometimes waiting for hours in a long line circling the block to gain admission. They shared and circulated her extraordinary images across countless networks, and beyond the United States, triggering an avalanche of questions: What motivated the artist? What did she want to achieve? Who writes art history? Who gets to be in a canon and who doesn't, and why?

In this book, I explore these and many more questions as I attempt to shine a light into corners of af Klint's life that she systematically left in the dark. What she bequeathed to posterity is like a large house with countless rooms, chambers, and hallways. Hilma allowed some of the rooms to remain brightly illuminated, whereas in others she turned off the light, and sometimes even locked the door and threw away the key. The earliest document she left us dates from 1879, when she was seventeen years old. Her last notes are from 1944, the year she died at nearly eighty-two.

It is an exceptional stroke of luck that af Klint's artistic oeuvre has been almost completely preserved. The traces of artists who had only modest success during their lifetimes tend to disappear once they are dead and are then nearly impossible to recover. Af Klint took early action to prevent this from happening, but she never would have succeeded had her principal heir, her nephew Erik af Klint (1901–81), not preserved her work. Following her instructions he stored the paintings and notebooks in the attic of the apartment building where he lived in Stockholm. There they remained for more than two decades, until 1966, when the boxes were opened and the canvases unrolled and photographed. Six years later Erik af Klint founded the Stiftung Hilma af Klints Verk, and the Anthroposophical Society in Sweden provided space to store the estate. In 1979 Gustaf af Klint, Erik's eldest son, took over management of the foundation. Johan af Klint, the younger brother, followed in 2011 and saw to it that his great-aunt's estate was transferred to professional museum storage in 2017.[9] Today, the foundation is headed by Ulrika af Klint, Gustaf af Klint's daughter.

When I first visited the archive with Johan af Klint, I met with a surprise. I had traveled there planning to write a biography and hoping to close a few gaps in the literature. Instead I found documents that didn't at all fit with what I believed I knew about the artist. The more research I did, the clearer it became that much of the art-historical literature was based on assumption, and several claims I had taken for fact were simply not true. It became clear that I too had been subscribing to a fallacy that had persisted over the years in books, articles, and catalogues about the artist.[10] In many respects, therefore, I had to start over from zero. I learned Swedish and made this biography my primary occupation.

The Hilma af Klint I ultimately discovered in the archive was hidden beneath layers of obfuscation. The first layer was the doing of the artist herself, as archivist and editor of her own writings. Considering her work to be far more important than she was, Hilma allowed many facts of her private life to disappear. The archive contained little that offered a sense of her daily life—no diaries, only a few letters. The more than one hundred notebooks she saved primarily record her insights into higher worlds and rarely allow conclusions to be drawn about other matters, such as goings-on in Stockholm, on the island of Munsö, or in other places where the artist spent time. It was more important to her to make space for the visions and voices that accompanied her and that, she was convinced, gave her access to higher spiritual planes. As a result, her archive presents a rather impersonal facade.

The rare self-portrait included in this book is an exception (see plate 1). As far as we know, it is the only surviving likeness Hilma made of herself. That it bears no date is telling.[11] Going about her day in a plain dark dress, af Klint had little regard for her appearance, and capturing it for its own sake would have struck her as a waste of time. The self-portrait therefore does not depict her in ordinary clothes, but rather during a séance, wearing a cloak, in front of an atmospheric blue background. Presumably she painted the watercolor as a present for one of the friends who played a major role in her life and without whom everything would have gone quite differently.

The second barrier to knowing Hilma derives from a welter of stereotypes and biased historical expectations of women. She is hardly the only female artist to have dismissed the idea of chronicling her own life. It's the art that matters, many say even today, and the formalist methods of art history reinforce this. The consequence can be an underestimation of both the person and the work, especially if the reception during an artist's life was negligible. Without context, an oeuvre can shrink; it becomes smaller and smaller until it seems narrow and trivial.

The result is that Hilma's early abstract painting is often treated as a stroke of luck, accidental and unplanned. In contrast, the work of her male contemporaries is generally considered the product of prodigious skill and intellect. Af Klint has often been explained as a "crazy woman" by those who haven't troubled themselves to investigate further. This, as artist Rebecca H. Quaytman notes, was the easiest way to dismiss her. Quaytman also astutely points out that af Klint's works were long considered "worthless" in the literal sense, because they were not traded on the art market.[12]

My research has shown that many beliefs about af Klint are false and need to be dispelled from the outset. Here, in brief, are five important correctives:

1. HILMA AF KLINT EXHIBITED HER ABSTRACT PAINTINGS

One of the most persistent myths is that the paintings were meant to be "secret" and af Klint did not show them during her lifetime. The story can be traced to the 1988 text "Hilma af Klint's Secret Paintings."[13] The author, Åke Fant, was a Swedish Anthroposophist and art historian, and a great deal of our knowledge about af Klint derives from his research. But Fant was wrong on this crucial point. Af Klint did not keep her paintings secret. She was convinced that the paintings she started to make in 1906 were the best work she'd ever done, and she spent years looking for opportunities to show them. The first chance came in 1913 in Stockholm, in a group exhibition organized by the Theosophical Society, of which she was a member.[14] In 1928 she finally succeeded, after many attempts, in organizing her own exhibition in London. The hostile reactions the paintings drew prompted her to rethink her strategy. As mentioned, she reached the decision that her works were not to be shown until twenty years after her death. The exhibitions in Stockholm and London and their circumstances are described in this book.[15]

Two picture cycles that recently appeared on the art market also demonstrate that af Klint wanted to find an audience for her works. In 2021–22, David Zwirner Gallery in New York exhibited two versions of the *Tree of Knowledge* series, created in 1913–15. Af Klint gave one version to the Goetheanum in Dornach, Switzerland, around 1927, hoping that it would be exhibited there, though this never happened. It took nearly a century for that version of the *Tree of Knowledge* to become accessible to the public after the series was acquired by Glenstone, a private museum in Potomac, Maryland.[16]

2. HILMA AF KLINT TRAVELED

The literature, almost without exception, describes af Klint as an artist who rarely left Sweden and had little interest in the history of her profession.[17] Previous writers have recounted only her trips to Dornach, Switzerland, to visit Rudolf Steiner's Goetheanum, the center of Anthroposophy. Such accounts are grossly incomplete. In addition to London, af Klint visited Norway, Germany, Holland, and Belgium. She also traveled to Italy to see the great masterpieces of the Renaissance, which had a lasting impact on her work. Anyone who wants to understand her paintings must accompany her on these journeys and into the museums and churches she visited. Her itineraries are offered here for the first time.

3. HILMA AF KLINT DEVELOPED HER OWN SPIRITUAL UNDERSTANDING

A widely circulated anecdote about af Klint involves the Austrian Rudolf Steiner, the founder of Anthroposophy. According to the story, Steiner visited her studio in Stockholm in 1908. Af Klint did ask him to come—that much is true. It is alleged that Steiner sharply criticized the work and told her that her paintings wouldn't be understood for another fifty years. Yet there is no mention of the fierce onsite criticism or of Steiner's prediction in the artist's notebooks.

I explore other possibilities of when the meeting happened and how it might have gone, but mainly it is important to stress that af Klint cannot be reduced to any of the spiritual doctrines that interested her. Early on, she seems to have been influenced by the Rosicrucians; then she joined the Stockholm Theosophical Society in 1904, and later the Anthroposophists. But primarily the artist developed her own spiritual cosmology, which evolved throughout her life.[18] She confronted life's major questions with surprising texts and images. It is perfectly consequent, then, that her spiritual perspective should be at the center of our investigations into her life and her work.

4. HILMA AF KLINT HAD AN UNUSUALLY BROAD EDUCATION IN THE SCIENCES

This book is the first to address af Klint's scientific drawings from the turn of the twentieth century, which are housed in the Veterinary Museum in Skara, Sweden. She was commissioned in 1900 to illustrate a handbook on horse surgery. A keen interest in science pervades her many drawings, and several series are named for major discoveries of the time, such as the 1908 series *Evolution* and 1917's *Atom*. The artist saw no contradiction in her devotion to both science and spirituality. She was anything but one-sided, and her holistic worldview is at the heart of this biography.

5. HILMA AF KLINT INTENDED HER ART TO INSPIRE A SOCIAL REVOLUTION

Af Klint never realized one of her most ambitious ideas. She wanted us to view her paintings in a spiraling multistory building, proceeding all the way up to an observatory at the top. She called her sketches for this project "Designs for a Temple."

The exhibition that opened in fall 2018 at the Guggenheim Museum's famous Frank Lloyd Wright building came closer to fulfilling her vision than anything had before. Af Klint wanted a spiral-shaped building—and thanks to the Guggenheim, her works were shown in one.

Yet the temple building was only part of it. She also dreamed of a departure from the art world as we know it. She wasn't eager merely for a place in the history of painting. Her works, she believed, could help us leave behind everything that makes the world small and rigid: entrenched thought patterns and systems of order, categories of sex and class, materialism and capitalism, the binary view of an Orient and an Occident, and the distinction between art and life.

Stop. At this point, af Klint would raise an objection: too much has already been written about her as an individual. Despite what people think, she would insist she wasn't alone: she was moved by what she saw as contact with higher beings, and there were two great loves in her life—the artist Anna Cassel and the nurse Thomasine Anderson. Without these women, the story told here would have been unthinkable. Without love, af Klint was convinced, there could be no insight. To achieve wisdom, she wrote in December 1919, "two individuals must travel together, for the path makes it impossible for one person to proceed alone."[19]

She was sure we would read these words one day.

PART ONE

Family, Childhood, and Youth in Stockholm

Mary Wollstonecraft
Visits Sweden and Is Upset

What kind of world was Hilma af Klint born into in 1862? Which paths were set, which doors were closed, and which were open to a young girl? When the English feminist Mary Wollstonecraft visited Sweden at the end of the eighteenth century, she was appalled by what she saw. She already considered the treatment of women and girls in England and France to be deplorable, but Sweden took the cake. The Nordic country struck her as impossibly backward, and in her letters home she described, with equal parts astonishment and fury, "how far the Swedes are from having a just conception of rational equality."[1] Swedish society was marked by dramatic class differences, she noted. Everyone took out the indignities that they themselves had suffered on the class beneath them. In particular, "the men stand up for the dignity of man by oppressing the women."[2]

Nor did Wollstonecraft find any evidence of cultural refinement. "[A]ll the men of consequence," she wrote, had "a fondness for social pleasures" and drinking too much brandy. The long time spent sitting at tables seemed all the more incomprehensible to the Englishwoman as she considered Swedish cuisine inedible: "Their tables, like their compliments, seem equally a caricature of the French. The dishes are composed . . . of a variety of mixtures to destroy the native taste of the food without being as relishing. Spices and sugar are put into everything, even into the bread."[3]

What bearing might the Sweden that had so stunned Wollstonecraft have had on Hilma af Klint, born nearly seventy years later? Did it affect her path and the world she experienced? It wasn't until 1971 that an American art historian demonstrated that, even into the twentieth century, the course of an artist's career was inescapably determined by such indelible factors as gender. In her now-famous essay "Why Have There Been No Great Women Artists?" Linda Nochlin challenged ideas that had endured for centuries, such as the assumption that talent was the most important requirement for making great art and the logical fallacy that "there are no great women artists because women are incapable of greatness."[4] How could this be? Nochlin wondered. The answer, she proposed, was institutional. Even into the twentieth century, female artists weren't encouraged to take their craft seriously and in many countries weren't allowed to attend art school, which prevented them from developing the qualifications to win major commissions. A female artist, Nochlin polemicized, had no better chance of greatness than a tennis player who grew up at the North Pole.[5] Anyone who wanted to become someone had to first be white, male, and middle-class. Only then was talent pressed into service.

Nochlin also examined class in her essay. She explained that for members of the European nobility, it was nearly impossible to pursue an artistic career: this was a matter not of talent but of upbringing. It was considered improper for an aristocrat to do more than dabble in art, let alone make a living from it. It was thus perfectly consequent that the nobility had produced few artists of note.

Seventy years after Wollstonecraft's visit, the Sweden that Hilma af Klint was born into was still largely impoverished, and people's beliefs were monitored by an authoritarian state church. Sweden's achievements as a modern social state lay far in the future. The young Hilma would have been no more able to imagine Sweden's transformation into one of the richest and most progressive countries in the world than Mary Wollstonecraft had been. Nochlin herself would likely have been intrigued had she learned of the Swedish artist while working on her essay.[6] The painter fulfilled two of Nochlin's criteria for exclusion from artistic success: she was a woman and an aristocrat, her status designated by the two letters between her first and last names—*af* is the Swedish equivalent of the German *von*, a marker of nobility.

Yet af Klint managed to thrive as an artist, and to understand why we must look to her family and background. To what degree was she being carried along by a current, and to what degree did she have to fight against it? What did it mean to be female and noble in Sweden? What did it mean to belong to the af Klint family?

[2]

Birth

Hilma af Klint was born on October 26, 1862, in a rather austere location: the barracks of a military academy in northwest Stockholm. Housed in a former palace, the Military Academy Karlberg had once been run by Erik af Klint (1732–1812), Hilma's great-grandfather and the first seafarer of the family. His male descendants also served as officers and directors of the academy: Hilma's grandfather Gustaf (fig. 1) and then her father, Victor (1822–98). Stockholm was the family's primary residence, though they spent summers on the island of Adelsö, on the estates of Hanmora and Tofta.

Since home births were common, it is reasonable to assume that Hilma's mother, Mathilda, gave birth in the barracks. Mathilda af Klint (1832–1920) was born Mathilda Sontag; her family came from Finland where they had belonged to the Swedish upper class.

Hilma was the fourth child in the family (fig. 2). The firstborn, Anna, died before she reached the age of two. Then came a son, Gustaf (1858–1927), named after his grandfather, and a daughter, Ida (1860–1938). They were ages four and two, respectively, when Hilma was born. Another girl, named Hermina (1870–80), would be born eight years later.

Hilma's first six years were spent in the decidedly masculine environment of the military school. Each day she and her sister Ida would watch ships sailing in and out of the harbor. They were steeped in the knowledge and terminology of the nautical life, as all

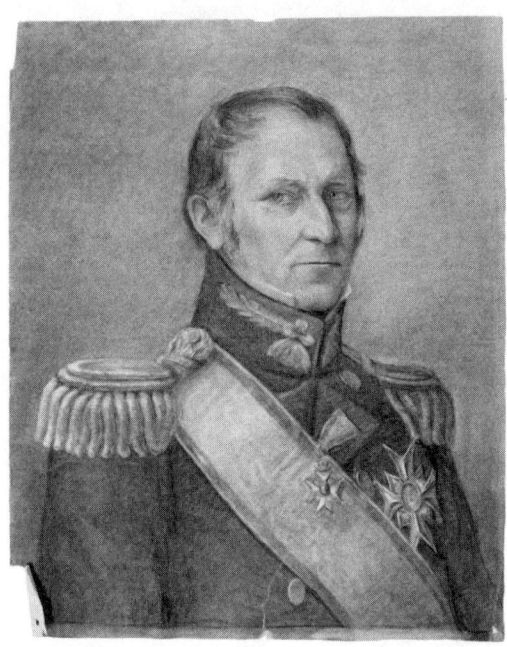

1. *Gustaf af Klint* (1771–1840), charcoal and chalk on paper, 59 x 48 cm,
Stiftelsen Hilma af Klints Verk, HaK 1222.

the af Klints had been since Erik had joined the navy when he was
eighteen. Prior to that, the Klint family had belonged to the bourgeoisie, the men working as farmers, civil servants, tax collectors,
pastors, magistrates, and notaries, with little chance of upward
mobility. In 1790, however, King Gustav III elevated the family to
the nobility in gratitude to Erik and his son, Gustaf Klint (1771–
1840), for their considerable contributions to the Battle of Vyborg
Bay, fought against Russia. The family was thereafter known as the
af Klints.

The stature the af Klint family came to enjoy was based not only
on their military service but on their fine reputation as cartographers, a legacy we can trace to Erik and Gustaf, who had surveyed
the Swedish coastline at the behest of the king. After the king's
death, Gustaf continued making maps on his own and without
payment or official support.[1] Charts of the North and Baltic Seas

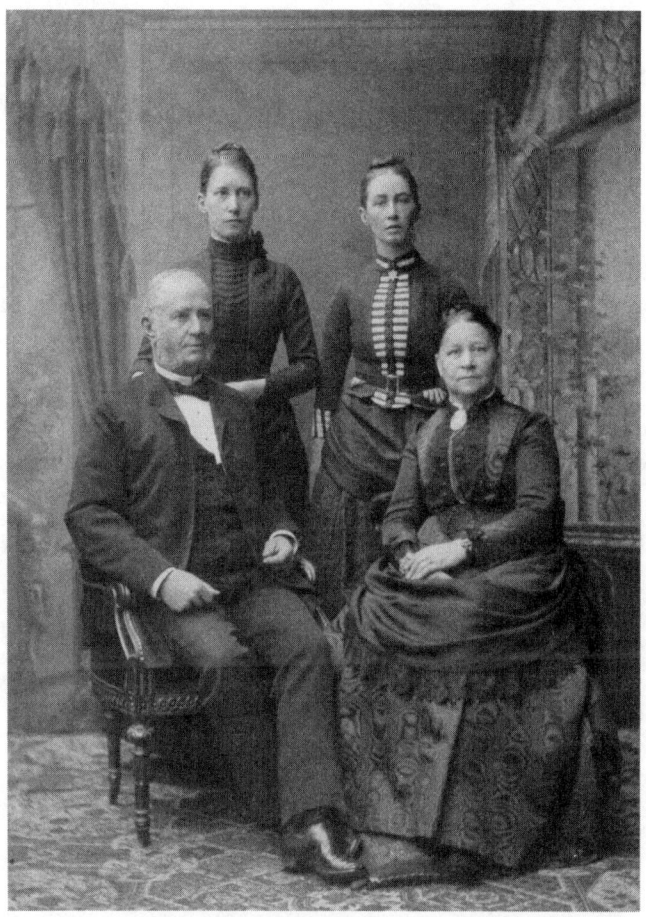

2. *Front row:* Victor and Mathilda af Klint. *Behind them:* their daughters Ida (*left*) and Hilma, ca. 1880. Note the nautical motif in Hilma's dress.

and a map of the Norwegian coastline as well as most of the larger Swedish lakes and various foreign bodies of water constituted his life's work.

Had Hilma been born a boy, she would have become an officer in the Swedish navy like her father, grandfather, and great-grandfather as well as her brother. Years later Hilma would paint a portrait of her father, Victor, as a gaunt man with friendly eyes, a high forehead, and sideburns. His descendants described him as a man who loved nature. In his free time, he played the violin and built miniature boats out of wood.[2]

Even though a naval career was out of the question for Hilma, nautical tradition was part of family life, and its influence can be seen in her work. In her notebooks, she recorded the routes of her journeys in the form of little maps. In 1906, the same period when she began work on the cycle *Paintings for the Temple*, she made an extensive inventory of lighthouses around the world. The nautical influence can also be seen in her paintings, above all in *The Ten Largest*, where cartographic symbols like those used by her fore-fathers appear.[3] Dashed white lines flit through the paintings of 1907, outlining hidden forms as if they were underwater reefs (see plate 2).

Making the invisible visible. This was to become a leitmotif in af Klint's work, and it is also a notable quality of nautical charts. Unlike land maps, nautical charts mainly depict underwater terri-tories that humans cannot access. Metaphorically, nautical charts work like hydraulic lifts, cranking the ocean floor up to the sur-face where it can be seen. Reefs, sandbars, rocks, and cliffs—all the things that lie under the surface—are made visible.

[3]

School and Religion

Hilma af Klint was six years old when her family moved out of the barracks and into an apartment in a large house on Norrtullsgatan, a long street that ran through the modern, bourgeois district of Vasastaden.[1] Victor continued to work at the military academy in Karlberg Palace, which was within walking distance of the apart-ment.

The population of Stockholm was barely 140,000—not much compared with Berlin, Paris, or London. But the city was growing quickly. People were moving from the countryside into the city to look for work in the factories. In the north provinces, people were starving. The cold and drought had led to crop failures, food became scarce for the people and their livestock, and prices soared. The newspapers sent illustrators to document the crisis. The papers were filled with sad sketches of emaciated families, a dying mother with her children, for example, all as thin as skeletons. It was rare in those days for newspapers to print photographs.

On Sundays, like most Swedes, the af Klints went to church. On religious holidays, they usually went down to the water and across to Stadsholmen, one of the islands of Stockholm's famous archipelago, where the royal palace and the cathedral, the Church of St. Nicholas, are located. Each visit was a trip back to the late Middle Ages, when the stucco church with its five aisles had been built. On the outside, the building looked broader than it was high, a fairly unspectacular house of worship.

But when the af Klint family walked through the heavy cathedral doors into the nave, they were met by an enormous wooden statue of Saint George, who still towers above the many rows of pews, swinging his huge sword over the heads of the faithful (fig. 3). He has reached the decisive moment in his fight against the powers of darkness, represented by a dragon, which lies on the ground, about to receive the death blow. Yet still the monster turns, its tongue shooting from its mouth like a jet of flame. George's wide-eyed horse lifts its foreleg to avoid the sword. The armor of horse and rider is coated in gold leaf. Created by the Lübeck-born sculptor Bernt Notke, the statue survived the iconoclasm of the Reformation only because Swedish Lutherans were more moderate than their Calvinist counterparts.[2]

The sculpture of Saint George in the cathedral made a great impression on Hilma and would later figure importantly in her paintings and texts (see plates 34 and 35). The knight with the pale, gentle face would become the artist's alter ego. When did she first sense the connection? When did she discover that George could help her to better understand herself and the uncommon gifts she possessed?

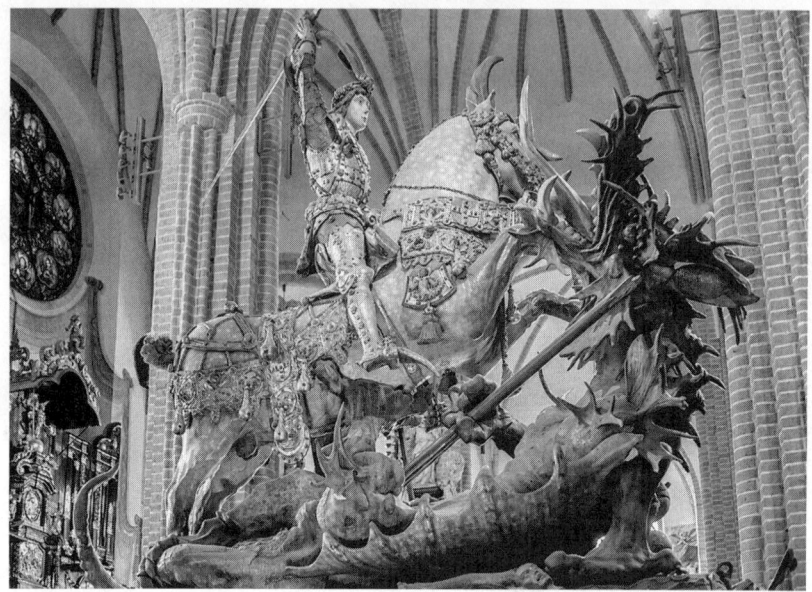

3. Bernt Notke, Saint George in the Stockholm Cathedral,
wooden sculpture, fifteenth century.

Despite his great size, the saint in the cathedral has a delicate look (rather like Hilma herself). Notke fashioned him with narrow shoulders and long arms and legs. The knight's slender build makes him almost seem too fragile for the violent task at hand. According to legend, Saint George slew a dragon that fed on human sacrifices, thereby rescuing a princess who was to be its next victim. Returning to the city with the princess and the slain dragon, he calmed the terrified citizens by assuring them he had been sent by God. In gratitude, the king and his people converted to Christianity. The sculpture illustrates the knight's miraculous victory over the dragon. His gaze is fixed not on his opponent but upward to the heavens. As if in response, light descends through the stained-glass windows of the church to surround him like an aura. The message is clear: George's strength comes from God, channeled through the saint's faith.

The sense of channeling something larger and more powerful than oneself would become familiar to Hilma even as a child when she had her first visions, as her nephew Erik reported after her death. From 1891 she also received messages from higher worlds, which she recorded in notebooks. Many years later she would tell her nephew: "I am so small, I am so insignificant but the force that flows through me is so powerful that I must go forward."[3] The words could just as well have been spoken by Saint George.

The cathedral featured another significant artwork, one the af Klint children certainly would have known, an oil painting hanging in the southern aisle, a few meters from Saint George and the dragon. Like the sculpture's, the painting's scale is impressive: 163 centimeters high—taller than Hilma would ever be. (As a grown woman, she was 1.57 meters tall.)[4]

The painting depicts a miracle that happened in Stockholm the morning of April 20, 1535. It shows the old town with the cathedral in the center, surrounded by the archipelago, the islands still wooded (see plate 6). The sky fills half the canvas, dwarfing the church and the houses, towers, and fortifications around it. Multiple suns appear in the sky, each surrounded by a gleaming halo.

At the time it happened, residents of Stockholm interpreted the phenomenon as a sign from God: a heavenly greeting to followers of the new Lutheran faith. There is eyewitness testimony that suddenly multiple golden rings sparkled in the sky over the city; a Protestant reformer commissioned the painting to document the event.[5] From an astrophysical perspective, the formation of such "mock suns" occurs when light is refracted by ice crystals in the atmosphere. The scientific perspective prevailed in what came to be the modern title of the work, the *Mock Sun Painting*. It is worth noting that a number of Hilma's paintings after 1907 include large orbs suggestive of mock suns, which roll like huge wheels across the canvas (see plate 7).

Like most Swedes, the af Klint family had been Lutherans for generations. Deviation was hardly imaginable. Lutherans in Sweden did not have to assert themselves against the Catholic Church. A state church had ruled since the late sixteenth century; services were held in spartan churches in accordance with a strict liturgy.

The richly decorated Saint George in the Stockholm cathedral was an exception.

Swedish church officials were as intolerant of religious diversity as the Papacy, and this changed little during Hilma's lifetime. The indigenous Sami, for example, who lived in the north of Sweden and had their own religion, were required to bury their dead in cemeteries; their traditional practices were forbidden. Jews were allowed to apply for citizenship starting only in 1870 and were prohibited from working in the civil service, as were Catholics. Higher public office was reserved for Lutherans well into the twentieth century. Society rested on a foundation of word and text, sermon and Bible. Religious assemblies where no clergy were present were forbidden until 1868.[6]

The congregation the af Klints felt most connected to was on the island of Adelsö in Lake Mälaren, where the two family estates were located. The little church, with its tower and thick stone walls, looked like a castle. In the cemetery stood the headstones of Hilma's grandfather Gustaf af Klint and his eldest son, Erik Gustaf, who drowned when his boat capsized in a storm off the coast of Cuba. The af Klints spent most of the summer on Adelsö. Sheep grazed in the meadows; beyond sparkled the blue water of the lake. The grave of a Viking king was discovered beneath a hill close to a rune stone a few meters' walk from the church, the two religions close in a way that was tolerated by the church because Viking religious practices were believed to be a thing of the past. No one prayed to the thunder god Thor anymore or honored the world ash tree, Yggdrasil. Or did they? That the old myths had been forgotten turned out to be false, and a nineteenth-century revival of interest in archaic spiritual systems would be reflected in Hilma's work.

Hilma captured the Adelsö church in a drawing she made while a student at the Royal Academy in Stockholm (fig. 4).[7] Another drawing looks into a different church on the neighboring island of Munsö.[8] Hilma drew the pulpit, the altar, the big cross in the window, the candelabrum, and the pews. That was all: there were no sculptures, no murals, no decorations. When Hilma was a child there was little to compete for her attention other than the huge

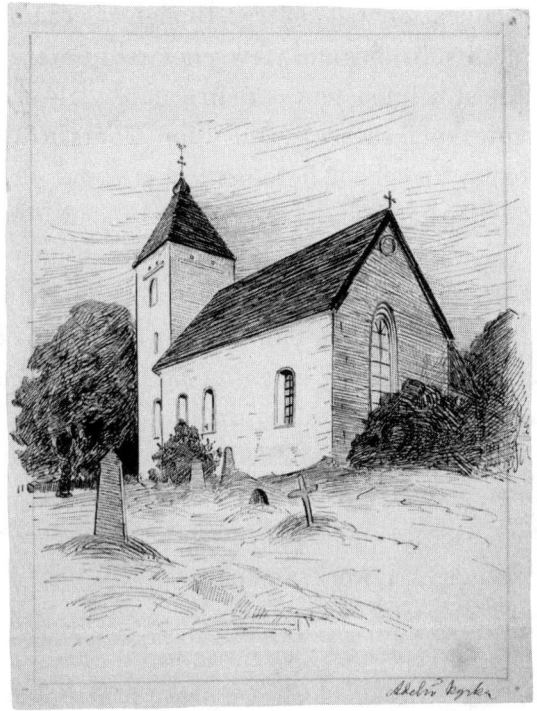

4. The church on Adelsö, ink and pencil on paper, 19.2 x 14.5 cm,
Stiftelsen Hilma af Klints Verk, HaK 1349.5.

nautical charts of her family. For years, they were the only images
that Hilma and her siblings consistently encountered.

From Norrtullsgatan, where the af Klints lived, it wasn't far to
the Royal Normal School for Girls that Hilma and Ida attended after
finishing elementary school. The sisters could walk to Riddargatan,
which led them into the neighboring district of Östermalm. The
number of horse-drawn buses on the streets increased every year,
and getting around Stockholm had become unimaginable without
them. Tracks were laid to improve traction. The horse dung on the
streets sometimes made it smell like the countryside. Hermina, the
youngest sister, was still too little and remained at home.

The secondary school for girls opened in 1864. (It was connected
to the Royal Seminary for the Training of Female Teachers, founded

in 1861.) The education was not free, though after fierce debate in Parliament, state subsidies and a few scholarships were made available. When the af Klint sisters were in school, girls and boys were far from having equal access to education. Their brother, Gustaf, didn't have to pay for school, because he was a boy.[9]

The inequality between the sexes would lead Ida to join the women's suffrage movement in 1887.[10] She became a member of the Fredrika Bremer Association, an organization that lobbied for women's suffrage in Sweden, named after the author of the 1856 novel *Hertha, or the Story of a Soul: A Sketch from Real Life*. The book was wildly successful, and within a few years the heroine, Hertha, managed to escape the confines of literature to become the role model for a new generation of women who wanted to join the fight she led in the novel: for equality on every level—before the law and in matters of education, work, and pay.

A photograph of Hilma when she was about twelve shows a schoolgirl with a long braid and a large taffeta bow. Her eyes are such a light blue that the image captures little more than the black of her pupils (fig. 5).

Anna Whitlock (1852–1930) was a reformer who taught at the Royal Normal School for girls when Hilma was there. In a photograph from the period, Whitlock wears glasses and a serious expression; her hair is parted in the middle. The picture is mounted on the beige cardboard used by the many portrait studios in Stockholm at the time. The age difference between teacher and student was a mere ten years. Whitlock turned out to be one of the sharpest critics of the Swedish educational system.

Her texts offer stark insight into the institution responsible for Hilma's education. Like many reformers, Whitlock believed in the progressive value of a scientific education. She used statistics to support her claims about what needed to change in the curriculum. One of her most important ratios was "1476 to 369," signaling the critical imbalance in schools between classes in religion and in nat-

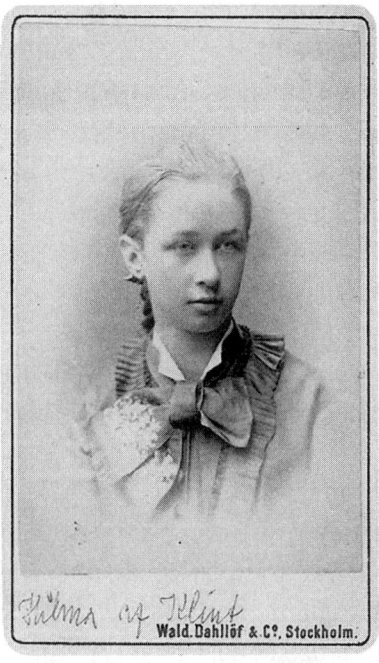

Wald. Dahllöf & Cᵒ. Stockholm.

5. Hilma af Klint as a young girl, date unknown.

ural history: A child who went to school until the sixth grade had to sit through "1476 hours of religious education," she observed furiously, while only 369 hours were dedicated to instruction in natural history—precisely one quarter.[11] In fact, Whitlock calculated, religious education received as much class time as natural history, history, and geography combined. Church and state together controlling education, she argued, involved a conflict of interest. Religious education was an exercise in deference to authority, while the state should have the goal of educating free-thinking citizens. The church's influence should be curbed, she argued. Moreover, girls and boys ought to be taught together, and taught the same subjects. For the majority of her contemporaries, such a proposition was unthinkable.

The good news for Hilma was that she grew up in a liberal family that allowed the girls to continue school past sixth grade and even pursue vocational training. Victor and Mathilda af Klint thought as little of the idea that only men should be allowed to take their fortunes into their own hands as Anna Whitlock did. And when it came to religion, they gave their daughters plenty of freedom. They rejected dogmatism and allowed the children to explore spiritual matters that were anathema to the state church. The af Klints also considered instruction in the natural sciences an essential part of any education. Mathematics and physics were as much a part of the seafaring life as the masts and sails of a ship.

The bad news was that Hilma had to endure the very education that Anna Whitlock criticized so sharply. Whitlock's decision to open her own progressive school in 1878 came too late for Hilma. In a society where even boys were expected to submit to authority, norms were even stricter for young women: they were trained to be obedient, good, and devout. Original, unconventional, or even exceptional female students were the last thing one could expect to come out of the Swedish educational system.

It is no wonder that Hilma did not remember her schooldays fondly. In 1943, looking back to her childhood from the advanced age of eighty, the first thing that occurred to her was how difficult she had found it to speak her mind. She hadn't dared to defend her opinions, she wrote in a notebook, calling her former timidity a "mistake."

The artist described her relationship to school in a single sentence: "I can't remember much more than that school caused me grief."[12]

[4]

An Exhibition in London

While the girl with the taffeta bow and light blue eyes was walking each day to the school that brought her so little joy, protests against the old authorities were happening across Europe. Sometimes they were public and highly vocal, and other times they attracted little attention. More and more people were demanding rights they had been refused by the state and church: workers, women, and non-Christians.

In 1871, two nearly simultaneous events worked to destabilize the old order. In France members of the Paris Commune toppled the city government and called on citizens to elect a new parliament. Meanwhile, across the English Channel, a London gallery showed an exhibition of watercolors by a female medium who claimed to be guided in her work by supernatural beings. The artist, Georgiana Houghton, belonged to an English spiritualist movement with ambitions of transforming society; adherents drew strength from the belief they had higher powers on their side.[1]

Most visitors to the exhibition did not know what to make of Houghton's futuristic, abstract art, and it was largely ignored.

We are fortunate that Houghton published a small catalogue for the show titled *Catalogue of the Spirit Drawings in Water Colours Exhibited at the New British Gallery, Old Bond Street*. "By Miss Houghton" appeared below, with a clarification in smaller print: "Through Whose Mediumship They Have Been Executed." The catalogue was produced in both simple and deluxe editions. Houghton sent Queen Victoria a copy of the deluxe version featuring pink paper and gold lettering bound in white calfskin.[2] Such production values were usually reserved at the time for classics and the Bible.

The comparison to the Bible would not have struck the artist as far-fetched. Houghton's concerns were artistic *and* spiritual. She was devout, prayed regularly, and attended Anglican services including those, by her own account, at Westminster Abbey. In this respect, she was an unremarkable Christian. Less usual were the spirits that regularly visited her home. They were not recognized by the Anglican Church, nor did they resemble the chain-rattling ghosts that haunted Gothic novels. Houghton's spirits were friendly, and they made their presence felt in various ways. At séances that the artist organized with friends, the spirits awed participants, for example, by making a banana suddenly appear, then a watermelon and a coconut. Other times dead people came and touched their living relatives— including Houghton's own sister, Zilla, who had died young.[3] It never seemed to be the apparitions' aim to frighten their hosts, and sometimes famous historical figures appeared—always with goodwill. According to the descriptions Houghton wrote on the reverse of her drawings, her hand was even occasionally guided by the spirit of great artists such as Titian and Correggio.[4]

It is easy to underestimate her from her photographs. She wore her hair severely parted in the middle and combed back, fastened by a barrette at the nape of her neck. She wore high-necked blouses and dresses with moderate ruffles; her gaze did not challenge the viewer but was pensively fixed on the distance. She did not try to attract attention. Her demeanor was modest, in keeping with social expectations for a middle-class woman.

Her biography is mostly unremarkable. She was born in 1814 in Las Palmas in the Canary Islands, but the family moved to London, where she spent most of her life. She lived alone off a small inheritance and never married. Her house at 20 Delamere Crescent was only a few minutes' walk from Paddington Station in west central London, though the building and street no longer exist.

Houghton's first séance took place in 1859 with her mother, though Georgiana was in her mid-forties, a mature woman. But she had never gotten over the sudden death of her sister Zilla in 1851. Both girls had received artistic training, though no further details of their education are known. After Zilla died, Georgiana summarily broke with conventional painting.

During the séance, Houghton and her mother sat at a table. They laid their hands on the surface and waited with paper and pen every day, for three months. The first messages that came were single letters of the alphabet. In less than two years, Houghton began to draw as a medium. Her circle grew and came to include artists such as William Holman Hunt, a founder of the Pre-Raphaelite movement. Hunt and his fellow artists often painted women to look as if they had fallen into a trance.[5] Typically the dreaming women's heads are thrown back, their gaze enraptured, their hair flowing in waves across their upper bodies.

Houghton, in contrast, looked within for her visions, which she captured in increasingly elaborate watercolors. She was interested not in outward appearances but rather in the phenomena that occurred when her consciousness gave up control of her body. The division of labor was clear: the Pre-Raphaelites concerned themselves with the outward form, while Houghton gave shape to an invisible inner life.

In artistic questions she relied on two sources for advice. One was an artist friend whom she referred to as Mr. L; his full name is not revealed in her autobiography, *Evenings at Home*.[6] Spirits were her other source; they counseled her not just about painting but also about practical matters. For example, they sent transit suggestions—she was to take "the Paddington omnibus" to visit friends—or they offered advice on her wardrobe, suggesting that on the day of her vernissage she should wear "a coat of many colors."[7]

It was Mr. L who suggested Houghton show her work publicly. "Why do you not exhibit?" Mr. L asked her one day, the artist reports in her autobiography. She responded by mentioning her rejection by the Royal Academy. Drawings that she had submitted for an exhibition had been rejected—twice, in fact.

"Oh! that is not what I mean," she has Mr. L reply. "Why not have an Exhibition of your own?"

"*Of my own*!!! What a bewildering thought!"[8]

Houghton delivers more protestations over the course of the dialogue. She was alone, weak, a woman, and she had no one who could help her with such an endeavor. She couldn't even think of what the first step would be—the very idea surpassed her imagination. Mr. L promised to help. He would assist in every way, as a mentor, admirer, and friend. Houghton's spirits advised her to accept.

The opening took place on May 22, 1871, in a central London exhibition space rented by the artist, at 39 Old Bond Street. The "New British Gallery" was well-known in the art scene. Houghton had placed ads in the newspapers and had posters put up around town. All of the 151 works that hung in the gallery were hers. None of them was particularly large—few exceeded 32 by 23 centimeters.

But each picture had an unconventional density and captivating effect. Her watercolors were composed of hundreds of overlapping, vortex-like lines. There were dark, mysterious paintings and bright red-toned paintings that exuded a fiery energy (see plate 8).

But the most extraordinary thing about the watercolors is what they show: nothing, according to conventional understanding. There are only colors and lines, layers, depths, and swirls. The artist distributed magnifying glasses so viewers could take a closer look at the delicate compositions. But what, many asked, were they supposed to look at? There were no people, no landscapes, no houses—no figures at all. Houghton's watercolors were nonrepresentational, abstract—though this concept was not developed until later.

The reactions, predictably, were largely hostile. The queen, who was the first to receive a catalogue, did not make contact, which is hardly surprising. Like most of the crowned heads of Europe, Queen Victoria had conservative tastes in art. She favored pictures of the royal family and the palace dogs.

Scathing reviews followed. The artist was ridiculed and her work denounced as a sham. Only one reviewer was appreciative, gushing over the "brilliancy and harmony of the tints" and urging his readers to think of the works as Turner paintings that "troops of fairies" had walked across, leaving traces of jewels behind them.[9]

But no one had eyes for Houghton's real discovery, despite the fact that she had hung the paintings in a way that she hoped would guide viewers. They were to follow the development from one picture to another. First came the works that were still representational, then the ones that abandoned recognizable forms for oscillating lines that told of their origin in the spirit world. Houghton called the forms in her paintings "fruits" and "flowers." She was convinced that the soul grew and developed like the fruits and plants she used as metaphors. What she captured on paper were the coils of feeling, intellect, and temperament that twined together to form the thicket of inner life.

Houghton associated each painting with a person: sometimes dead acquaintances or relatives, sometimes famous people such as the artist William Blake, whose work was also admired by the Pre-Raphaelites. The artist does not always prove a reliable interpreter of her own work; her explanations fluctuate and sometimes even contradict each other. No, she writes at one point, her paintings were "not simply allegorical" as she first assumed, but rather "real objects" created by the spiritual world. A few pages later she nonetheless writes of the "Sacred Symbolism" of her work as its primary characteristic, as if this did not conflict with what she had previously written.[10] Sometimes she notes the meaning of individual forms on the back of her pictures, but then she rejects any attempt at interpretation and declares the paintings the signs of a secret code, a "Spiritual cypher" that would remain enigmatic because its "glorious hues" went beyond human language.[11]

Since no explanation could be exhaustive, the painter did not spend time resolving the paradoxes. Her paintings are simultaneously symbolic and real, interpretable and mysterious. In their contradictions, the small watercolors resemble the kind of great works of art that remain in the viewer's mind precisely because they pose insoluble riddles.

Her works, Houghton knew, were "art without parallel" in the world. There was nothing comparable, either among her contemporaries or in the past. Like great artists before her, she had the craftsmanship and will to practice for years in order to reach something higher. The gift of being able to record the invisible had to be trained, she claimed. It required not only talent and calling but patience and hard work. "No person can spring, at one bound, to a pinnacle of art perfection," the artist explains, "any more than an acorn can in one season become a widely spreading oak." Houghton said she was present for some of the best moments of her exhibition. Visitors emitted cries of joy in the face of the "new beauty" that was revealed to them.[12]

Houghton sold only a few paintings—too few to cover the high cost of the show. The proceeds from the price of admission were also less than expected. "The result was in God's hands," Houghton writes soberly. "I never received the shadow of a promise as to mundane success." But the artist was able to make distinctions and understood that the commercial flop did not mean that she had failed across the board. "I . . . had many evidences," she wrote, "that it did a good work in the true sense."[13]

When Houghton took down the work, her hope of inspiring a new direction in painting vanished. Her dream of a society for spiritual art was shattered.[14] But she remained convinced that her works were superior to anything else on offer from London's art scene. With the support of friends who got up a collection to help cover her losses, she was soon back on her feet and determined to document for posterity what she called her "bold experiment."[15] She wrote a book about herself, her art, and the exhibition. The more her trust in the present dwindled, the more faith she had in the future. In publishing her autobiography, she made sure that future generations would learn about her experiences and could take example from them.

While Houghton was working on her manuscript, she learned that her exhibition had been mentioned in two other books. One author, Sir Henry Yule, a Scottish engineer, geographer, and orientalist, had seen it and been reminded of images he knew from a different culture: Chinese Buddhism. In his view, the paintings depicted the kind of dream apparitions that mystics from East Asia described. The scholar was impressed by the similarities and described them in his 1875 book about the explorer Marco Polo. The book was honored with the gold medal of the Royal Geographical Society.[16]

Notably, the other author was Helena Petrovna Blavatsky (1831–91), the Russian mystic and best-selling author. Blavatsky had founded the Theosophical Society in New York in 1875, along with two Americans, Henry Olcott and William Quan Judge. She detailed the society's program in two volumes, comprising more than a thousand pages, under the title *Isis Unveiled*. The book was translated into many languages, including Swedish. Blavatsky quotes Yule on his visit to Houghton's exhibition and the comparison to Buddhist dream apparitions. The mention is only a footnote, but a footnote in one of the most influential books of the nineteenth century.[17]

Both Blavatsky and Yule studied Eastern mysticism, so it is no coincidence that they refer to Houghton's exhibition. Their esteem for Eastern thought also inspired a political agenda. When Blavatsky moved the headquarters of the Theosophical Society to India, adherents of Theosophy began to support the independence movement there.[18] Yule, too, expressed his opposition to English colonial rule. As vice president of the Royal Geographical Society, he refused to greet Sir Henry Morton Stanley, the famous explorer who, as an agent of the king of Belgium, had employed brutal methods to suppress the inhabitants of the Congo.

Houghton wrote in her autobiography that she was pleased to be mentioned by Yule and Blavatsky. It struck her as a good omen. A friend assured her: "Pioneers are always sufferers in Earthly things, and they sink a capital of this World's goods, to realize both capital and interest in the next."[19] Houghton could wait. In the late 1870s, word of new paintings originating from other planes and recorded by mediums spread through Europe's spiritualist circles like subterranean seismic waves.

[5]

Bertha Valerius and the Dead

The adolescent Hilma wore her light, shoulder-length hair held off her forehead with a headband.[1] She dressed simply, and the simplicity sent a message: the af Klint daughters were not dolls dressed up for the marriage market. They were to be educated so they could lead independent lives. After she finished secondary school at age seventeen, Hilma took painting classes at the Technical School (Tekniska skolan) in preparation for her application to the Stockholm Royal Academy of Art.

Even as a teen, Hilma ran in artistic circles. That may have been how she met a woman nearly forty years her senior, Bertha Valerius (1825–95). Valerius would have been in a position to introduce her to a wide swath of Stockholm society.[2] She was one of Sweden's first independent female photographers, with a successful studio in town.[3] Every day, members of the bourgeoisie came to have their portraits made: priests, captains, officers, entrepreneurs, merchants, actors and actresses, housewives with their daughters and sons. She counted members of the aristocracy and the royal family among her clients, as well as many suffragists and advocates for women's rights.

Valerius had to fight for her professional success and personal freedom. As a young woman, she and other like-minded women had demanded and won the right to study art. In her mid-twenties, she was accepted to the Royal Academy through an exceptional admissions process that initially allowed just a few women to study. Only fifteen years later, in 1864, did the Academy change its policy and set up facilities especially for female students in a so-called ladies' department.[4] The decision was unusual. Most state academies in Europe held to tradition and did not admit women until after the First World War.

As soon as Valerius completed her studies, she went abroad to Düsseldorf, Dresden, and Paris for further training. Returning to Stockholm, she opened a photography studio and was appointed a royal portrait supplier in 1864. Her paintings were also in great demand, and she painted the royal family, among others Karl XV and Oscar II. Valerius was unmarried and childless and happy to stay that way.

Like Georgiana Houghton, Valerius put little stock in her appearance. One of the few surviving photographs of her shows an old woman, her gray hair parted and pinned up, her dress black though not overly severe. The lace inserts suggest she belonged to the upper class, or at least that she ran in those circles.[5]

Tracking her leads to the oldest document in the af Klint archive, a notebook of 170 pages created by Valerius; its crumbling black binding is labeled 1879 to 1882. The first page announces "Communications through Bertha Valerius." The notebook contains no explanations that might be helpful to researchers. Notes on the place and time of recorded events are the only anchors to the quotidian world; the rest are messages from the beyond. Valerius wrote her notes in black ink using a simple script. She was probably among the first mentors to help Hilma navigate the realm of the spirits.

The notebook documents a séance on July 26, 1879, when Valerius channeled a voice for the first time. The spirit's name was Ulla. She got straight to the point, paving the way for all the voices that would speak in later sessions. She criticized the state church and pointed to "falsehoods in the theological doctrine." According to Ulla, it wasn't right to consider the Bible the sole basis of faith. Jesus was sent by God, as was well-known, "and returned to him when his mission was completed."[6] This made her happy, she explained, and those listening understood her meaning. (Finding biblical examples that supported the possibility of communication with the dead was almost a sport in those circles.) Heaven was open, and not a one-way street. Jesus could leave and return. Why should he be the only one, or the last to do so?

Ulla was not alone. The notebook records her as being joined by others in such lively succession that it was as if Valerius, as medium, had opened not just a window to another world but a revolving door. A spirit named Johan came on the seventeenth of August, according to the notebook; then, that same day, Carl Otto and someone with the initials C. F. The spirits were cheerful and carefree, though they spoke of the last things. As a young man, Johan reported, he had been afraid of death. But after the "heavenly dwellings" had been revealed to him, he hurried to depart, for they were "peaceful and enticing" and had filled him with happiness.[7]

A few pages later, Sweden's most famous botanist, Carl Linnaeus, addressed the séance participants. "Dear friends," he began; he wished to speak for a while.[8] During his life, he had been a kind of translator of the plant world, and he was happy that his research was now respected. Linnaeus was followed by Voltaire, the eighteenth-century French philosopher with whom Gustav III had exchanged letters.

If af Klint had imagined guests from the realm of the dead as gloomy figures who returned to haunt the living, she would have learned better at the séances. Ulla, Johan, and Carl Otto were not scary graveyard ghosts, nor was Linnaeus or Voltaire. They were also nothing like Shakespeare's revenants who came to plague the consciences of those who wanted to forget their misdeeds. On the contrary, the spirits that Valerius called during the séances came in friendship. They brought good news from the beyond: news of love, joy, and happiness.

Valerius never described the method or gift that allowed her to open her consciousness to messages from the beyond. She did not say whether she could see those who spoke to her or whether she heard voices or whether her hand was guided as she wrote. Only the results were documented.[9] All who gathered around Valerius believed that communication was possible between the living and the dead. Starting in 1883, the circle was called Klöverbladet, Swedish for "cloverleaf." Hilma's parents seem to have been open to experiments with the spiritual world since they allowed their daughter to participate in sessions. Erik af Klint, Hilma's nephew, would later report that his aunt had taken part in séances from 1879 on and was a member of several spiritualist associations over her lifetime. Valerius's notebook is the only document from this period in Hilma's estate.[10] Most likely it was a present to the girl from her mentor.

Nothing the seventeen-year-old could have heard or seen at the sessions was meant for outsiders. Trust was essential, and no one in the circle wanted the meetings to become public knowledge, which could lead to a scandal. The state church did not countenance messages from the dead, so they were treading on dangerous ground. Ulla had alluded to this when she spoke of the "false doctrines" of the church, but had not elaborated on the profound contradictions involved. The séances seemed to challenge the biblical foundations of the participants' religion, according to which souls would be resurrected on Judgment Day. How, then, could they be getting in touch now? It was no small question, and not one to be raised with a Lutheran pastor.

Claiming to speak with the souls of the dead had been the downfall of great scholars in the past, Emanuel Swedenborg being a prime example. The scientist had been granted a noble title for his many accomplishments and was respected far beyond his homeland of Sweden. But when he shifted his research away from the things of this world and toward the world beyond, his career came to a swift end. Books in which Swedenborg discussed the realm of the dead, blithely describing their daily lives, their beautiful cities, and married love in heaven, were not well received by the scholarly community.[11] Swedenborg insisted that it was easy to speak with the dead; he himself was in regular contact. Scorn came from all sides, but Immanuel Kant was particularly virulent. The philosopher from Königsberg called Swedenborg ripe for the asylum and dedicated the critical text *Dreams of a Spirit-Seer, Illustrated by Dreams of Metaphysics* to him. Swedenborg died in 1772 during a trip to London.

No one in Bertha Valerius's circle believed the time had come to take up the cause again. Still, there were signs that views were starting to relax. There was a trend toward agnosticism, particularly in England, with many arguing that there were phenomena that could neither be proven nor disproven. According to this view, scientific methods are unsuitable for explaining some phenomena or concepts, particularly when they touch on matters of faith. The existence of God or spirits, for example, was something researchers could neither prove nor disprove given the limits of their field. Thus the only way to refute spiritualists was to convict them of deception. Their circles were rife with fraud in the second half of the nineteenth century.[12] Valerius nonetheless maintained a spotless reputation. From an agnostic perspective, this meant that her experiences could not be refuted. At the same time, nothing had been proven.

The meeting places for the secret society suggest members were worried about their reputations. "Gripsholm" is mentioned early in the notebook; it is one of Sweden's oldest castles.[13] To use its rooms for séances would have required connections to the royal family, which Bertha Valerius, as court painter, had. As far as we know, no list of the séance participants survives. King Oscar II, who had been in power for seven years, was sympathetic to spiritualism and corresponded with the medium Huldine Beamish. He personally met with representatives of the Theosophical movement in the 1890s.[14]

Gripsholm Castle was easy to reach from Stockholm. Secluded on the banks of Mälaren yet within easy reach of the city, the fortress-like building was the perfect meeting place. Kurt Tucholsky gushed over the uninhabited landscape in his novel *Castle Gripsholm*.

Valerius's spirits were unconventional not just in speaking from beyond the grave. Their behavior also broke with social norms. The spirits or souls, who often had masculine names, directed their messages primarily to women, an unusual preference in the nineteenth century. Important matters would typically be discussed between men, who set the tone in all things and kept their mothers, sisters, wives, and daughters silent, by either law or convention. In séances, however, women often had leading roles as hostesses, mediums, or note takers. Valerius was not the only one to adopt a central role. In both Europe and America, it was common for mediums to be female.[15] All over the world, spiritual visitors seemed uninterested in the old gender hierarchy, which contributed to the popularity of spiritualism in some circles. In others, this break with societal rules made spiritism all the more off-putting.

Such unusual practices were not viewed sympathetically by the state church, any more than was the claim that the dead could speak to the living. On the subject of women and their relationship to higher spheres, the church's position was clear: Metaphysics was not a subject for women to mess about with, and it was unsuitable for them to concern themselves with questions of God or faith. Women were prohibited from studying theology. While the first female medical student in Sweden entered medical school in 1873, the church continued to bar women from joining the clergy. This did not bother the circle at Gripsholm Castle. They had carved out a space for their activities and turned their backs on the strict doctrines, rules, and prohibitions of the church. They kept their new freedoms to themselves. For the moment.

If af Klint was among the participants, she was largely silent in the meetings. Nothing suggests that she received or recorded messages herself. Valerius made a clean copy of the messages she had been sent in the notebook so that everything was clear and neat, but she did not edit them at all.

Then, in February 1879, an entry appears that deals neither with the past nor with the dead characters who surfaced from it, but rather with the future.[16] A spirit named Charles spoke of a new epoch in art. The time was approaching, he said, and it would involve men and women artists equally. Charles said: "The priests and priestesses of art need no materials other than the fine waves that surround them, which resemble the air around them. To create works of genius they must only develop the strength that lies in the pure will . . . , to be beautiful and free of all the defects that one finds in the work of earthly artists. To paint is to let the light shine that the artist forms in his own spirit."[17] To make his prophecy more vivid, Charles turned to a musical analogy. What had already been achieved in art, he said, resembled the chirping of insects. What was to come would sound like organ music in comparison. This raised an obvious question. Who would play the organ? Who would be the new geniuses?

At the time, few thought of Valerius as a candidate. She kept her own project secret for the time being. For several years she had been working on a painting that she received medially, stroke for stroke, in the seclusion of her studio. The work, which she hoped would one day outshine the rest of art as it was then known, was titled *Christ Painting*. It would not be completed for more than another decade (see fig. 15).[18]

Eight years had passed since Georgiana Houghton's 1871 exhibition in London. The show had not been a success, but nor had it been forgotten, thanks to mentions by Henry Yule and Helena P. Blavatsky. Much of what Charles now said echoed the way Houghton described her art, as "without parallel in the world" and as the "summit of art."

Nor was Houghton the first or the only artist who had experi-

mented in the spiritual realm. Automatic drawing had been practiced in séances for years. Camilla Dufour Crosland, also from
England, had reported on her supernatural experiences in words
and images in 1857. Her book *Light in the Valley: My Experiences
of Spiritualism* features innovative representational and abstract
illustrations, including biblical and spiritual figures as well as
ellipses, circles, hearts, and enigmatic forms that seem cautiously
to probe their surroundings as if with antennae (see plates 9 and
10). Crosland had collaborated with two artists, a mysterious gentleman she called "Confidence" and the trained painter Anna Mary
Howitt. She had much in common with Howitt. Both were staunch
spiritualists and feminists. In her novella *The Sisters in Art* Howitt
had described a female art collective similar to the circle of friends
with whom she had studied in Munich.[19] Moreover, Howitt had connections in Sweden through her mother, a writer and translator.
Among the books her mother had translated were the collected
works of Fredrika Bremer, including the influential novel *Hertha,
or the Story of a Soul: A Sketch from Real Life.*[20] She had received
a silver medal for her translations from the Literary Academy of
Stockholm. Anna Mary Howitt counted her parents among the *Pioneers of the Spiritual Reformation*. Mediumship ran in her family.
And Fredrika Bremer had been a spiritualist, too.[21] Thus the trans-
national exchange on these questions was established early.

In the upper-class milieu in which Valerius and af Klint moved,
there were many channels that carried news back and forth across
Europe. People in those circles generally spoke and read several
languages and would have spent time in London, Florence, or Paris.

———

Hilma would keep Valerius's black notebook all her life. The notes
testify to the fact that tidings of a quiet revolution in art had already
reached Sweden through "Charles" by 1879. What forms it would
take were uncertain. But all who believed in the new art, from
Charles to Houghton to Crosland, were convinced it would draw
power from higher sources and would turn away from the material

world. The task was to paint the spirit, not matter. They were also in agreement that the path would be long and rocky. No one involved expected quick appreciation. Valerius kept her work secret, and in 1882 Houghton wrote: "A large proportion of newspaper critics know nothing in the world about *Art*; they can look at pictures, where they see that a horse is a horse, and they gather from the talk of the studios what is to be said of such or such a production, but my Exhibition baffled them utterly, therefore they sometimes took refuge in unseemly words about what they did not understand."[22] Reservations couldn't dampen the euphoria. Participants believed spiritual painting could be a fresh start, on the canvas and beyond. "In the ages that are to come, Developed Woman will be the great artist," Camilla Dufour Crosland wrote optimistically in 1857.[23] She was convinced that female artists had special abilities to receive signals from other worlds.

Some had already started: Howitt and Houghton in England and Valerius in Sweden. The future could begin.

[6]

Kerstin Cardon's Painting School

When Hilma af Klint decided to become an artist, she had to learn to accept contradictions. On the one hand, she had participated in séances, possibly even in those where a new epoch in art was being predicted. On the other hand, she was trained in traditional painting. Charles, the incorporeal messenger of Valerius's notes, spoke of the light from which the new works would emerge and contrasted this with the "flaws" still found "in the work of earthly artists." Nonetheless, the earthly craft now had to take center stage.

Beginning in 1879 af Klint attended classes several times a week at Stockholm's Technical School as she prepared to apply to the Royal Academy. She also enrolled at a painting school for women.[1]

The way there led down Norrtullsgatan toward the city center, past the municipal observatory and its park. A few blocks later began Drottninggatan, an old seventeenth-century street. At number 52, stairs led to the top floor, where the artist Kerstin Cardon ran a private school for female painters. She modeled the school on the ones in Paris where she herself had trained.[2]

When the seventeen-year-old Hilma opened the door to the studio, she was greeted by a teacher who was herself still young, not yet forty. A later image of Kerstin Cardon shows her in a plain, dark dress. Her hair is pinned up, and her posture is as erect as if she were sitting on a horse. Her soldierly bearing was appropriate: most of her commissions came from the aristocracy and from officers in the military. She immortalized barons, counts, and lieutenants in oil on canvas, as well as members of the royal family, including Oscar II.

Cardon had much in common with Bertha Valerius. Like Valerius, Cardon had graduated from the Royal Academy in Stockholm, continued her education abroad, and then returned to Sweden to make a living in the 1870s. Both worked in a conventional manner that reflected the taste of their clients. Cardon's portraits do not betray the fact that in Paris, where she lived for several years, art had begun to change. Her art has nothing to do with impressionism, or modernity, much less with the light, waves, and power Charles had spoken of and with which Valerius was secretly experimenting. Cardon served a market with traditional tastes. The new kinds of paintings produced abroad by Édouard Manet or Claude Monet interested only a few artists in Stockholm. Most of the commissions Cardon painted for her upper-class clients could have been made a hundred years earlier.

Nonetheless, at her school, the future was approaching: young women learned the craft of painting—a new generation stood before the easels, canvases, and stretchers, wielding brushes, mixing paints. For the first time in Sweden's history, women were being taught to paint by another woman.[3] Female professors were still unthinkable at the Royal Academy; female students were taught exclusively by men. But not in Cardon's studio. She was a pioneer—

not as a painter, but as an independent entrepreneur with a paint-brush in her hand.

In December 1878, barely a year before af Klint enrolled at Cardon's school, another innovation arrived in Sweden: the science fiction novel. The first one in Swedish, by Claës Lundin (1825–1908), received considerable attention in the press.[4]

Lundin, it turned out, was an admirer of Kerstin Cardon. He set his story in the year 2378 in a futuristic Stockholm filled with gigantic skyscrapers. The main character, Aromasia, is a wealthy single artist. She invests her money in the stock market and has a doctorate in finance from the University of Göteborg.[5] The book was titled *Oxygen and Aromasia*, after the heroine and the young man with whom she falls in love.

Lundin's novel is many things at once: utopian vision, satire, criticism, moral portrait. He creates a vast panorama of the society to come. Though set in the future, the plot is full of allusions to recent events and innovations. Young women, in particular, would have recognized the many reforms that were taken for granted in Aromasia's futuristic world. The self-determined life of Lundin's heroine, for example, would have been unthinkable without the legislative change that took effect when Hilma af Klint was eight years old. The new maturity law declared unmarried women over the age of twenty-five to be legal adults and gave them the right to pursue a profession. The law was conceived only to help mitigate a crisis: too many men had emigrated to escape hunger, poverty, or religious suppression, leaving their mothers and sisters without legal representatives. When Parliament passed the law, few legislators had any idea how much women would relish the new freedom. In a few decades the proportion of unmarried women in the population rose to nearly forty percent.[6] Valerius and Cardon counted among them; they were later joined by Selma Lagerlöf, the first female winner of the Nobel Prize for literature, and Ellen Key, the world-famous author of *The Century of the Child*.

As it happens, Lundin bestows upon his heroine great artistic talent. Page after page, she is described as a virtuoso, a wunderkind, the Mozart of her field. Importantly, Aromasia invents the art form at which she excels. She composes works called "scent symphonies," which she performs on a device called a "scent organ." The compositions constitute pleasant aromas that engulf the audience, throwing them into raptures. Audience members could smell the art of the future—but they could neither see nor hear it. It was Lundin's playful answer to the question that also concerned members of spiritual societies: what form would the masterpieces of the future take? Just as Crosland predicted that "Developed Woman" would be the "great artist" of the future, Lundin makes Aromasia the inventor and most important interpreter of the future's masterpieces.

Beyond his science fiction, Lundin hoped for a different and better world. He was a genuine progressive. Tellingly, he did not consider talent and genius solely the province of men. Many years after Hilma left Cardon's painting school, Lundin celebrated it as a prime example of female achievement. In 1894 he visited the school to report on it for the women's magazine *Idun*. Lundin's article started with a profile of the school's director, discussing her most famous paintings and clients, including Sven Hedin, an explorer whose portrait Cardon had painted. Then Lundin turned his attention to the pupils. What he saw convinced him that female artists were in no way outranked by their male colleagues: "The living example of these young art students, their great effort and delightful skill, is a contribution to the oft-disputed view that even in the field of fine art, woman is well able to compete with man."[7] But back in 1879 Sweden's leading artists held a very different view from Lundin's. They read his novel as a satire in which the world was turned upside down. Female genius was seen as a joke, a view articulated in the art magazine *Palettskrap* by Carl Larsson (1852–1919), who would become one of Sweden's most important artists. He had been asked to write an obituary of the artist Anna Nordlander, one of the few women to study at the Royal Academy. Nordlander died at thirty-six. Instead of writing a respectful obituary, Larsson used the space given to him to rant against female artists in general, inveighing against what he saw as their lack of aptitude. Weeping crocodile tears, he wrote that it broke his heart to watch the futile efforts of female artists. They were incapable of creating lasting art. "It takes the strength of man to create a Parthenon frieze or paint the Sistine Chapel!"[8]

Larsson was pleased with the sentence, ending it with an exclamation point. In his opinion, it couldn't be said often or loudly enough. Things needed to remain as they were.

[7]

Hermina's Death

Hermina, Hilma's youngest sister, died on October 17, 1880, at the age of ten. As far as we know, no one painted or photographed the girl during her lifetime. Much suggests that she died unexpectedly.

The cemetery where she was laid to rest was primarily reserved for members of the navy and their families. It was located in the south of the city, in the Djurgården, the former site of royal hunts. Trees shaded the graves, and the shore was just beyond the cemetery walls; the naval fleet was anchored in view. Hermina had no headstone; she was buried in the family plot, her name and date of birth preserved in the cemetery records.[1]

She was not the first daughter the af Klints had lost. Their first child, Anna, did not reach her second birthday. The af Klints had five children: Anna was followed by Ida, Gustaf, Hilma, and Hermina. Now both the eldest and youngest daughters were gone.

We do not know why Hermina died, though the most likely cause was pneumonia. Adelaïde Nauckhoff's 1905 book states only that she was "born in Stockholm on January 3, 1870, died there on October 17, 1880, buried in the naval cemetery at Galärvarfvet."[2] That same month Hilma celebrated her eighteenth birthday.

The af Klint family was hardly alone in the trials they endured. In nineteenth-century Sweden, pneumonia, bronchitis, and tuberculosis were the most common causes of death. Children also died of mumps, measles, and scarlet fever. Medical care was poor, particularly in rural areas where there were few doctors and people had to travel long distances to see one. Cases of leprosy were regularly documented in Dalarna County and in the province of Hälsingland.[3] Like other parts of Europe, Sweden suffered epidemics of cholera and typhus. The artist Carl Larsson wrote that the winters of the late 1860s saw such rampant cholera in Stockholm that he and his father had to fumigate the stairwells and hallways of their home several times a day.[4]

Hunger also killed many people, the last great famine occurring in the late 1870s. The rate of child mortality was higher on the coasts than inland and lower in cities than in the countryside. Nonetheless, in comparison with the rest of Europe, Swedish children had a good chance of surviving at least to the age of five.[5]

Though the af Klints lived in the city and enjoyed a good income, they were more vulnerable to disease than others of their class because the men were in the navy. Harbors were gateways for bacteria and viruses. With every shore leave, sailors carried germs into port and brought different ones back onboard. Because he trained cadets Victor af Klint did not have to go anywhere to encounter foreign-born disease; his students brought it to him. There were many deaths in his immediate family because so many of the men were in the navy. Out of fourteen cousins, five—more than a third—died as children or adolescents.[6]

What toll did Hermina's death take on the family? How did Hilma deal with the loss? As far as we know, she made no record of her feelings at the time, but many years later in a notebook entry from December 1934, we find an inscription accompanying a series of watercolors: "Made in remembrance of her who was dear to you." When Hilma later edited her notes, she added the sentence: "Refers to the death of sister 1880, Hermine."[7]

Erik af Klint, Hilma's nephew and chief heir, would later say that his aunt actually came into contact with "the beyond" years before Hermina died: "She told me that as a young girl, one morning she saw two coffins in her room. Above each stood a year. In those [specific] years she fell gravely ill and was close to death."[8] Hilma would always hold a door open for her dead sister. She hoped that hidden connections that led to the beyond could one day be widely accepted, a wish fueled by contemporary science. Advances in physics, chemistry, medicine, and biology were proving that the invisible could be made visible, revolutionizing knowledge and technology. Hilma was two years old when the Scotsman James Clerk Maxwell described light as an electromagnetic wave, and she was four when the first transatlantic telegraph cable was laid between Ireland and Newfoundland. She was nine when, in England, Charles Darwin described the relationship between humans and apes, while, in America, Alexander Graham Bell submitted a patent application for the telephone. When she was eleven, the German physicist Ernst Abbe published his theory of the resolution limit, which greatly improved microscope technology. The year of her eighteenth birthday and Hermina's death also marked the invention of the photophone—a wireless light-telephone that transmitted sound over long distances.

And that was only the beginning. The discovery of the pathogens that cause anthrax and tuberculosis would follow, along with the discovery of X-rays and the invention of wireless telegraphy. The electron was described, the theory of radioactivity developed; scientists speculated about isotopes and the possibility of splitting the atom. Nothing remained as it had so long seemed. Things that had once been concealed or invisible could be seen.[9] In America, even Thomas Alva Edison, inventor of the lightbulb, believed the day would come when he could engineer a device for calling the dead. He called the machine, which was never finished, a "spirit phone" and gave interviews about it in the *New York Times*.

And art? From her earliest séances, af Klint understood that detecting the invisible powers of the universe was not just the task of scientists. Artists, she knew, had capacities, elevated senses, that would allow them to apprehend phenomena that eluded other people—rays, waves, and vibrations. She shared this view with other unusual artists of the century, including Houghton, who had also lost a sister, and Edvard Munch (1863–1944), the Norwegian painter almost exactly the same age as Hilma, whose mother and sister died when he was young.[10]

Af Klint, Houghton, and Munch shared the experience of loss and the feeling of responsibility that grows out of it. The dead had left them in tense silence. It was for them, the living, to remain vigilant, pen and brush in hand. If there were a crack in reality that could bring them into contact with the beyond, they would find it. And if signs came from higher worlds, in whatever form, they would not fail to register them. Their losses had turned them into living seismographs.

PART TWO

Study at the Academy and Independent Work

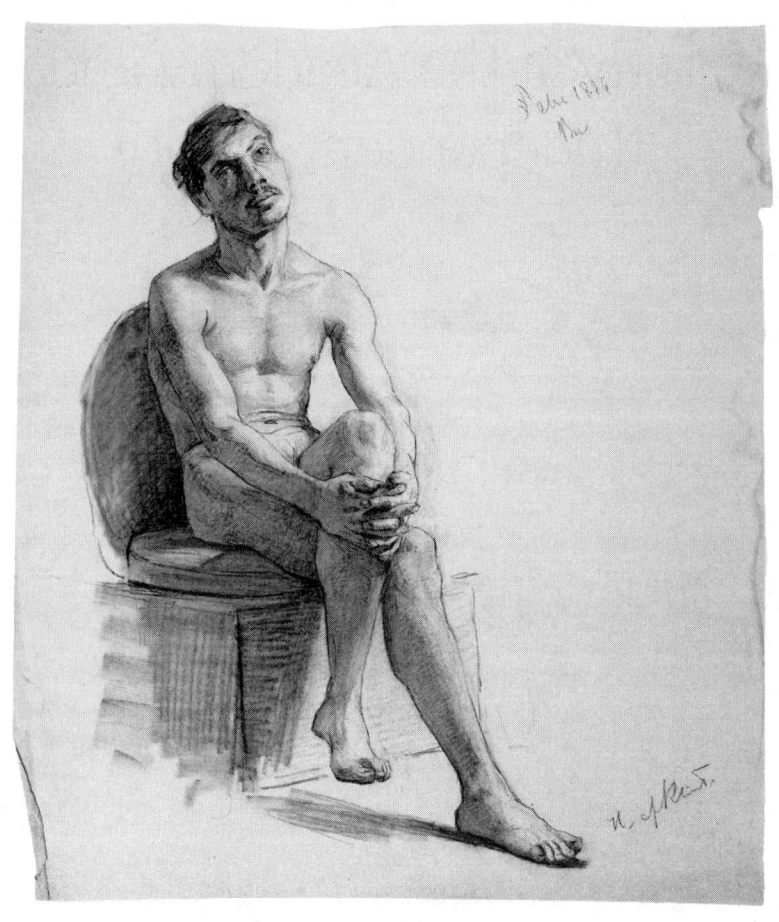

6. Male nude, charcoal, chalk, and pencil on paper, 61.3 x 46.7 cm,
Stiftelsen Hilma af Klints Verk, HaK 1243.

The Academy

Hilma af Klint, wearing a high-necked dress, looked at men wearing nothing but a cloth and drew them (fig. 6). More than a dozen other female students would have been in the room, too, clothed women drawing naked men. It was a highly progressive arrangement for the 1880s, when af Klint was studying at the Royal Swedish Academy of Fine Art in Stockholm. Across Europe, many male artists and professors protested that it was both indecent and unnatural for women to be in a room with naked men, observing and drawing them; the matter was used to help advance the argument that women should be barred from studying art altogether.[1]

What was or wasn't seemly for a female artist seems not to have concerned af Klint. Her sketchbooks depict fully nude men, including in frontal view.[2] The models are young, her strokes easy and loose. Even before she entered the Academy on September 4, 1882, she had demonstrated a decided facility for drawing. A sketch from 1880 is one of the earliest documents in her archive: a pencil drawing of a spiral staircase, fanlike with elegant curves and shading.[3] The archive also includes drawings of vases, plaster ornaments, and lamps—all made when she was taking preparatory courses at the technical college and with Kerstin Cardon. Years later she would remember her art studies fondly, in contrast with how she remembered her primary education. "Then I started out on the path of art, which made me happier," the eighty-year-old painter wrote in 1943. "The task consisted of reproducing. I had no ideas of my own."[4] But ideas were not required of a woman studying at the Academy.

―――――――

Human figures first appeared in Hilma's drawings after she entered the Academy, renderings in charcoal or pencil. One sketch depicts human hands; a more developed scene features nuns and a monk.[5]

The archive contains no drawings from her childhood or adolescence; nor have stories come down through her family to suggest that Hilma made any art as a child. Of course it may be that her juvenilia were destroyed at some point, but, in any event, as a young adult she quickly mastered the principles of traditional rendering: perspective, value, composition. After 1882 we find dozens of her sketches executed with perfect assurance.[6] The student was drawing everything: houses, sailboats, landscapes, human figures, sheep, insects.

Hilma's drawings from the Academy also document the daily life of an artist-in-training—the routines of art instruction. The most important techniques the students learned were watercolor, oil painting, and drawing. There were also anatomy lessons and practice drawing plaster copies of classical sculptures. At least once Hilma drew the class itself, depicting her fellow students at their easels (fig. 7).[7] After an exercise was completed, the student's name and date were written on the paper. Then the teacher arrived to make corrections and sign off with his initials.

Men and women were instructed separately at the Academy— this had not changed since 1864, when women were first admitted. There were no coed courses, and spaces for men and women were strictly separated. Only men were hired as teachers. The painter Carl Larsson would later say that the female students were so sequestered that he never found out exactly where they were. Only the "constant smell of coffee" hinted at the general direction. Even after he left the Academy, Larsson couldn't manage to speak of his female colleagues without disparaging them.[8]

Fortunately af Klint had very good luck with her professors. In conversations with her nephew, she mentioned the genre painter Carl Behm and Georg von Rosen (1843–1923), who specialized in large-format history paintings. Von Rosen was one of Stockholm's leading artists, advancing from professor to director of the Academy. In portraits he presents as a man of the world, sporting a carefully groomed mustache and a tuxedo with medals on the lapel— awards for his work.[9]

Hilma and von Rosen shared interests beyond making art. Both

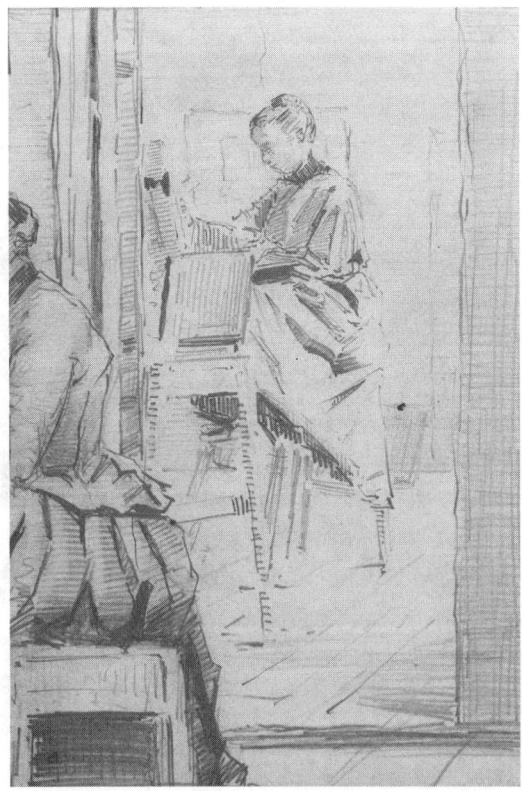

7. Sketch of a classroom with fellow students at the Royal Academy, undated,
pencil on paper, Stiftelsen Hilma af Klints Verk, HaK 1489.

attended spiritual meetings. Von Rosen is mentioned as a partici-
pant in the protocols of Valerius's Cloverleaf Society in the 1880s.[10]
Among his paintings we find mythical creatures such as a blood-
thirsty sphinx lying in wait for prey on the edge of a cliff. The history
of seafaring also interested him. During the time he was teaching
Hilma, he painted the Swedish cartographer and polar explorer
Adolf Erik Nordenskiöld, the first person to traverse the Northeast
Passage along the north coast of Siberia.

Hilma began to study life drawing during her third year. The
male models struck classical poses, standing and pretending to
be archers or spear throwers, or sitting relaxed or lost in thought.

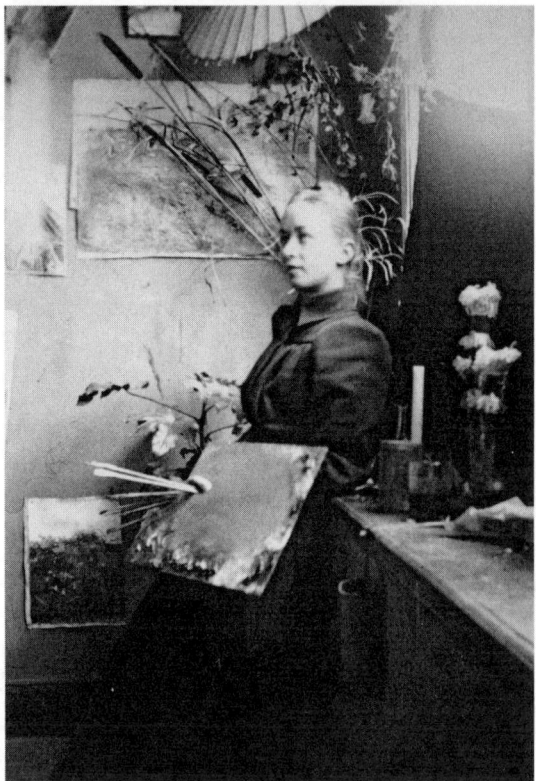

8. Af Klint as a student at the Royal Academy, ca. 1885,
Stiftelsen Hilma af Klints Verk.

Hilma worked economically, just a few strokes to suggest different
parts of the model's anatomy. Proportions were studied, muscles
modeled. She learned to see beneath the skin. In one drawing the
male body is transparent, the bones carefully rendered as in a medical illustration. As a student Hilma received an award for her skill
in "plastic anatomy."[11]

There is only one photo of her from her time at the Academy
(fig. 8). She leans on a stone ledge, palette and brush in hand, as
if taking a short break from painting. Her bearing is relaxed; she
smiles. She wears a simple black dress without a single frill—when
painting in oils, one couldn't worry about getting dirty. Oil sketches

hang on the walls, small landscapes. A Japanese parasol hangs from the ceiling. The young artist's gaze is fixed on a point beyond the photograph's frame.

For female students, learning to draw the nude figure marked an important opportunity. It gave them the skill to produce history paintings, by far the most prestigious genre. According to tradition, the greatest artworks portrayed important historical or religious events, such as the death of King Gustav Adolf on the battlefield at Lützen in 1632. These scenes required the ability to realistically depict the human body in motion. Academic societies set great store by history paintings as evidence of artistic genius, and they earned the best fees and received the most public attention.

For af Klint's contemporaries, the idea that future generations would forget the monumental paintings of the day was unthinkable. Yet many huge canvases would disappear into museum storerooms soon after the turn of the century, while paintings showing not a single king, general, warrior, or soldier were starting to make waves across Europe.

[2]

Guardian Spirit

In her fourth year at the Academy, af Klint continued to refine her skills. She mixed paints, primed canvases, and built stretchers. Making art required knowledge across multiple fields from chemistry to aesthetics, the latter learned primarily by copying the Old Masters.

Tensions arose in her relationship to spiritualist circles in the 1880s, as her nephew Erik af Klint reports. According to him the "spiritist path" did not suit her "healthy and truthful essence," and she began to distance herself after taking part in séances from 1879 to 1882.[1] Erik does not specify the date or occasion of her disenchantment. But his remark indicates an important distinction:

the dead who spoke to Valerius with cheerful speeches and descriptions of the afterlife often seem downright naïve compared with the voices af Klint and her friends began to record a decade later. Those spirits were more philosophical and sincere, and they were very often higher spiritual beings rather than dead people. (The speaking dead would nevertheless accompany her for a lifetime.)

––––––––

Archival records indicate that in the summer of 1886 Hilma was probably still attending some spiritualist meetings. A "Hilma" appears in the protocol of a particularly eventful meeting, but without a last name.[2] If it was Hilma af Klint, the artist had accepted an invitation that drew her away from her studies. On June 22, instead of going to the Academy, she may have walked to a magnificent building with a stucco façade and bel étage in downtown Stockholm, not far from the opera, at Blasieholmstorg 11.[3] Maypoles were already set up in the city to celebrate the summer solstice the following day. The hours when the sun reached its highest point had mystical significance. Girls were told to pick seven different flowers and place them under their pillows to conjure dreams of their future husbands. Houses and barns were decorated with greenery to invite fertility, health, and prosperity. On the day the sun didn't set, people danced, drank, and sang. Farm girls put on their best dresses and let the colorful ties of their aprons fly as they danced in circles in the most riotous celebration of the year.

It was not a celebration of the sun that the "Hilma" of the protocol had been invited to, but an intimate séance. Valerius, the photographer, painter, and author of the notebook in Hilma's future archive, was there to act as note taker. The gathering was hosted by Huldine Beamish (1836–92), a fifty-year-old Swede born in Ireland, where she had married the heir to a brewery six years before.[4] When married life began to bore her, Beamish moved to Sweden, her homeland. She was friends with Valerius, who had made a portrait of her at her Stockholm studio. The photograph shows Beamish seated, her light eyes fixed on the distance. Her hair falls over her neck in tight curls, and her shimmering taffeta dress is topped with a black lace bodice.[5] The other guests at the séance were presumably members of leading Stockholm families, as Beamish, like Valerius, belonged to an upper-class milieu.

The event featured three main characters: Valerius, who documented the occurrences in text and image; Beamish, who received a vision and rose in the following years to become a key figure in Stockholm's spiritual scene; and a woman named "Hilma," who was addressed in the séance.

The voice that spoke called himself Lorentz, and he directed his speech to a single person. "I am here," was the first sentence that Valerius recorded in her lined notebook. "I want to speak to Hilma."[6] The voice was appeasing. "I am your guardian spirit," he said to Hilma, "and your perfection is my task."

As far as we know, this may have been the first recorded direct message to af Klint from the spirit world. For this reason, it is given here in full:

> God be with you, my child! A clear light has come to your path. Do not let it be shadowed by the darkness of doubt, but wander happy and humble in its glow, thanking the Lord for his infinite love. Do not fear, even if you hear voices that want to frighten you, because of the light. These are the temptations that you must reject, for a child that believes need never fear.[7]

The protocol, consisting of several pages, also includes a small sketch (fig. 9). Lines crisscross the page, finally exploding like fireworks. A single sentence comments on the events: "Hilma, you have been brought here for this!"

The rest of the meeting was also documented. Beamish had a vision in which she walked through a dark cave until Jesus appeared as a flash of lightning, illuminating everything. "It was as if Jesus was standing next to her [Hilma] and was pressing her to his chest and saying: 'I convey your mother's blessings to you,'" Beamish reported, and Valerius wrote it down. An "Anna" who participated

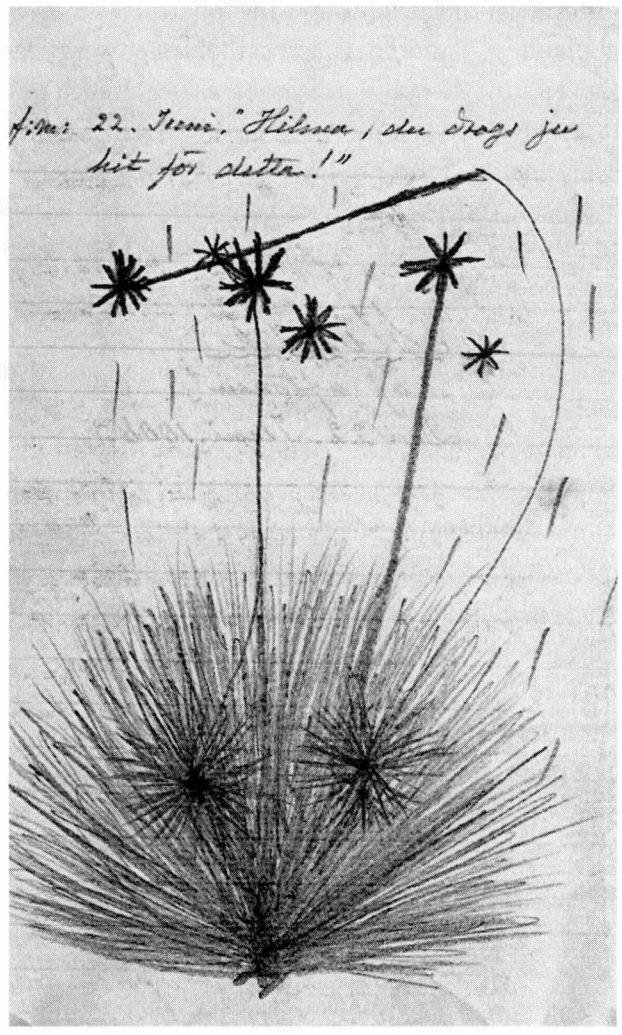

9. Automatic drawing by Bertha Valerius, June 22, 1886.

in the séance also received blessings via Jesus, "him who watches over you like a star in the spiritual world." Af Klint's best friend from the Academy was named Anna Cassel.

That day, Beamish employed all her skills. She channeled the voice of the guardian spirit Lorentz. She saw Jesus in a vision. And, according to the notebook, she passed along a message telepathi-

cally from a mother to a daughter via Jesus, presumably from af
Klint's living mother to her, assuming she was the Hilma present
that day.[8]

———

The notes do not answer the most important questions. How did the
Hilma addressed react to the experience? What did it mean to her?

If Valerius or Beamish helped af Klint understand what had
just happened, they must have done so orally (there is no written
evidence). The women certainly had far more experience with
séances than she did. Only a month before, in May 1886, Valerius
had anonymously published a book on the messages she received
from the "invisible world" as a "writing medium," as she called
herself. Only a privy few could guess who was behind the initials
"B. V." Hilma owned a copy of the text and wrote her name in it.[9]
The book contained important messages for artists: a voice bearing the name "Eon" predicted a future in which the artist would be
equipped with "great power" and would "revive the sacred fire on
the altar of art." Af Klint would have read: "The temple of art will
then no longer be desecrated by sensual images, since music and
painting will harmoniously reproduce the higher pure inspiration."
This had unpredictable consequences for the form. As Valerius's
Eon explained, "completely different expressions will emerge from
the practitioners of art."[10]

As the messages show, Valerius was still preoccupied with the
development of spiritual art, as in her 1879 séance. Eon described
the coming time as a movement, not as the task of a sole individual.
Maybe Valerius hoped the young af Klint could become a companion
or soul sister. "Sister Bertha" is Valerius's name when she appears in
af Klint's notebooks many decades later. "She feels a lot for you," the
aged Hilma was informed by the spirits talking to her in December
1943.[11]

In 1886 Hilma was still just an art student. But Valerius's "temple of art" and the "completely different expressions" of art she
predicted were to become her calling.

3

The Prize

In the fall of 1886 surprising news came from Finland, this time through conventional channels in the form of a press release. Helene Schjerfbeck, a young woman, had won one of the country's most important prizes for a history painting titled *The Death of Wilhelm von Schwerin*. Presented at the annual exhibition of the Finnish Art Society, the work shows a fallen young lieutenant laid out in a barn, the glistening white cloth under his dark uniform glowing like a halo. The painting features five men and, in the background, a peasant woman feeding livestock. The theme, composition, and execution were so unusual for a female artist that the painting was much discussed in the press. There was praise, but criticism as well. A "female painter of battle scenes," one writer complained, was a contradiction in terms. A woman couldn't have any conception of combat.[1]

In her final year at the Academy, af Klint also began to explore history painting, possibly inspired by the Finnish woman who had dared to paint a dying soldier. Perhaps she saw similarities between herself and the artist in Helsinki. Both were born the same year, and Schjerfbeck belonged to the Swedish minority in Finland, like the Sontags, Hilma's mother's family.

In late 1887 or early 1888, af Klint embarked on an ambitious plan to paint a major mythological scene.[2]

Andromeda, the daughter of the Ethiopian king Kepheus, is about to be sacrificed to the sea monster Ketos (fig. 10). She is naked and chained to a rock by both arms, waiting for the monster. Between her and the mainland there is only open sea. The wind blows through Andromeda's hair, and her exposed body is bright against the dark stone.

The dramatic story of how the beautiful princess was saved by Perseus from a gruesome fate has been painted by such major art-

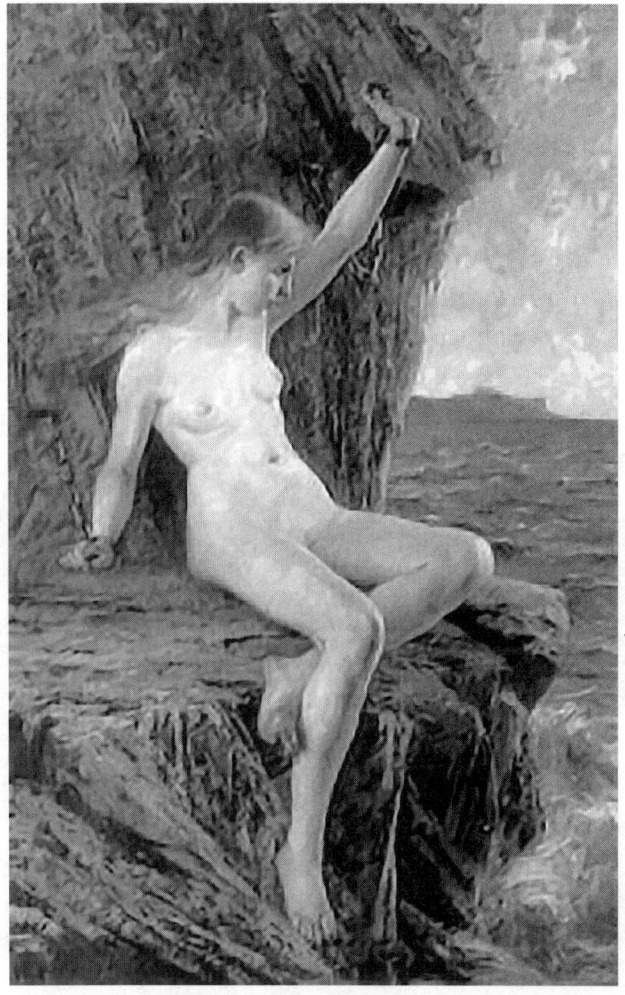

10. *Andromeda by the Sea*, 1888, oil on canvas, 133 x 88 cm.

ists as Vasari, Titian, and Rubens. Like her predecessors, af Klint painted the cliffs, the sea, the iron manacles, and the disrobed virgin. But that is where the similarities end. Af Klint took some decisive liberties. Where is the monster that most artists included? Where is Perseus, whom other paintings show rushing to the rescue? But above all: where is Andromeda's fear? Af Klint did not render the princess with eyes wide open in terror, seeking the viewer's gaze, helpless and pleading. Her Andromeda turns her head to the sea; she seems cool, rational. Nothing betrays the fact that she is in a life-threatening predicament. The victim has been transformed into a heroine, master of her situation. If af Klint needed a model for Andromeda's expression, she didn't have to look far. Across from the Academy was Stockholm's old town with the Church of St. Nicholas and the sculpture of George the dragon slayer that the artist knew from her childhood. The saint in the sculpture also keeps his composure while fighting the dragon. His childlike features are calm, his gaze fixed on the distance.

The princess also resembles her creator: she has the same delicate youthfulness one sees in early photographs of af Klint, the same high forehead, fine nose, narrow face. Perhaps this accounts for Andromeda's look of composure. She seems imbued with the courage and experience of a family that had gone to sea for generations, and it is probably no coincidence that the sea and cliffs in the painting also figure in the af Klint coat of arms.

The artist submitted her painting to the Academy jury in the category of "history painting." But that prize went to a fellow student named B. C. Heppe, who had also entered a painting of Andromeda. Af Klint's painting was honored in the less-prestigious category of "[life] model painting," according to the newspapers. She received 100 crowns.[3]

When af Klint's *Andromeda* appeared at auction in Stockholm in 2002 it sold for little money. Even in Sweden the artist was still relatively unknown, and the hammer price did not even reach the low estimate.[4] It was purchased for roughly 3,600 euros and disappeared into a private collection. If we had to depend solely on the af Klint archive, we would know nothing of the painting today. The artist did not write a word about it, like so many other things that shaped her life without leaving a trace.

As to taking a minor prize for the painting, af Klint had to content herself with this modest success. Her contemporaries continued to argue over the abilities of female artists in general. Many continued to give more weight to the sex of the person who created

a work than to its quality. Carl Larsson's contempt for female students at the Academy grew over the years into cold rage. In an 1889
letter he wrote that he would prefer to kick the lot of them out of
the institution: "Woman must go. Immediately. . . . Has a single
one of these weak women at the Academy become an artist? For me
there is not one who has any value at all."[5] But the clock could not be
turned back. In 1888, the year af Klint graduated, there are newspaper reports of a group exhibition featuring one of her paintings as
well as works by her former teacher Kerstin Cardon. The show was
organized by Sveriges Allmänna Konstförening (Swedish General
Art Association), located in the heart of Stockholm's art district,
overlooking the Kungsträdgården.[6]

[4]

Anna Cassel

From the time they were both students at the Royal Academy, Hilma
and Anna Cassel were best friends. Anna Maria Augusta Cassel
(1860–1937) was born into a wealthy family and entered the Academy in 1880, two years ahead of Hilma. The two had met earlier
when they were both taking preparatory courses at the technical
college.[1] But by the time they were at the Academy, they shared
nearly everything: the dream of becoming artists, a belief in the
accessibility of higher worlds, the ideal of a free society. Together,
they would become convinced that gender was less rigid than generally assumed: masculine qualities were intrinsic to femininity,
and feminine qualities intrinsic to masculinity. The borders could
be fluid.

Only a few letters and a single postcard from the lifelong friendship have survived. The letters were all written by Cassel in Stockholm when the two women were nearing their seventies, and saved
by Hilma, who by then was living in Uppsala and Lund. Cassel's
letters talk about their shared work, including the joint notebooks

created between 1909 and 1915. The letters also cover practical matters: repairing a door, money for the housekeeper, greetings from friends, health.[2]

The postcard from af Klint to Cassel was sent from England on July 17, 1928, when the breakthrough both were hoping for seemed close at hand: finally, af Klint's paintings were to be publicly shown abroad. The message is cheerful and high-spirited.[3]

Anna Cassel saved the postcard.

How did the friendship begin? Cassel was two years older and beginning her third year when Hilma started at the Academy. Cassel lived close to the school, in the central neighborhood of Östermalm, on the elegant Engelbrektsgatan, with her mother and three of her four sisters. There were no men at home: her father, Per August Cassel, had died, leaving his wife, Josefina, and five daughters a large fortune made in the iron- and wood-milling industries.[4]

Anna was the third daughter. Since the death of her husband, Josefina Cassel had cared for the family alone—the estate was enough to provide for everyone. Anna's will, written in 1937, contains an impressive list of holdings, including securities worth 300,000 crowns, comparable today to about 8.5 million crowns or nearly one million euros.[5] Af Klint would paint her wealthy friend several times. A photograph shows Anna in middle age, looking at the camera with a serious expression, her hair pinned up (see plate 11).

The first evidence of artistic exchange between the two women dates from 1887 and 1888: two paintings, made in quick succession, the first by Cassel, the second by af Klint.[6] *Country Lane and Boy, Adelsö*, painted by Cassel, depicts a scene on the island where the af Klint family's estates were located. The painting shows low clouds above a child walking down a narrow lane toward the viewer. The colors are muted; the beauty is in the inconspicuous details—stones covered with lichens, the wildflowers and grasses typical of Sweden's landscape.

As if in response, the following year Hilma painted a similar scene (see plate 12). In her version, the boy is a man, and he walks in the opposite direction, away from the viewer, deeper into the landscape. Once again, the sky is overcast, but pink and violet now appear amid the dark brown and green tones of the landscape. The title is *Summer Landscape (Summer Evening on Öland)*. Öland, too, is an island, in the Baltic across from the town of Kalmar. The similarities between the two landscapes are unmistakable. The country lane, the earthy colors, the solitary figure. Only the formats differ: af Klint's canvas is somewhat larger than Cassel's,[7] as they tended to be.

The friends were further linked by what separated them from other students. Together, they decided not to go study in France, the path taken by so many colleagues. In the 1880s, more than fifty female Swedish artists went to France.[8] While af Klint and Cassel visited the Swedish islands, their classmates were enthralled by Paris and the Louvre. Some of them practiced plein-air painting at the art colony at Grez-sur-Loing. Since French state academies did not admit female students, the Swedish women studied at the private academies of Filippo Colarossi or Rodolphe Julian, hoping their paintings would nonetheless be accepted to the annual Salon, the most important exhibition in Paris. "Real art and true good taste cannot be expected from the Nordic climates," it was said of Sweden at the end of the eighteenth century, and the view was still common during Hilma's time at the Academy.[9] Her native landscape was deemed too cold, too harsh, and too monotonous to be the subject of beautiful paintings, and the majority of artists believed they needed to go south in order to advance their careers—to France, Italy, or at least Germany.

But there were good reasons for the friends' decision not to go to France. Cassel suffered from asthma, and one notebook even mentions tuberculosis.[10] She spent considerable time at health spas. For Hilma, the cost of studying in Paris may have been an issue. From 1879 on, the af Klint family lived at Stora Bastugatan 13, still near the city center, and had enough money for a servant.[11] But they had no fortune like the Cassels. Paris cost money. Courses at the private academies that were so popular with Swedish women were expensive. The prices were significantly higher for women than for men, though they studied side by side.[12]

While Cassel was in her final year at the Academy, French influence nonetheless arrived in Stockholm. In the fall of 1885, dozens of canvases by Swedish artists emerged from the city's studios, still smelling of fresh paint. They were loaded onto horse-drawn carts or carried under arms, along the riverbanks, past the opera, through the city park, past the wondering guests at Theodor Blanch's legendary café, and into the building next door, to Blanchs Konstsalong (Art Salon), the premier address for independent art exhibitions in the city. The space, a former theater with high ceilings and splendid stucco decorations, had been rented out for a month by a group of artists seeking to escape the rigid academicism that dominated the Stockholm art world.[13] The exhibition ran from mid-September to mid-October. Paintings were hung cheek by jowl: there were portraits, landscapes, genre paintings, and paintings of animals. The exhibition's title—*Opponenterna*, or "the opponents"—made it clear that the show was an attack on the antiquated customs of academic art.[14]

One of the "opponents" was Carl Larsson, who had spent several years in France and who alone showed eight works at Blanch's Art Salon. Larsson had already participated in a show with a more conciliatory title, *From the Banks of the Seine*. Most of the works chosen for that show as well as for *Opponenterna* were strongly influenced by French realism and impressionism. Artists like Larsson wanted the Royal Academy to include more plein-air painting in the curriculum, more scenes of everyday life, bolder colors and more light. Organizers hoped that the fact that many of the participants came from the Academy's own ranks would not be lost on the instructors and directors. The show occasioned Sweden's first illustrated catalogue, with a title page designed by Larsson.[15] Alas, the Academy was unresponsive; the curriculum did not change.[16]

The most unusual painting in *Opponenterna* was also the one that came closest to the understanding of art that af Klint and Cassel would one day champion. The painting by Ernst Josephson (1851–1906) did not include anything that could be seen in nature with the naked eye. The motif came to the painter in a dream, he

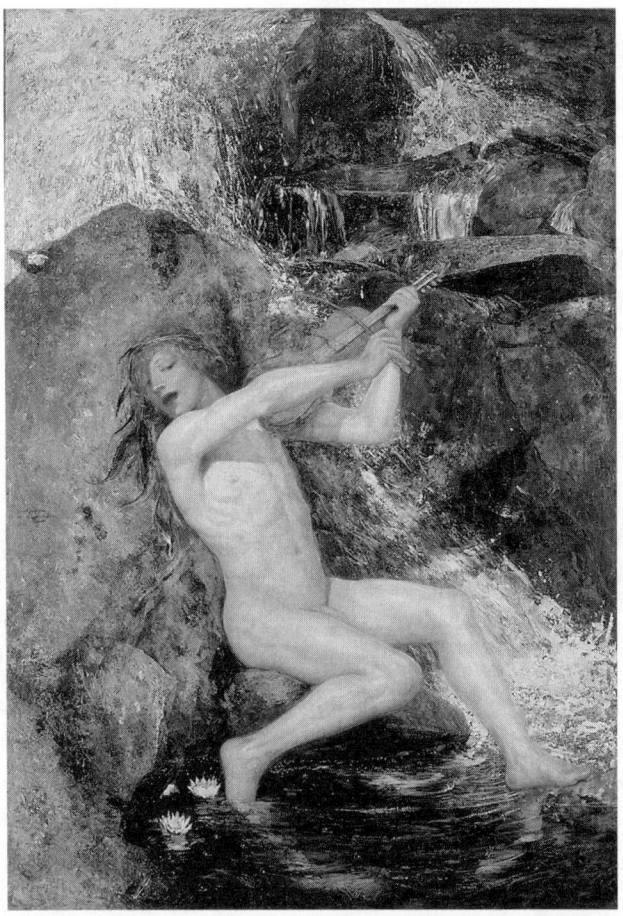

11. Ernst Josephson, *Water Sprite* (*Strömkarlen*), 1884,
oil on canvas, 216 x 150 cm.

said, as a vision during a trip to Italy after the death of his mother
and sister.[17] The piece was called *Strömkarlen*, or *The Water Sprite*,
and it shows an enraptured male nude playing the violin in a fiercely
cascading waterfall (fig. 11).

Josephson was a leader of the Opponenterna, which is why his
water sprite was included in the show. Josephson had already built
a successful career in Paris, but as a genre painter of subjects such
as laughing blacksmiths or a gang of jolly vagrants. His reputation

meant no one could prevent him from hanging *Strömkarlen* on the wall at Blanch's Art Salon, though even his closest friends disliked the painting and tried to talk him out of it. To Josephson, his vision was worth more than the opinions of colleagues. He was interested in the invisible disembodied powers that could travel through space and time, not unlike conversations on the newly invented telephone—of which there were now several hundred in Stockholm. The second work that Josephson exhibited with the Opponenterna was in fact titled *On the Telephone*.[18]

Like af·Klint, Josephson sometimes attended séances. The number of spiritual societies in Stockholm was increasing year by year. Bertha Valerius had founded the Cloverleaf Society.[19] Huldine Beamish would name the group that she organized in 1890 the Edelweiss Society. Af Klint and Cassel would join the Edelweiss Society, and they would also have contact with the Theosophists, who first established a group in Sweden in 1888, then later an independent section, which Lotten Cassel, one of Anna's sisters, joined in the mid-1890s.[20] In 1890 the Swedish Society for Psychical Research was founded with the goal of investigating supernatural phenomena through scientific means. One of its members was Georg von Rosen, Hilma's painting teacher at the Academy.[21] Also active was a much older initiative, the Spiritistiska Lånebibliothek, opened in 1877. An important protagonist in spiritual circles was also Oscar Busch (1844–1916), a writer and adjutant at the Karlberg naval academy run by Hilma's father.[22] Busch has been described as the "driving force" of another society, the Spiritistiska Litteraturföreningen, and started publishing books on spiritual matters as early as 1888.[23]

Since the two women were still quite young when they first became acquainted with spiritual communities, they may have found their way along Karlavägen, a wide street in the city center, to the home of Sweden's most famous writer, Viktor Rydberg (1828–95).[24] The author, scholar, and translator was more than thirty years older than they were, wore a mustache with twisted ends, and regularly opened his home to guests to debate questions of religion and spirituality. Here men and women, members of the nobility and the bourgeoisie, scientists, artists, Jews, and Christians all mingled. The circle interested in Theosophy first met at Rydberg's home in 1888; four months later the Swedish branch of the Theosophical Society was established.[25]

———

Cassel and af Klint kept their eyes and ears open. They didn't need Paris or France for inspiration. While the French style of painting was creating an uproar in leading artistic circles, Stockholm had enough to offer them. Their travels took them to other dimensions, and for that they needed neither ships nor trains.

[5]

"My First Experience with Mediumship"

It is one thing to be around people who speak with the dead or with higher beings. It is another thing to receive messages oneself. Many years after the fact, af Klint described the first time this happened to her in one of her rare autobiographical notes:

> My first experience with mediumship occurred in fall 1891, when the painter Valborg Hällström was using a psychograph in her studio and my interest was aroused. I asked if a few words could be said to me through the instrument. It was said immediately: Go calmly on your way and when I wanted further explanations they continued through life.[1]

The spirit message is underscored in the note.

The "psychograph" that af Klint mentions was a widely used device in spiritualist circles, including that of Valerius and her Cloverleaf Society.[2] The instrument consisted of a wooden frame over a plate that contained the letters of the alphabet. To receive messages from the other world, a hand would be placed on the frame, which was equipped with an indicator. During a séance, the hand would unconsciously guide the device. The indicator would thus point to letters which could then be formed into words.

According to Hilma's account, she first simply listened to the messages that Hällström received through the psychograph. But then she took a more active role and did not need a device: the messages came "through life," as she wrote, addressing her directly for the first time.

Later in the fall, she reported using the psychograph again to try to get in touch with the other world, at the house of the Helleday family, friends of the af Klints who also had an estate on Adelsö. This time the message that came was that Hilma should take better care of her health. Shortly thereafter she fell out of a horse-drawn cart and took to her bed "with bad pain." The accident is recorded in a sketchbook, next to a small portrait that was crossed out.[3] The messages then instructed her how to treat her bruises: with cold compresses. Once she had recovered, she received welcome news:

> It was said to me: <u>Hilma will receive a great gift, if she never forgets the power of the highest</u>.[4]

This sentence, too, was underlined in the notebook.

[6]

The Young Artist

After af Klint graduated from the Academy, her name appeared in the press with some frequency, mainly in regard to exhibitions organized by the Sveriges Allmänna Konstförening, the Swedish

General Art Association, an umbrella organization for the fine arts headed by Georg von Rosen. Starting in 1886, she participated in group exhibits, showing work up to several times a year.[1] The shows were generally well attended.

The exhibition space was located in the center of Stockholm, on the second floor of a three-story building at Hamngatan 5. Windows faced a square featuring a statue of King Karl XIII surrounded by four lions. Above the Konstförening's rooms were spacious studios where Hilma would one day paint some of her most important works.[2]

People coming to see shows would pass by the cosmopolitan Blanch's Café on the ground floor. The owner and operator, Theodor Blanch, had won a prize at the world's fair in Vienna for his excellent cuisine, and since then had enjoyed an international reputation. Colorful awnings vaulted over the entrance and terrace of the café, where there was live music in the summer.

When Hilma left the building after a show, as she turned toward home she would pass Blanch's other establishment, the Art Salon where the Opponenterna had presented their work in 1885. Theodor Blanch's Art Salon was the most prestigious address in Stockholm's art world, and according to the newspapers af Klint showed there at least once in a group exhibition. In 1891 she showed *Evening Mood*, a landscape with a glowing red sky,[3] and her friend Anna Cassel showed the painting *Hoarfrost*. Af Klint's painting seems not to have sold, as it appeared two years later in the exhibition Birger Jarls Basar at Norrmalmstorg.[4] In 1890 another article mentions that she had two landscapes in a show organized by Nya Idun, a women's cultural society cofounded by Anna Whitlock, Hilma's former schoolteacher.[5]

Blanch's establishments were not only important sites for art and music but also portals to the modern era in Sweden. Blanch's Café featured Stockholm's first electric lighting. The city's first cinema would open in the building near the turn of the century. The café offered foreign newspapers, and the waiters wore tailcoats in the Parisian style. Many artists were regular customers. Musicians performed the newest compositions, and once an all-female orchestra visited from Bohemia, causing a sensation.[6]

Over the next few years the art world transformed before af Klint's eyes. As a student, she had watched the Opponenterna create a stir with their French-inspired ideas, producing scenes of daily life in the sunny style of the impressionists. They were led by Carl Larsson and Anders Zorn. Af Klint later owned a small book by Zorn containing illustrations of naked bathers.[7]

Less than a decade after the Opponenterna exhibition, the tables turned, and Scandinavia had become the inspiration for artistic innovation. Art lovers and critics no longer seemed to mind that the barren harshness of the north had once been judged infertile ground for art. Now the opposite was true. When Ernst Josephson's *Strömkarlen* was displayed at Blanch's Art Salon for the second time, in 1893 in a solo show, it was a great success. The same painting had provoked only head-shaking and embarrassed silence when it had first been shown with the Opponenterna (see fig. 11). This time the water sprite was purchased by the young Prince Eugen, the greatest art patron in Sweden, who also painted—primarily Nordic landscapes. And the Swedish artist Richard Bergh published an essay in the art magazine *Ord och Bild* praising *Strömkarlen* as a masterpiece.[8] The water sprite, Bergh wrote, was a testament to Nordic will and deep insight. He read the painting as the manifesto of a new generation of Swedish artists who no longer needed to seek inspiration abroad. The general enthusiasm for Josephson continued even with his latest work, painted following a nervous breakdown in France, which necessitated a stint in an institution. Since then, his pictures had been populated with light beings that appeared in gleaming aureoles, bright and glistening, painted in thick impasto. The dazzling light of impressionism was transformed in Josephson's work into the eternal inner light of the divine. The artist signed his works with the names of Old Masters, from Holbein to Michelangelo to Rembrandt.[9] They had guided his hand, he claimed. The visitors to Blanch's Art Salon were awed.

Then, in October 1894, the large paintings of a young Norwegian, Edvard Munch, were presented at Blanch's. They had no trace of the sparkling light of French impressionism. Instead the colors were dark, the themes heavy. A painting of a pale man staring out to sea was called *Jealousy*. A painting of a woman whose hair flows over her lover like water bore the title *Vampire*. In *The Scream*, the subject seems to hold his own skull in his hands.[10] No one guessed that these pictures would one day be world famous. The rumor mill buzzed with stories of a scandal in Berlin, where the artist's show had to be closed the day after opening. Munch's growing fame, at that point, rarely resulted in sales.

At least two of the grim scenes that hung at Blanch's might have struck a chord with Hilma. In *The Sick Child*, Munch painted his own sister shortly before her death; the girl died three years before Hermina af Klint. In *Summer Night's Dream (the Voice)*, a lonely figure in white wanders through a wood, listening intently to the voice of an invisible being. Af Klint would later describe an almost identical event when she jotted down the words of an invisible speaker in the woods of Adelsö.[11]

Like many other famous contemporaries who exhibited at Blanch's, Munch is not mentioned in af Klint's notes. The single exception is August Strindberg (1849–1912)—a loose sheet in the archive deals with his previous lives and incarnations.[12] The playwright and the artist may have met at Huldine Beamish's home, as Strindberg sometimes attended her salons and séances.

Only one surviving picture by af Klint concerns the cultural life of Stockholm. The oil sketch shows a couple at a museum, a woman in a hat on the arm of a gentleman with a top hat, standing in front of a marble statue of a woman.[13] The couple could be at the National Museum, in the antique collection donated by Gustav III. (Founded in 1866, the museum still exists.)

Another small drawing in the archive offers a hint of the subjects that interested the artist when she was young. The sketch shows a canal bridge with a swan swimming past; in the background, the silhouette of a cathedral stretches toward the sky. "Bruges" is written on the reverse, there is no date (fig. 12). It is a travel sketch,

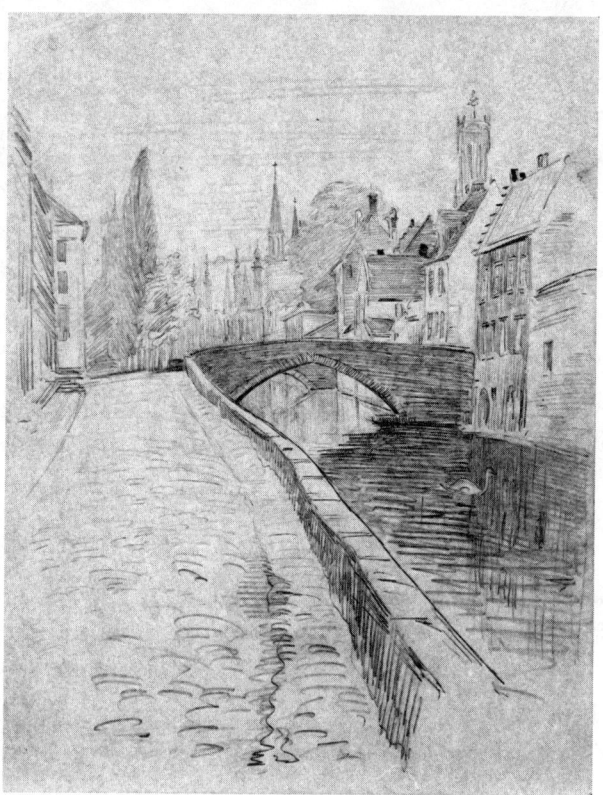

12. Sketch of Bruges, pencil on paper,
Stiftelsen Hilma af Klints Verk, HaK 1633.

made quickly. In the 1890s the artist regularly traveled to other countries, but only the occasional sketch survives. There were many reasons for a trip to Bruges. One of the city's most famous artworks is Michelangelo's *Madonna of Bruges*, acquired by rich merchants when the city was called the Venice of the North.

In 1892 there was another reason to visit Bruges. The Belgian author Georges Rodenbach published the book *Bruges-la-Morte*, which was translated into many languages. The title page, designed by the Belgian painter Fernand Khnopff, is remarkably similar to af Klint's sketch with the canal, bridge, and church in the background. But instead of the swan that glides past in the sketch, Khnopff's image shows a woman's corpse, her long hair flowing around her like water. Rodenbach's novel deals with the woman's murder by her lover; the decaying city in the background reflects the state of his soul. The success of Rodenbach's book turned Bruges into a popular destination, particularly for artists seeking the mystical and mysterious who were known as "Symbolists."[14]

Was af Klint one of them? It could be argued that her impassive *Andromeda* had been executed in a Symbolist vein: it inscribed a modern viewpoint on a classical mythical figure, just as Gustave Doré and Gustave Moreau had done before her in France: they, too, had portrayed Andromeda as they paved the way for Symbolism. (Af Klint later owned an edition of *The Divine Comedy* illustrated by Doré.)[15]

Her estate also includes a small oil sketch depicting the triumphal procession of Bacchus. The god of intoxication and ecstasy rides through the night on a tiger, attended by fauns and maenads.[16] In Sweden, the Swiss artist Arnold Böcklin was much admired for his Nordic-looking paintings populated with hybrid creatures. His red-cheeked water gods splash amid the churning gray waves of the North Sea, and the centaurs and fauns are covered in thick winter fur. Af Klint's library would later contain a book by a Swedish art historian who extensively discussed Böcklin's work.[17]

Two symbols that would soon play a central role for af Klint were emblems of the Symbolist movement in Paris: the rose and the cross. Like lodestars, they graced the catalogues and posters of the exhibitions that Joséphin Péladan (1858–1918), the author, critic, and founder of the Mystic Order of the Rose + Croix, began organizing in 1892. Named after the secret society of the Rosicrucians, the Salons de la Rose + Croix brought together works by such Symbolist artists as Ferdinand Hodler, Félix Vallotton, Khnopff, and various students of Gustave Moreau.

For Péladan, Symbolism offered a way to resist the present, and his agenda was unapologetically retrograde. He denounced scientific materialism, instead exalting the Catholic faith, the Middle Ages, and monarchy. The impresario of Symbolism even styled himself as a priest, wearing long robes and the pointy beard of a magician.

One of the Swedish artists who had seen Péladan's grand project firsthand was Tyra Kleen (1874–1951), a painter, graphic artist, writer, journalist, and regular at Edelweiss Society séances. Kleen visited Péladan's last salon in 1897 and came away with an unequivocal judgment: the Rosicrucian movement and its exhibitions were ridiculous.[18]

The young Kleen exemplified the rift that was dividing the spiritualist movement into two camps. At first glance, she would seem the perfect fan of Péladan's salons. She loved dramatic presentation, her tastes tended to the mysterious and mystical, and she was eccentric, well educated, and talented. She was at the start of her career and had studied in Karlsruhe, Dresden, and Paris. Her works are peopled with classical heroes and mythic beings like sphinxes and elves. She read Symbolist literature by Charles Baudelaire and Paul Verlaine, whose portraits she saw in the Rose + Croix salon in Paris.

The difference between Kleen and Péladan can be discerned in their approaches to time. Péladan turned to the Rosicrucians to escape the present, training his gaze back to the past. His mysticism referenced ostensibly supreme laws, and his understanding of the old order was overtly misogynist. "No work by a woman will ever be exhibited or commissioned," declared a statute of Péladan's fraternity. In fact, some female artists did hang work in his salons, but under male pseudonyms.[19]

Tyra Kleen, on the other hand, looked to the future. Photographs show her riding a bicycle or dressed in male garb—knickerbockers and a sports jacket. Her face betrays her pleasure in the dawn of the new era. Kleen wished to escape the rigidity of social conventions through engagement with higher spheres. Her mysticism was futuristic, fueled by the drive to change, transform, move. In her art, she revised traditional motifs with an eye toward a brighter future. For example, in her illustrated book *En Psykesaga*, from just after the turn of the century, she offers a new take on the ancient myth of

Eros and Psyche. In Kleen's version, Psyche rebels against the old order, challenging her father:

> If you are my father, what gave you the right to give me life? If you have no better gift for me than this existence, then take it back. Either give me light and freedom or kill me.[20]

Psyche ultimately escapes the narrow confines of patriarchal tradition to make her own way.

Kleen traveled too much to encounter Hilma regularly in Stockholm's spiritualist circles.[21] It is nonetheless likely they met in the 1890s, though it would be years before they got to know each other well.

Documents from Hilma's early years as a professional artist are extremely scarce and offer only fragmentary impressions. After she graduated, her relationship with the Academy seems to have remained copacetic, as she was awarded a study grant in 1891.[22] She liked to travel, judging from the sketches of Bruges and from trips along the Rhine and to Holland, Germany, and Norway.[23] Traveling had become easier by the end of the nineteenth century. There were ferries from Sweden to Denmark and Germany, and cities on the continent were connected by extensive railroad networks. Hilma, who liked innovation of every sort—both spiritual and earthly—made regular use of them.

[7]

Dr. Helleday and Love

For a moment it looked as if Hilma af Klint would do, after all, what any nineteenth-century woman was expected to do. According to family lore, a man came into her life with a view toward marriage.[1] The circumstances couldn't have been better. Doctor Helleday, who was said to fancy the artist, and she him, came from a family that had been noble for hundreds of years longer than the af Klints. Dr. Helleday's first name has not been passed down; Hilma's relatives seem to have been more interested in his academic title. His education and family background made him a good match for the young artist. The Helleday family originally came from Scotland, but they had emigrated to Sweden in the seventeenth century and were even distantly related to the af Klints: in the mid-nineteenth century, one of Hilma's aunts had married into the Helleday family. The wedding had taken place in the church on Adelsö.[2] Hilma and Dr. Helleday therefore likely first met *en famille*.

There must have been plenty of opportunities for the two to see each other: at society gatherings or at outings to the theater, opera, or exhibitions, or on walks through Skansen, the world's first open-air museum—a miniature Sweden in the middle of the city. The attraction, which opened in 1891, brought together traditional farmhouses from every region of Sweden for city dwellers to marvel over.

It is also possible that a meeting was arranged on Adelsö, where the Helledays also had an estate.[3] The island was reached by ship from Stockholm. The rest of the way to the estate could be traveled by carriage or on foot, through the fields and meadows of billowing grass or through the woods that Hilma so loved.

She had long since reached the age when a woman was expected to marry in Sweden. She was now in her thirties. But in her circle, social expectations had begun to change. For one thing, she knew women who had decided against marriage entirely, like Bertha Valerius and Kerstin Cardon. The law granting single women legal majority gave Swedish daughters a freedom they did not give up easily: a husband was superior to his wife in legal matters, too high a price for many women.

In addition, ideas of what "love" meant were shifting in artistic and socially progressive circles. Richard Bergh's (1858–1919) painting *Knight and Virgin* (fig. 13), first exhibited in May 1897 at the General Art and Industrial Exhibition in Stockholm, exemplifies the mystery and complexity of the feeling.[4] At first glance, the painting shows a classic romantic scene: a huge knight and a childlike vir-

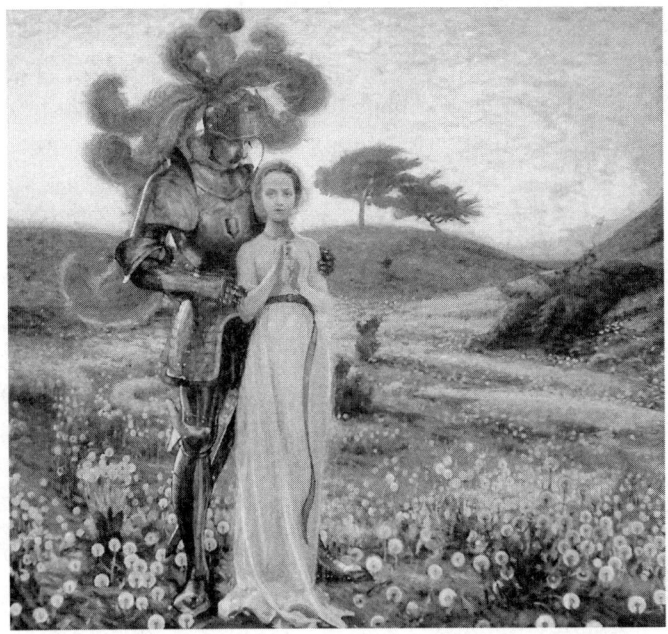

13. Richard Bergh, *Knight and Virgin*, 1897, oil on canvas, 197 x 212 cm.

gin stand together in an autumnal meadow studded with overblown
dandelions that stretch to the horizon. She is delicate, dressed in
white, and holds a dandelion in her hand, looking forward as if she
were unaware of the knight behind her. He, a giant in armor, bends
down to her, the huge, gleaming red feathers that seem to grow
from his helmet dancing enigmatically around him. The knight's
headdress enshrouds the lovers, and the wild motion transports the
scene, as if it were taking place in a liquid environment.

But Bergh's *Knight and Virgin* depicts no ordinary couple. The
figures are embodiments, messengers, and inhabitants of a spiritual landscape that melds dream and reality. The coming together
of the two characters unites opposites: past and present, nature and
culture, male and female.

"All true art," wrote Bergh, who had been so enthusiastic about
Josephson's water sprite, "is the result of an emotional outburst."[5]
Bergh headed the Konstnärsförbundet, an association that had

evolved from the Opponenterna movement. Bergh's paintings were, in a sense, love letters to Sweden: the rugged beauty of the landscape and a history that reached back to the Vikings.[6] *Knight and Virgin* was also a nod to the secret society of the Freemasons. According to their tradition, "knight of the red feather" (*eques a penna ruba*) was the pseudonym of an influential head of the Freemasons in the eighteenth century.[7]

In the esoteric literature that af Klint read, love played a no less important role than in Symbolist art. Texts emphasized compassion, tenderness, and devotion, describing love in all its variety. Carl du Prel (1839–99), a German writer, spiritualist, and Theosophist, wrote of "feelers." This was his term for an organ that was underdeveloped in most people, that had to be trained, he emphasized, in order to discover the secret face of the world, what one sensed in a dream and forgot upon waking. Two of his books from 1890 were in Hilma's collection, heavily underlined.[8]

Love in all its forms was also hugely important in the Edelweiss Society, the Stockholm spiritualist group founded by Huldine Beamish. "Love" and "Purity" were framing concepts, according to the society's 1890 charter.[9] When the group first gathered for séances, they met at Beamish's old apartment on Blasieholmstorg, but eventually the séances were held on Valhallavägen, a grand boulevard with a wide green median in the Östermalm neighborhood.

Beamish's circle had become better organized. There was now an altar and a chapel, a guestbook, member rosters, and running minutes of the meetings, with messages from the beyond scrupulously recorded.[10] The séances had earned a reputation far beyond Sweden. Beamish had admirers in England, met Tolstoy in Russia, and exchanged letters with Oscar II, the king of Sweden.[11] Since she knew several languages, her circle was as international as it was distinguished, and she traveled to ancient sacred sites in Egypt, Constantinople, and Jerusalem in order to develop her own understanding of religious history. Her spiritual salon increasingly attracted artists and intellectuals, including, as mentioned, the writer August Strindberg.

Beamish, who now dressed all in white, continued to cross boundaries set by the state church. She understood her society to be Christian and often quoted the New Testament. Yet she also believed that she had direct access to the divine and that she could facilitate such contact in others. It was no accident that the edelweiss flower was chosen as the movement's emblem. The plant, which grows high on mountain ridges, where heaven and earth meet, had come to her in a vision. Members of the society wore the flower as a badge, the women as a brooch, the men on their watch chains.

Beamish also believed in the possibility of multiple incarnations—which was not part of traditional Christian dogma—and understood herself to be the reincarnation of Saint Catherine of Siena, a fourteenth-century mystic. This claim went too far for several members of the society, including Bertha Valerius, who criticized her for it.

But it was not only in religious matters that Beamish deviated. In questions of love, as well, she left societal norms behind: her ideal of love was one of the few mandatory tenets of the Edelweiss Society. Beamish's followers were urged to seek out a soulmate of the opposite sex. The two halves had to find each other in order to form a unity, like the pieces of a puzzle. But the soulmate to whom Beamish referred was not a spouse. Though married to Captain Richard Pigott Beamish, she had found her soulmate in Carl von Bergen, a well-known writer, translator, and founder of the previously mentioned Swedish Society for Psychical Research. Von Bergen and she, Beamish reported happily, were "a pair of twins sent from heaven to earth."[12] The two had met in 1887 when Beamish attended a lecture given by von Bergen on the Theosophical movement. At their next meeting, suggested by Beamish in an enthusiastic letter, they recognized each other as "dual souls." Von Bergen was also married, but he did not see this bond as standing in the way of a celestial connection. When Beamish died suddenly on December 24, 1892, von Bergen wrote a passionate obituary for his fifty-six-year-old friend in the magazine *Idun*, comparing her to the "angelic Catherine of Siena."[13]

The names Hilma af Klint and Anna Cassel come up repeatedly in one of the Edelweiss Society's black notebooks. On August 31, 1895, Hilma's presence as a guest is noted in elegant handwriting. The text goes on to discuss a drawing that would become "valuable," followed by the instruction to initiate the artist and accept her into the Edelweiss Society. According to the society's records, Hilma joined in the summer of the following year, and Anna Cassel joined that December.[14] By the time the two friends joined the society, Huldine Beamish was already dead, and her daughter, Huldine Fock, had taken over the group.

Borders between spiritualist movements were hazy in those years; they were not yet battling for territory. Spiritualists were on an expedition together and were discovering other worlds that had long existed without anyone's being aware of them. They were euphoric about what they were learning. Hilma was a member of the Edelweiss Society but also had connections to the Theosophical Society, which Lotten Cassel, Anna's sister, joined in 1895. The Theosophists met regularly at Jakobsgatan 16, just a few minutes by foot from Blanch's Café, at the Medical-Mechanical Institute run by Gustav Zander (1835–1920). The doctor and pioneer of physiotherapy was a member of the Academy of Sciences and, since 1889, president of the Theosophical Society in Sweden.[15] Ideas about the unity of masculine and feminine souls similar to those of Beamish were common among the members, though the accompanying theory was more sharply formulated: on the one hand, Theosophists believed that each person had both masculine and feminine characteristics; on the other, man and woman alone were understood to be incomplete if they weren't able to develop their other side. According to the Theosophists, there wasn't a strong and a weak sex, but rather two weak sexes that could be strong when they joined together.

The Theosophists' chief source for this was none other than the Greek philosopher Plato. Plato's *Symposium*, in which the comic playwright Aristophanes propounds his idea of round beings, was an important reference. In the text Aristophanes maintains that in the early days of creation, there had been round beings with two sexes, four arms, and four legs, and they had been the happiest creatures imaginable. But the gods were jealous of their courage and strength and decided to destroy this aggravating perfection by dividing the round beings in two. The beings fell apart like the two halves of an orange, into man and woman. Since then, they had always longed to become one and return to their original form.

Blavatsky, the founder of Theosophy, retells the story in *The Secret Doctrine*, her three-volume magnum opus. The first volume appeared in Swedish translation in 1895, and the second followed three years later. Af Klint owned both.[16] Blavatsky explained that the dual-sex round beings had been called "androgyni." This, she declared, had been humankind's original state. From that state, wrote Blavatsky, "Humanity became distinctly hermaphrodite or bi-sexual," then evolving, "finally, to distinct men and women."[17] Blavatsky surveyed the plant and animal kingdoms seeking evidence and concluded that bisexuality predominated. Many animals had both male and female sex organs, Blavatsky explained, and the consequences were far-reaching. In nature, the sexes were combined in all kinds of ways. There were insects who didn't even need a male mate for reproduction, Blavatsky wrote, her excitement resonating through the lines:

> The Aphids or plant lice keep house like Amazons, and *virgin parents* perpetuate the Race for ten successive generations.[18]

Blavatsky had no interest in pitting myth against science. On the contrary, she meant them to be understood together, and she subtitled her book "the synthesis of science, religion, and philosophy." She connected Plato with biology and leapt from antiquity to Darwin's theory of evolution.

The freer the ideas about sex and gender became in spiritual circles, the more urgently conservative forces worked to restore the old order. For example, prominent figures in medical science had been waging a campaign for years against attempts to expand the role of women. Many were bent on proving that the women's rights movement was detrimental to the health of females. In Sweden, the theories of the Austrian psychiatrist Richard von Krafft-Ebing (1840–1902) found great resonance.[19] Krafft-Ebing was nettled by the fact that more and more women were attending institutions of higher learning and pursuing professions. He explicitly warned against a woman's "learning an art or science, or any profession at all . . . , if doing so would bring her into competition with man in the public sphere." The consequences? Nervous disorders, he said, the results of which could be fatal. He claimed that in the fight for jobs with the male sex, "the number of defeated and dead" women was very high.[20] Education and work brought with them sickness and death for the female sex—such was the conclusion of a scientific profession that claimed its arguments were based on empirical data.

The societies Hilma frequented gave her plenty to think about when it came to the type of bond she wanted to enter into and with whom. In the end, she never married, and "Dr. Helleday" never appears in her notebooks. Only once is the daughter of a cousin named Gustaf Helleday mentioned, with whom she spent an afternoon on Adelsö.[21] Nonetheless, over the course of her life, Hilma sought to investigate the mystery of love in all its forms.

The year 1895 ended with a message for her. On September 5, the minutes of the Edelweiss Society record an announcement by the then-deceased Huldine Beamish. Bertha Valerius had died in March, and, according to Beamish, she wanted "Hilma" to receive her "sign," in the form of Valerius's edelweiss brooch.[22] It was now Huldine Fock who channeled messages from the two souls who had cared so much about Hilma's future spiritual development.

[8]

The Five

For af Klint, 1896 marked the start of a new era that she wished future generations to know about in detail. That was the year she joined with Anna Cassel and three other women to found a group called De Fem, or "The Five." It came into being during a séance of the Edelweiss Society, on Easter Sunday, April 15, 1896. Thenceforth The Five recorded their own separate sessions in nine notebooks spanning 1896 to 1907, which are preserved in af Klint's archive and deal exclusively with spiritual experiences.[1] Bertha Valerius's notebook from 1879 to 1882 is the oldest document in the archive, followed by a long gap. But from 1896 to the artist's death, not a year would pass without assiduous notes being preserved for us by Hilma. The minutes of The Five signal the onset of the chronology that would come to mean so much to her.

Whereas the first notebook contains messages both to The Five and to the Edelweiss Society, the next notebook of The Five beginning on October 8, 1896, is independent. The first entry is cryptic: "I am not leaving my child, I am just gaining an associate. He has grown, has come to the point at which another help can achieve more than that which I leave behind."[2] Who is speaking? Who is the child? What help, for whom? The messages begin and end abruptly, without explanation, something that persists through many hundreds of pages. There are no derivations, no questions or comments. The reader must ascertain the logic of the text for herself.

There are patterns, however: for one, a number of voices return again and again. In the beginning it is Gregor, the namesake of the first book of The Five: "Gregors bok." In a later entry Hilma describes him as a priest who lived during the time of Pope Gregory VII and shared his views. Pope Gregory's politics led in the eleventh century to the Investiture Controversy over who could install high church officials. The Gregor who spoke to The Five wanted to free the church from "Catholic heresies," the artist noted.[3] From the beginning, they were consorting with dissenters and deviators; the entry makes that clear.

Being a dead priest, Gregor behaved as one might expect of a ghost from the Middle Ages: he referred to himself only by his first name—like a saint, pope, or prophet—and whether he would speak at all was anyone's guess. When he did, his Swedish was sophisticated, but his messages did not build on one another, and their significance was anything but clear. Hundreds of years separated

Gregor from The Five, and sometimes it seemed that only fragments of speech were coming through, as if parts had broken away on the long journey through space and time.

For Hilma, it was the start of a challenging time. She was given a subordinate role in The Five even though she had already received some messages herself. She was treated like a novice and at first neither operated the psychograph nor received messages by any other means.

The leader of The Five was Sigrid Hedman (1855–1922). She was seven years older than Hilma and a married mother of five. Many of the messages sent to The Five were transmitted through her. She received them while asleep or in a trance, the notebooks explain.[4] Like the rest of The Five, Hedman also belonged to the Edelweiss Society, regularly attending sessions, and until 1897 the lines between the two groups were blurry: for example, Bertha Valerius came with messages to The Five, always introducing herself as "your old friend Bertha."[5]

Mathilda Nilsson (1844–1923), at fifty-two the oldest member, also played a central role. Nilsson had many years of experience in spiritual matters. In the 1880s she had belonged to Valerius's Cloverleaf Society.[6] For the past five years she had been publishing the monthly magazine *Efteråt. Tidskrift för Spiritism och dermed Beslägtade Ämnen* (*Afterwards. Journal for Spiritism and Related Topics*). The journal ran until 1922 and had a good reputation. When the English Theosophist Annie Besant visited Stockholm, Nilsson interviewed her for the magazine. Besant, who traveled to Stockholm several times in the 1890s, was already a celebrity, known far beyond spiritualist circles. Daily newspapers reported on her lectures, and photographs circulated of Besant wearing bright saris, in homage to India, whose independence movement she supported. For her, the spiritual was political and the political spiritual. Besant spoke up for the rights of women, workers, and colonized peoples. Af Klint read her books and underlined them copiously.[7]

Like Sigrid Hedman, Mathilda Nilsson was married. Her husband was a captain in the navy.[8] Nilsson also received messages, though her body was not the instrument as Hedman's was when she fell into a trance. Nilsson used the psychograph. She laid her hand on the wooden frame and let the higher powers guide the indicator to letters. She also usually was the one to record the messages and later make a clean copy of the notes.[9]

The Five also included Nilsson's younger sister, Cornelia Cederberg (1854–1933), who was unmarried. Cornelia lived with Mathilda and her family. There was also a connection between Cederberg, Anna Cassel, and Hilma: Cederberg, too, had trained in art at the technical college.[10]

The Five usually met weekly in one of their homes.[11] The women prayed before a session; a document from the early days lists Bible passages that were read at the start of a séance.[12] The women would hold hands to form a "chain," like an electrical circuit.[13] Eventually they came to study Theosophical books together, such as Blavatsky's *Secret Doctrine* and Charles Leadbeater's *Invisible Helpers*.[14]

Unlike Beamish's circle, which was conducted like a literary salon where guests were welcome, The Five generally remained closed to outsiders. Only rarely did others attend a meeting, such as Oscar Busch, the writer and adjutant who had founded the magazine *Efteråt* together with Mathilda Nilsson and who ran his own society. Busch brought along Charlotte Busch and two other participants.[15] This particular configuration was known as the "Friday group," and it met several times. Busch was clearly interested in opening up the movement to literary and artistic circles. He had dedicated his first two books to the distinguished novelist Selma Lagerlöf and had corresponded with her on spiritual matters for more than twenty years. Carl Larsson and Anders Zorn, Sweden's two most famous painters, were among his close friends.[16]

The ebullience of the early years of the spiritualist movement was beginning to wane in some quarters; several high-profile leaders were starting to come under criticism. Blavatsky, for example, was accused during her lifetime of plagiarism, forgery, and fraud. The allegations served to undermine the authority of her texts, and the debates continued after she died in 1891.[17] And there could be deleterious consequences for those who participated in spiritual-ism: August Strindberg, for instance, began to suffer hallucina-tions, then underwent the "Inferno crisis," named after his 1897 autobiographical novel. The book's main character attempted alchemical experiments in Paris until the connection to mysterious powers resulted in paranoia and depression—which also happened to the author.[18]

Nor was there good news from the artist Ernst Josephson. His exhibition at Blanch's Art Salon in 1893 had been a success, and his painting *Water Sprite* continued to garner acclaim. But the painter could not enjoy the recognition; he, too, now suffered from depres-sion and paranoia—supposedly triggered by his participation in the séances of a famous medium in France.[19]

And as a new century approached, the sciences that dealt with the changing states of the soul were gathering force. The profession of psychiatry was deeply skeptical of the supernatural. Visions and apparitions were seen as expressions of nervous illness, also called hysteria. In Sweden, more and more mental asylums were open-ing, and women were being locked away twice as often as men.[20] The women's emancipation movement, which encouraged women to study and work, was viewed by many psychiatrists as particularly harmful to the female mind. Unmarried, educated women such as Hilma af Klint, Anna Cassel, and Cornelia Cederberg were seen as being especially susceptible to nervous complaints.

Despite the growing skepticism about spiritualism, the circle of voices who spoke to The Five expanded. Gregor was often relieved by Agnes, and they were followed by Georg, Amaliel, and Clemens. The spiritual beings that spoke to the women understood themselves as messengers from higher authorities, de Höga, or "the High ones," as the listeners were one day told: "We who speak to you are only servants, whose superiors you must seek elsewhere."[21]

Were The Five aware of the similarities between their beings and the deities of other religions? Blavatsky, for example, favored the inclusive polytheism of Hinduism and claimed to receive her insights from a kind of council made up of several spiritual leaders, the so-called Mahatmas in Tibet.[22] The Five followed her in this respect. De Höga also comprised several godlike beings who formed a kind of consortium.

At the same time, Gregor, Agnes, and the other voices tended to behave more like the saints of Roman Catholicism: intermediaries between the earthly and the divine, The Five and the High Ones. Adopting concepts from other religions did not prevent the women from praying to "God, the Lord," as if they were still in Protestant territory.

The messages from the higher worlds reached the women in the form of words and images. The drawings were understood to be automatic: spirits guided the drawer's hand. Many drawings had been produced during Edelweiss Society sessions, always in pencil, so there was never any need to interrupt the process for refilling ink. It was the same with The Five. The dozens of drawings in the large notebooks are as light and delicate as spiderwebs on some days, and as dark and concentrated as thunderclouds on others.[23] Sometimes the long lines wave over the pages like lianas or algae underwater; then suddenly it looks as if the drawer has received an electric shock and the pencil starts to move in jerks, angular zigzags, juddering and scratching.

A device called a "planchette" was also sometimes used. Here the pencil would be clamped into a small wooden board and steered, producing lines with a more mechanical aspect. The Edelweiss Society had a luxury version of the device made of brass, with four little wheels. In a photograph from af Klint's archive, the little vehicle rolls across the séance table, past two portraits of Huldine Beamish.[24]

The higher powers were never more playful than when they drew. The variety of forms that materialized session after session and page after page seems inexhaustible. Geometric elements included spirals, circles, ellipses, grids, and diagonals. Flowers, leaves, trees, fruits, eyes, vases, and stairs appeared on the paper. The images were created quickly, in daring strokes, without any of the care that Hilma, Anna Cassel, and Cornelia Cederberg had learned in their

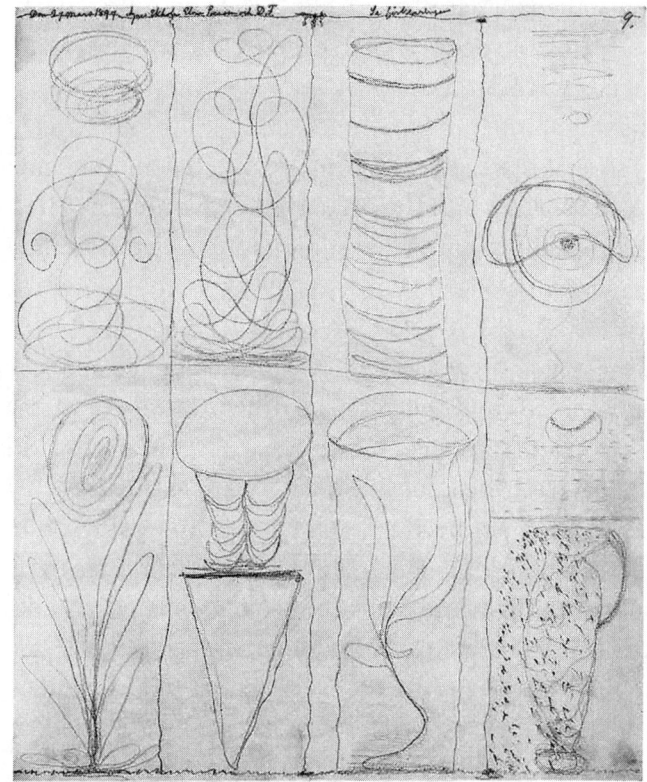

14. Automatic drawing by The Five, March 27, 1897,
Stiftelsen Hilma af Klints Verk, HaK 1515.

drawing lessons. Letters often fly from one corner to another; some-times they form whole words or sentences.

None of these works is easy to understand, and The Five often looked at their handiwork in perplexity. When one day Gregor talked about a drawing (fig. 14), he urged the women not to be frustrated. "It is life, friends," he said, "a rich mixture of the simplest with the most beautiful, the struggle and the joy, calculations, proofs, the striving toward thousands of species, a diverse jumble to the external observer—but behind it all, a unity."[25] There was no talk of a new kind of art. Programmatic announcements like those by Charles and Eon at Valerius's séances in 1879 and 1886 did not come to The Five, at least not while they were led by Hedman and Nilsson.

The group had none of the extroversion or theatricality of Valerius's events; it began modestly.

At the end of the nineteenth century, af Klint was exhibiting less frequently, and Cederberg, despite her training, worked as a seamstress. The hope that making advanced training available to women would herald a new era was dwindling among female artists. Disappointment was spreading. Important commissions continued to be awarded almost exclusively to men. Women had to accept that, in group exhibitions, their work would be installed in a back room or hallway rather than in the main salon. They were still not welcomed into networks dominated by male artists.

The artwork that Cassel and af Klint saw most often in those years was Bertha Valerius's *Christ Painting*. It took Valerius until 1895, the year she died, to complete the painting she had been working on for more than three decades. The original hung in the chapel of the Edelweiss Society. The Five owned a reproduction, which they displayed above an altar constructed from a pedestal, table, and lace tablecloth (fig. 15).

On first inspection the *Christ Painting* seems far from spectacular. Jesus turns his head to the side, his hair falls in waves over his shoulders, his eyes are rimmed by strikingly long lashes. He gazes upward and is illuminated by rays of light. What made the beautiful son of God into a sensation even beyond Sweden was Valerius's assertion that she had received every mark as a medium. Her Jesus had been sent from another dimension, from above, in meticulous detail.

The *Christ Painting* circulated widely throughout Europe, attesting to how interconnected spiritualist groups were across national boundaries and denominations. The work would count among its admirers the biologist and clergyman George Henslow in England, who believed in the connection between science and religion that so many artists and researchers were investigating around the turn of the century. Henslow opined that evolution would lead out of materiality and into the spiritual realm. His theories were given some credence because he had studied science and came from a famous family of researchers: his father was John Stevens Henslow, Charles

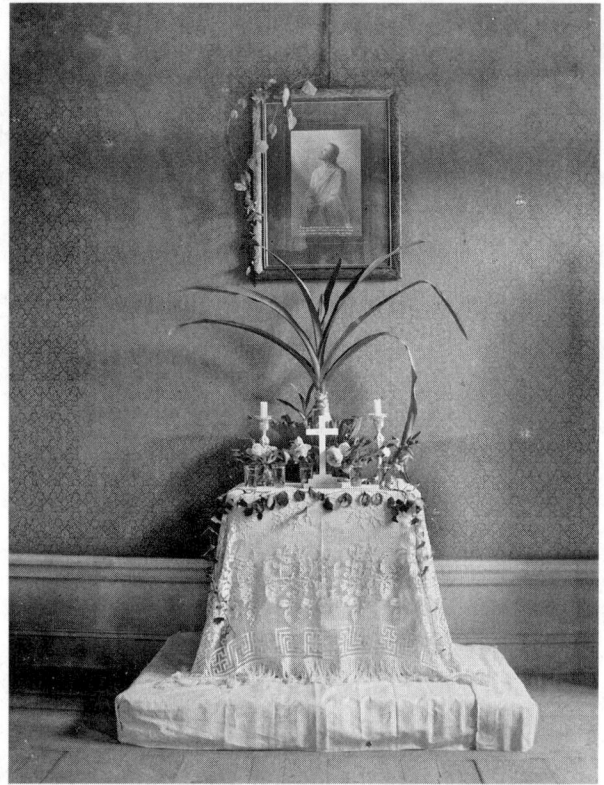

15. Altar of the Five with copy of
Christ Painting by Bertha Valerius.

Darwin's mentor and friend. As a child, Henslow junior had met
Darwin, and as an adult, he corresponded with him about botany.
Henslow attempted to corroborate his ideas about higher worlds by
collecting case studies, which he presented in the book *The Proofs of
the Truth of Spiritualism*. Valerius's "Prince of Peace," as Henslow
called it, was one such proof, and the book contained a full-page
reproduction.[26]

   In addition to the reproduction, The Five had a small, original
drawing by Valerius.[27] The sketch has the same content as the *Christ
Painting* and had probably been donated to the Edelweiss Society
as an early draft. The gift may have been meant as a reminder that

the ways of art are sometimes unfathomable or as encouragement to move beyond the limits of academic painting.

For Hilma, was this what Charles, the prophet of the "fine waves," had meant when he spoke of the "works of genius" of the future? Or the "higher pure inspiration" for the "temple of art" foreseen by Eon?

Since Charles's first predictions at the 1879 séance, the fantastical styles that had come to circulate in groups like the Edelweiss Society and The Five were as disparate as they were distant from those of the official art world. And the automatic drawings were often nonrepresentational. It was one thing for Valerius to draw the face of Jesus but something quite different when it was not the bearer of messages who was depicted, but the messages themselves. The communications, revelations, or disclosures came from another dimension where the spirit had freed itself from matter, from objects and things. It was therefore no longer an issue of depicting something. If content determines form, abstraction is the natural mode of the spirit.

The profusion of drawings and diagrams in Theosophical texts testify to this. The *Teosofisk Tidskrift* published by the Swedish Theosophical Society often included circles, squares, triangles, or pentagrams to introduce readers to the "symbolic language of Theosophy." An article from May 1893 showed how wayward the signifiers could be. First the signs are shown in a row so that each seems to evolve into another: dots become circles and then lines, like the images in a flip book.[28] When Annie Besant visited Sweden in 1897, the magazine printed one of her texts under the title "Occult Chemistry." The piece included a series of diagrams tracing the transformation of matter into spirit (fig. 16).[29]

These particular forms have nothing in common with conventional symbols with fixed meanings. The signs disperse and transform incessantly as in a chain reaction. Blavatsky and Besant were convinced there was a law of the series in the spirit realm, a kind of evolution that both paralleled and furthered the organic one, leading higher and higher, into the spheres of the divine. Everything was

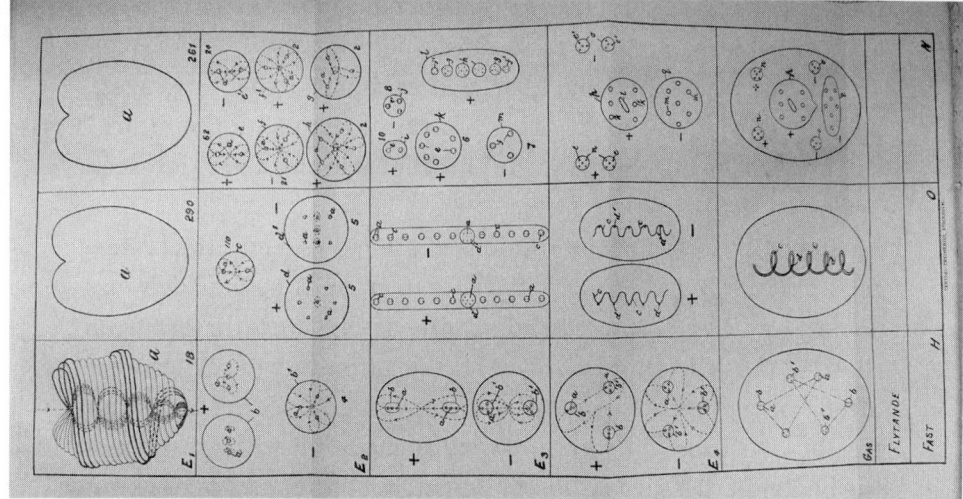

16. Annie Besant, "Occult Chemistry," *Teosofisk Tidskrift*
(Swedish Theosophical Society, 1897).

in motion, everything flowed in this world and in the beyond: two realms connected through the eternal wheel of incarnations. This concept of continual progression is reflected in af Klint's choice to work exclusively in series from 1906 on.

[9]

Art from the Orient

Near the end of the nineteenth century Stockholm's population had grown to almost 300,000, and the country was beginning to define itself as a modern industrial nation. In May 1897 the General Art and Industrial Exposition, a world's fair, opened with a bang, comprising hundreds of buildings and pavilions. The exposition aimed to show that Sweden and Norway, which still formed a union, had much more to offer than forest, water, and natural resources.

Sweden, in fact, embodied the very spirit of invention. Modernity. Industry. The fair featured a state-of-the-art sawmill, a mine, a fishery hall, and an armory. One could inspect ships of the Swedish fleet, including the historic *Amphion*, where Gustav III had signed the document ennobling Erik Klint more than a century before.[1]

The Lumière brothers traveled from Paris to make a film about the exposition: the first ever created on Swedish soil. The filmmakers had astonished the world by filming a train pulling into a station, and their reputation preceded them. In Stockholm they filmed everything from visitors arriving by streetcar, ferry, and train and streaming jubilantly into the fairgrounds to a military parade heralding the arrival of the king and crown prince. The minute the film was finished, it became a main attraction of the fair. At the Lumières' cinema, viewers watched Oscar II ascend the staircase of the main building in full ceremonial dress, followed by Crown Prince Gustaf, in continuous loop. Again and again, the wind blew through their bicorn hats, ruffling the ostrich feathers, which danced around the father and son like those of the knight in Richard Bergh's painting (see fig. 13), which was hanging in the fine arts section.[2]

The af Klint family had good reasons to visit the exposition. Hilma's brother, Gustaf, had achieved the rank of captain in the navy like his father, grandfather, and great-grandfather. The marine section of the fair showed their world, and the *Amphion* was part of family history. And then Ida, Hilma's sister, was affiliated with the Nordic Museum, which opened a new building in connection with the exhibition, allowing folklore collections from all over Scandinavia to be united under a single roof.[3] Ida worked for the museum as a typist, and Hilma had once painted a medieval tapestry from the museum's collection; the unfinished piece is in her estate.[4]

Hilma does not mention the world's fair in her notebooks, but two shows must have elicited great interest in spiritualist circles. One was a display of X-ray images, shown to the Swedish public for the first time. The images made by the mysterious rays that had been discovered just the year before seemed to confirm the spiritualists' intuitions. Hadn't they long believed in spectral powers that could penetrate matter? The phenomenon had become a central argument for the existence of invisible worlds in Theosophical literature.[5]

The other sensation was a simple white building with a flat roof that might have been a harbinger of the modern architecture soon to come, were it not for the arched windows and ornamented door. Once inside, visitors found themselves in rooms covered from floor to ceiling in carpets and fabrics and filled with a labyrinth of cabinets and display cases. In the middle of the structure stood a wooden horseman wearing a turban, atop a decorated steed. The sheer number of objects packed into the small building was overwhelming: golden bowls from Mosul; lamps from Byzantium; Persian faience; funerary ornaments from Samarkand; old Turkish weapons; doors from Turkmenistan.

The exhibition was a paradise for Theosophists. For them, wisdom and insight constituted a mosaic; understanding had to be pieced together from the world religions, supplemented by the findings of science. The Christian parts of the mosaic could easily be found in Sweden, along with the newest scientific research. What was missing was direct access to the other countries then lumped together under the term "Orient." Such traditions could be read about in the books of Blavatsky and others, and spiritualist magazines regularly printed essays on Hinduism, Sufism, and the teachings of Mohammed.

Now, for the first time in Sweden, an abundance of works from this region were being presented to the public in an evocative display of the collection of Fredrik Robert Martin (1868–1933). In addition to mundane articles—lamps, doors, and vases—there were many cult objects: Persian prayer rugs; an old canvas from Upper Egypt with the woven inscription "all power belongs to Allah"; a piece of black silk that veiled the Kaaba in the Great Mosque of Mecca; a "unique and extremely valuable manuscript of the Quran on parchment with Kufic letters, probably from the eighth century," according to the booklet for the exhibition.[6] There were also sumptuous miniatures, painted during the Mughal period, when the Muslim rulers of the Indian subcontinent employed skilled artists in their courts. Rembrandt van Rijn had been a great admirer of the Mughal painters and collected their works.[7] But that had been a long time ago, and Swedish visitors to the exhibition were seeing the images for the first time.

What was set in motion in this building was no passing fad. The pieces in the exhibition would influence art history far beyond Sweden. It was not only the exquisite artifacts themselves that were unusual, but also the appreciation with which they were received. The booklet repeatedly refers to "masterpieces," a term normally reserved for European artworks. The reassessment set a precedent, and when the same collection was shown a decade later in Munich, it had been significantly enlarged and was accompanied by a detailed catalogue. "Masterpieces of Muhammadan Art" lured artists from all across Europe to the Bavarian capital. Edvard Munch came from Norway, and Henri Matisse from Paris. Franz Marc, Gabriele Münter, and Wassily Kandinsky also attended; it wasn't far for them, as they lived in the area.[8] Kandinsky wrote a panegyric on the show, and Franz Marc dreamed of one day hanging works by Kandinsky alongside the carpets of the exhibition. Marc wrote: "Why do we so marvel at and admire this oriental art? Does it not mockingly show us the narrowness of our European understanding of painting? The artistry of its color and composition is a thousand times deeper and puts our conventional theories to shame."[9] In 1910, the artists of the avant-garde were unanimous: they had seen the art of the future, and it came from the past.

———

But back to the Swedish exposition of 1897 and the collection of oriental art belonging to Fredrik Robert Martin. Martin was not yet thirty at the time. He moved in artistic circles and was close to the painter Anders Zorn, who is highlighted in his memoir.[10] In a portrait by the Swiss artist Ferdinand Hodler, Martin is a dark-haired man with a full beard, double-breasted suit, orange tie,

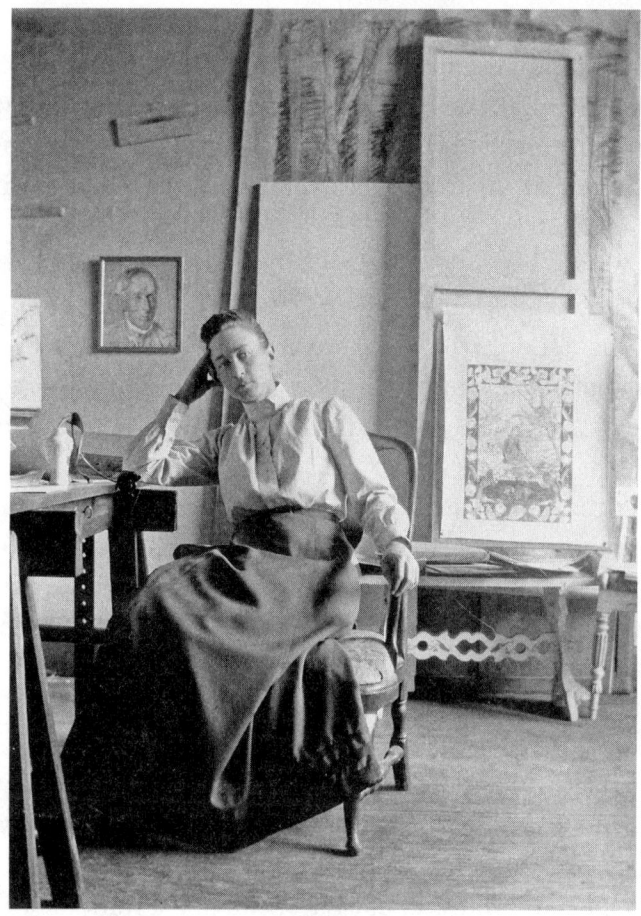

17. Af Klint in her studio around 1902, Stiftelsen Hilma af Klints Verk.

and an appraising expression.[11] Martin was a dealer, explorer, and autodidact whose mania for collecting is attested by the glut of publications he wrote. His magnum opus, *The Miniature Painting and Painters of Persia, India, and Turkey. From the 8th to the 18th Century*, was a work of such distinction that Carl Larsson purchased both volumes. Larsson owned an Indian miniature given to him by Harald Bildt, a diplomat and member of the Theosophical Society who in 1913 would organize a group exhibition that included works by af Klint.[12]

When af Klint was photographed in her studio at the beginning of the century (fig. 17), the camera captured a confident young artist.[13] Curiously the conventional attributes of her craft—paintbrush, palette, easel—are absent. Instead, the painter seems lost in thought, her head tilted toward the portrait of her late grandfather that hangs in the background. Before her on the table is a wilted flower, its petals dropped. The circular arrangement of plant, portrait, and face might be seen to form the cycle of life and death as in a mystical wheel of incarnations.

For those of Hilma's contemporaries not interested in spiritual matters, the photograph would signal the painter's respect for her family heritage. The seafaring af Klints had secured a place in Sweden's history, especially Gustaf, the cartographer and young marine of the battle of Vyborg, pictured here. The young woman in the photograph looks like someone with big plans for her own future.

[10]

Rose and Cross

In 1898 things took a decided turn for The Five. On April 5 Sigrid Hedman had a vision in which the women were summoned to prepare for a new apprenticeship: she saw three steps leading up to an alcove with a "painting in dark colors" in the background.[1] Gradually a white cross appeared, followed by the message "three months as novitiates." Next, the symbolism of the three steps was explained; the training the women were to undergo would last three times three months. Each phase was assigned a concept: "word," "thought," and "rosary." The last was understood in a double sense, as a request to pray and as a reference to the rose.

The women were told little more. Previous messages had talked of love, unity, and humility—virtues that could just as easily be extolled in a Protestant sermon. Now, something new was hap-

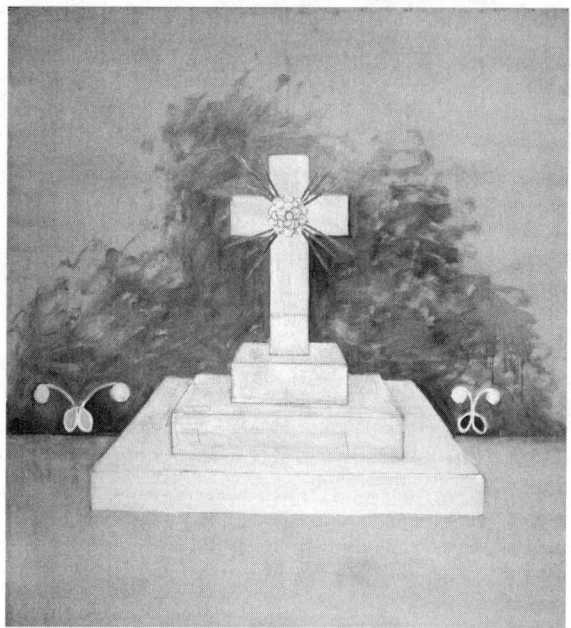

18. *The Altar of the Five*, in *The Large Figure Paintings,
No. 9, Group III, WU/The Rose*, 1907, oil on canvas,
Stiftelsen Hilma af Klints Verk, HaK 47.

pening. The Five were to view themselves as a fellowship, having
received a sign of their perfection: the rose and cross. The women
turned Hedman's vision into reality, building an altar of wood and
glass. A pane of glass with a gold border was inserted into the middle
of the cross. The glass was engraved with the rose used by Robert
Fludd in 1629 as the frontispiece of his book *Summum Bonum*. In
the book, the English scholar and doctor defended the ideas of the
Rosicrucians, though stressing that he himself was not a member
of the secret society.[2]

Af Klint preserved a preliminary sketch of the rose in a small
white leather folder printed with the edelweiss flower of Beamish's
society. She changed the number of petals from the seven in Fludd's
drawing to five, matching the number of women in the group. The
artist later made a painting of the altar (fig. 18).[3]

Af Klint frequently associated herself with the Rosicrucians both in documents and in public, though it is unclear what this meant to her. We do not know if she belonged to a lodge, but she obviously saw herself and her friends as belonging to a tradition of dissenters. The Five met under the symbols of a secret society that understood itself as the origin of Christian reform movements. It was said that Frater Christian Rosenkreuz, the eponymous founder of the Rosicrucians, died the same year that Martin Luther was born.[4] According to the Rosicrucians, Martin Luther had steered Christian teachings back onto the right path. Their task was to amplify the teachings with ancient wisdom, drawing on the Kabbala, Hermeticism, and alchemy. Hilma followed their syncretic approach but primarily combined the religious principles of Buddhism and Hinduism with Christian ideas.

The leather folder in which Hilma kept the rose drawing also contained photographs and assorted documents, including the typed minutes of a séance, headed with the artist's name, "Fröken af Klint." The minutes describe a vision dedicated to af Klint that involved the spirits of two dead people, a man and a girl, possibly family members. What is most interesting is that the typescript is in English, suggesting that af Klint continued to participate in international groups, well beyond The Five. She may have met the English-speaking person who typed the document through the Edelweiss Society or through the Theosophists, but their name remains a mystery.

In adopting the rose and cross, af Klint associated herself with the same symbols as Joséphin Péladan and his order "de la Rose + Croix du Temple et du Graal" in Paris. Péladan organized a series of exhibits of Symbolist art known as Salons de la Rose + Croix. The salons were closely followed by the Swedish press until the final one in 1897.[5]

But the differences between af Klint and Péladan are more decisive than the similarities. Whereas Péladan understood his movement as a kind of church exercising influence on society at large, The Five, by contrast, resembled a cloister. They did not seek an audience for their séances or promote the insights they gained. They were still a fledgling group with no mandate to expand.

In studying the Rosicrucians, af Klint read texts by Franz Hartmann (1838–1912), a German Rosicrucian and Theosophist. His book *Magic, White and Black* had been translated into Swedish in 1889 by the Theosophist Victor Pfeiff, and a copy can be found in the artist's library. To disabuse readers of any misunderstanding caused by the sensational title, Hartmann wrote in the very first sentence: "Whatever misinterpretation ancient or modern ignorance may have given to the word *Magic*, its only true significance is *The Highest Science, or Wisdom, based upon knowledge and practical experience*."[6] Anyone who embraced this wisdom could set in motion the "spiritual powers" that all people possessed though few understood. This was the essence of mysticism. Spirit could move matter; it was more powerful than matter because it was the source and cause of all things. The beings who spoke to The Five were of the same opinion. In November 1898, Mathilda Nilsson received a message through the psychograph explaining the white cross. The symbol stood for "the descent of the spirit into matter—the rising of matter through spirit."[7]

The af Klints spent the summer of 1898 on the island of Adelsö. On August 9, Hilma's father, Victor, died at the family estate of Hanmora. He was buried in Stockholm, in the cemetery where Hermina already lay. Hilma painted a posthumous portrait.[8]

[11]

At the Veterinary Institute

When af Klint and Cassel arrived for work at the Veterinary Institute in the summer heat, the stench of decay was overwhelming. The dissection rooms were transformed into chambers of horror as the flesh of dead animals turned slimy and the meat hooks dug deep into the eye sockets of the heavy horse cadavers that hung from the ceiling on chains. The artists had to hurry as they drew in order to make out the different tissues before they deteriorated. Books depicted reality with too much order and cleanliness. The technical literature that the women consulted to prepare for their work showed bodies without fluids, like dry models. Some veterinary students made the whole bloody business into a joke: two knives had recently been found sticking out of the corpse of a cat, as if they'd been aimed there by knife-throwers.[1]

John Vennerholm (1858–1931), a longtime professor at the institute and now its director, would not countenance such levity. Vennerholm was a thin, grave man with a beard and a high forehead who looked older than his forty-some years. No one was more disgusted by the sorry state of the institute than he. To him coarseness and brutality were repugnant, particularly because such behavior seemed to come naturally to many of the students. He admonished the ones who disrespected the animals. He understood the mission of the veterinarian—to relieve pain and heal ailment—to be a "lofty and noble task." "This duty," he told his students, "is made no less important by the fact that we are dealing with animals who cannot thank us."[2]

Few shared this view around the turn of the century. Most understood animals, especially livestock, to be machines that carried heavy loads or supplied the population with meat, milk, and eggs. The doctors who cared for livestock were viewed not as full-fledged doctors but rather as specialist mechanics who could repair the cows, horses, and pigs when they broke. Vennerholm was convinced that animals could feel pain. In essays published both in Sweden and abroad, he urged veterinarians to use anesthetics during surgeries. The profession reacted stubbornly.

The low standing of the veterinary profession was reflected in the cramped facilities of the institute. It was located in the center of Stockholm, on the tree-lined Karlavägen, just a few blocks from Blanch's Art Salon. The school lacked toilets, so nature's call had to be answered in a stall by everyone from professors to animal keepers. Surgeries were performed outdoors in the back courtyard or, in inclement weather, in the riding hall. Since there was no heating, temperatures could fall well below freezing. Owing to the lack of space, the directors of the clinics for small and large animals taught in the same room. Instructors had no assistants, so they cleaned and sterilized their instruments themselves after surgery. Students tended the animals at night. At the time, veterinary medicine was not a discipline that granted doctoral degrees.[3]

Nonetheless, Vennerholm was an unshakeable optimist. His decision to hire Cassel and af Klint to produce technical drawings was part of a larger plan: he knew that an argument based on ethics or animal rights would not earn his discipline more respect. Instead, he found that people were willing to listen when he spoke of the usefulness of animals—and how their health affected humans and what the dangers and economic risks were if research in veterinary medicine was neglected. The danger amounted to diseases and epidemics; many pathogens did not discriminate between humans and animals. The field of bacteriology was advancing. The "rapid developments in microbiology and hygiene" made a new, modern veterinary establishment urgently necessary in Sweden, according to Vennerholm.[4] Such an argument was difficult to counter.

Vennerholm watched developments abroad, particularly in Germany, where new research institutes were springing up. In Berlin, Robert Koch had just moved into a huge building, the Prussian Institute for Infectious Diseases. The doctor and pathologist Rudolf Virchow was working on founding another establishment, the Institute for Pathology, also in Berlin.

Stockholm was a different story. Vennerholm knew he would have to wait for his new institute. Negotiations with the king and members of Parliament were taking forever. But he could do something in the meantime, namely, write cutting-edge veterinary books that would set a new standard for the discipline. Like Robert Koch's books, they were to be of the newest typographical standard. Vennerholm imagined first-class illustrations accompanying high-level texts: standard reference works that could hold their own abroad. He planned to write a book on horse surgery, his specialty, for which he had invented a number of new instruments. The artists he chose to produce the illustrations for the textbook were Anna Cassel and Hilma af Klint; the latter had already been recognized for her skill in anatomical drawing while a student at the Academy. The illustrations produced by artists would replace the clumsy depictions that were so common in veterinary literature.

When the women went to work at the institute, a new century was just beginning. They had been out of the Academy for more than a decade. In 1900 af Klint turned thirty-eight and Cassel forty. The two friends were ill prepared for the job that awaited them. The horses they were to render precisely were not the same animals ridden by kings and heroes in artworks. Their task was to illustrate the beast of burden, the maltreated animal in all its sad manifestations: with respiratory illnesses, ulcers, abrasions, colic, rashes, wounds, and broken bones. The two women accepted the assignment.

Over the next months they drew their subjects in pencil. They hatched, shaded, and outlined. At the institute the most they could produce were sketches, which they then had to develop in the studio. Their drawings turned horses into puzzles that could be separated into individual pieces. Skulls. Bones. Vertebrae. Eyes. Hoofs. Organs. Sex organs. Tendons. Muscles. Tissues. The artists couldn't always overcome their aesthetic training, giving the world they were depicting more glamour than it really had. In their drawings, Vennerholm's operating tools shine like swords and a horse skull resembles a vanitas still life by an Old Master (fig. 19).[5]

At the Veterinary Institute, the two women were surrounded by men. There were no female students or teachers. But this seems not to have been a drawback. The spirit of improvisation and even the chaos of the environment gave the two friends opportunities. They saw into a world never intended for high-born women. They studied the penises of stallions and learned how testicles were removed during castration. They drew the vaginas of mares and studied the reproductive process from fertilization to birth. They experienced the blood, mucus, and excretions of the animals. They learned about the methods and tools of medical research: heightened observation,

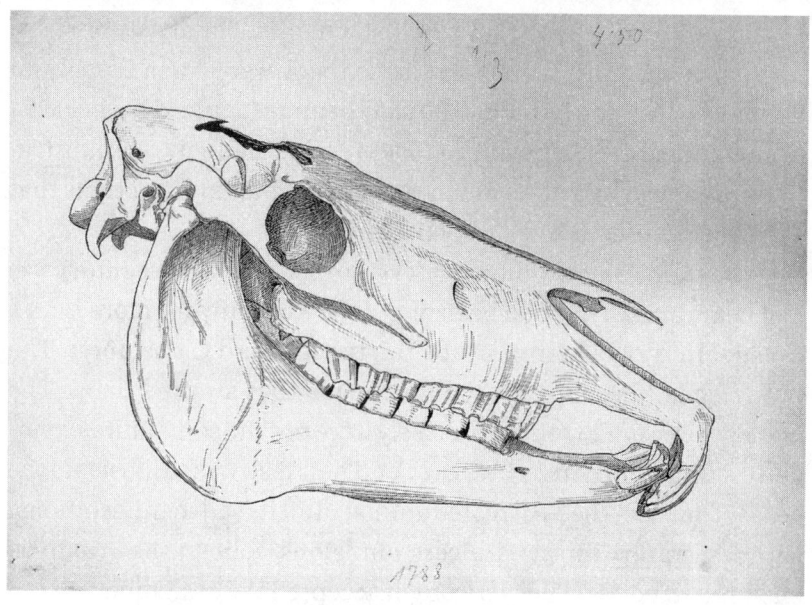

19. Anatomical drawing of a horse's skull by af Klint or Anna Cassel, ca. 1900.

illustrations, measurements, cross sections, models, highly specialized instruments. They would never again see as many pictures of ovaries, sperm, uteri, and sperm ducts as they did in the single year they spent with Vennerholm, who wrote scientific papers with titles like "Diseases of the Female Sex Organs and Mammary Glands." This left a lasting impression on af Klint: reproductive organs would later be a motif in her paintings.

Vennerholm had also acquired teaching models of human embryos, little wax figures that stood on lacquered bases like statues. The models transformed the inside of the womb into a museum that exhibited all the stages of human development, from fertilization to birth. The models were produced in Germany with great care and scientific accuracy by a specialty firm in Freiburg. They looked astonishing.[6] At certain stages, the human fetuses had coiled tails, the oversized heads of tadpoles, and the long bodies of amphibians. For most of their development they looked less like humans than like fish or amphibians. For precisely this reason, the German

zoologist Ernst Haeckel saw more in them than simply the development of a single individual. He understood the sequence of forms
as a spectacle of evolution, a visual recapitulation of the history
of mankind, the stages of mammalian development in time lapse.

The splendid plates of his *Art Forms in Nature*, published in
series between 1899 and 1904, proved a sensation. A passionate
exponent of the theory of evolution and a gifted draftsman, Haeckel
translated Darwin's teachings into an ecstasy of colors and forms.
He ennobled our predecessors from the sea with baroque beauty.
Jellyfish sported lavish skirts and veils that pulsed through the
water; single-celled radiolarians looked like fairy-tale castles with
hundreds of towers and bays. Those who feared that Darwin's theories would denigrate humankind and rob it of its noble origins could
be persuaded to the contrary through the beauty of Haeckel's work.
The pedigree that Haeckel presented to his readers seemed to be of
the first rank.

At Vennerholm's institute, af Klint and Cassel encountered the
biological literature often referenced in spiritualist books. Haeckel's theses were a particularly popular topic with the Theosophists:
some of them were seen as useful, others less so. "No Occultist,"
Blavatsky wrote, "would deny that man—no less than the elephant
and the microbe, the crocodile and the lizard, the blade of grass or
the crystal—is, in his physical formation, the simple product of the
evolutionary forces of nature."[7] But the idea of evolution had to be
expanded to include the soul and its evolution. Haeckel had missed
this, according to Blavatsky, and as a scientist, he told only the first
part of the story. The second part, which began after the evolution
of homo sapiens, was the responsibility of occult research.

Scientists also debated the boundaries of what could be explained
by biology. In England the researcher Alfred Russel Wallace held
the view that the soul couldn't be purely a product of blind natural
forces, and he attended séances to learn more about the spiritual
realm. His word carried weight. He had formulated a theory of evolution at the same time as Darwin and had presented alongside him
at the Linnean Society in London in 1858.[8]

Hilma kept three drawings from her time at the institute. One shows a surgical instrument. The second depicts an infected hoof. The third portrays a dental procedure in which holes had to be drilled in the upper jaw and forehead of a horse to reach the interior of its mouth (see plate 13).[9] She and Cassel made dozens of such drawings, which were sent to the printers to be made into plates. The original drawings are now archived at the Veterinary Museum in Skara, in boxes containing Vennerholm's estate. The drawings show cross sections of equine legs and eyes, the position of organs, sores on the anus, and adhesions of the hoofs. Vennerholm did not wish to part with the pencil drawings, some of them colored. He kept them his entire life.

One technical innovation that af Klint encountered at the institute later found its way into some of her paintings: the petri dish. The device was named after its inventor, Julius Richard Petri, who worked under Koch in Berlin. Petri dishes are circular, shallow glass vessels in which microorganisms are cultivated for examination under a microscope. The process that took place in them was photographed at every stage. The photographs' black backgrounds set off the bright circle of the petri dish where the tiny life forms swarm and grow. Hilma would later use the composition in the 1907 series *The Large Figure Paintings*, which looked at the world as if through a microscope (see figs. 26 and 27).

Vennerholm's textbook appeared in 1901 and contained 168 illustrations and four colored plates. The title in English was "Textbook of Specialized Operations on Horses for Veterinarians and Students." It was published by Norstedts, Sweden's oldest publisher, and subsequently translated into German, becoming a standard reference for a number of years.[10] Though the first automobiles had already reached Sweden's streets, the number of horses continued to rise even after 1900, as in all industrial nations. The more goods were exported from the country, the greater the need for transport from the mountains, mines, and woods to the streets, train stations, and harbors.[11]

Vennerholm thanked af Klint and Cassel by name in the foreword to his book. They, on the other hand, seemed not to view the illustrations as major accomplishments. Illustrating a textbook was hardly proof of success for two Academy graduates, notwithstanding the knowledge they gained from the project. They did not sign any of the drawings made for Vennerholm.[12]

[12]

Children's Books and Decorative Art

The turn of the century found The Five making slow progress. The nine months prescribed for their apprenticeship had ended, yet the séances were producing irregular results. Af Klint failed several times to receive communications through water in a glass, a common device in séances. Nor did Cassel or Cederberg discern more than water in the vessel.[1] Sigrid Hedman found the trances increasingly exhausting and was resorting more often to the psychograph.[2] Automatic drawing continued. Cederberg is mentioned several times in the notebooks as executor, though the group often signed the pictures collectively.

New voices joined Gregor and Agnes: Georg spoke up in October 1897, Amaliel in September 1899, followed the next year on April 22 by Ananda, a name that broke the mold. The other beings had all borne the names of Christian saints, whereas Ananda wasn't a Western name at all but an Indian one belonging to the Buddha's favorite disciple. According to tradition, Ananda was a particular friend of women, having convinced the Buddha to allow them to found religious orders as Bhikkhuni. For the first time The Five were not sure how to spell a name. Amanda? Arnanda? The word is rewritten several times in the notebook.[3]

In October 1901 Hilma tried, for the first time with The Five, to record medial messages herself. The experiment failed, and Hedman took over with the psychograph.[4]

The notes suggest that Hilma played a passive role in The Five for a very long time. The early successes of her professional life had receded into the past. She continued to live with her mother at Brahegatan 52, where they had moved after her father died. The apartment was light, with high ceilings and windows. There was even a telephone connection, and "Hilma af Klint, artist" was listed in the Stockholm directory.[5]

In a photograph of the artist in her studio, a picture leans against the wall behind her, not far from the portrait of her grandfather. It is the draft of an illustration for a children's book (see fig. 17). Af Klint regularly accepted such commissions: one of the books she illustrated was *Little Knut*, another *Maria the Ladybug*. The latter was written by Anna Maria Roos, an author, critic, songwriter, Theosophist, and harsh critic of the Lutheran church. "The watercolor by H. af Klint" was published in the magazine *Julklappen* in December 1902.[6] It is the draft for this picture that we see in the photograph of the artist's studio.

The next year she published a Christmas picture in the journal *Friskar Vindar*.[7] A year later she contributed ten illustrations to *Lille Lapp-Natti*, a children's book by the successful writer Laura Fitinghoff.[8] Developing motifs and compositions came easily to her. The little protagonists are shown amid seas of animals and flowers that surge across the pages. Her estate contains dozens of watercolors of plants, primarily wildflowers, which would have provided the artist with plenty of material (see plate 15).[9] The art nouveau era had begun, and in Sweden, too, books, magazines, paintings, furniture, even whole houses were covered with botanical ornamentation.

Hilma now counted among her friends Ottilia Adelborg (1855–1936), one of the most successful children's book authors of the time. Adelborg had also studied at the Royal Academy and illustrated her own books. Their paths frequently crossed. In 1891 both artists had received grants from the Academy, in 1902 both supplied illustrations for fairytales written by the aforementioned Roos, and they both had sisters who were prominent women activists and had jointly run the Stockholm office of the Fredrika Bremer Association.[10]

Adelborg's children's books had a political agenda. Like the writer Ellen Key, Adelborg believed that children developed into well-adjusted adults when raised sensitively and with freedom. In response to the German *Struwwelpeter*, a popular book that promoted strict methods of upbringing, Adelborg created the character Pelle Snygg, a lovable companion who always wears a white Pierrot costume and treats the children in his care with humor and empathy.[11] He became one of af Klint's favorite characters.

A leather-bound album suggests that af Klint worked on other commissions as well. It contains sketches of embroidered designs: flowers, droplets, stripes, dots. No such embellishments could be found in her wardrobe of simple, plain clothes. The designs were probably shown to customers in a needlework shop. The album was discovered at a Swedish flea market in 2017.[12] Af Klint seems not to have valued it enough to keep it. The nonrepresentational motifs that appear in her later paintings have nothing in common with the tame ornaments in the album (see plate 14).

The artist's estate contains no account books, but the illustrations from the Stockholm Veterinary Institute constitute the largest documented commission. Af Klint was paid by the page: a drawing of a horse's skull is labeled "4.50" crowns.[13] Her name sometimes appears in the press in lofty company, for example in 1902 when her illustrations appeared in the same issue of a magazine as works by Prince Eugen, the painting and art collecting son of Oscar II. A 1903 newspaper article notes the sale of "nine watercolor studies" by Hilma to the group that rented the space above Blanch's Café, the Sveriges Allmänna Konstförening.[14] But none of this suggests resounding professional success.

At the turn of the twentieth century, there were other things to engage Hilma's interest. On March 12, 1901, Erik Viktor Philip Gustafsson af Klint was born, a blond boy with blue eyes who quickly earned a special place in his aunt's heart. Erik was the son of Hilma's brother, Gustaf. Hilma would later leave her life's work to him in her will.

Wilhelm Conrad Röntgen received the first Nobel Prize for Physics, awarded on December 19, 1901, by the Royal Academy of Sciences in Stockholm. Röntgen initially wanted to send his assistant to the award ceremony, because he suffered from stage fright, but finally traveled himself. A journalist who visited him in Bavaria described him as a tall, thin apparition in a dark blue suit whose hair "stood straight up from his forehead, as if it were permanently electrified by his own enthusiasm." During a visit to Röntgen's lab the same journalist asked him, "Is the invisible visible?" Röntgen answered, "Not to the eye; but its results are."[15]

———

Something else happened in 1901. One of the higher beings who normally visited The Five began to speak to Hilma outside the group. "I am Gidro, as you have known me for a long time," the voice introduced itself in the spring, about half a year before Hilma would try to channel messages in The Five and fail.[16] Gidro promised support: "Give yourself completely, I will help you, you will soon become a medium."[17] The breakthrough did not come immediately. "You are not satisfied," the speaker noted soberly in August 1901, citing "the fire" as a primary cause. The connection is not further elaborated in Hilma's notes. However, a new name appears in the same paragraph: Sigrid Lancén's, a gymnastics teacher about ten years younger than the artist. Hilma would later enter into a relationship with Lancén, both physically and mentally. In the same entry Hilma was told to worry less about "useless things." It ends: "It was said that S. L. was my supporting friend."[18]

In summer 1902 she switched to a vegetarian diet. Perhaps she was moved by Vennerholm's research into the ability of animals to feel pain, or perhaps she was following a Buddhist command not to inflict suffering on other sentient beings. In any case the higher ones who spoke to her were unequivocal on the issue: "You cannot imagine what great harm you are doing to yourself by eating meat."[19]

It became increasingly apparent that the higher beings had a larger plan and that the artist might play an important role in it. At the end of June, they enumerated their expectations for a medium: first, restraint, with regard to the "increasing physicality of the past years"; second, to "battle against all falsehood and for the good"; third, an "eager and satisfied spirit."[20] The artist recorded everything without comment.

A legal document from 1903 suggests that a turning point in af Klint's life was imminent. It states that an engraver by the name of Robert Ludvig Haglund was to pick up some designs from her studio.[21] There are no details that indicate which designs, but Haglund was to make plates of them and the document allowed him to carry on in her absence.

She was planning to leave Stockholm on a long journey—the longest she had ever made. She would make it with her good friend Anna Cassel.

[13]

Italy

Finally, Florence. Af Klint had brought along a small sketchbook in which she drew Brunelleschi's dome for the Basilica of San Lorenzo, the great marvel of the fifteenth century that towered above all the other buildings. The basilica's sacristy contains the famous tombs of Giuliano di Lorenzo de' Medici and Lorenzo di Piero de' Medici designed by Michelangelo.[1]

Af Klint's room was on the fourth floor of a building at the corner of Via Nazionale and Via Dell'Ariento, just a few minutes from the train station. Yet all she had to do was open the window to gaze into the historic center of the city (fig. 20). She sat on the windowsill to sketch the dome.

The buildings of Italy fascinated her. No other notebook evinces such unbridled enthusiasm. "Vacker" (beautiful), she wrote,

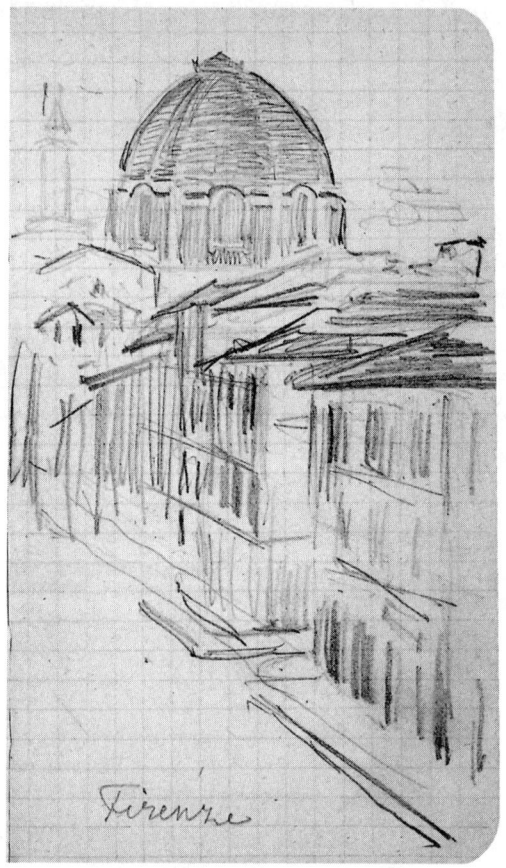

20. Sketch of San Lorenzo from a hotel room in Florence, pencil on paper, 12 x 7 cm, Stiftelsen Hilma af Klints Verk, HaK 1151a.

"mycket vacker" (very beautiful), and "utomordentligt vacker" (extremely beautiful), the latter referring to the Milan Cathedral. Her trip through northern Italy took her to Venice, where she sketched the gondolas on the Grand Canal; to Verona, where she drew the bank of the Adige; to Milan, where, at the Brera Art Gallery, she marveled at the paintings of Raphael and works by Leonardo da Vinci. She saw his famous *Last Supper* in the church of Santa Maria della Grazie, on the wall of the refectory. Her enchantment grew with each city she visited.[2] In Rome, she and Cassel bought a necklace for Magdalena Augusta ("Gusten") Andersson (1862–1936), a friend in Sweden who would later play an important role in her life.[3]

Af Klint had with her a travel guide of Florence by Theodor Bierfreund, an art historian from Copenhagen. No other book in her library shows as much wear. The cover has fallen off; the pages are curled. Though written in Danish, the guidebook was widely purchased in Sweden. One of its countless readers was the Swedish writer Selma Lagerlöf (1858–1940), who wrote to her friend Valborg Olander from Naples at the beginning of the century: "I also wanted to ask you if you could get me a Danish book by (Theodor) Bierfreund that is called Florence or at least contains a description of the city. I've been told that it's good and I'd like to read it while we have a little time here, in order to prepare for our time in Florence next month."[4]

Lagerlöf's route from Sweden to Italy suggests the path Hilma may also have taken. Lagerlöf documented every stop on her journey in diary entries or postcards. She traveled from Göteborg to Copenhagen, through Germany to northern Italy.[5] Af Klint, too, stopped in Germany: a drawing of the Wartburg Castle in Thuringia from 1903 survives as proof.[6] Hilma did not draw the famous east side of the castle with its massive stone buildings from the Hohenstaufen period, where Lagerlöf was photographed standing on the walls. Her drawing goes inside the complex to capture the first castle courtyard with its half-timbered structures. There is good reason for her choice: that was where Martin Luther lived in protective custody after he was excommunicated in 1521 when he refused to recant at the Diet of Worms. The Reformer used his time there to translate the New Testament into German. "Luthers bostad"— Luther's residence—the artist noted on the back of her sketch, which is accented in watercolor.[7]

Was af Klint alone in the castle courtyard when she made the sketch? Or did she and Cassel draw side by side? Cassel left no records of the journey. But Gusten, who was gifted the trinket from Rome, noted on a scrap of paper that it had been purchased by the two of them.[8] The gift and Gusten's note are the sole evidence that the two painters made the trip together. Af Klint left only a small square notebook labeled "Italian Journey."

But the character of her notes and sketches indicates that she was more than a lady on the Grand Tour. As one of The Five, she was attuned to artworks beyond those covered in the guidebooks. For example, in Bologna at the Pinacoteca Nazionale, she sketched the *Padre Eterno*, the "Eternal Father," a little-known painting by Ludovico Mazzolino from 1524 (see plates 16 and 17). In the painting, God the Father's eyes are closed, and he raises his right hand while resting the left on the globe; the Holy Spirit floats over it in the form of a dove. A storm sweeps through Mazzolino's painting, driving the clouds and making God's cloak billow around him. While the cosmos oscillates, the creator seems to contemplate his creation through his mind's eye. The unmoved mover operates as if in a dream or "trance," as the state was termed in the friends' notebooks. His power comes from within, his spirit affects matter. He performs the process symbolized by the white cross of The Five: "the descent of the spirit into matter—the rising of matter through spirit."[9]

Though Hilma was studying works hundreds of years old, the journey to Italy turned out to be a journey into the future. When the painter's train had pulled out of the station in Stockholm, her mind was filled with the writings of Rosicrucians, Theosophists, and Spiritists. She knew the literature that set out how the supernatural manifested in daily life, and she was well aware of the skepticism that surrounded it and how easily a practitioner could be ridiculed or even accused of fraud; her late mentor Bertha Valerius had good reason to publish her text on the "invisible worlds" anonymously.[10]

The dispute was equally bitter among scientists. No one had hammered out a formula for where matter ended and spirit began. The polemics are reflected in the range of authors found in Hilma's library, from Blavatsky to du Prel to Hartmann. One day a researcher would cause a stir by claiming his field would soon be able to prove there was an invisible world that penetrated the substance of the one we know, perhaps even forming it and steering its movements. That claim would instantly be dismissed by scientists arguing against it, for example by Rudolf Virchow, a doctor, pathologist, and anthropologist from Berlin. His terse remark that he had dissected thousands of corpses without ever finding "a trace of the human soul" seemed to say everything.[11]

But what would Virchow have to say in Italy, in the Church of San Lorenzo or viewing masterpieces in the Uffizi or Mazzolini's painting? As Hilma arrived in Verona, Milan, Florence, and Rome, she was continually entering environments that confirmed the incursion of the divine into daily life. That seemed ever present in Italy: in the churches, chapels, and museums, even at the souvenir stands and in the train station bookstores. Wherever she went, miracles and saints were taken for granted, their glowing, radiant reality depicted a thousand times over. The question was not whether miracles happened but how they could best be captured with paintbrush, chisel, or bare hands; as frescoes, oil on canvas, in marble, plaster, gold, terra-cotta, copper, or bronze. For Hilma, who had been raised with the austerity of Protestant churches, the density of art in Italy must have been staggering.

There was more. The artists in the Middle Ages and the Renaissance believed that painting was to be practiced in service to a higher power and that it participated in higher spheres. The way of insight led from the visible to the invisible, "per visibilia ad invisibilia," as Saint Augustine had put it.[12] Art was a gateway that humans could access to apprehend the divine world.

———

After Hilma and Anna returned to Stockholm, The Five picked up their regular meetings again.[13] But power was shifting—the younger women, including Cornelia Cederberg, were becoming more active. It was said of Cornelia one day that she "drew so fiercely" that the session had to be interrupted.[14] Hilma, too, began to produce drawings during the sessions. On December 8, 1903, she was encouraged by a being named Esther to "Take the pencil, Hilma." The artist did as she was told, and a few lines later the minutes confirm that "Hilma drew and wrote."[15] The painter received a rectangle and a sphere, along with an explanation of the meaning of the forms. They were "the expression of life."[16] Though modest, it was a beginning.

[14]

Genius

While Hilma was traveling with Anna Cassel, visiting churches and museums and enjoying the views of Florence, a book published in Austria was being celebrated in many quarters of Europe. The book asked, among other things, what contribution women could make to the history of ideas. Were they capable of making exceptional paintings? Writing enduring poetry? Making scientific discoveries?

The book, which answered each question in the negative, was *Sex and Character*, written by the twenty-three-year-old intellectual Otto Weininger (1880–1903). Weininger was born of Hungarian-Jewish parents in Vienna, though he converted to Protestant Christianity. His book presented afresh what had been claimed for centuries—that women were inferior to men both physically and mentally. None of Weininger's ideas were new, but now, as the women's movement was gathering steam, the old theses found fertile ground among those who feared for their privileges. Many had been waiting for someone to take up the crusade which had become more urgent now that women had entered the universities and were pursuing careers and demanding suffrage. Weininger castigated the masculinization of the female sex that, in his view, was inevitable when women went to work, pursued an advanced education, conducted research, participated in politics, or made art. And he warned men against their own feminization, which he blamed on the women's rights movement.

One of the ingredients in Weininger's weak brew was a collection of letters and symbols that were meant to give his text the appearance of an indisputable scientific study. His formula for the ideal man, for example, was the following:

Mμ (the truly male part in the "male") + Mω (the truly male part in the "female") will equal a constant quantity, M, the ideal male

He described "ideal woman" with the following formula:

Wμ + Wω (the ideal female parts in respectively the "male" and the "female") will equal a second constant quantity, W, the ideal female

It was all nonsense, of course. And his conclusion can be summed up in two sentences: Men possess genius. Women do not. In Weininger's words: "The abstract male is the image of God, the absolute something; the female, and the female element in the male, is the symbol of nothing."[1] The author also attempted to use history as proof. He wrote: "It is enough to make the general statement that there is not a single woman in the history of thought, not even the most man-like, who can be truthfully compared with men of fifth or sixth-rate genius, for instance with Rückert as a poet, Van Dyck as a painter, or Schleiermacher as a philosopher."[2] His views found many admirers, including the writer Karl Kraus, the physicist Ernst Mach, and the Swedish playwright August Strindberg.

Weininger committed suicide in October 1903 in Vienna, with a shot through the heart, in a rented room in the house where Beethoven had died. He did not live to see his claims refuted: just two months later, the Nobel Prize committee in Stockholm awarded the prize in physics to three people, two men and a woman. The female scientist was Marie Curie (1867–1934), a Polish-born physicist who lived in France with her husband, Pierre Curie. The couple received the award with Henri Becquerel, and the news made waves around the world. A woman had won the Nobel Prize! There was a female genius in physics! In Sweden, newspapers printed portraits of the winners. *Dagens Nyheter* published a photograph of the Curies in their Paris lab, with Marie operating the device that measured radioactivity.[3]

The disordering of the sexes promoted by the Nobel Prize was met with curiosity, joy, and celebration—but also with annoyance and criticism. In Sweden it ruined Strindberg's interest in the phenomenon of radioactivity to have a woman connected with it. "A woman, of all things," a friend of the writer summarized Strindberg's displeasure, "had to give Strindberg and the world the pleasure (Madame Curie) of the discovery of Radium."[4] When he learned of Weininger's death, Strindberg wished to "lay a wreath" on the grave of the "brave, masculine thinker," the Swedish press reported.[5]

In France, the Academy of Sciences even tried to undermine the awarding of the prize to Marie Curie. The conspiracy was foiled owing in part to the intervention of two Swedish researchers. One of them was the physicist Knut Ångström, whose portrait af Klint would later paint.[6]

At the end of 1903, the question of female genius was a hot issue. On one side was Weininger with his invented formulas that nonetheless made sense to enough intelligent men to keep his book in print for years. On the other side stood Marie Curie, the Nobel Prize Committee, and the decision that just barely came to be.

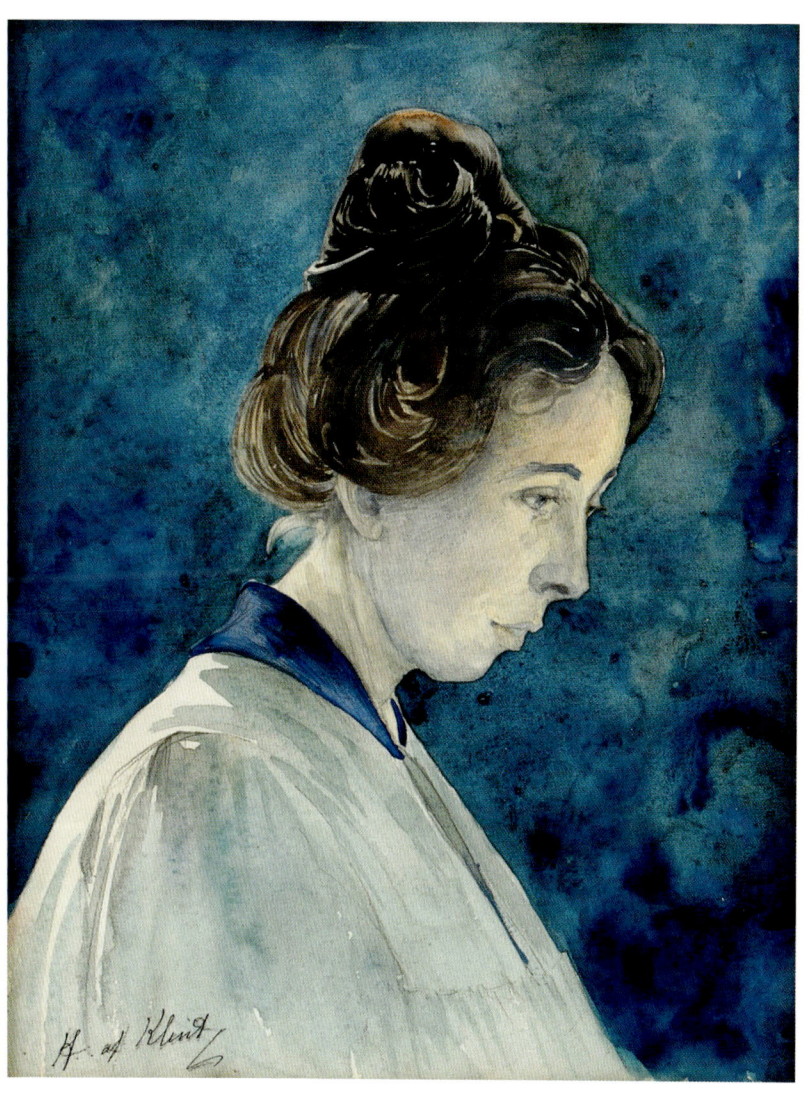

PLATE 1. Hilma af Klint, untitled, undated, watercolor on paper, approx. 27.5 x 21.5 cm. © Antonia Ax:son Johnson.

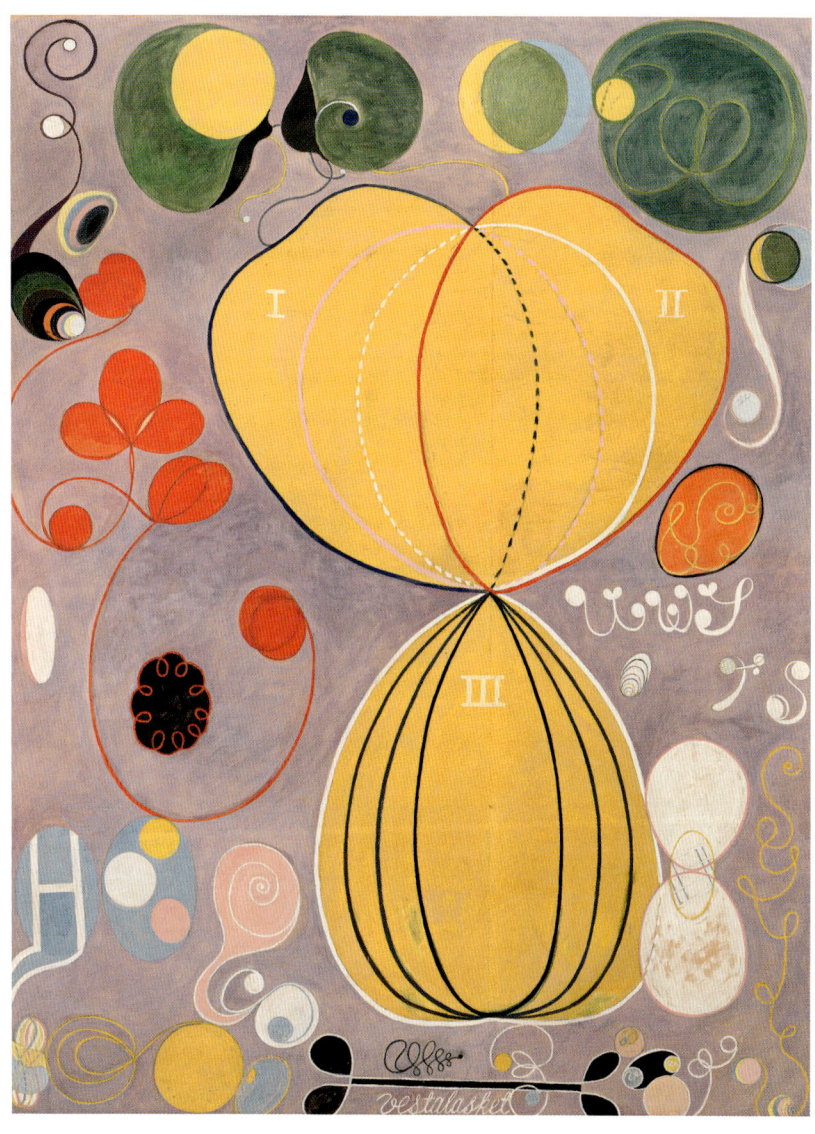

PLATE 2. *The Ten Largest, No. 7, Adulthood, Group IV,*
1907, tempera on paper pasted on canvas, 315 x 234 cm, Stiftelsen
Hilma af Klints Verk, HaK 103.

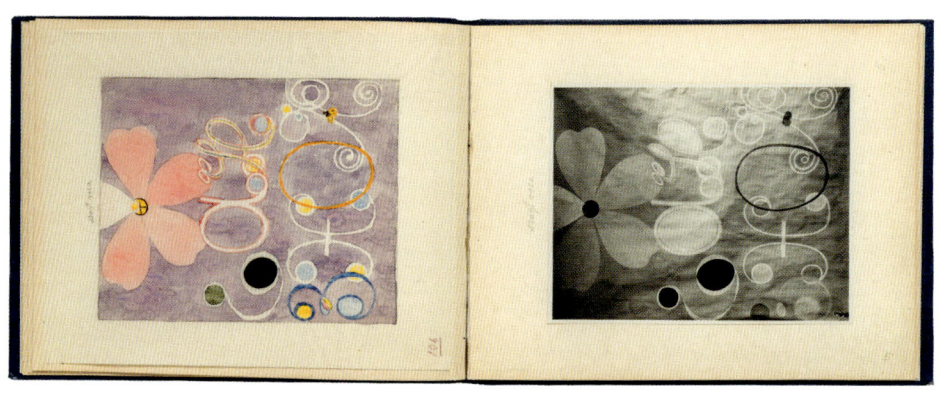

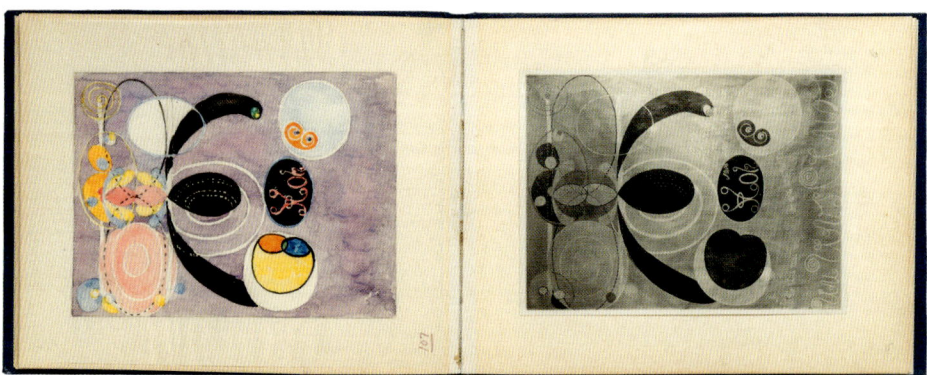

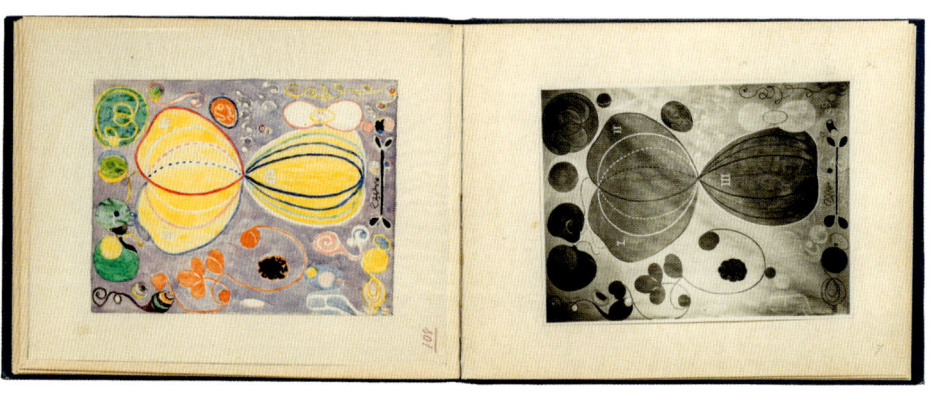

PLATES 3, 4, AND 5. Hilma af Klint's Suitcase Museum: small-format reproductions of *The Ten Largest, Nos. 5, 6, and 7,* in blue album, Stiftelsen Hilma af Klints Verk, HaK 1174.

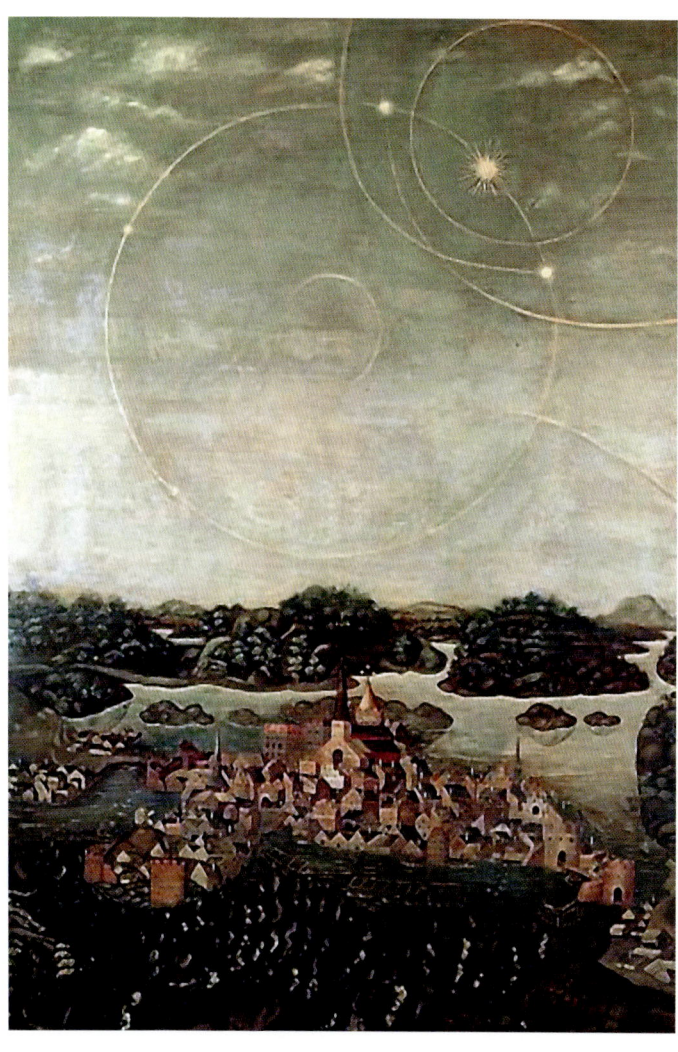

PLATE 6. The *Mock Sun Painting* from the cathedral church
in Stockholm, oil on wood, 1630s.

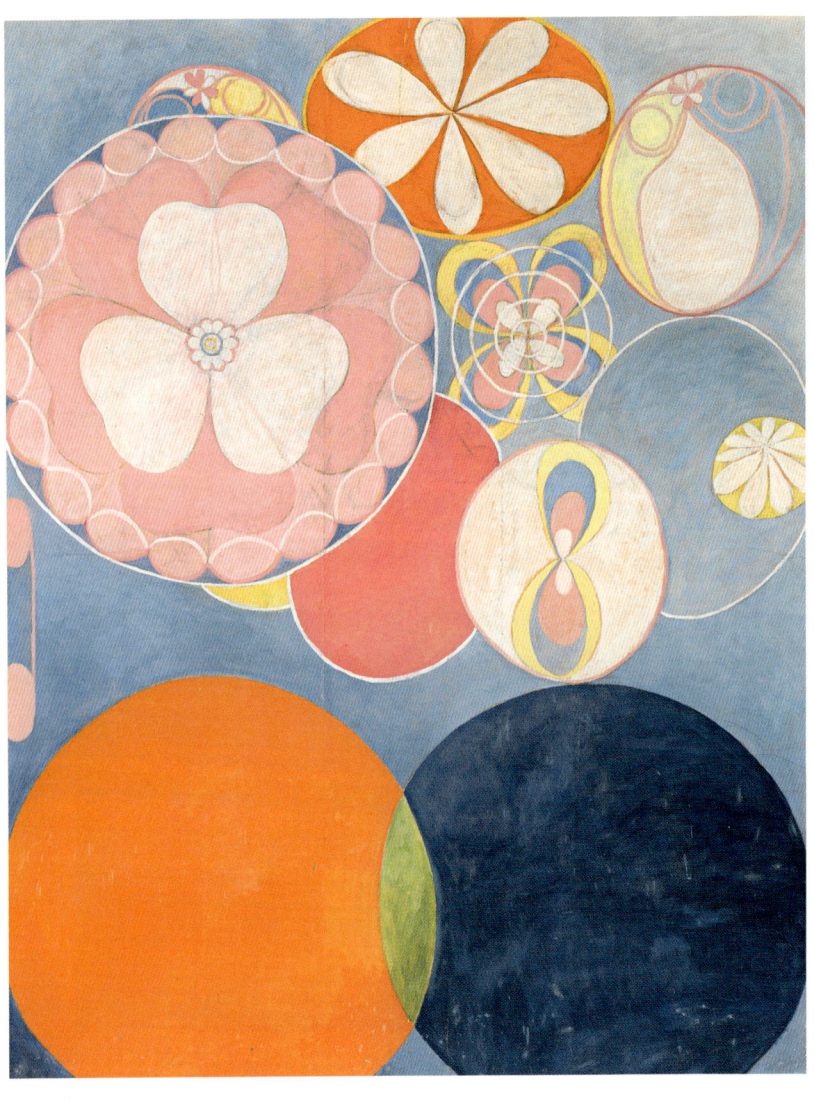

PLATE 7. *The Ten Largest, No. 2, Childhood, Group IV*, 1907, tempera on paper pasted on canvas, 315 x 235 cm, Stiftelsen Hilma af Klints Verk, HaK 108.

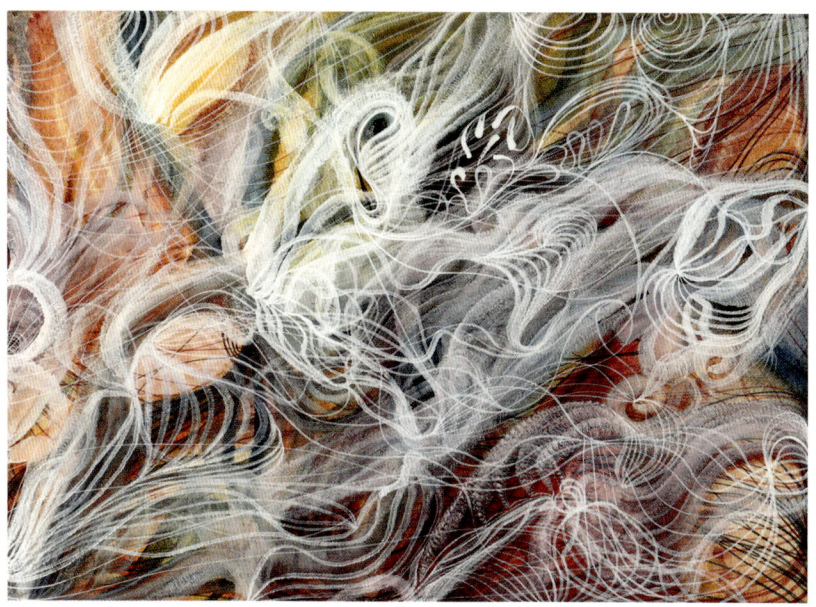

PLATE 8. Georgiana Houghton, *The Love of God*, August 3, 1864, watercolor and gouache on paper, 23.7 x 32.6 cm, Victorian Spiritualists' Union, Melbourne.

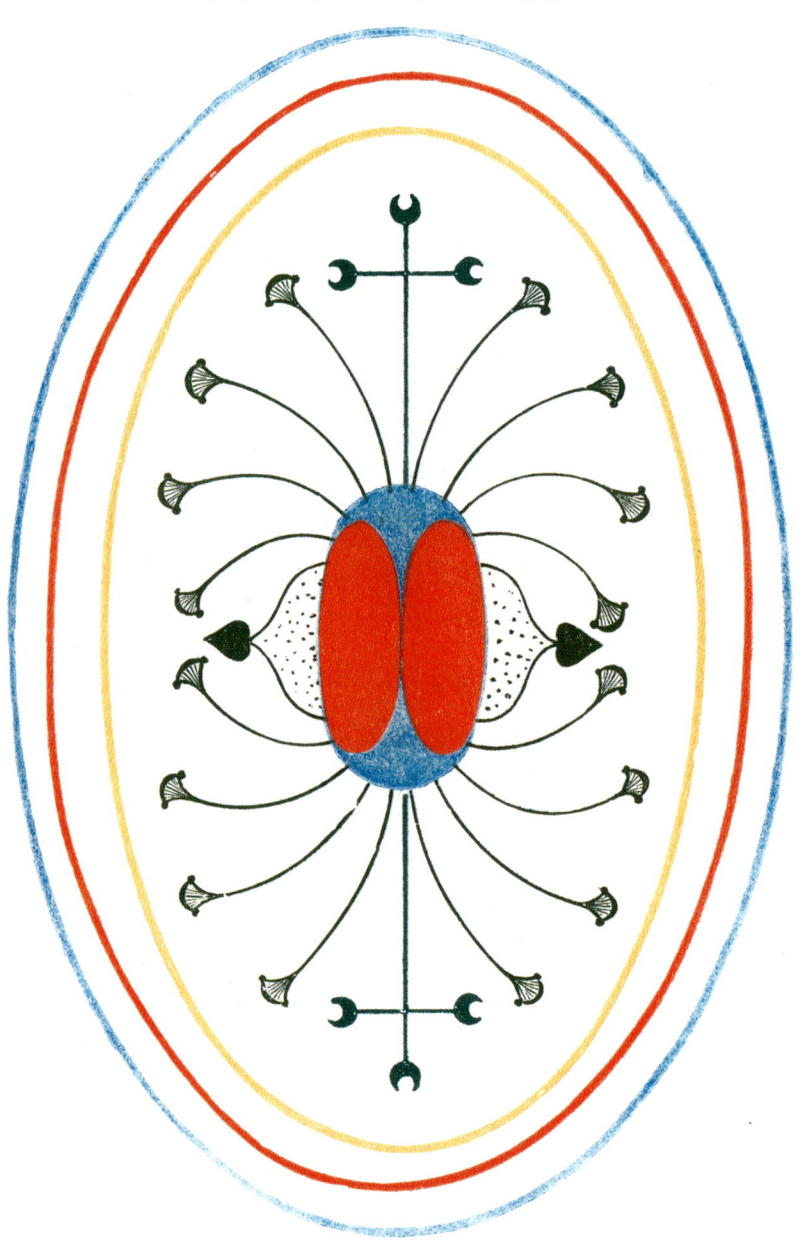

"Sustainer"

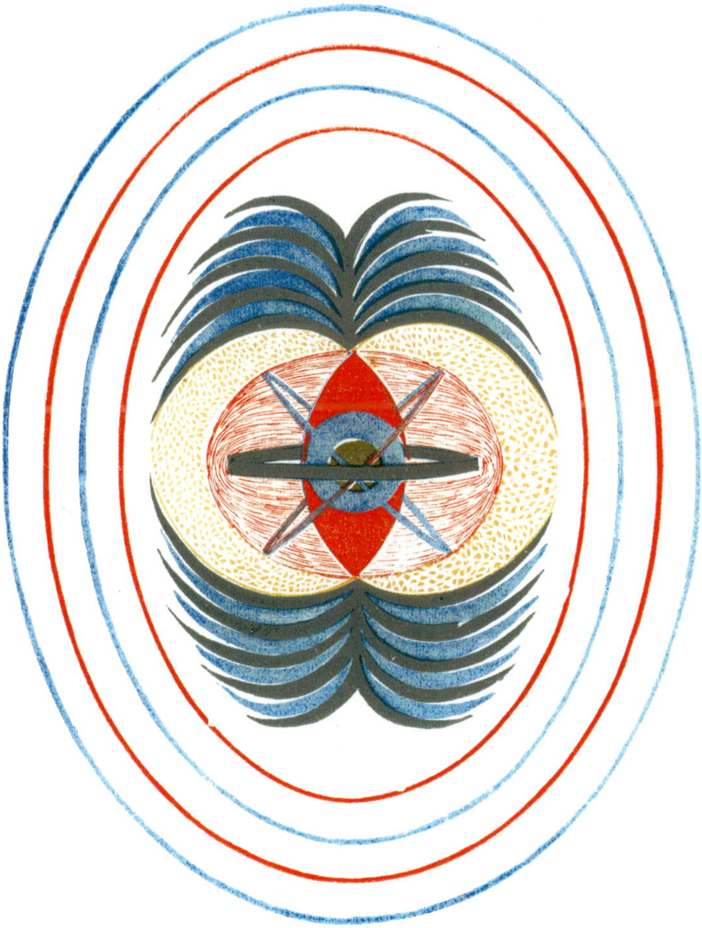

PERSONAL SPIRIT-EMBLEM.

"Introvision"

PLATES 9 AND 10. Anna Mary Howitt, book illustrations
Sustainer and *Introvision*, from C. D. Crosland, *Light in the Valley:
My Experiences in Spiritualism* (London, 1857).

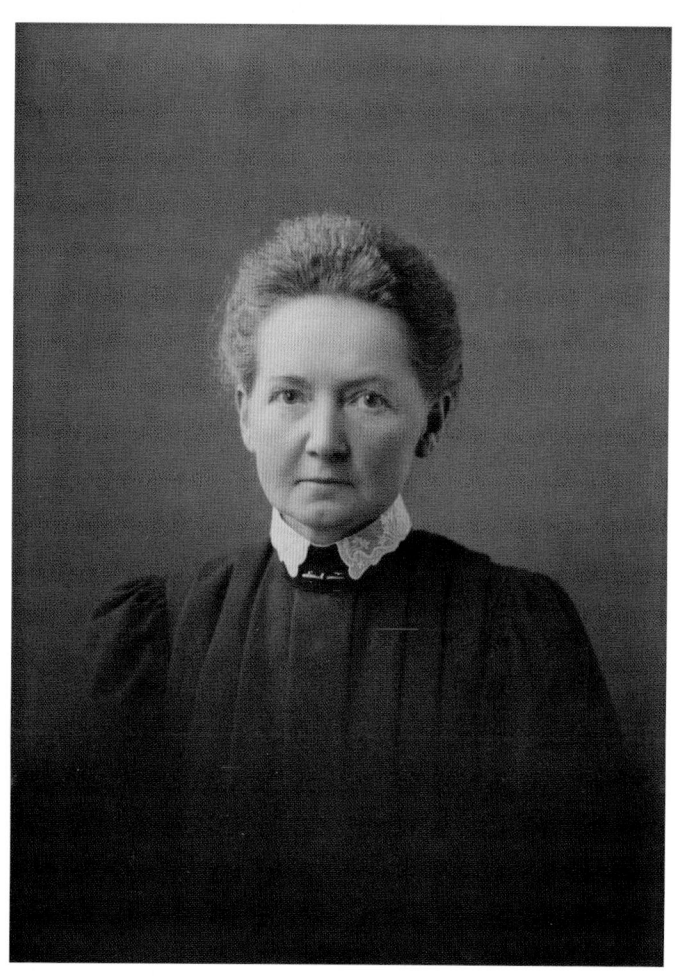

PLATE 11. Anna Cassel, undated, Stiftelsen Hilma af Klints Verk.

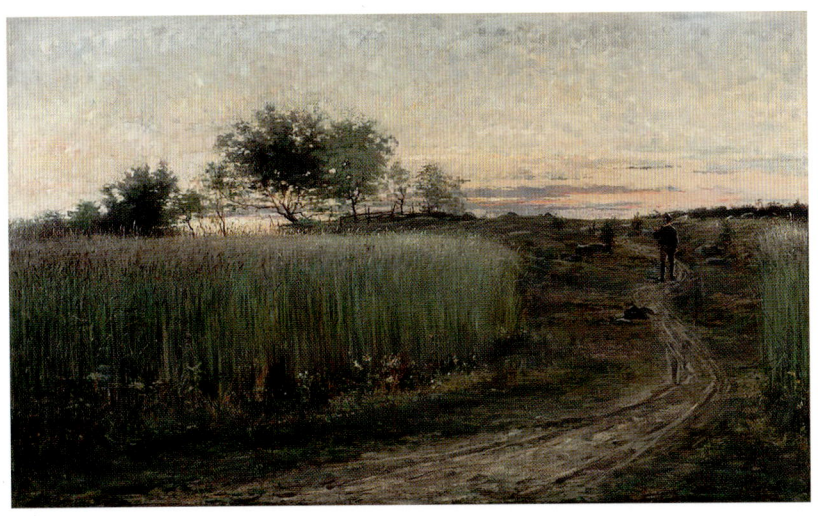

PLATE 12. *Summer Landscape (Summer Evening on Öland)*, 1888,
oil on canvas, 88 x 148 cm, Dorsia Hotel, Göteborg, Sweden.

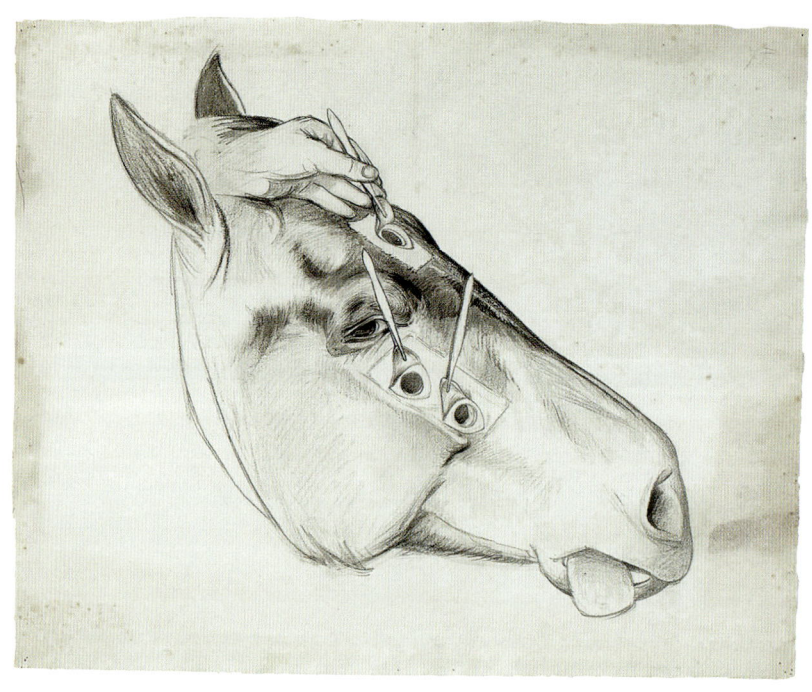

PLATE 13. *Dental Operation for a Horse,* chalk and pencil on paper, 35 x 43 cm, Stiftelsen Hilma af Klints Verk, HaK 1299.

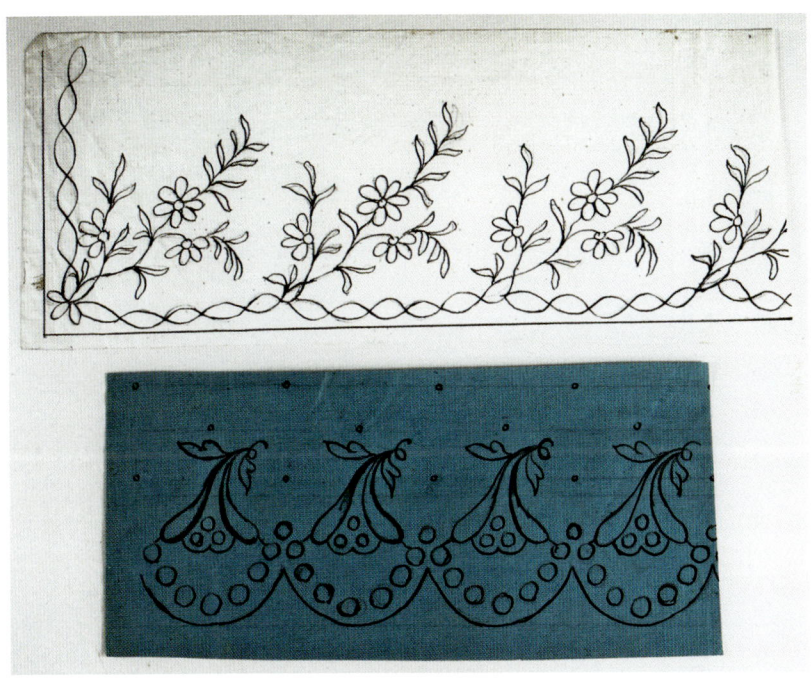

PLATE 14. Pattern book for embroidery, probably 1890s,
labeled "belongs to the artist Hilma af Klint."

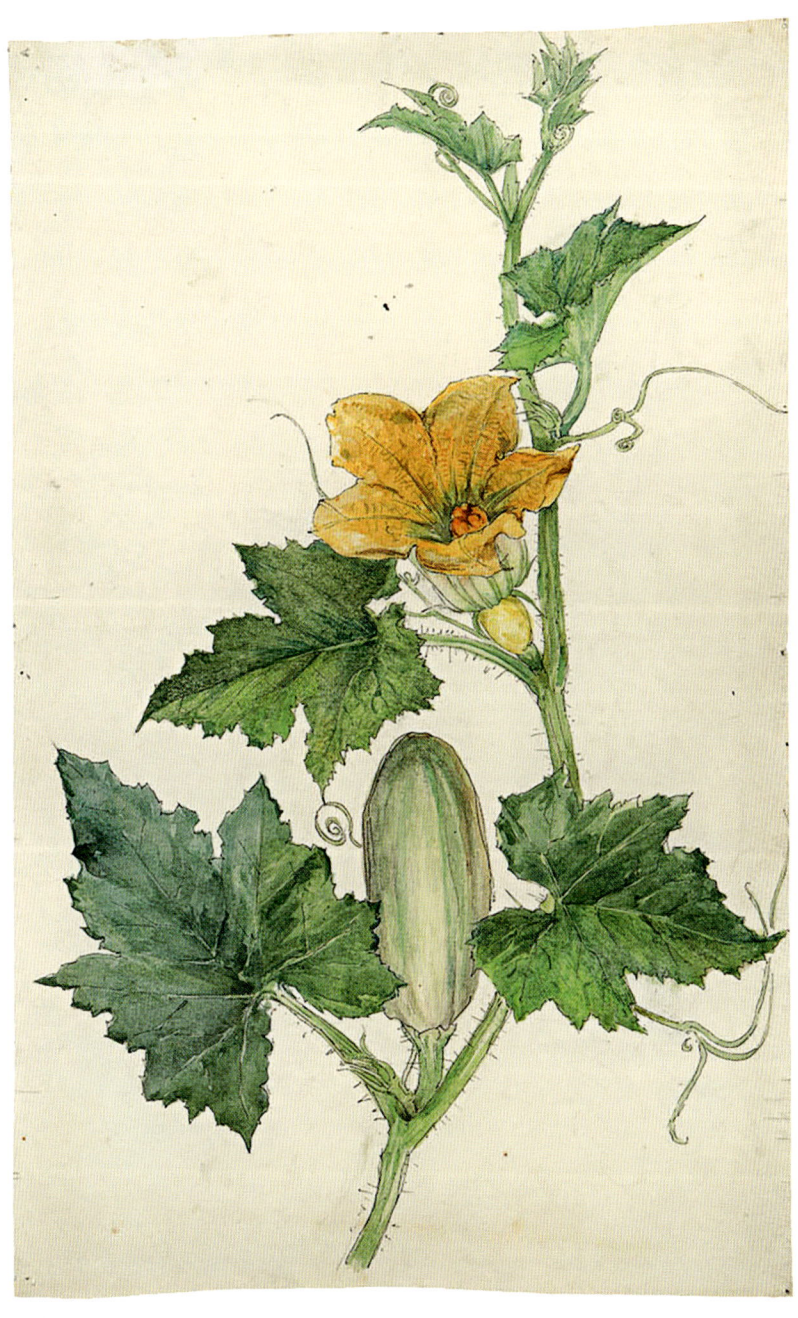

PLATE 15. Zucchini, 1890s, watercolor, pencil, and
ink on paper, 22.4 x 35.6 cm, Stiftelsen Hilma af Klints Verk, HaK 1327.

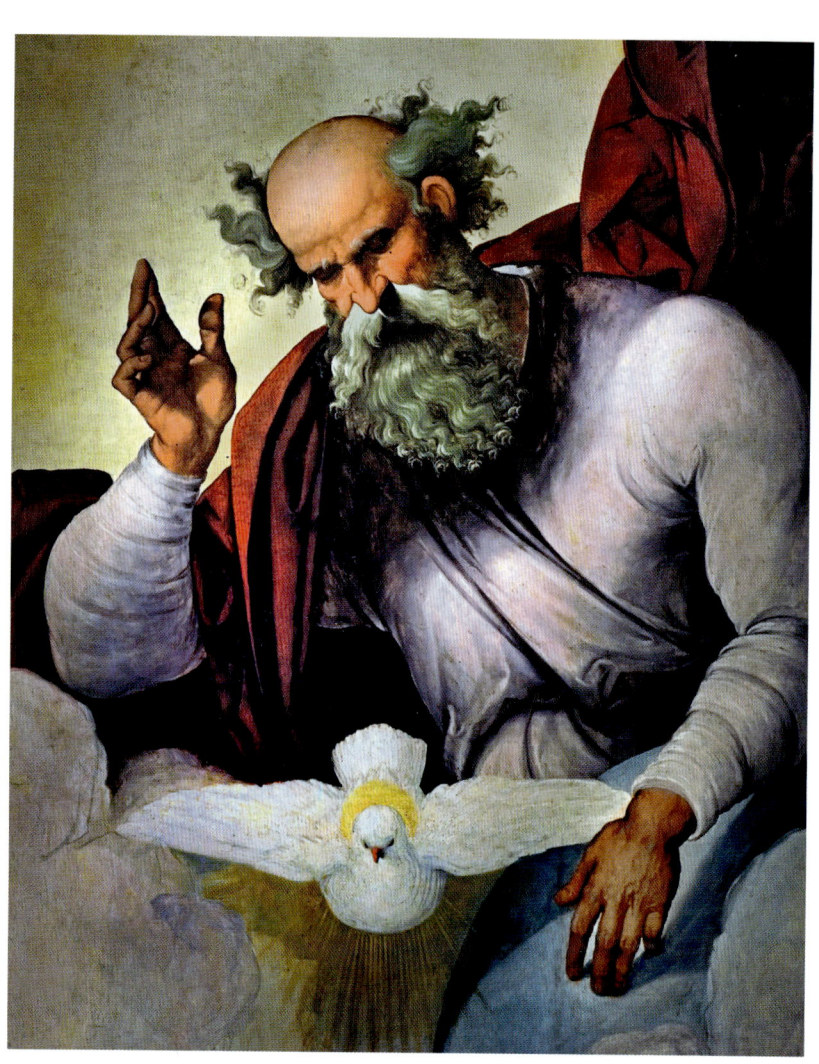

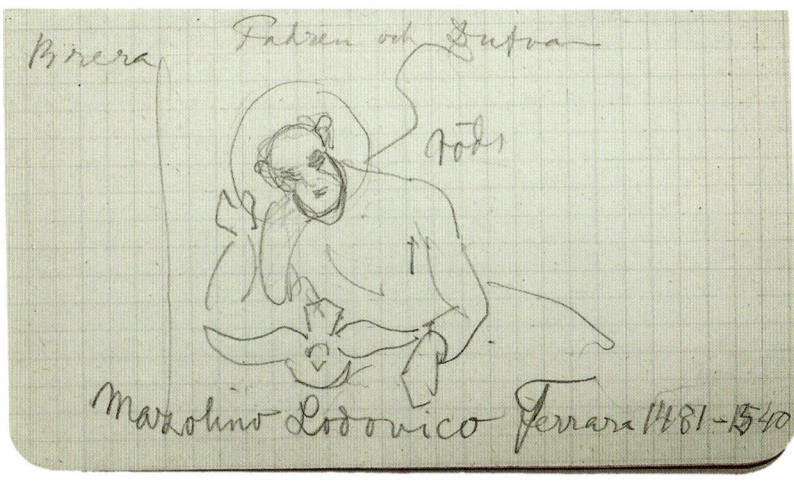

PLATES 16 AND 17. *Opposite*: Ludovico Mazzolini, *Eternal Father with the Dove of the Holy Ghost*, 1524, oil on canvas, 101 x 103.5 cm, Pinacoteca Nazionale di Bologna; *above*: af Klint's sketch of Mazzolini's painting, undated, pencil on paper, 7 x 12 cm, Stiftelsen Hilma af Klints Verk, HaK 1151a.

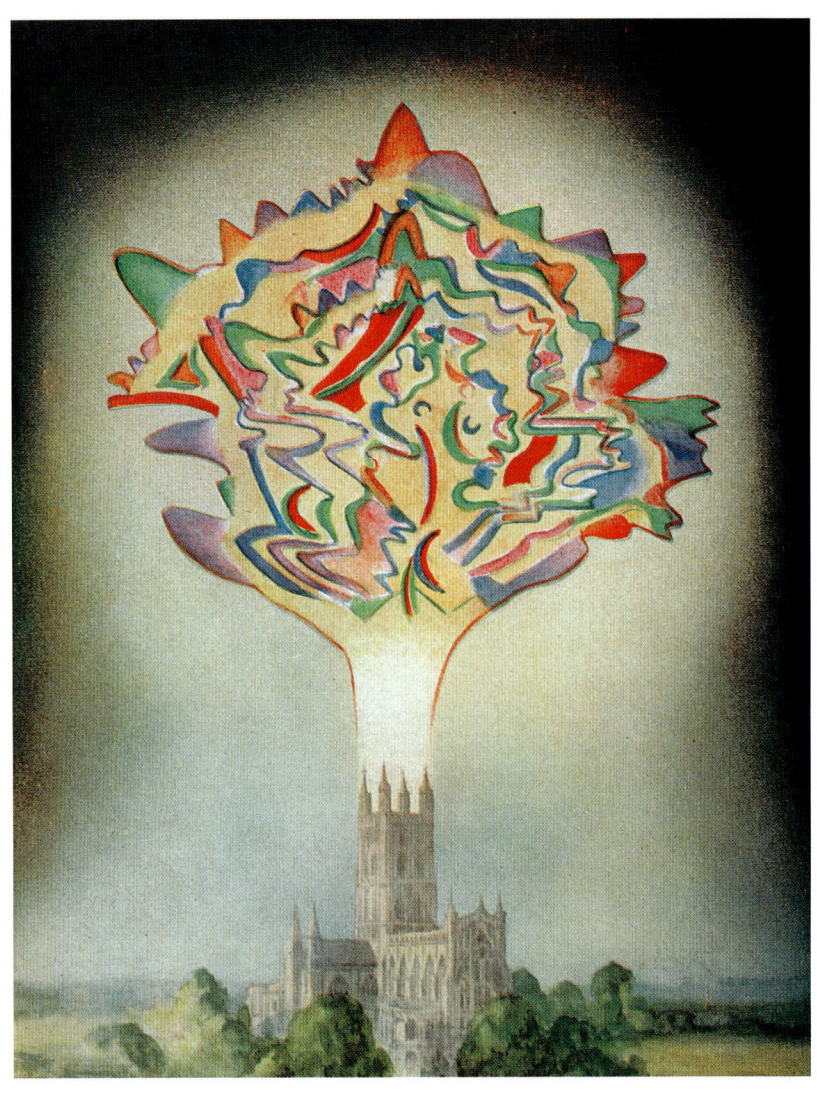

PLATE 18. Music by Gounod, illustration from A. Besant and C. Leadbeater, *Thought-Forms*, 1905.

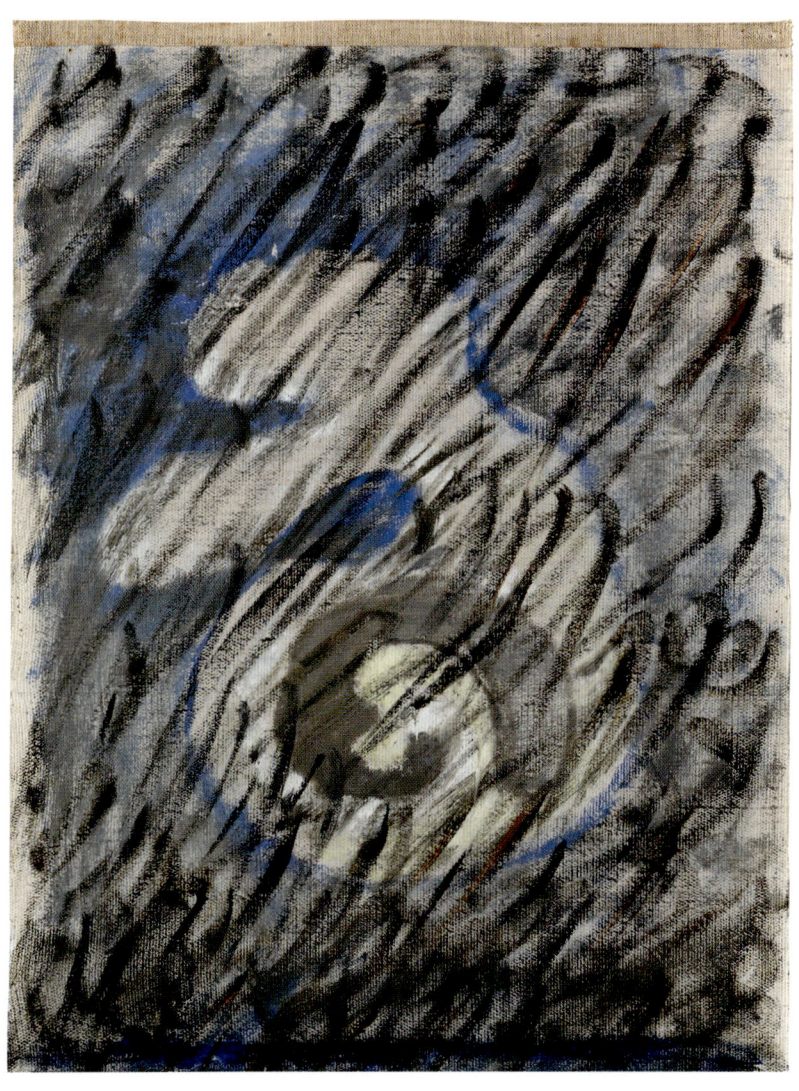

PLATE 19. *Primordial Chaos, No. 1, Group I, Series WU/The Rose*, 1906, oil on canvas, 53 x 37 cm, Stiftelsen Hilma af Klints Verk, HaK 01.

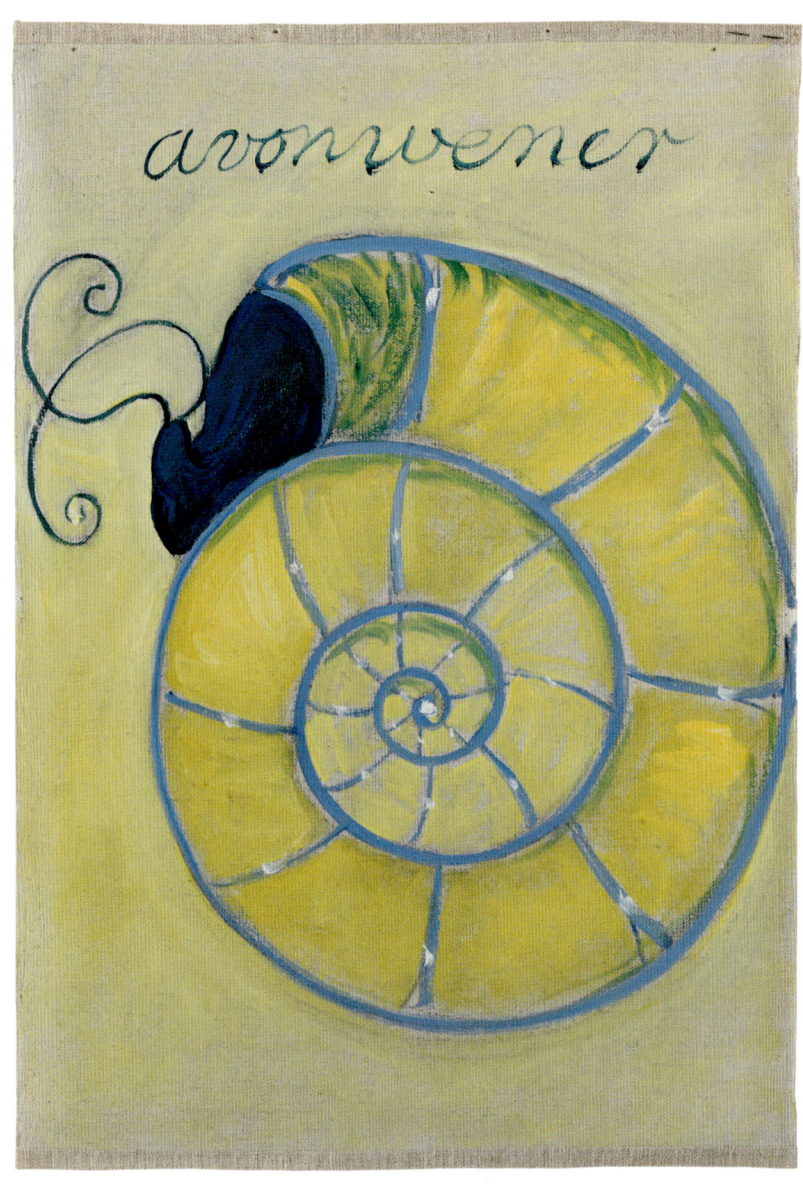

PLATE 20. *Primordial Chaos, No. 8, Group I, Series WU/The Rose*, 1906/7, oil on canvas, approx. 52 x 37 cm, Stiftelsen Hilma af Klints Verk, HaK 08.

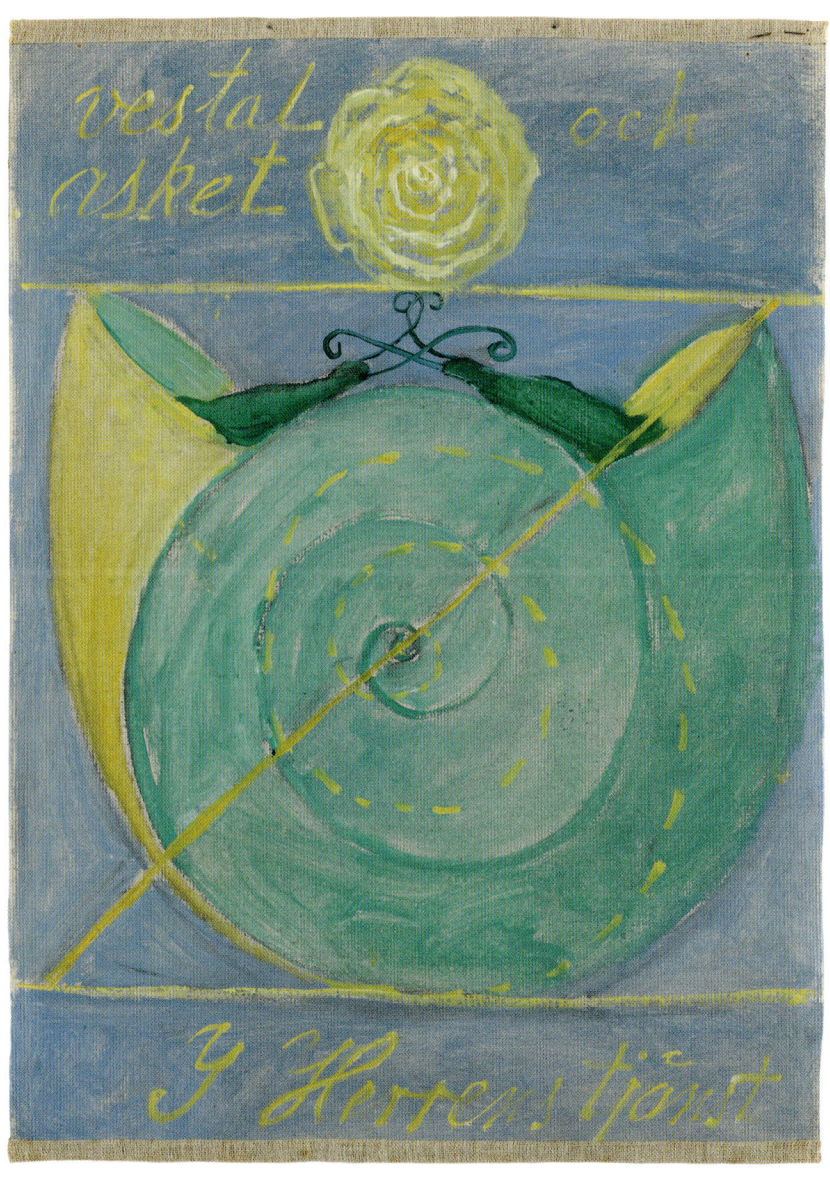

PLATE 21. *Primordial Chaos, No. 9, Group I, Series WU/The Rose*, 1906/7, oil on canvas, approx. 52 x 37 cm, Stiftelsen Hilma af Klints Verk, HaK 09.

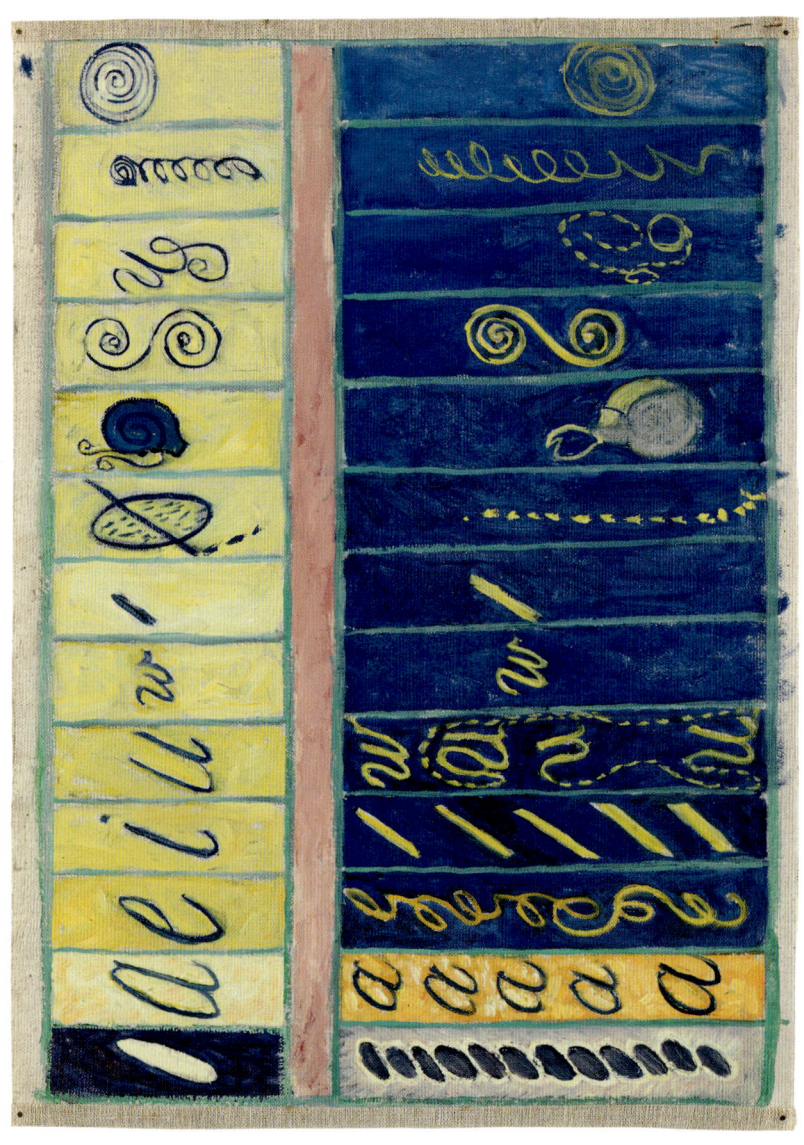

PLATE 22. *Primordial Chaos, No. 10, Group I, Series WU/The Rose*, 1906/7, oil on canvas, approx. 52 x 37 cm, Stiftelsen Hilma af Klints Verk, HaK 10.

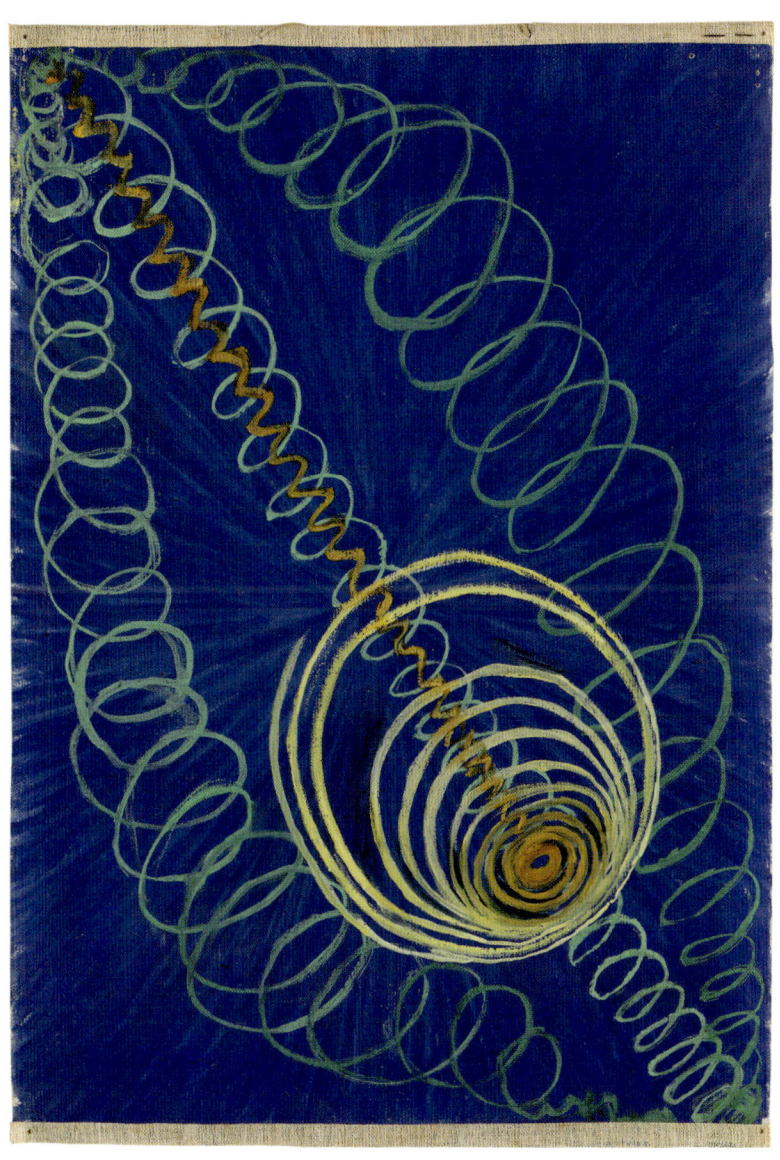

PLATE 23. *Primordial Chaos, No. 16, Group I, Series WU/The Rose*, 1906/7, oil on canvas, approx. 52 x 37 cm, Stiftelsen Hilma af Klints Verk, HaK 16.

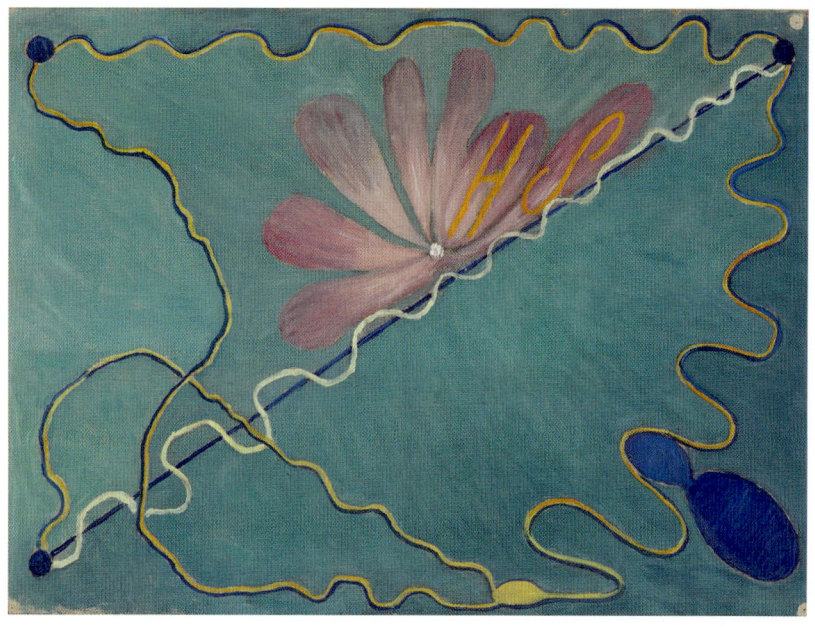

PLATE 24. *The Eros Series, No. 2, Group II, Series WU/The Rose*, 1907, oil on canvas, Stiftelsen Hilma af Klints Verk, HaK 027.

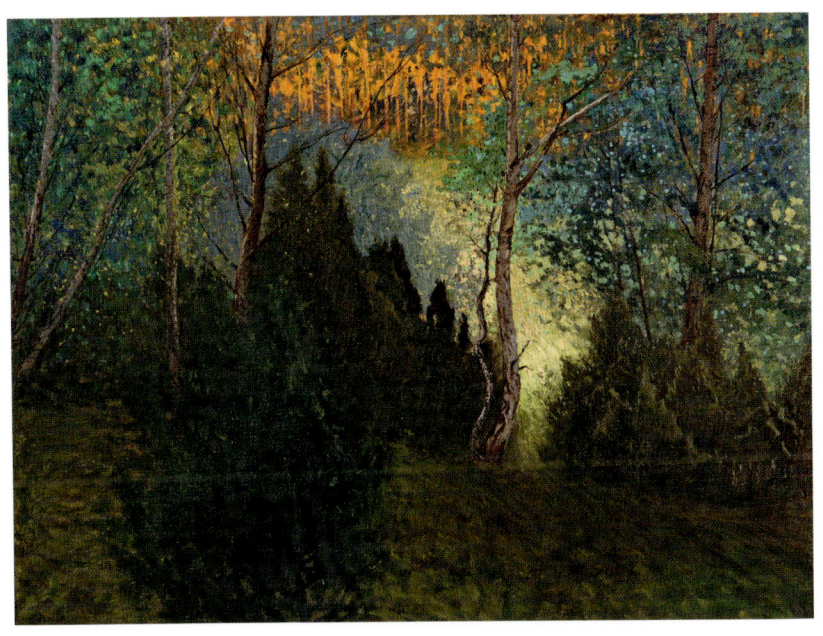

PLATE 25. *Evening Calm*, 1907, oil on canvas,
Stiftelsen Hilma af Klints Verk, HaK 036.

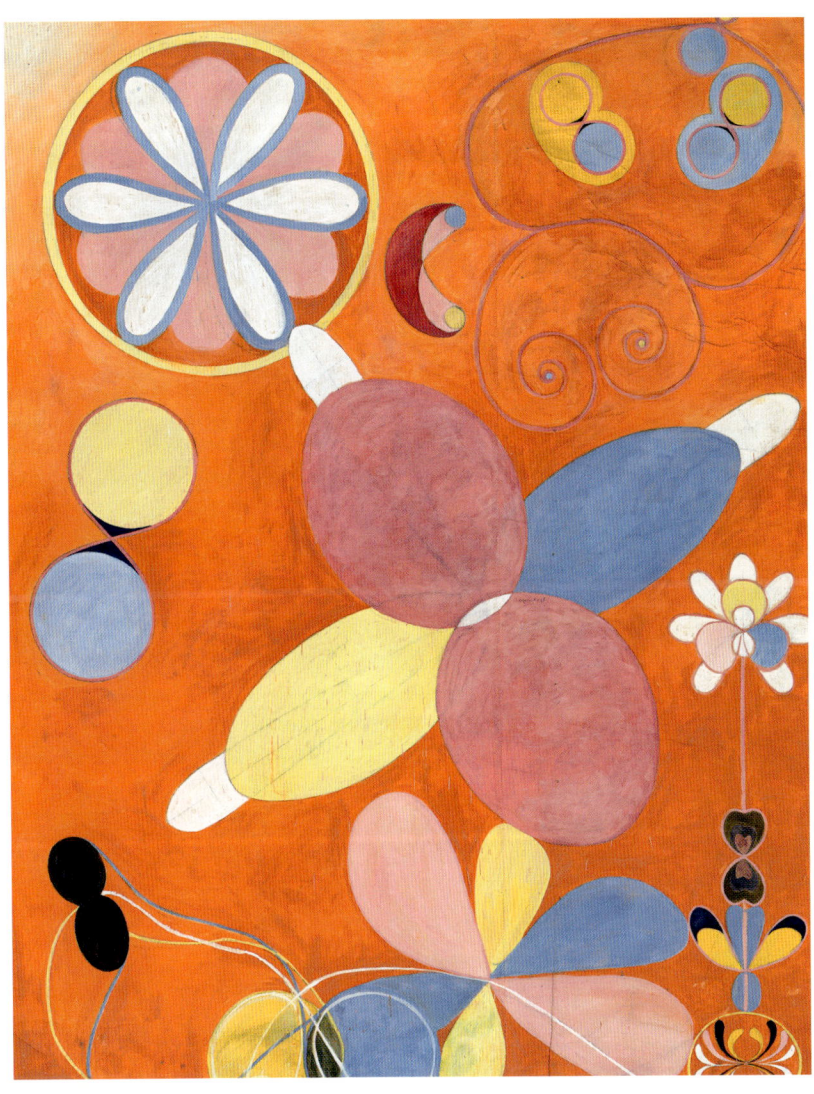

PLATE 26. *The Ten Largest, No. 4, Youth, Group IV*, 1907, tempera on paper pasted on canvas, 315 x 234 cm, Stiftelsen Hilma af Klints Verk, HaK 105.

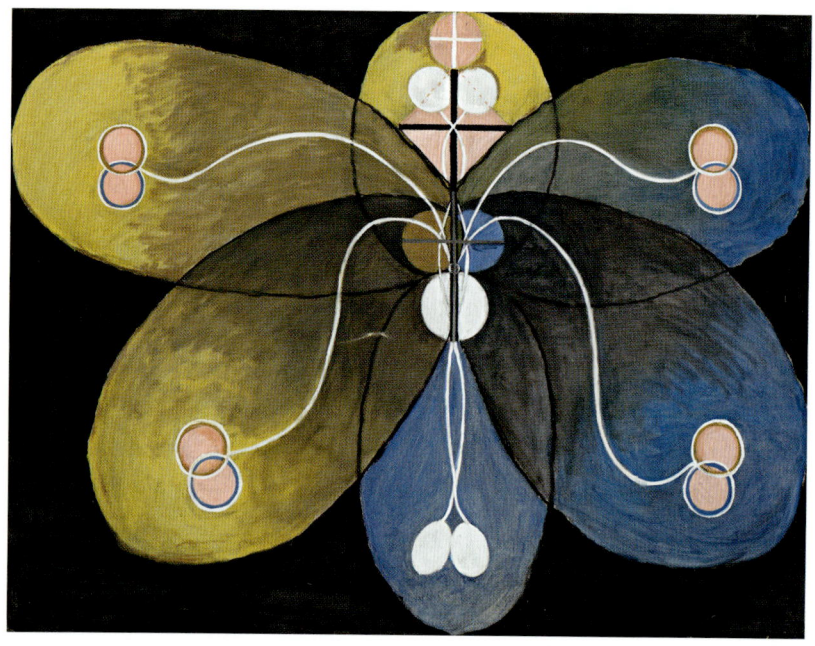

PLATES 27 AND 28. Above: *The Evolution, No. 9, Group VI*, 1908, oil on canvas, 101 x 131.5 cm, Stiftelsen Hilma af Klints Verk, HaK 77; opposite: *The Evolution, No. 11, Group IV*, 1908, oil on canvas, 102.5 x 133.5 cm, Stiftelsen Hilma af Klints Verk, HaK 79.

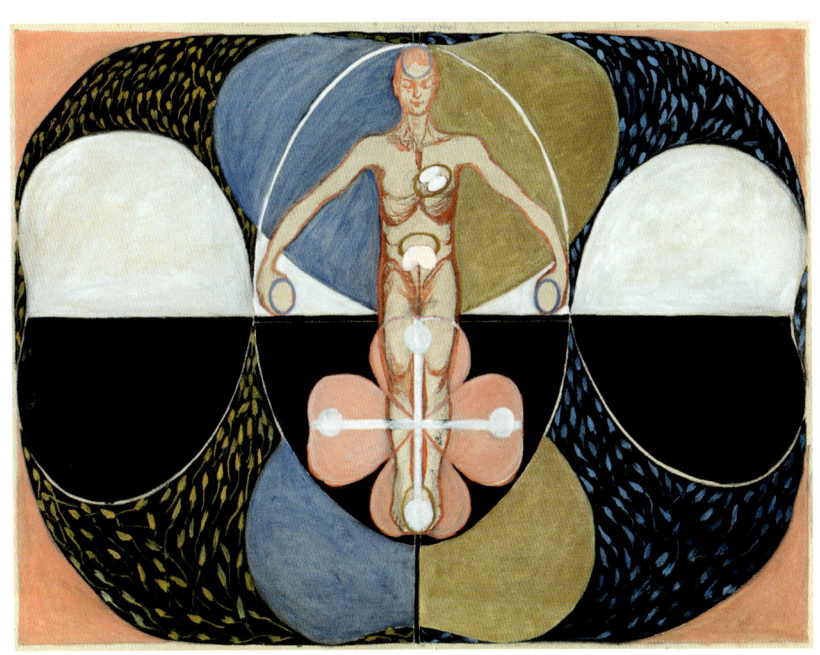

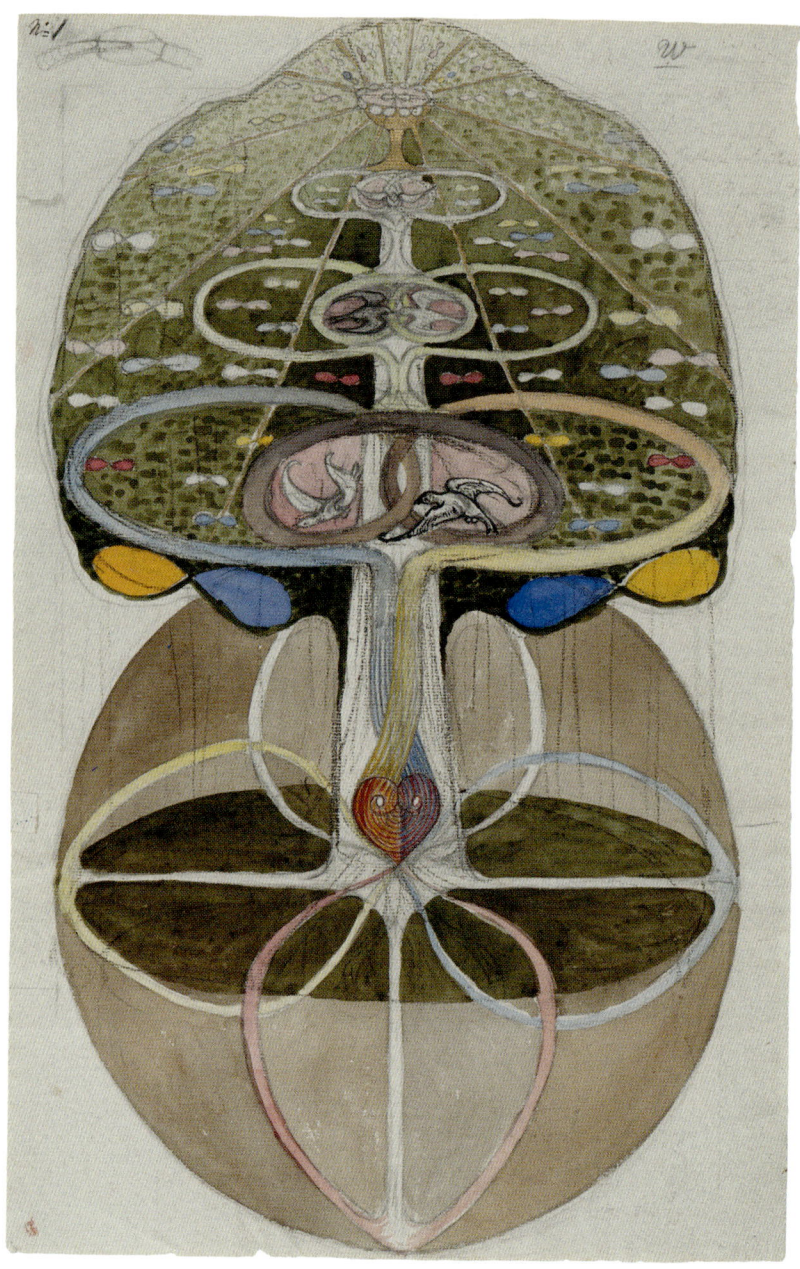

PLATES 29 AND 30. Above: *Tree of Knowledge*, 1913, watercolor, gouache, pencil, metallic paint, and ink on paper, 45.7 cm x 29.5 cm, Stiftelsen Hilma af Klints Verk, HaK 133; opposite: *Tree of Knowledge*, 1915, watercolor, gouache, pencil, and metallic paint on paper, 45.8 x 29.5 cm, Stiftelsen Hilma af Klints Verk, HaK 137.

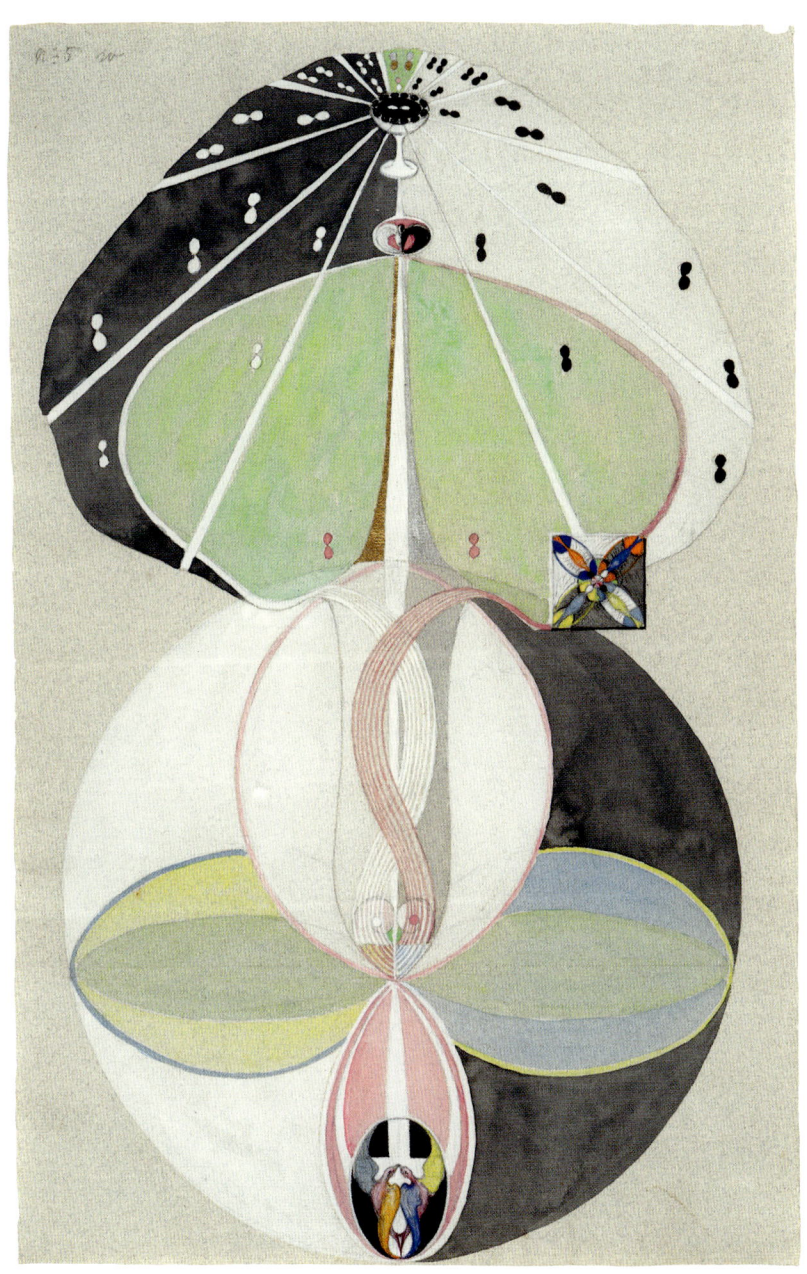

Paintings for the Temple

[1]

Old Images

The meeting of The Five on April 12, 1904, was distinguished by
something so unusual that it changed the group forever. For eight
years the women had been gathering for séances and recording messages in words and images. They had filled hundreds of pages in
notebooks and sketchbooks. They had built an altar with a white
cross and a rose. They had prayed together and read such esoteric
literature as Blavatsky's *Secret Doctrine* and Leadbeater's *Invisible
Helpers*. They had developed their own rituals, sometimes dressing
in long white robes when they met.[1] They now also wore a brooch,
like the badge of an order: a silver cross with a rose at its center.
Hilma's nephew Eric would later recall that she wore the brooch
the rest of her life.[2]

As The Five saw it, they were being rewarded by the spirit world
for their perseverance. Their pencils recorded spirals, circles, and
zigzags as well as flowers and crosses and sometimes even the outlines of boats, people, or eyes. The pages of their notebooks were
peppered with letters and occult signs. Even the younger members,
Cassel and af Klint, now actively participated in the séances, writing and drawing messages along with the others.

What was evident to the group was that the High Ones' inten-
tions toward them were benevolent. The texts they recorded always
suggested a friendly attitude, talking of peace, love, modesty, humility, or apprenticeship and tasks to come. Over the years, the messages had varied in content, leading to shifts in the group but never
to turbulence. Sometimes a message would indicate that a time of
preparation was dawning, that The Five should ready themselves,
but for what? Specifics were never articulated, and the topic would
eventually be dropped. So most of the group took little notice when
the following message was spelled out by Cassel using the psychograph:

> Ananda also prays for you, Hilma. You should rest for days, quiet and
> still. Look toward images, old ones, images that wait for you. Just
> have patience, then you will be guided, calmly and surely, to the goal
> that lies before you.[3]

Nothing about the message seemed unusual: the spirits often
addressed a specific member, and "goals" were frequently vague.
But two of the members heard this particular message differently
from the others.

For Cassel and af Klint it marked the beginning of something new.
The message seemed to announce an additional channel through
which communications would come to them directly and without
distortion. Almost immediately they saw the need to record the
communications in their own notebooks, separate from The Five.[4]
Hilma had actually been doing this since 1901, and now she had a
comrade in arms. The notes they made are rendered in a new style:
they are neither vague nor noncommittal. They do not hesitate or
defer; the messages are concrete and meant to lead to actions. The
main purpose of the séances, which had been difficult to pinpoint,
suddenly became clear. It was not just a matter of developing one's
own spiritual capacities and slowly approaching a higher truth.
Now there was a goal, a purpose, a mission. And they, Anna and
Hilma, would accept it. Hilma would later summarize: "Prophecies
of the creation of astral paintings came through Ananda beginning
in 1904."[5] The "images, old ones," of which Ananda spoke came to
be called "astral paintings." Their execution was declared the goal.

———

In ordinary conversation, when a person speaks and listeners come
away with different understandings, it is generally because some of
them have misinterpreted the content. But the conversations of The
Five were not ordinary. Messages from the High Ones were understood to be truths, revelations of wisdom, and all five listeners knew
that these communications required interpretation. That was the
challenge. In this respect, what seemed clear to whom was not inci-

dental; they believed that the person who most clearly understood a message had been chosen and was closest to the higher powers.

April 12 therefore marked a change for everyone, not just for Hilma and Anna. The balance of power had shifted. It seemed to the other three women that Hilma and Anna were rushing forward on their own and putting the words they wanted to hear in the mouths of the messengers of the High Ones. Hedman, Nilsson, and Cederberg did not embrace the new mission and continued as before. From the perspective of Hilma and Anna, the other three were hesitating to turn word into action, despite the urgings from on high; from the beginning Anna and Hilma were convinced that the assignment was directed at all five women. Cederberg, who was also trained in art, would have been capable of fulfilling the wishes of the High Ones, Anna and Hilma believed—but she lacked the will.[6]

Hilma had been only seventeen when Bertha Valerius had hosted the séance in which a new kind of art was discussed and it was announced that, one day, to paint would mean "to let the light shine that the artist forms in his own spirit." She had been twenty-four and a student at the Academy when Valerius had channeled the prediction by the spirit Eon that the paintings of the future would "reproduce the higher pure inspiration" and "completely different expressions will emerge from the practitioners of art." She was twenty-nine when, in 1891, she was assured that she should go "calmly" on her way and that she would receive a gift. At thirty-two she joined the Edelweiss Society, and at thirty-three she and her friends founded The Five, where automatic writing and drawing were the order of the day. For decades, then, she had seen and created images that, for her, originated in higher spheres.

In the same year that Hilma received the exciting new message, The Five—except Cederberg—joined the Theosophical Society Adyar, named for the place in India where it had been headquartered since 1882.[7] The vocabulary that af Klint used when speaking of "astral paintings" came from Theosophy. Charles Leadbeater explains the term in *Man Visible and Invisible*. According to Leadbeater, reality consists of seven planes, leading up to the highest

PLANES OF NATURE

7 MAHÂPARANIRVÂNIC		FIRST	TRIPLE MANIFESTATION	
6 PARANIRVÂNIC		SECOND		
5 NIRVÂNIC	ATOMIC / PIRIT	THIRD	HREEFOLD PIRIT in AN	
4 BUDDHIC	ATOMIC / The Reincarnating Ego or Soul in Man	INTUITION		
3 MENTAL — ARUPA / RUPA	ATOMIC	NTELLIGENC CAUSAL BODY / MENTAL BODY		
2 ASTRAL	ATOMIC	ASTRAL BODY		
1 PHYSICAL	ATOMIC / SUB-ATOMIC / SUPER-ETHERIC / ETHERIC / GASEOUS / LIQUID / SOLID	ETHERIC DOUBLE / DENSE BODY		

21. Planes of Nature, from C. Leadbeater,
Man Visible and Invisible, 1902.

level of being, the spiritual (fig. 21). The "astral world" is the first step on the way to the spiritual; it is a "higher and more refined world, though a world which is still material."[8]

Henry Steel Olcott, a founder of the Theosophical Society, had described Ananda as the Buddha's favorite disciple. Ananda had been appearing regularly in the notes of The Five, and he was now commanding af Klint to "look toward images, old ones." In *Buddhist Catechism*, Olcott tells a story in which Ananda encounters a "pariah," a girl from the caste of the untouchables. When Ananda asks the girl for water, she says modestly that she is too impure to serve him, to which Ananda answers, "I ask not for caste but for water." He drinks the water the girl gives him.[9] Like the histori-

cal Ananda, the voice that spoke to Hilma and Anna was not interested in traditional social categories and was ready to entrust an
important task to two women—unlikely candidates, according to
the conventions of the time.

Near the end of 1904, as Hilma and Anna prepared for the
assignment ahead, The Five held a session in which they produced
an image that looked like a volcano erupting.[10]

[2]

Revolution

In 1905 everything changed in the countries bordering Sweden.
Revolution broke out in Russia when 150,000 workers participated
in a general strike and marched to the Winter Palace, provoking
loyalist soldiers to shoot into the crowd. Norway declared independence from Sweden, first in Parliament, then by popular vote. King
Oscar II of Sweden bowed to the vote, averting war at the last minute. In Finland workers joined together in calling a general strike;
the country still belonged to Russia as an autonomous grand duchy.
The Finnish workers demanded universal suffrage, explicitly for
both men and women. European leaders worried that the sparks of
revolution would catch elsewhere as well.

The events would have been much discussed in the af Klint
household. What was happening in the neighboring countries had
links to the family history. Mathilda af Klint, Hilma's mother, came
from Finland, where her family belonged to the Swedish minority. Erik and Gustaf, Hilma's great-grandfather and grandfather,
had been sent to war in the eighteenth century to determine where
Russia ended and Sweden began. Catherine the Great and Gustav
III had decided to end the fighting because revolution had broken
out in France, and both feared that it could spread. Now it seemed
closer than ever.

Ida, Hilma's older sister, undoubtedly followed the developments in Finland, especially the demand for universal suffrage. She
had worked for the Fredrika Bremer Association for fifteen years.
At that point New Zealand and Australia were the only countries
that allowed women to vote. What if Finland were to follow their
example?[1]

While the af Klints would have been interested in the situation
in Finland, changes were also brewing at home. The workers' movement was gaining strength as industrialization swelled the ranks
of the proletariat. Workers were organizing; unrest was growing.
Europe's old political order had suffered a serious blow, even if some
conservative forces still believed or hoped the turbulence was only
passing or could be stopped—with violence, if necessary.

There was talk of a "revolution" in science as well. No one
attempted to downplay *this* revolution; on the contrary, it was
received with open arms by the broader society. Researchers in
physics and chemistry were winning one prize after another, as we
have seen. In June 1905, Pierre Curie (1859–1906) came to Stockholm to outline the implications of his recent discoveries in a Nobel
lecture, which he delivered two years after he and his wife, Marie
Curie, had won the prize. The journey had been postponed several
times—for professional reasons and owing to Marie Curie's poor
health. Applause swept the Academy of Sciences when Pierre Curie
took the stage. Every seat was filled. Marie Curie stayed in the audience, too weak to share the stage with her husband.[2] Everyone was
curious to hear about the mysterious powers that the Curies had
dubbed "radioactivity." The discovery of radiation had opened the
door to phenomena that had previously been considered impossible. Elements, Curie explained to the audience, were mutable, and
the idea that the atom was indivisible had been refuted. There was
a "continuous and irreversible disaggregation of the atoms of the
radioactive elements," Curie explained in the speech.

He stressed that the consequences could not be dismissed. He
warned the audience of the forces unleashed by splitting the atom
and then asked a crucial question: did "mankind benefit from know-

ing the secrets of Nature"? "Radium could be very dangerous in criminal hands," he explained, concluding: "I am one of those who believe with Nobel that mankind will derive more good than harm from the new discoveries."[3] But this was hardly the end of the story.

The Five would not have needed to hear Curie's lecture or read about it in the newspapers to know that the foundations of physics and chemistry had been shaken. The decay of the atom was an alchemist's dream come true, at least as the Theosophists saw it, and they never missed a chance to point out that mystics had always known that physical matter was mutable. Charles Leadbeater, for example, wrote: "Occult science has always taught that these so-called elements are not in the truest sense of the word elements at all; that what we call an atom of oxygen or hydrogen can under certain circumstances be broken up."[4] Leadbeater also addressed the mutability of elements in a book he published with Annie Besant in 1905. "Röntgen's rays," they wrote, "have rearranged some of the older ideas of matter, while radium has revolutionised them."[5]

According to Besant and Leadbeater, the theoretical revolution would be followed by a revolution in practice, in application of the knowledge. The invisible powers of nature, they were convinced, corresponded with the powers of the human spirit. In the book *Thought-Forms*, they taught readers how to develop these powers. The title *Thought-Forms* is a play on words: it is both a compound word and a statement. Thought *forms*, the authors explained. The spirit could alter matter, kneading it and reforming it. Most occult doctrines agreed on the point that spirit was superior to matter. Consciousness determined being. The challenge was to understand how.

Besant and Leadbeater published their book as an introduction to the art of making visible the forms of thoughts and feelings. Once learned, this ability would enable humanity to affect matter through the power of thought—not unlike the invisible rays newly discovered by scientists. For the authors, the natural manifestation of these spiritual powers was abstraction. The book was accordingly equipped with a number of nonrepresentational illustrations. Every thought and feeling has a color and a form, they wrote, but one has to learn to see them—it is just a matter of practice, they assured the reader. The states of "affection," "the Intention to Know," and "anger" are illustrated with images, as are works of music by Charles Gounod (see plate 18) and Richard Wagner, among others. "Thoughts are things," the authors write, things on a spiritual level, and whoever can perceive them can have power over them.[6] Besant and Leadbeater wanted to make this insight available to all, and their book became quite popular.

In Munich, the artist Wassily Kandinsky was one of the readers. Hilma af Klint did not own a copy but could easily have borrowed it from the lending library run by the Theosophists in Stockholm. She would later write repeatedly about "thought forms" when describing the beings with which she was in contact (see fig. 48).[7]

Amid the stream of political and scientific change came more news from the High Ones, this time channeled directly to af Klint and Cassel. According to their notes, in August 1905, three of the messengers got in touch: Amaliel, Esther, and Georg. The messages were telegraphic: "Promise to receive work in the service of the mysteries," the women wrote in their new notebook, separate from the notebooks of The Five.[8] These personal notes came more frequently, as if the two artists had finer nets to catch messages from the astral world.

They still met with The Five and received messages there as well. In a drawing made by Cassel, af Klint, and Cederberg at a séance in November 1905, a huge nautilus shell appears on the paper, covered with signs and letters (fig. 22). A dark shape swells out of the shell and long tentacles strew dots into the air, not unlike Morse code. The being is labeled "Annanda," with two n's.[9] Anna and Ananda seem to have become one in this session; no one had ever come closer to the High Ones. "Ask Anna to interpret" is written under the drawing. It was not the first time that Ananda had preferred Anna as a vehicle. Once, for example, the messengers of the High Ones had instructed Mathilda Nilsson and Hilma to lay their hands on Anna's head to help her speak in a trance. It was to convey messages from Ananda, her namesake.[10]

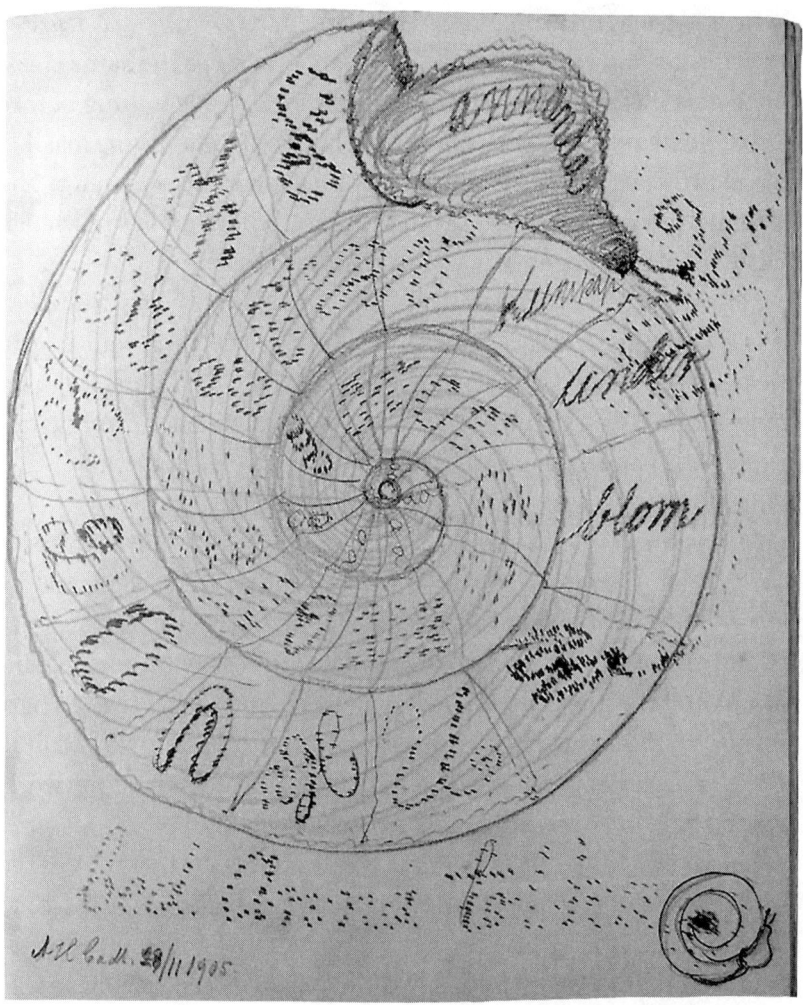

22. Automatic drawing by The Five, November 28, 1905,
Stiftelsen Hilma af Klints Verk, HaK 1526.

Ananda had spoken in the previous year of the "old images" with
which Hilma was to rest, "quiet and still," to be led to the "goal,"
and now, perhaps, the prophecy was beginning to be fulfilled. No
motif recorded by The Five is more archaic than the nautilus. The
spiral-shaped animal led the women deep into prehistory, millions
of years ago to the cephalopods. The zoologist Ernst Haeckel had

dedicated a magnificent plate in his popular *Art Forms in Nature* to the nautilus and to ammonites, an extinct taxon of the same class. Since nautiluses had inhabited the primordial ocean long before humans existed, they were sometimes referred to as "living fossils." The nautilus unites geological eras—it is both old and young. The new emerges from the past, from the primordial flow of knowledge that The Five had been tapping into in their sessions.

Cassel and af Klint pressed forward. A new name began to appear in their notes: Undan. The name refers to the recipient of the necklace Anna and Hilma had bought in Italy. Magdalena Augusta Andersson was nicknamed "Gusten," the short form of "Augusta," and her arrival in the notes heralds change—that instead of five women, the meetings increasingly included six.[11]

In December the notebooks indicate that Hilma wanted to know more. What was meant by the "old images" that Ananda had mentioned? What work was to be taken on "in the service of the mysteries"? She sensed that her artistic skills might be required, and she formulated the question accordingly when she turned to the High Ones. The information was furnished promptly, and she wrote: "Direct answer to my question whether I had transferred my work into the field of painting: the response was yes."[12]

The last trace we have of Hilma in 1905 relates to a birthday party hosted by Ottilia Adelborg, the children's book author and artist, who was turning fifty. She rented a large hall in Skansen, the open-air museum, for the festivities. (Af Klint knew the location, as she had worked on a popular album about Skansen, painting an old bell tower on the site.)[13] The artists were linked by a close friendship, which af Klint would refer to twice in old age. Looking back, she wrote: "She [Ottilia] was brave, preserving, strong, and true. What has been the millstone around her neck was her orthodox being. In the next incarnation she must fight to overcome this."[14] What af Klint would have liked to see from her friend is an open question. The difference between the two is attested by a photo of Adelborg's birthday party published in the women's weekly *Idun*. Adelborg famously collected traditional clothing, so all the guests dressed

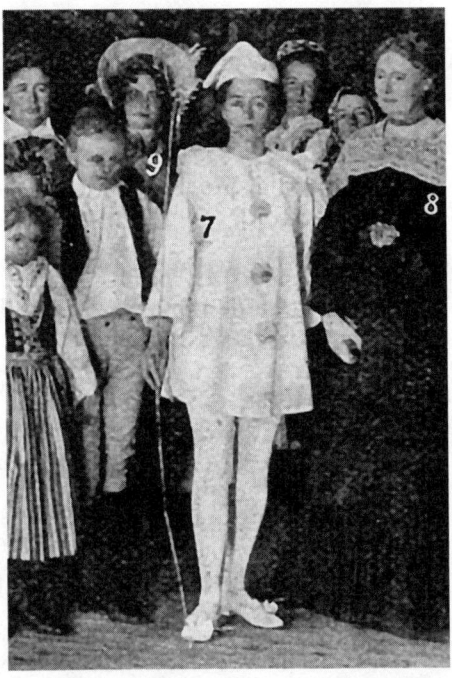

23. Af Klint in a Pierrot costume at a birthday party in December 1905.

accordingly, with one exception. Af Klint stands next to Adelborg in the middle of the well-wishers, glowing in a white tunic, tights, and hat (fig. 23), costumed as Pelle Snygg, the character from Adelborg's most popular children's book.[15]

Instead of bowing to tradition, she looks like a visitor from a different world.

[3]

Primordial Chaos

Blue, green, yellow. These were the principal colors af Klint used for her first series in oil on canvas: twenty-six paintings collected under the title *Primordial Chaos*, begun on November 7, 1906. The artist had just turned forty-four; congratulations from the astral world are recorded in her notebook.[1] *Primordial Chaos* begins with a curved figure that floats over the waters like the spirit; it then undergoes progressive transformations in the paintings that follow (see plate 19). Circles, wheels, and spirals alternate with squares, lines, and charts, accompanied by rays and oscillations. The muted blue and gray tones of the first paintings disappear until golden light seems to radiate from the canvases, contrasting with the dark backgrounds (see plates 20–23).

Several of the paintings are abstract, while in others, letters and even whole words float in pictorial space. Figures appear here and there: roses or the nautilus. There are similarities to some of the collective drawings by The Five, in which flowers, spirals, crosses, and circles appear. Those, however, mainly lack color and the certainty and clarity of the new works. The drawings of The Five also perform individually rather than in series.

The images of *Primordial Chaos* form a sequence, a succession, in some ways reminiscent of the processes described by Pierre Curie in his Nobel lecture. The glow of radium in the darkness. The decay of atoms and the creation of new elements. Number 10 in the series resembles a scientific table, with formula-like symbols (see plate 22). The artist herself compared the paintings to "charts and logarithms for a seaman."[2] There were more parallels: her father's research ship was called *Snäckan*, Swedish for "snail," a name insinuating the slowness with which the waters were traversed to take magnetic and meteorological measurements. The spiral shells of snails and nautiluses would be a leitmotif in af Klint's work going forward.

These first works were accompanied by an explosion of drawings that were burned decades later when Hilma and Anna decided to make clean copies of their notes and to destroy the originals.[3] They claimed to fill thirty notebooks in the months before and after *Primordial Chaos*. The material was later transferred into two notebooks labeled "Preliminary Work on the Paintings" and "Descriptions of the Symbols, Signs, and Images." In these documents, the friends retrospectively bestowed order and logical form on the rush of material, with future readers in mind.

Is it hyperbolic to speak of these works as revolutionary? Hilma and Anna did so: in their notebooks they drew parallels to revolutions in the external world. They referred to a "turning point in history," the "Russian Empire," and the "blind powers" that were destroying it. "The work," they wrote, referring to their own creations, "must be carried forward by the people of the earth, the work refers to liberation from the oppression of the higher classes."[4] The two women were not simply interested in the revolutions in the world around them; they understood themselves to be part of the process.

The friends began to present themselves in the notebooks in various guises. "Asket" referred to af Klint, the name ("ascetic") suggesting abstinence and self-control. Cassel was called "Vestal," after the priestesses of ancient Rome who tended the fire in the temple of Vesta and, like the goddess, practiced chastity. The masculine "Asket" forms a unity with the feminine "Vestal." "Vestal-asket" appears frequently in the notes as well as on canvases of *Primordial Chaos* (see plate 21).[5]

Asket and Vestal were not just roles the pair took in the present moment; they also saw them as vessels of past lives. Memories of previous incarnations became an important aspect of the notebooks; time ceased to be understood diachronically. The spirit was seen to be able to slip into various bodies, rather like the Hindu god Vishnu in his avatars. Reincarnation was also a teaching of Theosophy.[6]

The new freedoms went further. It was not just the boundaries of space and time that had been ruptured, but those of sex as well. In 1906 af Klint was already exploring gender shifts, as the male Asket. In her circles this was not unusual. The artist Lotten Rönquist was said to have been a "priest in Syria" in a previous incarnation, when Asket ruled as "king of the land."[7] When spirit could shape matter, the old systems were voided.

The secret powerhouse behind the metamorphoses was the

paintings. The works did not just depict processes, they set them in motion. The shell of the nautilus in number 9 of *Primordial Chaos* (see plate 21) is doubled: there are two exits; out of both emerge forms that resemble snails. The animals stretch forward to entwine their tentacles. The rose of the Rosicrucians springs from the point where they touch. None of this is coincidence. The nautilus brings the past into the present and unites the sexes. In nature, the snail is hermaphroditic, possessing both male and female sex organs. Af Klint inscribed the painting with "Vestal" and "Asket."

The notebooks also describe a creature known as "dual being," which emerges from the longing for unity, the original state, when man and woman were one.[8] Hilma designated other forms that look like swimming sperm cells in one of the paintings "the man" and "the woman" (number 15). She assigned the two sexes the colors blue and yellow and retained this symbolism throughout her work. Blue often stands for the female principle, yellow for the male, but the color code can switch. Rigid rules did not fit af Klint's world of metamorphosis and fluid transitions.

While the spirit was penetrating matter on the canvases, boundaries were melting in daily life as well. The messengers of the High Ones no longer waited for scheduled séances. They simply got in touch without warning, and they had a lot to say. They became so unpredictable that Hilma turned to keeping paper and pencil at hand, just in case. One of the notebook pages is labeled "In the woods of Adelsö." Another is labeled "Engelsberg" for a town in a mining district several hundred kilometers northwest of Stockholm.[9] An artist colony had formed there around 1900, perhaps accounting for Hilma's visit.[10] The notes, however, do not mention any resident artists.

4

Eros

Primordial Chaos set in motion a chain reaction. Each painting required another to follow it. The first series was not yet finished when the next, *Eros*, was begun. *Eros* comprises eight paintings, the first executed in January 1907, the last in September.

For af Klint, *Eros* was the natural continuation of *Primordial Chaos*. The blue and yellow lines that snaked through the first series continue to explore uncharted terrain on the new canvases, though here pink tones predominate. "Asket" and "Vestal" appear again; the combination of forms changes continually. Lines intersect and form ovals, then come together in shapes reminiscent of flowers or clover leaves before separating again, like a swarm of migratory birds flying in various formations (see plate 24).[1] The pastel colors lend the paintings an innocent, platonic air, though they have a deeper meaning. "Eros is the fusion of all colors," Hilma writes, "and announces, among other things, understanding in love."[2] Mixing, melting, connecting, dissolving: it is chemistry on the canvas and beyond.

Eros is the Greek name for the god of love, called Amor in Latin. According to the story told by Apuleius in his *Metamorphoses*, Amor was in love with the beautiful princess Psyche, whom he married when Jupiter granted her immortality. The theme has been interpreted by numerous artists in marble, on canvas, and in fresco, from Raphael to Rodin. In 1907 Edvard Munch painted a work titled *Amor and Psyche*, and just a few buildings away from the studio where af Klint painted her *Eros*, Julius Kronberg (1850–1921), a former professor at the Stockholm Academy, was painting a large-scale fresco based on the same tale. Kronberg had received the commission from the Royal Dramatic Theatre, which wanted a painting above the stage in their new building on Nybroplan, scheduled to open in February 1908 (see fig. 33).[3]

Nothing in af Klint's painting is reminiscent of classical models: her approach is even more radical than the one for *Andromeda*, her fearless princess of 1887. The *Eros* series involves no literal figuration, no nudes about to kiss as in Munch's rendition. There is no winged Amor as in Kronberg's version, no vaporous tresses of Psyche fluttering around him. Rather, af Klint treats the myth as a play of colors and forms in a new configuration. Amor and Psyche, masculine and feminine principles, have transformed into Asket and Vestal, who unite to transcend matter, made immortal like Psyche in the old story.

"Cupid or love in his primitive sense is Eros, the Divine Will, or *Desire of manifesting itself through visible creation*," Blavatsky wrote in *The Secret Doctrine*.[4] The world had not seen so joyful and exuberant a treatment of the theme as Hilma's series, and the messengers of the High Ones advised her to leave it that way, at least for the time being. "As long as it is necessary," they said, "the paintings must remain hidden from the eyes of the general public, until the time to come forward is possible."[5]

[5]

Medium

Hilma af Klint and Anna Cassel found themselves in a maelstrom. They were used to drawing and writing as mediums, but modestly, with paper and pencil, and guided by more experienced women. The High Ones and their messengers had never once tried to incite The Five to artistic feats; they had never mentioned painting. Now, however, the wishes and ideas that came to af Klint and Cassel were precise: paintings there would be; even the dimensions were prescribed. There was also mention of "museum walls" for which the works were to be made. The point was taken up again in the notebooks two decades later, when Hilma wrote about her plan for "a museum to show what lies behind the forces of matter" and asked the higher forces for help "to lay the foundations for a building."[1]

The painters had decided to document their process with the intention of parsing it once the situation had calmed. They could more easily describe what was happening than understand it. Their wonder never diminished. When Hilma was an old woman, she received a letter from a young friend who, with his wife, had visited her studio on Munsö. His wife, the enthusiastic friend wrote, wanted to know more about the letters that appeared in the paintings. The artist answered in her typically dry style: "How is your wife? If she's wondering about my letters, then tell her that I am doing the same."[2]

Cassel and af Klint dealt with the abundance of images, signs, and messages by dividing the labor. Painting fell primarily to Hilma, while Anna wrote.[3] The task assigned by the High Ones had two parts—one visual, one narrative. As to the latter, the pair were not only to take notes but to prepare an extensive, stand-alone text. A message directed to Cassel in 1900, and recorded in a notebook of The Five, had already referred to this:

> You should read the documents—not written by human hands, but engraved in the finest material of human life. For you should know this: For those who have eyes to see, there is a living text in everything, a diary of the changing fates of worlds, you are to look at the many lives of individuals and a fraction of this text.[4]

The "living text" is given various names in the friends' notebooks. Sometimes it is referred to as the "Akasha Chronicle" after a concept from Theosophy. Other times it is called the "Tale of the Rose," connecting their task to Rosicrucian symbolism.[5]

While Cassel was to "calmly study the Akasha," as it was formulated at the beginning of the first notebook, af Klint was to paint, ever more and ever faster, in steadily growing formats. The powers that guided her seemed to relish variety. A message from March 1907 said abruptly: "Take your palette and begin. Expect a surprise!"[6] Three paintings followed in May, including two landscapes:

in one the sun is rising, in the other it is setting, light dripping from the sky like lava (see plate 25).[7] That same month the astrological symbol for Jupiter appeared to Hilma above her easel, "powerfully illuminated and lasting several seconds."[8]

A third series followed *Primordial Chaos* and *Eros*. It would include nine paintings and be called *The Large Figure Paintings*.[9] The canvases were starting to be taller than the artist herself.

Hilma had moved into a new studio to execute the work. The address was Hamngatan 5, as she wrote in her notebook.[10] The studio was on the top floor above the exhibition rooms of the Sveriges Allmänna Konstförening, where she had participated in group shows. Blanch's Café on the first floor was still a hotspot for Stockholm's art scene.

Hilma shared the studio with two other female artists, Alma Arnell (1857–1934) and Lotten Rönquist (1864–1912), both graduates of the Royal Academy. They were the first to give feedback on the new work. "Unsuitable," they declared, and Hilma recorded the comment.[11] Most of her contemporaries probably would have agreed: the most recent large figure painting showed a man and a woman—he yellow, she blue[12]—their bodies connected by a glowing red organ that seemed to combine ovaries and sperm ducts. "I was told," Hilma wrote, that the painting should remain "unseen," hidden from the eyes of other people.[13] It's not difficult to imagine what a tempest would have otherwise ensued: an artist who painted reproductive organs and believed she had been a man in a previous incarnation?

In her notebooks she called the paintings "groundbreaking" and wrote that "the attempts I have undertaken . . . will astound humanity."[14] The time for that was in the future, she realized; she had to be patient. In the meantime the astral world was in such a hurry, there was no time to think about an audience. She spent four hours every day just painting, to say nothing of the time spent on the texts and sketches in the notebooks.

Af Klint repeatedly referred to her way of working as "mediumistic."[15] She wrote, "the images are painted directly through me, without preliminary sketches, with great force."[16] But this was only half true; the artist could not have been merely a passive instrument. From the beginning, the process had been a dialogue, with questions and answers traded between spheres without direct commands. "Amaliel offered me the work and I instantly answered Yes," the artist wrote, describing how the work began.[17] In November 1907 she went into more detail about the collaboration: "It was not that I should blindly obey the lords of the Mysteries, but that I should imagine them always standing next to me."[18]

What's more, collaboration with higher powers did not free her from the standard requirements of painting: planning, choosing, executing. Of the thirty-four pencil sketches that preceded the canvases of *Primordial Chaos*, only twenty-six turned into paintings. The process was repeated for *Eros*: of eighty-four sketches, only eight made it onto canvas.[19] In her notebooks, the artist also records the exuberant praise sent by the higher powers. The paintings had "succeeded beyond expectations," according to one note.[20]

The energy and concentration she expended on the work over several months brought her to the brink of collapse. The notes indicate that she took comfort in the fact that her seafaring ancestors had also undertaken ambitious projects, more or less alone, proceeding from the "research and toils of a single person," as her grandfather Gustaf had written in 1816 of his work on the *Sveriges Sjöatlas*. She, the granddaughter of the man whose portrait hung in her studio, painted images like "charts and logarithms for a seaman." One notebook ends with a list of several dozen coastal towns that have lighthouses. Some are in Sweden, but most are scattered around the globe. Cannes, Palermo, Alexandria, Port Said, Cape Ducato, and Funchal—each, according to Hilma, had a particular meaning in the spiritual history of the world, which she briefly explains next to each place-name on the list.[21]

The notebook thus ends like a logbook. Gustaf, the seafarer and cartographer, had measured the vastness and shoals of the water of Sweden. His granddaughter had the task of charting the spiritual realm.

6

The Ten Largest

As August 1907 drew to a close, it was Amaliel who began to guide the sketches for the next series, to be called *The Ten Largest*. It was no exaggeration—the dimensions had doubled since the previous series: the new paintings would measure up to 328 by 240 centimeters (12.9 by 7.8 feet) and be as big as barn doors (see plates 2, 7, and 26).

Af Klint had never worked on such a scale. She had been impressed by paintings of a similar magnitude when she visited the churches and museums in Italy. In Florence, for example, Giotto had chosen a nearly identical height for his famous *Madonna Enthroned* in the Ognissanti Church. The early fourteenth-century work was thoroughly treated in Bierfreund's guidebook, which Hilma read so many times it practically fell apart.[1] But her higher beings seemed to want something even grander: not just one work standing alone on an altar, but ten. "What I needed was courage, and courage was promised me," she wrote in her notebook.[2] Of course she needed more than just courage to complete the assignment. Paint had to be purchased, and canvases and stretchers; space had to be made in the studio, and quite a lot of it. The artist began working on large-format "architect's paper," taking single sheets and pasting them together on a canvas.[3] She sometimes sketched in the design on a table, sometimes on the floor. Thin pencil lines are still visible if you look closely. "Yellow," she wrote on one canvas, as instruction. "Madder lake," a red hue, is written in another place.[4]

Hilma painted with unprecedented speed. She used tempera pigments mixed with eggs, and the farmers on the family estates were astonished at how many she used—that fall and winter she needed the clutches of several coops.[5] The paint was so fluid that it dripped from the brush, running down in long ropes and splashing on the paper like rain in a downpour. She had to lay the paintings on the floor to work on them, as they were much too large to fit on an easel.

She started the first of *The Ten Largest* on October 2 and finished the last one on December 7.[6] Ten paintings in two months with a total area of eighty square meters. Eighty square meters of painting without people, landscape, buildings, foreground, or horizon. But there were colors: blue, orange, violet, and pink.

She succeeded in doing what had seemed impossible: she gave visual character to spirit and found enduring forms to show how everything changes, moves, and flows—buzzing, floating, fertilizing, mating, oscillating, flipping, gliding, growing. Everything happening at the same time, to the great and to the small; something is in motion in every corner, spinning. "The form is the waves," Hilma af Klint wrote later, "behind the form is life itself."[7]

Though enormous, *The Ten Largest* offer no clues to the visual scale of the painted forms. One moment the viewer feels that she is huge and gazing down into the tiny world of a petri dish. The next she might feel tiny herself, at the center of the Milky Way, looking into the vast universe of planets, comets, and stars.

These comparisons are wrong, of course. Outer space isn't orange, and what is the odd, pumpkin-like form doing there (see plate 2)? Are the rings and circles on the canvas related to the mock suns that she saw as a girl in the painting at the Church of St. Nicholas (see plate 6)? What are the letters supposed to mean?

The assiduous notes made by Hilma and Anna as the paintings were produced can be just as inscrutable as the works themselves. The texts are not instructions or explanations of what appears on the canvas, but two themes run through them—first, Ernst Haeckel's theory of embryonic recapitulation, which Hilma invoked when she called the works "evolution paintings."[8] Like the Theosophists, she believed that every individual carries the history of their previous lives within them, and she understood this doctrine of reincarnation as an extension of Haeckel's theory that every embryo recapitulates its own phylogeny in the womb.

The other theme leads away from science and the Western world, toward mysticism and the East. Hilma repeatedly mentions "Ararat's Brothers," named for the mountain in Turkey where Noah's ark was said to have come to rest, as the origin of *The Ten Largest*. She also invokes the "Mahatmas," masters of wisdom said to be from Tibet (referred to by Blavatsky in her books).[9] Here the artist is establishing an affinity with religious practices wherein the design of letters in sacred texts is as important as it is in her own work. On the canvases, she sets writing and the pictorial in parity, like an Arabic calligrapher. Her inspiration may have come from Fredrik Robert Martin's collection of oriental art, displayed at the General Art and Industrial Exposition of Stockholm in 1897. She also owned a book describing the Jewish mystical tradition wherein combinations of Hebrew letters carry esoteric meaning.[10] In the first of *The Ten Largest*, the orange lines are reminiscent of Viking runes, such as those engraved on the runestone on Adelsö.[11] Af Klint explained some of her own letter combinations—for example "wu" signifies "evolution," "mwu" means "faith," and "ws" stands for "work in the matter." Other combinations of signs are more difficult to grasp, and af Klint never succeeded in assigning them stable meanings; she was continually creating new glossaries with hundreds of entries.[12]

The spiritual commissioners of her paintings praised the artist effusively. They were more than satisfied, she wrote in the notebooks—the paintings couldn't have turned out better. *The Ten Largest* were judged "paradisaically beautiful."[13] When they were finished in early 1908, Hilma records the spirits telling her: "You've now completed such glorious work that you would fall to your knees if you understood it."[14]

But there was also a dark side. Hilma desperately needed the euphoric approval: she was suffering, in doubt, and at the end of her strength. According to the notebooks, her condition didn't escape the notice of the messengers, and they addressed it repeatedly. Sometimes they were soothing, assuring Hilma that doubt was the power that prevented "false information" from being transmitted, and she couldn't be criticized for it.[15] The advice was that she "shouldn't be critical" of herself.[16] But once *The Ten Largest* were finished, who knew how much longer the higher powers would make demands on her? New commissions arrived constantly with no end in sight. Rules of conduct were also prescribed. The artist was to eat no meat, no salty food, and "no tainted foods," according to the notebook.[17]

The commissions led to tension among The Five. The more Hilma engaged with the higher world, the more it disrupted her life in the real one. By 1907 the closed circle of The Five had expanded to seven women, and in May the number increased to eleven. Instructions for the group's "reorganization" came through Hilma. She received messages in a "half trance," according to one of her notes, and the spirits gave her "carte blanche." "Anyone Hilma thinks should be part of the group is to be included," they said.[18] In addition to Gusten Andersson, other new members were Lotten Rönquist and Alma Arnell, who shared the studio with Hilma and who, only a short time earlier, had deemed the paintings "unsuitable."[19]

For the first time, some of the members refused to comply with what Hilma said the higher powers wanted. The conflict came to a head over the membership of Gusten Andersson, alias "Undan." When, in August 1907, the messengers repeated through Hilma the request that Andersson be added to the group, Sigrid Hedman, Mathilda Nilsson, and Cornelia Cederberg openly balked. "Inspired resistance," Hilma wrote.

The higher beings came down harshly on the ones who defied them: "I am asked to tell S. Hedman that she doesn't know Asket," Hilma wrote in the notebook; Hedman was to receive the host "for the last time."[20]

The tension that had been brewing erupted just before Hilma started *The Ten Largest*. It continued as she worked, creating a burden when what she needed was physical and emotional support. Worse, Cassel was being "no help," Hilma wrote.[21] On the canvases, "Vestalasket"—the dual nature of the two friends—continued, but otherwise the relationship lost its intensity and they ceased to function as a unity.

Luckily Cederberg stepped in to help with *The Ten Largest*, at the explicit request of the messengers.[22] Among The Five, Cederberg had most frequently rendered the images coming from the astral plane. Since she was a trained artist, from October through December 1907 she supplied whatever Hilma needed, from automatic drawing to painting.

Yet from Hilma's perspective, Gusten Andersson was even more helpful. As the project started, Hilma noted that Gusten had been in her studio for seven days to "further the work through prayer."[23] And it was Gusten who had made a medially directed drawing involving roses and lilies, the very flowers that appear in the first of *The Ten Largest*. The rose and the lily refer to the "conquest of the pain of duality," according to a comment in the notebook.[24] Other notes explain that the coming together of rose and lily signified "completeness" and that the rose and lily came from the "language of the ancient image" in connection with the command that Hilma and Gusten develop the flowers within themselves—Hilma the rose, her friend the lily.[25]

To the artist this simply advanced a theme from 1906 when she had made a portrait of Gusten "as a nun." In the painting Gusten sits with a lily in her hand in front of the altar of The Five, where the axes of the white cross meet and where a rose rested on the altar (fig. 24). Hilma picked up these motifs again in October 1907 when she painted whirling circles of roses and lilies on the first canvas of *The Ten Largest*. The wreaths of flowers also touch another circle in the painting, which contains the letters *a* and *v*—the initials of Vestalasket, Hilma and Anna's dual nature.[26]

Was Gusten the reason for Anna's distance? Did Anna think the communion of rose and lily displaced her own unity with Hilma as Asket and Vestal? Af Klint seems to work through her relationships with Anna and Gusten in the paintings: the two dual natures associated with them are not mutually exclusive. The rose and the lily—like the ascetic and the vestal—are free entities that travel

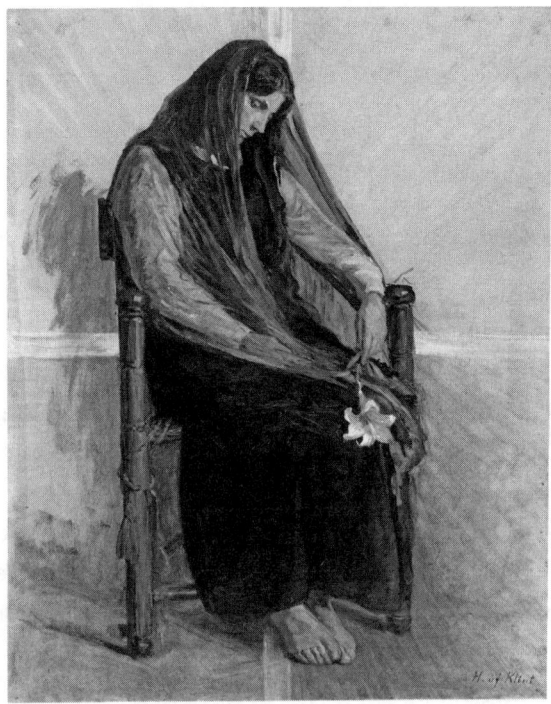

24. *Portrait of a Woman with a Lily*, 1906, watercolor on paper,
50 x 35 cm, Stiftelsen Hilma af Klints Verk, HaK 05.

through the tiered world, shifting back and forth from the astral
to the physical planes as divine symbols, avatars, alter egos, or
embodiments of the male and the female. Since rose and lily come
from the "language of the ancient images," they also connect past
and present—like the nautilus. But what created harmonic vibrations on the canvas caused dissonance beyond it. It didn't escape the
group that Gusten had not only become part of a second dual nature
with Hilma but had also brought a new element into The Five. On
October 26, 1907, during work on *The Ten Largest*, one note reads:
"She [Gusten] so gave herself over to desire that she must abstain
to the last drop of blood."[27]

When work on *The Ten Largest* was finished and a new series
begun, tensions reached a boiling point.

7

"I Was the Instrument of Ecstasy"

An erotic element had been approaching slowly, like a will-o'-the-wisp flickering among the shadows of a forest. In January and February 1907, curved forms with openings vaguely resembling vulvae began appearing in the notebooks of The Five. The images were drawn by Sigrid Hedman, Mathilda Nilsson, and Cornelia Cederberg.[1]

Then, in March, a head with a Phrygian cap appeared in one of af Klint's sketchbooks, captured with the electric strokes of automatic drawing. The baggy tip of the cap recalls the material the Phrygians used for their hats—the tanned skin of bull's testicles; the cap had last been fashionable among French revolutionaries in 1789. A second Phrygian followed in the same sketchbook (fig. 25), a full, naked figure in forward motion with an oversized penis and testicles swinging between its legs.[2] Intriguingly, the ancient domain of the Phrygians had included Mount Ararat, so the seemingly aroused man could possibly be an envoy from "Ararat's Brothers," beings frequently mentioned in the notebook. A third sketch in April ends the series. Here the figure is dressed in priestly garb, with the headdress and beard of a pharaoh.

The allusions continue. A notebook entry from September 1907 states: "The eyelet was hooked into by the hook." The metaphor refers to man, woman, and their union.[3] Blavatsky writes in *The Secret Doctrine* about "Yoni" and "Lingham," the tantric terms for the female and male sex organs.[4] As af Klint went to work on *The Ten Largest* in October, the paintings started to teem with forms that, though abstracted, recalled ovaries, sperm ducts, and testicles, and their attendant processes—insemination, fertilization, union, and coupling (see plates 2 and 26).

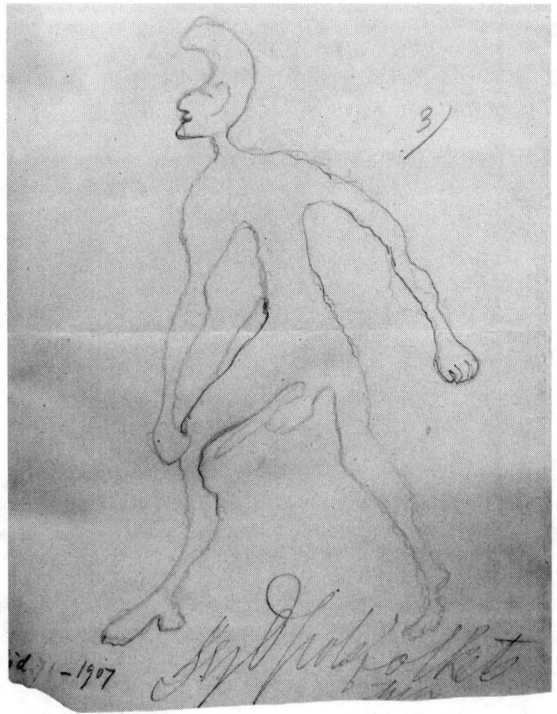

25. Automatic drawing of male figure, 1907.

The months-long slalom around sexual processes ended in December 1907, when af Klint concluded *The Ten Largest* and returned to *The Large Figure Paintings*. In number 6 of the series, a man and a woman appear, both naked (fig. 26). The woman sits on the man's lap, and a cross rises from their shared center, flanked by two white circles. Symbols once again reminiscent of stylized sex organs appear within the circles: eyelet and hook, as af Klint refers to them. The female and male principle unite in the literal sense: the image depicts sexual intercourse. The artist commented in her notebook: "The image of the man was me, that of the woman, Gusten."[5] The Phrygian man returns in the second-to-last of *The Large Figure Paintings*, now with a phallic headdress, floating in a bubble that resembles a womb (fig. 27). The final painting shows the altar of The Five, as if the insight symbolized by the cross had

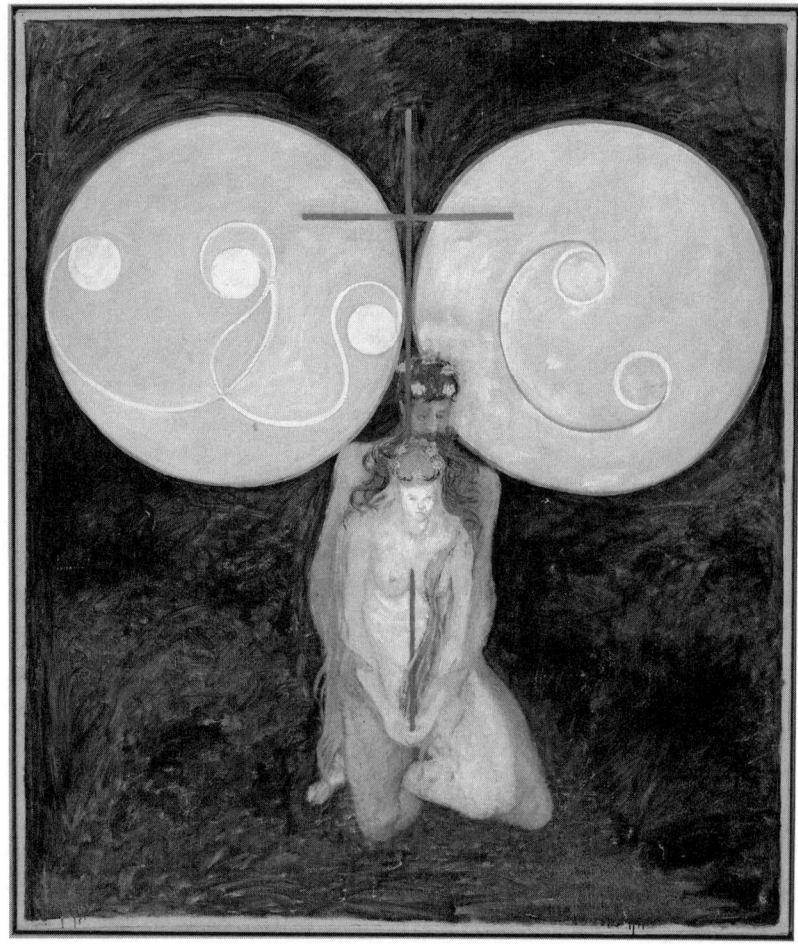

26. *The Large Figure Paintings, No. 6, Group III, Series WU/The Rose*, 1907, oil on canvas, 158 x 138 cm, Stiftelsen Hilma af Klints Verk, HaK 43.

been birthed from the womb in the previous painting (see fig. 18).

"The essence of my life," af Klint wrote in the notebook on December 9, "was a Spartan truth versus Gusten's Spartan love."[6] The women seemed to disagree about the nature of their relationship. The designation "Spartan" keeps coming back in the notebooks—a reference to Plutarch, who mentions the homosexual practices of Spartan women in his biography of the Spartan prince Lycurgus.[7]

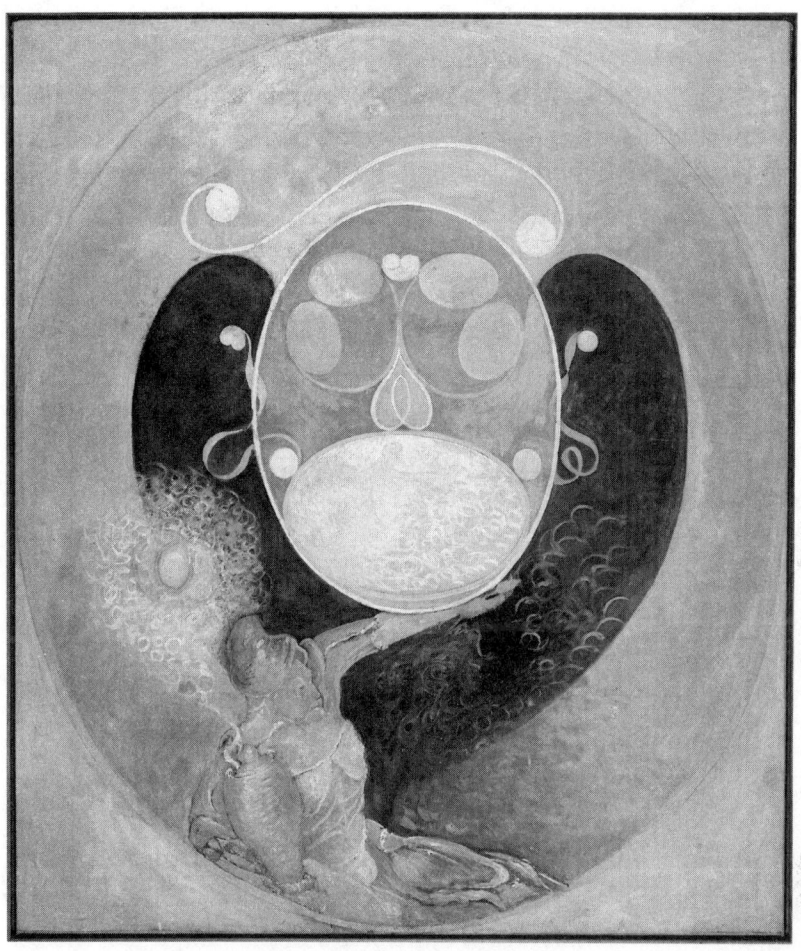

27. *The Large Figure Paintings, No. 8, Group III, Series WU/The Rose*, 1907, oil on canvas, 158 x 138 cm, Stiftelsen Hilma af Klints Verk, HaK 46.

Gusten's own words have also been preserved and took an equally creative form. While af Klint was painting, Gusten wrote about her turbulent feelings. She dedicated an entire notebook to sister "H a K," starting with a poem, "Desire," in 1905. Some pages later, she calls Hilma the "Mountain King." His doors, Gusten wrote, would open only to those "who knew the right moment and the right word." By summer of the following year, Gusten had lost her optimism. She notes the story of "The Broken Soul," in which "the one whom my heart loves has broken my heart in two."[8]

The relationship between the two women created friction among The Five, which escalated when Hilma suggested the group perform a ceremony to mark the completion of *The Large Figure Paintings* in 1907, on Christmas Eve. Gusten was to be included. This was what the higher powers wished, the artist recorded in her notes. In a spiritual vision, she saw herself and Gusten on two chaises, one blue and one yellow, like the female and male principles. They were holding hands, and according to the wishes of the spirits, Sigrid Hedman was then to lead them to the altar. But nothing came of the plan. "Reluctance from the others," the artist noted.[9] The ceremony did not take place, but that did not end the conflict. At the meeting on Christmas Eve, Hilma felt isolated from the others, as if they were turning away from her. Even Gusten "left me during that time," she wrote.[10] The crisis lasted months. When the artist edited the notebooks years later, she had still not forgotten how miserable she had felt. It had been "terribly difficult," she wrote in a margin, and she would have been "destroyed" without her work.[11]

Models for some of af Klint's motifs can be found in works on magic and alchemy. The physical union of man and woman often serves as a symbol for the marriage of opposites and the conquest of matter. Christian Rosencreutz refers to a "chymical wedding" in his book of the same name, in which he describes the seven steps of his transformation, culminating in a mystical wedding of king and queen.

The resolution of duality is often illustrated figuratively in alchemical books—for example, as a copulating couple who unite in a vial instead of in a bed, to suggest transformation, the conversion of matter to spirit. There are also illustrations of divine hermaphrodites with breasts and a penis, uniting the sexes.[12] In mysticism, as in art, the border between eroticism and insight has always been fluid. Painters across the centuries have depicted enraptured believers and saints trembling as they receive divine messages. "I was the instrument of ecstasy," af Klint wrote in January 1906 in the notebook that she and Cassel began when they split off from The Five.[13] Faith and sex are the two experiences most often said to be capable of inducing such a state.

Af Klint's explanation that the man in the painting depicts her and the woman depicts Gusten is followed by another sentence: "The image of the man in the painting is meant to portray desire without sensuality."[14] But the others in The Five seem to have interpreted the painting differently when they refused to hold the ceremony.

For af Klint it was becoming increasingly difficult to maintain a normal daily life. A note suggests that she continued her studio work and still accepted commissions. "At the same time, I was working on a portrait; the division of my personality was almost unbearable," she wrote in January 1908. Works she painted in the traditional academic style continued to appear in exhibitions, for example in 1906 at the Art and Industrial Exhibition in Norrköping, and in 1907 in a show of the same name in Lund.[15]

It is not clear from the notes where the border lay between wish and reality, whether or when spiritual ecstasy turned into physical desire or vice versa. The painter had left behind most conventions of representation and had recently departed from alchemical ones as well. When she turned to Theosophical symbolism or to that of older mystics like Jakob Böhme, the models shine through cautiously, like light in a misty dawn. Ever since *Primordial Chaos*, she had mainly been forging a path alone. She treated the old motif of union in a new way, with humans, snails, flowers, plants, symbols, signs, letters, and organisms that look like protozoa or bacteria. There had never been anything like it in painting. She was creating her own cosmos, breaking new aesthetic and thematic ground.

Her claim to a male role was likewise out of the ordinary. With Cassel she had been the ascetic at the side of the vestal virgin— abstinence was a central tenet of their spiritual understanding. With Gusten Andersson she was the unclothed male figure on whose lap the female sits. Everything had begun to shift: desire traveled between worlds, from the spiritual plane to the physical and back again.

By the end of 1907, the longing for union and for the conquest of duality took many forms in her work, leading to new associations and alter egos: Asket and Vestal, Rose and Lily, Phrygians, Spartans, eyelet and hook. Like a centrifuge, the work on "dual being" flung out three further series, more than fifty paintings in total. One series was called *Evolution* and showed armies of sperm in blue and yellow, the colors of the male and female principles (see plates 27 and 28).

[8]

Rudolf Steiner Visits Sweden

When Hilma af Klint's letter reached Rudolf Steiner in June 1908, it was simply one of a countless number. Steiner, a thin man with dark hair, only a year older than af Klint, had already soared to Theosophical stardom. Just answering his mail would have been a full-time job; his workload was practically inhuman. There were daily lectures—sometimes more than one—plus a stream of publications.

Steiner's great popularity could not have been predicted by his earlier, relatively modest achievements. After studying mathematics and science, he had been a private tutor in Vienna, teaching a child with a serious learning disability. From there he went to work in the Goethe-Schiller archive in Weimar, painstakingly editing Goethe's nature writings, a task that took over a decade.[1]

When Steiner joined the Theosophists, he was already forty-one years old and his talents soon became obvious. In 1902 he took over the direction of the newly founded German section of the society, with the assistance of Marie von Sivers, who would later become his second wife. Membership skyrocketed. The congresses that Steiner planned as general secretary attracted large audiences. His marked aesthetic and creative drive helped: from the programs to the lecture halls, every aspect of these events was designed by Steiner himself.[2]

Steiner first appears in af Klint's notes in early 1908.[3] The notes indicate that she attended one of his lectures in Stockholm while she was working on the series *Evolution* and *The Seven-Pointed Star*. On the evening of March 30, a Monday, she arrived at the elegant auditorium of the Swedish Society of Medicine to hear Steiner speak in German on "Goethe's Theosophical Answer to the Riddle of Humanity." Lectures followed on Wednesday and Thursday, titled "Guiding Themes in the Ring of the Nibelung" and "The Initiation."[4]

It seems she may have approached Steiner after one of the lectures to ask several questions she recorded in the notebooks. She wanted to know if he could put her in touch with the Rosicrucians and asked whether he thought her work might already be influenced by the secret society.[5] The history and meaning of the Rosicrucians was one of Steiner's areas of expertise. He had already delivered lectures on them in Munich, under the title "The Theosophy of the Rosicrucians."[6] Steiner's answers to her questions are not documented in the notebook.

The artist had probably already formulated a plan to invite the scholar to her studio. The exact chronology cannot be determined from the notebook, but it is clear that af Klint and Steiner corresponded briefly in the summer of 1908, several months after they met.[7] Af Klint sent a letter to Norway by post on June 26. Steiner was in Oslo, then called Christiania, where he frequently spent time and was well connected to the local Theosophists.

The letter was short: af Klint started each sentence on a new line. "Doktor Rudolf Steiner!" she wrote, as if calling out to someone hurrying along the street. From her "guide and teacher," she wrote, she had received the last paintings around the twenty-eighth of April. She wanted to know if Steiner could possibly stop in Stockholm on his way back to Germany: "The paintings are many and great and I cannot go to you."[8]

His travel costs would be reimbursed, she promised—she had consulted with the Theosophical Society in Stockholm on the matter. The letter is written in imperfect English. Someone must have assisted her since she did not speak the language herself. She came quickly to the point, her need for his presence being urgent: "My teacher," she explained, had sent him to her, "and I think it is for helping me understand the work."[9]

Steiner's answer arrived from Oslo a month later and suggests he had read the letter with dismay. Him, the great Steiner? Sent to her, Hilma af Klint? By her teacher? To understand her work? He didn't see it that way at all. "It is not evident," he wrote in English, "what I should do in your case, as it must be supposed that you have full confidence in your teacher."[10] As long as she had a teacher's support, Steiner argued, she didn't need him. "But if you need me for some occult advice, I will stand at your disposal."[11] The last sentence is conciliatory, but firm. He underlined three words in the letter. No. Task. Me.

Still, Steiner seems to have complied with Hilma's request after all. The notebooks do not indicate when the meeting took place, as the artist did not date those notes, nor did Steiner. Nonetheless, various loose pages and pieces of paper are preserved in the archive labeled "Doctor Steiner's notes" and "original drawing by Doctor Rudolf Steiner."[12] Af Klint repeatedly stressed in retrospect that Steiner had seen some of her early spiritual paintings. During a 1924 lecture she gave at the Anthroposophical Society in Stockholm, she said that the visit had occurred "14–15 years ago [when] he had looked at the first two series which were then finished and gave detailed explanations about them."[13] Accordingly the visit must have taken place in 1909 or 1910. And indeed, Steiner had visited Stockholm for almost two weeks at the beginning of 1910, from January 3 to 15. He lectured at the Academy of Science and offered a course on the Gospel of Saint John, attended, a newspaper reported, by a hundred participants.[14]

What happened when Steiner finally walked into af Klint's working space and found himself in the midst of her paintings—the monumental canvases, intoxicating colors, and pulsing forms? Did he feel the current of life flowing through it all? Did he recognize the dual being in the rose and the lily or in Vestalasket? Did he understand the eyelet and hook? There is little to suggest the visit took the legendary course reported in later literature. According to a much-repeated anecdote, Steiner is supposed to have predicted that the paintings would be understood only fifty years hence and to have criticized Hilma for using her mediumship to paint. This threw her into a crisis, as the story goes, and she stopped painting for four years.[15]

But af Klint never wrote about being disappointed or that Steiner had suggested her paintings would only find an audience half a century later. She did not describe the encounter at all. Therefore the few archival documents featuring Steiner's notes have to speak for themselves. The comments are sparse. On one paper scrap ripped from a letter envelope, Steiner made a small pencil drawing, no larger than a postage stamp. Its shape resembles a hanging flower, "male" and "female" are written next to it in German. A cosmological diagram in his handwriting is noted on another sheet, mentioning the sun, the earth, the moon, and the planets Mars, Saturn, Neptune, and Venus.

The two sketches appear again in identical form, but in ink, on two lined pages torn from a notebook. Af Klint's superordinated series "WU" and "WUS" are listed including "Primordial Chaos," "Eros," "The Large Figure Paintings," and "Evolution." Quantities of paintings are given; however, they do not correspond to the counts we have today. The list is followed by three short equations in Steiner's hand:

S = Snake = ormen
U = a = alfa
w = ω = omega

That's it. Not much. Yet the few remarks allow some conclusions. On the one hand Steiner quickly grasped the main features of af Klint's work: its relation to the macrocosm; the examination of the male and female principle;[16] the stream of evolution symbolized by the letters *wu*, which he relates to a quotation from the Bible: "I am Alpha and Omega, the first and the last, the beginning and the ending" appears in the Gospel of Saint John, on which Steiner lectured in Stockholm.[17]

On the other hand he was in a hurry. He scribbled his notes on random pieces of paper. The situation was probably less than ideal: af Klint had given up her studio at Hamngatan 9, so Steiner was confronted with an overwhelming multitude of works, presumably in a cramped space.

Perhaps he excused himself quickly, citing a busy schedule. Perhaps he was simply at a loss for more words in the face of the paintings, which did not resemble any kind of art that had ever been seen before. Whatever happened, the encounter did not diminish Hilma's later enthusiasm when she traveled to Dornach in Switzerland the first time in 1920 to visit the Goetheanum, Steiner's new center for spiritual teaching and research. On the contrary. Ever since they had met she seemed to want more contact.

Steiner was actually much more interested in another Swedish artist. On his first trip to Sweden in 1908, he encountered an oeuvre that would preoccupy him for a considerable time. In Göteborg he visited the studio of Frank Heyman (1880–1945), a sculptor who, like Hilma, belonged to the Theosophical Society. Heyman wasn't yet thirty when he met Steiner. A photograph from the time shows him as a young bearded man with an extravagant pompadour and a piercing gaze.[18] Steiner was carried away by his work. "This is something that is sensed from another world," he gushed. Heyman chiseled blocky, monumental sculptures that represented the life of the soul, "the whole inner life of humanity, including our reverence for the divine" (fig. 28).[19] Heyman had put it similarly in a manifesto he'd written in 1906. The artist had to chart the "inner life," he claimed; the academic tradition had become superfluous. "Depicting the outer nature does not lead to art."[20]

For Steiner, Heyman's sculptures were the realization of what he had longed to see in art. Before visiting Heyman's studio, he had written: "That's what it comes down to, that currently no artist has the capacity to reproduce life. And so there is only a choice between the formal abstract suggestion of inner life and substance

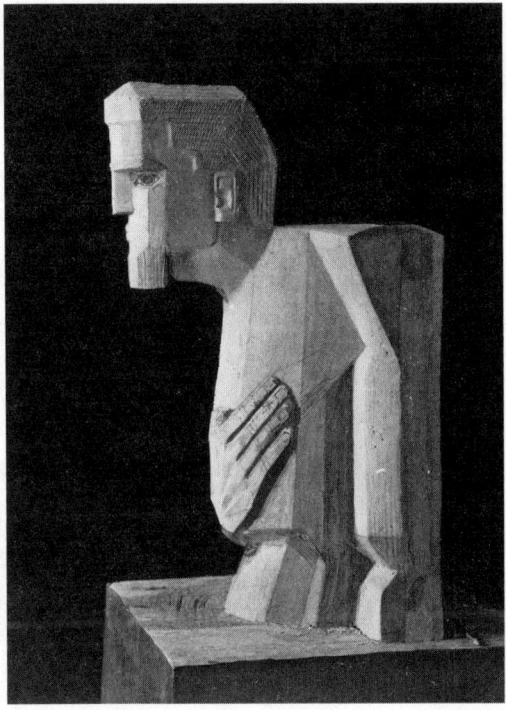

28. Frank Heyman, *Listening to the Inner Voice*, 1904, sculpture.

with outwardly inartistic form, or the dead forms and schemes that are frequently called artistic nowadays, which have approximately the same effect on one familiar with real life as corpses that are supposed to simulate life."[21] In Heyman, Steiner had finally found confirmation of his own understanding of art. The artist held the simple imitation of nature in as low esteem as he did.

That was in 1908. That same year brought another notable force for a new spiritual movement in art. When Steiner returned to Munich, he might have come across the latest issue of *Der Kunstwart*, a well-known art magazine published in the Bavarian capital. The August issue contained a special supplement with prints of seventeen drawings—black-and-white ones full of dark lines and vortices.

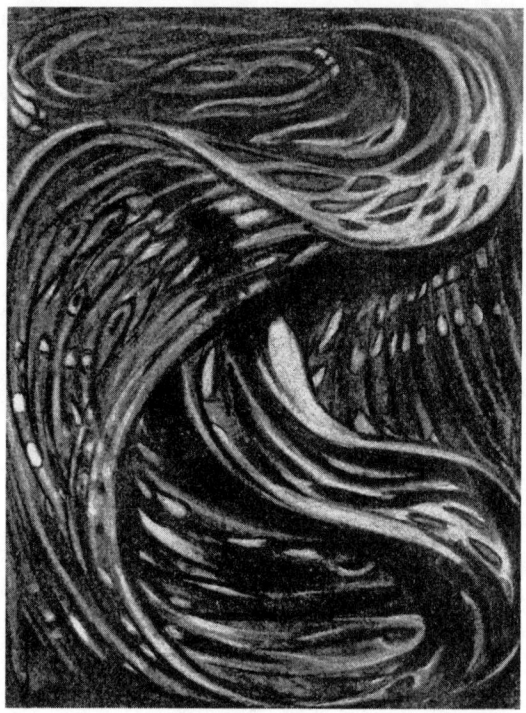

29. Katharine Schäffner, *Passion*, 1908, lithograph in *Kunstwart*.

Forms pulsed across the pages, billowing and towering like clouds in a stormy sky yet not depicting any recognizable subject (fig. 29). Art, according to the accompanying essay, was breaking away from "forms of reality" to communicate "spiritual values" through "light or color or line as such." The drawings were made by Katharine Schäffner (b. 1884), a Prague artist. She was praised in the strongest terms by Ferdinand Avenarius (1856–1923), the founder and publisher of *Der Kunstwart*, who in the essay became one of the first critics to write in favor of nonrepresentational painting.[22] According to Avenarius, a "new language" spoke in Schäffner's works. He predicted a great future for her.

But Katharine Schäffner, whom Avenarius praised so highly, proved a shooting star, disappearing from the empyrean of art as quickly as she appeared, for reasons still unknown. She vanished so

completely that even the year of her death is unknown.[23] Nonetheless, Schäffner had introduced the readers of *Der Kunstwart* to a
kind of art that was spiritual and antinaturalistic. In the next years,
she would be joined by many others. Wassily Kandinsky in Munich
and Hilma af Klint and Frank Heyman in Stockholm would publicly
stand up for the value of such art. And Steiner, who until then had
primarily been a writer, began to plan a *Gesamtkunstwerk* of his own.

[9]

The Young Ones

A new artists' association was organized in Stockholm by a generation of students returning from Paris who were about twenty years
younger than af Klint. They had trained at the Académie Matisse,
Henri Matisse's private painting school, and like him, they wanted
to paint in colors that came from within, from feelings. Matisse
described his approach in the essay "Notes of a Painter": "What I
am after, above all, is expression."[1]

The Stockholm artists who took up the cause of *l'expression*
called themselves "de unga," the Young Ones. They were the self-
declared antagonists of the Konstnärsförbundet (Artists' Association), which had emerged from the Opponenterna movement,
bringing the local art revolution full circle: twenty-five years earlier,
the Konstnärsförbundet had organized itself to counter the establishment values of the Academy. Larsson, Josephson, and Zorn were
now the old guard—and targets of the Young Ones.[2]

Their spokesperson was Isaac Grünewald (1889–1946), a
delicate-looking man with curly hair and large dark eyes. Photographs show him fastidiously dressed in an elegant double-breasted
suit betraying not a hint of his impoverished upbringing. The young
painter had been born in Stockholm, the son of a Jewish traveling
salesman from Poland. He was one of eleven siblings. At the first

exhibition of de unga, Grünewald's paintings introduced viewers to a Sweden that looked as if it were located in the South of France. The bay off Arild, a picturesque village in southern Sweden, glowed in bright colors; blue boats rested on the beach, the sun shone, and the sea gleamed. The exhibition was held in Hallins Konsthandel, an art dealer's shop at Norra Drottninggatan 22, near Kerstin Cardon's painting school. Spring was just beginning in Stockholm; it was early March 1909.[3]

When Grünewald and his friends founded de unga, he had not yet met Sigrid Hjertén (1885–1948), the artist he would eventually marry (and who painted the best portraits of him). Had the couple met sooner, de unga might have been different, but in March 1909, the founders were exceedingly proud not to include women and even wrote the exclusion into their charter. Thus, the self-proclaimed young ones behaved no differently than the "old ones." The female artists of Stockholm—including af Klint—took the exclusion as a declaration of war and readied themselves for a counteroffensive.

[10]

Sigrid Lancén

And yet Hilma was far too busy to become enmeshed in Stockholm's art scene. Her mother had gone blind after years of eye trouble, and it fell to Hilma to look after her. Her sister Ida and her brother, Gustaf, were each married with their own households to run. Hilma and her mother continued to share an apartment, and the artist gave up her studio at Hamngatan 9 to be close to her mother during the day. To make life even more complicated, Anna Cassel had suffered the tragic loss of her sister Lotten, who died in February 1908.

When the Young Ones celebrated their debut in Stockholm, Hilma had not painted for more than a year. In April 1908 she had finished a series of seventeen watercolors called *The Seven-Pointed*

Star and assigned the Roman numeral V. Starting with *Primordial Chaos*, the seven series she had painted also formed a larger cycle of 111 paintings in total. The paintings were numbered continuously, while each series was designated by a roman numeral. Additionally the series were grouped into two sections, which were labeled "WU" and "WUS."[1] The works were probably stored on the ground floor of Brahegatan 52 in a cramped workspace below the apartment where Hilma lived.

The women of The Five had recently produced several drawings in color, the last one executed in February 1908. It is impossible to know for sure the composition of the group at that point: the notes sometimes mention five women, but there is also talk of six or seven.[2] The notes also suggest that The Five stopped meeting in March 1908: "intense criticism of me," Hilma wrote.[3] The drawings in color were the last produced by the group.

Meanwhile, another woman began to appear more frequently in the notebooks. She had first turned up in 1901 when Hilma's spiritual tutors had called her a "supporting friend." Sigrid Lancén (1872–1946) was ten years younger than Hilma and worked as an athletics instructor, specializing in therapeutic exercise. She had trained at the Central Institute of Gymnastics in Stockholm, the oldest institution of its kind in the world.[4] In the telephone directory, she was listed as a "Gymnastikdirektör" living at Brahegatan 52, the same address as Hilma and her mother's. Lancén had become a lodger in 1904, which helped the af Klints stave off financial difficulty.[5] Mathilda af Klint's widow's pension was just enough to cover the rent and basic living expenses. Hilma had little income: in 1906 and 1907, newspapers mention her participating in only two exhibitions.[6]

Spatial proximity led to physical closeness; the first advances came from the younger woman. A note about this had appeared in December 1907, the troubled month when Hilma had finished work on *The Ten Largest* and argued with her friends over the ceremony with Gusten. In the middle of the chaos, the spiritual messengers warned the painter "not to come to harm through careless touches." The entry continues: "which S. L-n instigated."[7]

A year and a half later, Sigrid Lancén showed up in the note-book again, as someone in the spiritual circle around Hilma that had replaced The Five. A message arrived during a meeting on April 21, 1909, that suggested that Lancén should become the High Ones' new apprentice, side by side with the painter. The heart, it was said, had "never been given to anyone else" than her, Sigrid. Whose heart was meant was clarified soon afterward when Hilma and Sigrid were addressed directly by their first names: "To (S. and H.) heart with heart. The holiness of the room is best preserved thus."[8]

Over the next days, the spiritual messengers seemed unclear about what they were encouraging af Klint and Lancén to do. In one, they addressed Lancén directly (the message is recorded in Hilma's handwriting—like the entire notebook): "We want to explain the eyelet of the system to you (S), and through us you are to receive insight into the world of the mystery. The eyelet is an image of the female, the hook of the male. The eyelet has a deep occult meaning that no Spartan-minded person can sense without suffering for it. You must strive to be the eyelet, and Asket shall be the hook that connects you with the person you are fond of."[9] Several of the terms are easy enough to decipher, as the messengers had been using them for years. "S" stands for Sigrid, Asket is Hilma, the eyelet and hook were well established, and "Spartan" refers to the physical love practiced between Spartan women. The difficulty consists in understanding how literally the message is meant to be understood. Are these metaphors? Or was physical love part of the "world of the mystery" into which Sigrid Lancén was to be initiated? Could physical ecstasy turn into spiritual ecstasy, and vice versa? From the perspective of the Protestant church, this would violate God's laws in two ways: extramarital sex was forbidden as well as sex with someone of the same gender. But the women had left Christian orthodoxy behind when they began conversing with the dead. As to gender, they adhered to a theory of fluid borders. Hilma had mascu-line alter egos, such as Asket, making clear gender attribution moot.

In spring 1909, when the notes on Lancén appear, Gusten Andersson was also again pondering questions of love, and she too documented her thoughts in a notebook she called "The Blue Book," "written for Asket and dedicated to the dual work." Gusten signed the title page as "Sister Magdalena," perhaps referring to the beautiful nun with the long hair and lily, the guise in which af Klint had painted her in 1906 (see fig. 24).

"In love," Sister Magdalena, alias Gusten, explains in "The Blue Book," there was "every kind of tenderness and desire. The desire of the spirit, the soul, the body."[10] Despite great differences, they all sprang from the same cause, "the love of the infinite, the joy in creation of eternal life, the desire to multiply oneself."[11] The last sentence sounds like a description of some of af Klint's paintings.

The Five and the scrapped ceremony of December 1907, opposed by all the friends including Gusten, are not mentioned. Sister Magdalena remembers herself, rather than Hilma, as feeling alone and rejected during that time. "In the end I was thrown out of paradise," she writes. She had suffered "a crucifixion," executed "by you, Asket!"[12] The text vacillates from devotion to accusation, rage, submission, and passion. "I said to you once three years ago [referring to 1906, when Hilma had painted her portrait as a nun] that my love was strong enough for me to sacrifice my soul to you." Hilma's painting hadn't understood her, the author of "The Blue Book" writes several times. Without her, without her prayers, love, and spiritual support, without Sister Magdalena and Undan (another spiritual name Gusten took for herself), the paintings would have come "from evil."[13] Gusten, the lily who formed a unity with the rose, half of the hermaphroditic dual being, sounds sad and resentful.

While Gusten fought against losing a world, Hilma was creating a new one. Starting on Easter Sunday, the voices got in touch with new assignments, the first time in a year. They spoke of new thought-images, and the use of individual letters returned: "VWU" stood for life, matter, spirit, Hilma was told.[14] Cassel's name begins to appear more often again alongside that of Lancén, the new apprentice.

On the Sunday after Easter, April 25, 1909, the floorplan of a temple building appears in the notebook: a square with a circle in the middle. The round room is meant to be a workspace for initiates, a note suggests; a library was also planned. Another plan follows, larger and more ambitious, drawn on the same day. In this one, the building is surrounded by gardens, one for general use, another reserved for "Vestal and Asket."[15] This plan also features a library as well as rooms for "lärjunger": disciples, novitiates, like Lancén. The messages make it clear that communications from the High Ones were no longer to be private. The new circle headed by af Klint was to welcome outsiders and to share the teachings more widely: this was the purpose of the building.

The group grew until the women numbered thirteen. With the exception of Hilma and Cassel, none of the original Five were involved: Mathilda Nilsson, Sigrid Hedman, and Cornelia Cederberg had left. The Thirteen included Gusten Andersson and Sigrid Lancén, the latter as the eighth member.[16]

As to the building plan, the voices indicated that it fell to Cassel "to enter into the drawing." Did "enter into" mean to realize it, to build it? A few pages later Cassel is called the "caregiver" of the house.[17] Perhaps the High Ones were being practical. Cassel was independently wealthy; she would have had the resources to erect a building. The spiritual messengers sent more communications, almost daily through May, June, and July, when the entries suddenly break off.

[11]

The Association of Swedish Women Artists

Meanwhile, the Young Ones were shaking things up in Stockholm. Their debut met with scathing reviews; as with most avant-garde movements, the self-proclaimed rebels were ridiculed and scorned. But there was also some support. The day after the vernissage, on March 3, 1909, a critic wrote in the daily newspaper *Svenska Dag-*

bladet that the show marked the beginning of something new, a kind of painting reminiscent of Matisse, Munch, and Segantini, but with a clear Swedish bent.[1]

Among the female artists in Stockholm, the debate took a different turn. They were upset about the exclusion of women. Little seemed to have changed since af Klint had been a student. Women were still not taken seriously as artists or afforded access to professional networks. Works by women were disadvantageously installed in exhibitions, with the consequence that they received less attention from critics and the public. Major commissions continued to be granted almost exclusively to men.

That the Young Ones now boasted of excluding women showed how little had changed. In science Marie Curie had won the Nobel Prize. Selma Lagerlöf would become the first woman to win a Nobel Prize for literature later that year, but the visual arts seemed irremediably mired in the past.

Stockholm's female artists were disappointed, and their disappointment turned into anger. The solution was abundantly clear: they needed an association of women to counterbalance the associations of men.

In the beginning they met in their studios, led by Ida von Schulzenheim, Ellen Jolin, and Mina Carlson, all graduates of the Stockholm Academy, with years of study abroad and professional experience among them.

The Association of Swedish Women Artists (Föreningen Svenska Konstnärinnor) was founded in March 1910.[2] It was patterned after the Union des femmes peintres et sculpteurs in Paris and the Künstlerinnensektion des Dürerbundes in Vienna. Such groups offered the possibility of cooperation across borders and languages. The Swedish association began actively to recruit members.

The Young Ones opened their second exhibition in April, almost exactly a year after their debut, once again at Hallins Konsthandel. When Hilma walked from her house to the harbor to take a ferry to Adelsö, she would have passed near the gallery, but her notebooks do not mention it, the Young Ones, or their leader, Isaac Grünewald.

At the 1910 show a portrait by Grünewald of a sad-looking young man in front of a blue background created a sensation. *The Epileptic* confronted a malady thought to be most prevalent among urban dwellers, their nerves weakened by noise, distraction, and dissipation.[3] Grünewald also showed *Comrades in Art*. Predictably, the painting depicts only men, three members of the Young Ones posed importantly in front of a landscape, tugging at their lapels like statesmen.[4]

On April 13, 1910, ten days after the exhibition opened, af Klint applied for membership in the Association of Swedish Women Artists and was accepted.[5] She was following in the path of her sister Ida, who had fought for equal rights and suffrage for women through her work with the Fredrika Bremer Association. Hilma was fighting for emancipation in her own way, through art. The time seemed ripe for change. The worker's movement, which called for universal suffrage, was gaining ground in Sweden. In Finland women had been voting for four years; Finland was the first European country to make such a breakthrough. In the fall af Klint became secretary of the association, and in December Anna Cassel joined as well.[6]

Those close to af Klint were making great demands on her time. Her circle of friends was growing, and spiritual meetings now included up to twelve participants. Uppsala University commissioned her to paint a posthumous portrait of the physicist Knut Ångström, who had recently died at the age of fifty-three. One of Ångström's interests was solar radiation, a subject his father had also studied; wavelengths are still often measured in angstroms. Ångström had also been a supporter of the women's movement. As a member of the Stockholm Academy of Sciences, he had advocated for the Nobel Prize to be awarded to Marie Curie, and Eva von Bahr, the first female physicist at a Swedish university, worked in his department.[7]

In October 1910 af Klint's painting was hung in the building of Norrlands Nation, a student society. It shows an amiable-looking Ångström in bow tie, standing collar, and dark suit. The artist also painted another professor from the university, Johan August Lundell, a linguist. *Dagens Nyheter* mentioned both paintings by "the well-known artist Hilma af Klint," with accompanying illustrations.[8]

When the Association of Swedish Women Artists held its first exhibition at the Royal Academy in March 1911, af Klint participated with three representational paintings, one of them among the most expensive works in the show. She asked 1,000 crowns for an oil painting titled *Sotaren* (Chimney sweep), according to the catalogue. The price was roughly equivalent to the average annual income of an industrial worker, or the annual rent Hilma and her mother paid for their apartment. The catalogue included few other paintings in this price bracket; most cost less than half as much. Two of her other paintings were offered at much lower prices. The genre painting *At Work* was listed at 150 crowns, and a view of the bay from Riddarholmen, one of Stockholm's islands, at 300 crowns.[9] Anna Cassel also showed work: a landscape of the island of Värmdö and a sunset through rain. Both paintings were priced at 150 crowns.

For Hilma, life had split into two halves that were drifting farther and farther apart. One half was consumed with the business of daily life: taking care of her mother and working as an artist, painting landscapes, genre paintings, and portraits in the academic style. It was not important to her that future generations remember any of the works painted during these years: her notebooks say nothing about them or the exhibitions.

In the other half of her life, shared with friends, she painted works every bit as original and courageous as anything being created by the then avant-garde. She kept meticulous records of this side: every message, every assignment, and every work were noted. Yet it had been three years since she had painted any spiritual works: she lacked both space and time, so the break dragged on.

———

The women's exhibition garnered attention from the press, and one anecdote suggested a revolutionary dimension. The weekly magazine *Dagny* reported that the artist Charlotte Wahlström had met a "prominent theologist" at the show who had looked at the paintings in wonder and exclaimed, "If women can paint this well, then they really must have the vote."[10]

The Young Ones' third show, which opened on April 9, 1911, suggested a slight change of heart. Though there were still no female artists among their ranks, visitors to Hallins Konsthandel were greeted by a portrait of a female artist.[11] In the painting by Isaac Grünewald, the violet brim of a hat swirls around the face of Ise Morssing, a sculptor and painter. The exhibition turned out to be the group's last: Grünewald had met the artist Sigrid Hjertén, and the two were engaged to be married.

That same month, af Klint resigned from the Association of Swedish Women Artists. The association files state the reason as her obligation to care for her sick mother,[12] but her notebook says that she and her group should "only build for the youth."[13] In other words she was turning her gaze to the next generation, leaving the present one behind.

The first issue of the new magazine *Konst*, published by Ida Schulzenheim, appeared in Stockholm in November 1911. It was immediately apparent that the artists' association she had cofounded was oriented to the past rather than to the future.[14] The female editors invited Carl Larsson, of all people, to design the cover and to write a long essay. Schulzenheim and Larsson were united in their opposition to the Young Ones, even if their motives were different. Larsson was indifferent to the fact that Isaac Grünewald's group included no women, but he saw the young men as competitors. He obligingly railed in *Konst* against the "incompetents" and maintained that in their scrawlings it was impossible to distinguish a sunset from a portrait of the artist's grandmother.[15] The solidarity between the artist and the women of the association rested on the assumption that the enemy of one's enemy was one's friend.

Af Klint, on the other hand, was in no man's land. If she had hoped to find a forum for her spiritual art in the association, she was soon disappointed. She had as little in common with Ida Schulzenheim and Larsson as she did with Matisse acolytes like Grünewald.

While Larsson continued to belittle expressionism, the first Der Blaue Reiter (The Blue Rider) exhibition opened in Munich. Held in the Moderne Galerie Heinrich Thannhauser, it presented work by a group that included Franz Marc, Wassily Kandinsky, and Gabriele Münter. Kandinsky (1866–1944) showed a monumental painting with a religious title, *Composition V/The Last Judgment*. The surface is overrun with rhythmic, winding black lines. Beneath the lines are shapes vaguely reminiscent of a landscape with mountains—if they are reminiscent of anything. As if a brush could turn the visible world into mist, subjects dissolve in this painting. Like af Klint, members of the Blaue Reiter believed art's task was to contribute to the spiritualization of the viewer. Marc wrote of a "mystical-internal construction," Kandinsky of a "spiritual pyramid which will some day reach to heaven."[16]

It would take a while for news of the Blaue Reiter to reach Stockholm. When Kandinsky and Münter visited the Swedish capital in 1915, they became friends with Isaac Grünewald and Sigrid Hjertén.

[12]

Frank Heyman

Even though Hilma had left the Association of Swedish Women Artists, her work was featured in their exhibition, which, after a Stockholm premier, traveled to Lund in the south of Sweden. Many of Hilma's friends participated in the show, such as Ottilia Adelborg, Kerstin Cardon, and others she would have met at the Academy. Since part of the exhibition was dedicated to pioneering women artists in Sweden, it featured four works by Bertha Valerius.[1]

There was a lot of coming and going in Hilma's spiritual circle; more people were involved, both women and men. Anna Cassel continued to play a central role for Hilma, as did Gusten Andersson. Despite the growing network, only two people connected with the art world appear in the notebooks of this period. One is Natanael Beskow, a reformer, artist, school director, writer, and the husband of Elsa Beskow, a noted children's book author who is still popular in Sweden. Hilma reported a visit with Beskow in her notebook.[2]

The other artist Hilma notes is Frank Heyman, whose sculpture, Steiner had gushed, "was sensed from a higher world." Heyman called for a return to "the original image," and Hilma and Anna referred to him as "the great prophet."[3]

Heyman had recently moved from Göteborg to Stockholm, where he opened a studio. He and Hilma probably met through the Theosophical Society. The first time she mentions him is in September 1911. A few days later, according to Hilma's notes, her artistic momentum increased; the assignments became more concrete. She and Anna were now told that the temple should be built, and on the island of Adelsö.[4]

The notes cast Heyman in a most flattering light. He was twenty years younger than the two women, though this did not dim their admiration in the slightest. They were impressed by his "great occult powers" and trusted him in worldly matters as well. In December the messengers told Hilma, "You shall enter into the world of museums with him."[5] She was not to hesitate, but to surrender to his direction.

The spirits' exuberance was perplexing. Heyman had little to offer when it came to museums or any other exhibition venues: he couldn't even realize his own ambition to exhibit the monumental sculptures he had been forced to leave behind in Göteborg. Steiner was disappointed not to be able to show them outside of Sweden, but they were too heavy and massive to be moved: transport would have "required not just one freight car" but several.[6] Heyman was under no illusion about his stature in the art world. "From the beginning I felt myself a stranger among artists."[7]

Heyman had also designed a temple, a massive building of pure granite fifty meters tall. In reality the only thing he ever erected was a small plaster model.

"Take time with your teacher (Heyman) and ask him to guide you," the notes continue unswervingly. Again, the advice was directed to Hilma.[8] To her, success in the traditional sense hardly mattered: the spiritual guides had prepared her for a rocky path and had indicated the same would hold true for those close to her. "Anna shall also be scorned," the messengers had said in August 1906, before the first painting of *Primordial Chaos* had even been painted, "but less than Hilma, who is called to lead the fight."[9]

When Hilma, now nearly fifty, met the thirty-one-year-old Heyman, she realized at once that they shared a common language. She spoke of "ancient images" and he of "original images." She called her paintings "evolution paintings," and he explained that his sculptures represented the "evolution of the soul."[10] Heyman believed that genuine riches could be found only in the spiritual realm, and his lifestyle was intentionally simple. Hilma's alter ego was Asket, the ascetic, and in a later notebook she would write of the "riches" contained in her notes.[11] Both read Blavatsky and knew that a paradoxical movement was necessary to reach the ancient images they sought. Backward was forward, a leap into the past had to be taken to land in the future. Modern science pushed forward to discoveries long known to masters of the occult—or so Blavatsky claimed. The sculptor and the painter had developed strikingly different visual languages, but they were derived from shared convictions. Af Klint's forms are fluid, full of movement and life, while Heyman's are geometric and rigid, "distilled," as Steiner put it.

Heyman was not a Protestant and was thus in the Swedish minority. His father was a wealthy Jewish businessman from Göteborg; his mother, also Jewish, came from Hamburg. Heyman decided to become an artist when he saw the working-class neighborhoods of London during a business trip on behalf of his father. Coming face to face with the "hell of the poor" described by Jack London, he resolved to transform his life and went to Munich to study with the prominent sculptor Adolf Hildebrand.[12] Hilma would read Jack London's *People of the Abyss* when it was published in Swedish, probably at Heyman's recommendation.

Among Heyman's major works are two sculptures titled *Listening to the Inner Voice*, from the years 1902 and 1904 (see fig. 28). The figures have their hands on their hearts and their eyes are closed; their heads stretch forward as if straining to hear a faint sound. The angular forms would prompt some critics in the fifties, after Heyman's death, to describe the sculptor as a "cubist before cubism."[13] This posthumous glory was brief, however, and never extended beyond Sweden.

In January 1912 the High Ones and their messengers again encouraged Hilma to entrust herself to Heyman, though they also began to establish limits: "follow his advice in all things, but cleave to your guides."[14]

The notes also indicate that trouble was brewing. Heyman balked at the presumption that he was supposed to help Hilma interpret the messages from her spiritual teachers, just as Steiner had done. In March 1912 Amaliel tried to console her: Heyman would first find her actions "ignorant," but soon he would "surely understand" her. The next day she was told she should fight to find her own way of painting; Ananda would assist and not abandon her.[15]

The notes about Heyman become sparser as the artists' paths diverged. Looking back later, Hilma remembered that he had helped her move *The Ten Largest* "a few years after they were painted."[16]

As to the notes from 1912, Heyman makes a final appearance in June, when Hilma wrote that he stood "high above us," meaning herself and Cassel.[17] Too high, perhaps? The sculptor then vanishes from the notebooks. He died in Stockholm in 1945, his work largely forgotten.

But we have not yet come to that point.

Island Kingdom in Mälaren

Hilma was still in contact with Frank Heyman when she went back to work on her great project in early 1912. It had been four years since she had painted the last series and given up her studio at Hamngatan 9. Since then she had produced only conventional works like the portraits for Uppsala University and the paintings submitted to the Women's Association. Nonetheless, her notes continued; the connection to the higher worlds was never interrupted—her spiritual guides had simply stopped directing her to paint.

Af Klint referred to the seven drawings she was now creating as "preparatory studies for group 8." Executed in pencil and watercolor, they dealt with "the development of the soul" and were made between "2.19.1912 and 3.29."[1] They depict figurative scenes, people grouped around crosses with roses in the center or water lilies on top. Af Klint received support from an old friend: "Cornelia Cederberg helped me while the first series was done, partly through her interest, partly by being a model for the images I intuitively perceived."[2]

The artist was fifty years old. A photograph shows her soberly dressed (fig. 30). Like Heyman, she preferred to live simply. Younger relatives would later report that when Aunt Hilma came to visit, she liked to sleep on the sofa.[3]

The break from painting seems to have smoothed tensions in the group of women. Cederberg's support signals the return of one of The Five, though Nilsson and Hedman remained absent. Hilma's new group of friends decided to rent a summer house together on Munsö, an island in Mälaren so close to Adelsö that it could be reached by rowboat. The house and grounds belonged to the Giertta family, members of the nobility and neighbors of the af Klints on Adelsö. Emilia Giertta (1846–1924) regularly took part in the meetings; she was a member of the new circle that now comprised thir-

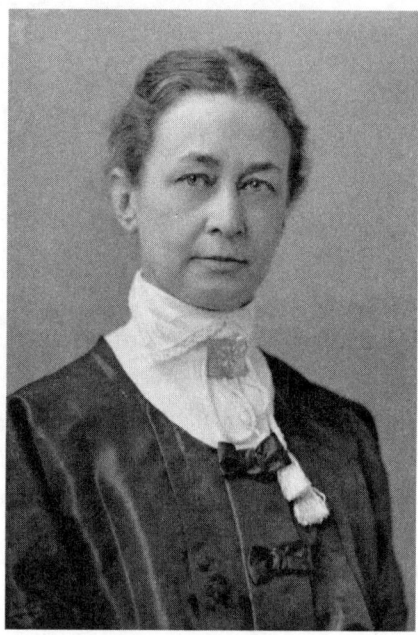

30. The artist around 1900,
Stiftelsen Hilma af Klints Verk.

teen women.[4] The following year, when af Klint unexpectedly came
into a large sum of money, she bought the lake house from the Gierttas. The house was called Furuheim, meaning "house of the pines."
The funds came from the artist's brother, Gustaf, who had bought
out his sisters' shares of the Adelsö property to consolidate ownership of the estate. Hilma purchased Furuheim on March 11, 1913,
according to the land register.[5]

Furuheim was picturesque, and the artist captured views of the
lake in several watercolors (fig. 31). In the summer, the trunks of
the pines glowed orange-red; from a distance the water sparkled
blue and from close up it was clear as glass. The island contained a
beautiful old church from the twelfth century with a round central
building and a slate-tiled roof. The congregation was small, like
the local population. Peace and quiet prevailed. The women had a
domain of their own, and the place, the expanses, and the privacy

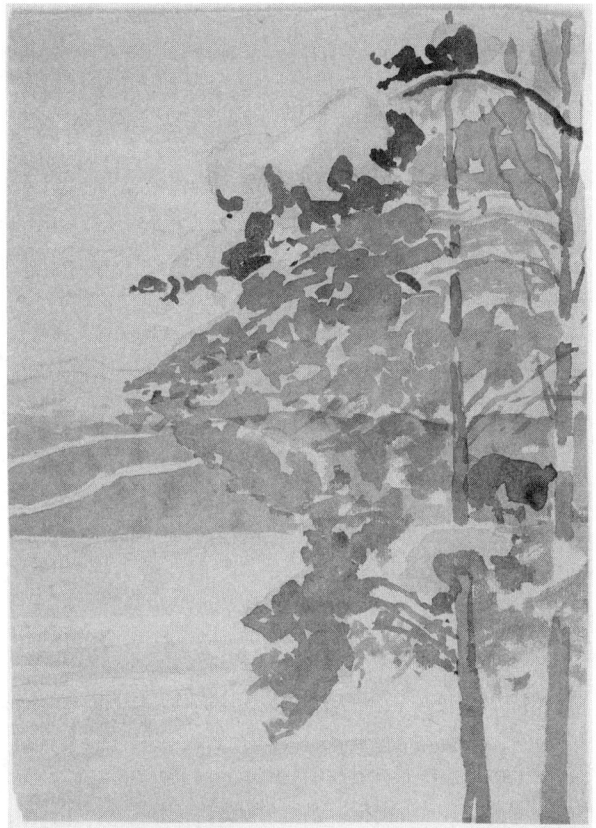

31. View of Lake Mälaren, watercolor,
Stiftelsen Hilma af Klints Verk, HaK 1207.

offered an excellent environment for new projects. Hilma's "pre-paratory studies" were just the beginning. Major work was starting again, and this time, it was not just she and Anna who believed in a mission that involved painting.

As the new phase began, over the course of which eighty-two new paintings were created, the notes become more narrative, but also more aggressive and militant. They describe struggle, battle, and pain as well as blood that was to flow. Egoism would soon make its last stand, the notes proclaim.[6] But the war in question was not beginning but ending. There is almost no further mention of internal conflict. On the contrary: the notes say the group had to be strong, to stick together in order to survive and to advance their project. Each woman was to contribute her strengths; together they had power. The higher forces assigned different characteristics to each of the women, as if they were putting together a team. Hilma is associated with "power, humility, love, smallness, also the word is yours." Gusten's qualities are specified as "humility, gentleness, patience, and peace."[7]

May was a high point for the group. During Pentecost they took the train to Norrköping, an industrial city about 150 kilometers south of Stockholm. Rudolf Steiner was speaking at a congress organized by the Theosophical Society; his lectures were to address "theosophical ethics." No reference to a personal exchange with Steiner can be found in the group records, which are written in different hands. A notebook indicates that beyond the lectures, the women held their own private sessions in Norrköpings Grand Hotel, recorded for three consecutive days. It is Hilma who speaks; Anna, Gusten, and Hélène Westmark listen. For one session they are joined by two people referred to as "W and wife."

"The powers come from within, not from without," Hilma explained and drew a parallel to the shell in which a simple grain of sand can grow into a pearl.[8]

The group now understood itself to be an avant-garde, a vanguard meant to reconnoiter the field of battle. The message came "to Hilma" that she had fought like a soldier, "but afterward you are to be assigned to a different domain, like a medic."[9] Direct references to contemporary events in the notes are rare, but they do appear. China is mentioned in the month that the 1911 Revolution broke out on the other side of the globe, forcing the Chinese emperor to abdicate. And in an earlier notebook Finland is mentioned when conflicts with the Russian czar's troops were reaching their zenith.[10] But the notebooks never describe concrete events.

Then the summer of 1912 arrived. It was unusually hot, and Sweden was hosting the Olympic Games for the first time. Tragically, a runner died during the marathon; the consensus was that the heat was to blame. The route of the cycling race circled Mälaren. The sun blazed, and temperatures reached Mediterranean heights. The unusual weather fit the general impression that change was in the air, but opinions differed on whether for better or for worse. It was clear from the Olympics alone that things had already shifted: for the first time, women participated in swimming and diving competitions. The youngest participant in the Games was Greta Carlsson, a fourteen-year-old Swedish swimmer.

"We have a mission," the notebook reports in July 1912. "Through us, a sensitive and fine new truth will be established for the generations to come."[11] Both sentences are underlined.

In October Hilma painted seven small pictures in oil of a woman dressed as if from another century. The first shows her letting a string of pearls glide through her fingers as she takes them from a jewelry box. In the last painting she wears religious garb and prays, eyes closed, before a blue and yellow background. The series recalls representations of the lives of saints, such as Elizabeth of Hungary, who lived at the Wartburg, renounced all earthly riches, and turned her attention to God. Hilma refers to the series as "A female series" and as "7 ascet pictures."[12]

For Anna Cassel, the situation also changed. In November she began to keep her own notebook, written in turquoise ink and illustrated with colorful images. She now interpreted her assignment to record the Tale of the Rose or Akasha Chronicle differently—instead of writing it, she wanted to paint it. Among her notes are sketches of boats and buildings, illuminated halls and dark tunnels at the end of which a rose appears like a light.[13] The notebook ends in February of the following year, 1913, and in March Cassel painted a series of her own—her first, as far as we know.[14] In the series, the forms free themselves from the lined pages and drift away from the letters and texts in the notebook to arrive on the larger surfaces

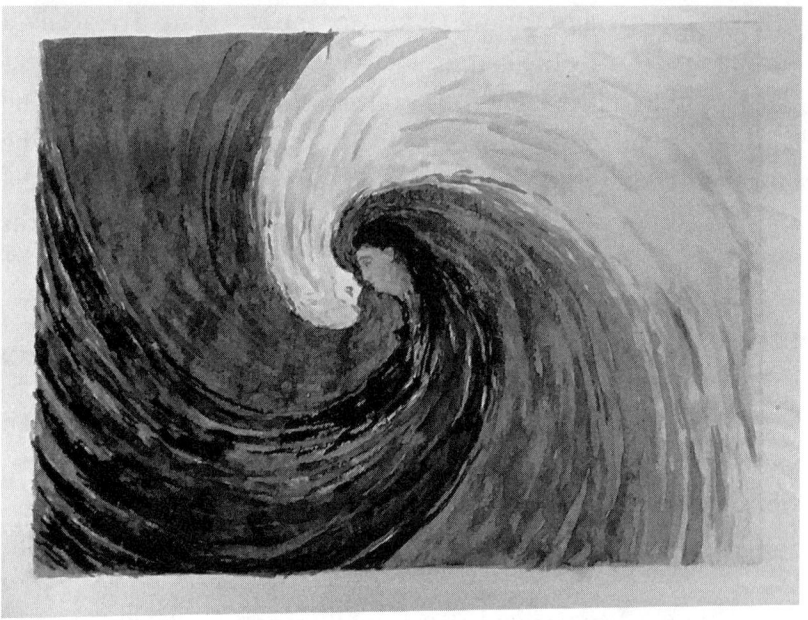

32. Anna Cassel, watercolor, 1913, Stiftelsen Hilma af Klints Verk.

of loose sheets of paper; they grow and become brighter and more colorful, as if brought to life. At the same time, the messengers from the spiritual world implored the group to remain unified. "None of you is greater than the others. You are one, one heart, one will, one thought, the word, one power,"[15] Cassel recorded the message.

Her series begins with swirls that twist into a spiral with two faces in the middle. They are so close that they seem bound to touch at any moment, to kiss (fig. 32). Two beings become one, blue and yellow, female and male, vestal virgin and ascetic; they form the divine hermaphrodite, the duality said in 1907 to be Cassel and af Klint.

The next painting features an explosion. Dark clouds swirl, and a cross-topped altar rises. Then, sheet after sheet, come a lotus blossom, the head of a sphinx, and the Rosicrucian cross of The Five. In the next drawing, the cross disappears down the throat of a monster.

Then it returns. Sometimes it is surrounded by flames, sometimes lapped by water; finally it sends out waves of its own. The series ends after twenty images.

Cassel worked feverishly. A second series followed the first in April, and a third in May. Each was longer than the previous one—first twenty pages, then thirty-six, and finally fifty. Some gouaches resemble tarot cards in the clarity and order of their symbols. Others are narrative. For example, there is a painting with two figures—one Egyptian, one Christian. Together, they walk down a long passage to arrive at a fountain surrounded by tiny lights, not unlike Robert Fludd's seventeenth-century illustrations of creation.[16]

Hilma was in an optimistic mood. When she gave a lecture in April 1913 at the invitation of the Spiritistiska Litteraturföreningen, she talked excitedly of the "elemental force" that would forge a path through each individual. "In ourselves we have great powers and capacities," she encouraged the audience; new life could now flow into the "withered branches" of the World Tree.[17] One should allow oneself to be filled with spiritual wisdom, the painter continued, "to the tips of one's fingers"—the very body part she used to manipulate a paintbrush or pen. As spring continued, she and her friends traveled more frequently to Munsö. A ferry left from Stockholm, and the departure times are carefully noted. In May 1913, when six of the thirteen friends arrived on the island by steamboat, the deeper meaning of the place where Hilma had bought the summer house was revealed to them. The ancient records had not correctly represented history, it says in the notebook: Christianity had first been preached not on the island of Björkö but on Munsö. This was why the women's work had to be moved there. The messages were received by Anna Cassel, Emilia Giertta, Gusten Andersson, and Hilma. They were told that they were now part of a tradition that included Saint Ansgar, the Apostle of the North, who was said to have brought Christianity to the Vikings in the ninth century.

Weeks later, the notes mention a new series executed by Hilma called the *Tree of Knowledge*.[18]

First Exhibition with the Theosophists

It was summer 1913. One year after the Olympic Games, Sweden hosted another international gathering, this one organized by Theosophists. Because the Theosophical Society had split into two camps, there were two events. The first took place in Stockholm and was organized by the section based in Adyar, India, and led by Annie Besant. The second event was organized by the American Theosophists from California, who invited guests to the island of Visingsö in Vättern, several hundred miles southwest of the capital.

Interest was high: two thousand people registered for the Visingsö event alone. Art exhibitions were featured in both programs, but the show in the American-organized event was much larger than the one in Stockholm. News spread quickly that Katherine Tingley, president of the Theosophists in Point Loma, California, had been given a monumental painting called *Eros* by Julius Kronberg, former professor at the Royal Academy and a leading recipient of public commissions (fig. 33). The painting was to form the basis of a collection Tingley was assembling for a new establishment, the Râja Yoga School at Visingsö. Kronberg was so enthusiastic that he donated several paintings as well as furniture, fabrics, and oriental rugs from his own collection.[1]

When the exhibition on Visingsö opened on June 22, 1913, the day before the summer solstice, Kronberg's *Eros* was the centerpiece.[2] Kronberg's representation of the Greek god is thoroughly academic, with wings, piercing gaze, and dark curls, surrounded by atmospheric swaths of smoke, in the style of the Paris Salon.

The newspapers couldn't contain their enthusiasm.[3] But the plethora of articles about events on the island came not only from

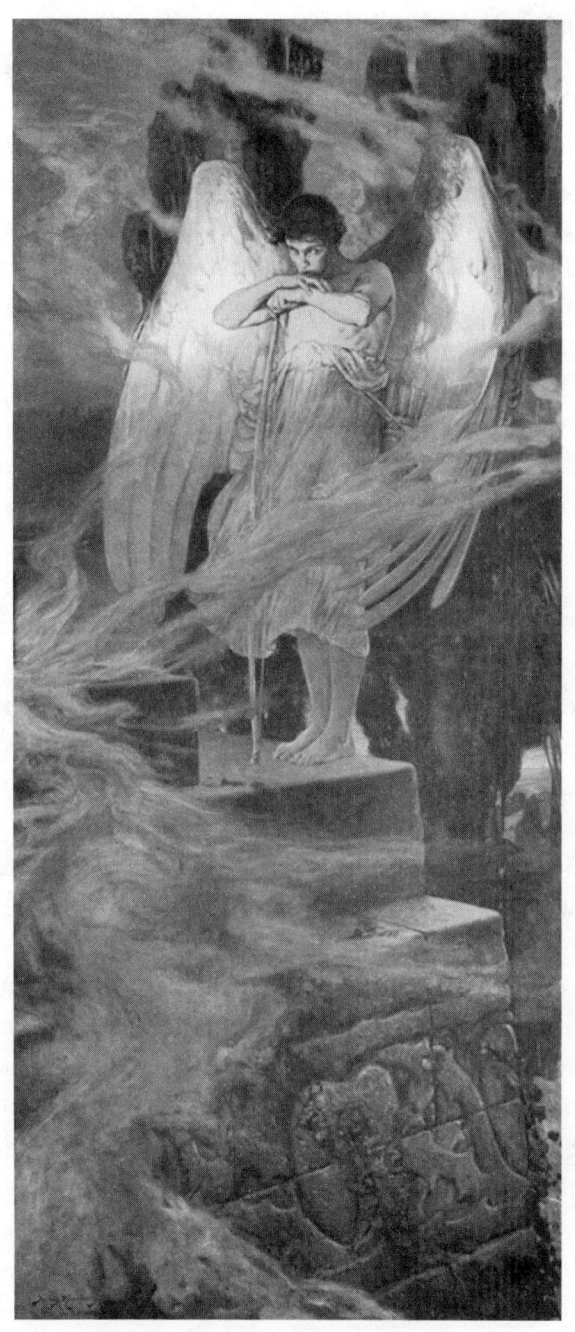

33. Julius Kronberg, *Eros*, 1912, oil on canvas.

interest in Kronberg's painting but from the fact that the American Theosophists in Sweden were extremely well connected, with ties to the highest levels of society. One of the founders was Karin Scholander, Kronberg's mother-in-law and the sister-in-law of Ferdinand Boberg, Sweden's most famous art nouveau architect, who had designed the Waldemarsudde for Prince Eugen. Anna Boberg, the wife of the architect and sister of Karin Scholander, was one of the few women who participated in the Theosophists' exhibition on Visingsö, along with Charlotte Wahlström from the Association of Women Artists. Carl Larsson and Anders Zorn participated, despite their spiritual apathy. Among the works included by Larsson was *Karin Peeling Apples*. Zorn contributed a painting titled *Girl Embroidering*.[4]

Af Klint had long since finished with the kind of painting celebrated on Visingsö, and she was not invited to participate. But if she had hoped to show her abstract works at the exhibitions sponsored by the Adyar Theosophists, she was deeply disappointed. The organizers chose three representational works by af Klint, titled *Sunrise*, *Evening Calm*, and *The Inner Domain*—two landscapes and a figure painting (plate 25 and fig. 34). All three works are from 1907, painted as a prelude to *The Large Figure Paintings*. The paintings were framed for the show in narrow wood moldings. For *The Inner Domain*, which depicts a praying woman in nun's habit, the frame was painted gold.[5] It was abundantly clear that the Theosophists around Annie Besant were no more progressive in their views about art than were members of Tingley's organization.

Among the more prominent painters who participated in the Stockholm event was Fidus, a German artist and longtime Theosophist who expressed his spiritual experiences in representational allegories. *Morning Miracle*, one of the paintings he hung, showed a winged woman emerging from a lotus flower.[6]

Tyra Kleen, now a member of the Women's Association, was also included in the exhibition. In 1911 she had shown works alongside af Klint and Cassel in an exhibition of the Föreningen Svenska Konstnärinnor, and now they met again at the Theosophists' show. Kleen

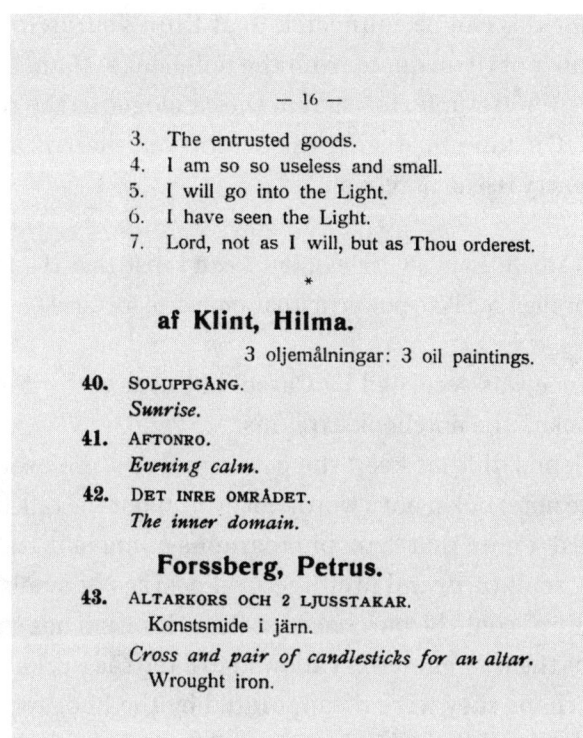

— 16 —

3. The entrusted goods.
4. I am so so useless and small.
5. I will go into the Light.
6. I have seen the Light.
7. Lord, not as I will, but as Thou orderest.

*

af Klint, Hilma.

3 oljemålningar: 3 oil paintings.

40. SOLUPPGÅNG.
Sunrise.

41. AFTONRO.
Evening calm.

42. DET INRE OMRÅDET.
The inner domain.

Forssberg, Petrus.

43. ALTARKORS OCH 2 LJUSSTAKAR.
Konstsmide i järn.

Cross and pair of candlesticks for an altar.
Wrought iron.

34. Page from exhibition catalogue
of the Adyar Theosophists in Stockholm, 1913.

contributed five drawings and a lithograph with titles like *Sun Worshipper* and *Rock Temple in India.*

In terms of sheer numbers, af Klint was one of the chief contributors. The three oil paintings were supplemented by two series of drawings and oil sketches. Cassel contributed a series of twelve drawings. According to the unillustrated catalogue, the two friends gave their works dramatic subtitles. Cassel's *Series of Suffering* included *Initiation to the Way of the Cross, Vanity of Vanities, In Expectation,* and *Peace.* Af Klint's *Series of Instruction* had subtitles like *Humiliation* and *Ecstasy,* while her *Series of Ascent* included oil sketches called *The Next Step* and *I Have Seen the Light.*

The subtitles can be connected to af Klint's surviving works,[7] and a number of them quote from the notebooks. "I am so useless and small," for example, is listed in the catalogue as the title of an oil sketch. On June 15, during the exhibition, there is an almost identical entry in the notebook:

> I am so small, I am so useless, but I can sense that the force that flows through me is so powerful that I must go forward.[8]

The sentence was recorded by Cassel but uttered by her friend. "Hilma spoke," the notebook explains.

The friends did not keep the catalogue, and the event is not cited in the notebooks: not a word, not even about the talk by Annie Besant. Just a note that "202 photographs of ancient Italian art, paintings, sculpture, and architectural designs of symbolic and mystic nature" could be purchased at the exhibition has survived.[9]

Perhaps the women weren't allowed to hang the works they preferred. Perhaps they were disappointed by the hodgepodge that crowded the art: fabrics, book covers, silver objects, architectural drawings, and a copper longcase clock—with "symbols," as the catalogue noted. It is possible that af Klint had offered monumental paintings—*The Ten Largest*, for example—which could have formed the centerpiece of the show. Instead, works were selected that were more suitable to the tastes of the day: representational landscapes, women praying.

But there may have been another reason they passed over the exhibition in their notes. All of the Theosophical Society events of June 1913 were overshadowed by sharp criticism coming from Rudolf Steiner, former general secretary of the Theosophists in Germany, along with his resignation from the society. In the run-up to Besant's and Tingley's congresses, Steiner had visited Stockholm with his wife, Marie von Sivers, and he sat for an extensive interview with the *Aftonbladet*. In the interview, published under the headline "A Theosophical Heretic," Steiner explained on June 9, 1913, his reasons for founding his new group, the Anthroposophical Society. "My work is based on science," he said, "and I find it impossible to watch what is happening within the society from a scientific standpoint."[10] In the photograph that accompanied the article, a crease in Steiner's forehead seems to amplify the anger behind his statement.

A few months later, in September 1913, Steiner laid the cornerstone of the Goetheanum in Dornach, Switzerland, to be the headquarters of the Anthroposophical Society.

[15]

Tree of Knowledge

What object is depicted in plates 29 and 30? A plant? A mushroom? A brain? Nerve pathways? A jellyfish? Are these representations of the metabolic system or of Yggdrasil, the world ash tree of Nordic mythology that connects heaven with the living world and the underworld?

When af Klint began a new series in pencil and watercolor on June 21, 1913, she titled it *Tree of Knowledge*.[1] But the essential form in the series only dimly resembles a tree: where tree roots would typically reach down into the earth, four leaflike structures are enclosed in a circle, from the middle of which a stem shoots up, radiating beams of light. Or are they tendons? The arches of a dome? Everything in this organism is in motion. Birds fly upward along the painting's axis, and colorful particles sink downward like the sparks of fireworks. Blue and yellow, the female and the male, merge into a sign: the infinity symbol, the lemniscate. What af Klint painted might be tiny, like a bacterium in a petri dish. But it could also have endless dimensions, like the universe itself.

The images can be traced to a single source: Rudolf Steiner. Af Klint attended his last public appearance as general secretary of the German Theosophists in May 1912, at the already mentioned

Pentecost Congress of the society in Norrköping. (She saved the tickets.) In December of that year, Steiner broke with Annie Besant and founded his own association, the Anthroposophical Society.[2]

The artist owned a transcript of the lectures he delivered in Cologne on the occasion of the founding of the Anthroposophical Society, and she underscored words and passages. The typescript is titled "The Bhagavad Gita and the Epistles of Saint Paul." In her copy the artist marked the word *brain* on the page where Steiner talks of the "cosmic tree."[3] According to Steiner, the brain is the gateway through which one reaches the cosmic tree. By ascending into the etheric body, one could see the body from inside out, looking along the spinal cord to the brain, which opened into the top of the world tree:

> One then looks upwards and sees how the nerves, which go through all the organs, are collected together up there in the brain. That produces the feeling: "That is a tree of which the roots go upwards, and the branches stretch down into all the members." That in reality is not felt as being of the same small size as we are inside our skin: it is felt as being a mighty cosmic tree. The roots stretch far out into the distances of space and the branches extend downwards.[4]

Steiner describes the tree as having "roots going upwards" and "branches going downwards"; its leaves "are the leaves of the Veda book, which, put together, yield the Veda knowledge," the holy teachings of the Hindus, about which af Klint had already made notes.[5]

Steiner's discourse stretches from India to Europe, from Hinduism to Christianity, from the Book of Revelation to medicine, from the etheric body to the spinal cord. His thought is a sediment formed of religion and science: compressed, drained, and dense.

Drawing on these teachings for the *Tree of Knowledge* series, Hilma added more layers and increased the density. Death and life meet in her world tree: structures reminiscent of bleached bones, and others that look like schools of fish. Her paintings exude stillness, yet one can almost hear humming and buzzing in the multitude of tiny forms. The artist offers the viewer a multivalent perspective, from the close apprehension of particles pumping through veins to a vast view of the firmament. The world is viewed through a microscope and through a telescope at once, as if dichotomies cease to exist. Even the biblical Fall is turned on its head. Adam and Eve are not thrown out of paradise. Instead, blue and yellow, female and male, whirl through the crown of the tree of knowledge as if united in a propeller or perpetuum mobile. The sexes are one and many, like Vishnu and his avatars. Af Klint captured world knowledge on a sheet of paper and compressed it into a diamond.

[16]

The Kiss

As the morning sun bathed Stockholm in the milky light that Hilma had painted in *Sunrise*, sometimes a door would silently open in the apartment at Brahegatan 52. A nightgown would rustle. Bare feet would patter over the wooden floor. Then another door would open and discreetly close.

It was Hilma leaving her bedroom to go to Sigrid Lancén, who had lived with her and her mother for nine years. It was Lancén, the friend, athletics instructor, and number 8 in the group of The Thirteen who wrote about it in a notebook of her own. The first entry is:

> H. slept by me for a while on the morning of July 25, kissed me incessantly, held my neck so tightly that I saw endless white flowers raining down, a white flower clock ticked above H.'s head. I prayed. Though her arm tried to hold me back.[1]

The next day, July 26, 1913, Lancén wrote:

Half of me felt the flash of joy in my heart when the other half met her dual soul.[2]

On July 28:

I felt a connection in those moments between my beloved H. and me that is the answer to the enigma of my life![3]

On July 29:

I was surrounded by H.'s arms, feeling an endless love, so that we could die together.[4]

On August 2:

H. and I sit next to each other, H., serious, embraces me gently.[5]

On August 28:

I never lived so intensely, so truly in bright light with H.'s soul as in this time.[6]

Was this the first time that the relationship led to kisses and embraces? Or was Lancén just beginning to record the experiences? As an athletics instructor, she would have been used to thinking about and describing the body; perhaps for this reason she was chosen to document the shared physical experiences. Six years had passed since Hilma was warned by her invisible companions "not to come to harm through careless touches" "which S. L-n instigated."[7] Four years had passed since the same messengers had urged Lancén to strive to be "the eyelet" in order to connect with the hook, Asket.[8] When the two friends came together in Lancén's bed, the warnings and euphemisms finally fell away. Physical love brought them closer to the mystery; the kisses and embraces passed into visions of raining flowers and light. The artist and her housemate opened further

gateways to the spiritual world—and not through trances, psycho-
graphs, or prayer. Lancén and af Klint became one in the literal
sense. The mystical term for this is "ecstasy." "I was the instrument
of ecstasy," af Klint wrote in 1907, with no further explanation.

When Lancén and af Klint were together, they experienced
voices joining them from the spiritual realm. On October 14, 1914,
the notebook records the following transmission through Hilma as
the two women held hands:

> Believe me, you are part of my being. You are flesh of my flesh, blood
> of my blood, soul of my soul.[9]

The language is a variation on a biblical text; in paradise, Adam says
to Eve, the helpmeet created for him by God: "This *is* now bone of
my bones, and flesh of my flesh: she shall be called Woman, because
she was taken out of Man."[10]

When af Klint was given Adam's words and spoke to Lancén as
Eve, the friends slipped into the roles of the first humans in paradise. They returned to the moment when Adam and Eve shared
a body and were one. Like Vestal and Asket or the rose and lily,
together they formed a dual being in which the artist occupied the
male position and Lancén the female.

Lancén's notes began on July 24, 1913. On July 25 she wrote about
the kiss. On September 10, the women sat together in a dark cinema
in Stockholm to watch *Quo Vadis*, the epic Italian film that tells the
story of the love between the kidnapped Princess Lygia and Marcus
Vinicius, a patrician.

On September 30, Hilma began to paint a new series in oil on
canvas, which she named *Group VIII, Series US*. In the first work,
she painted a slender figure turning on its own axis, illuminated
against a black background (see plate 31). Behind the figure, a white
cross is bordered by blue and yellow, the colors of the male and the
female, each color filling two quadrants of the painting. The central
figure, too, is half blue, half yellow. Everything oscillates, everything moves. A nautilus spirals from the figure's loins, and ovals

whirl like the wings of dragonflies. Four circular forms resembling chakras are painted on the being's upper body, at the height of the throat, heart, abdomen, and genitals.

When, years later, Hilma read Lancén's notebook, she drew a connection between the painting and her friend. On the cover, she wrote: "You, Nr. 8, were surely the one who inspired the *US Series*."[11]

On October 26, 1913, she celebrated her fifty-first birthday. In December she finished the *US Series*, less than three months after she had started it. From that point Lancén's notes become more sporadic, the last written on February 2, 1915. Then she and her kisses and embraces disappear from the notebooks for reasons that were never articulated.

[17]

Singoalla

As af Klint and Lancén were receiving one vision after another behind closed doors, the dead returned to the notebooks. Early 1913 brought a lively exchange with Lotten Rönquist, the painter with whom af Klint had once shared a studio. Rönquist had died suddenly a few months earlier, before she turned fifty, and the notes indicate that now she was advising Hilma's group to picture an apparatus in their minds similar to a telephone in order to contact her. "That will make it easier," Rönquist assured.[1]

In July a message arrived from Viktor Rydberg, the famous writer Cassel and af Klint knew from their Academy days. Though Rydberg had died in 1895, the circle of women was just now reading and discussing his novel *Singoalla*. It was the first and only literary work ever brought to the sessions, and two notebooks of commentary were devoted to it.[2]

Like the then-popular novel *Quo Vadis*, *Singoalla* is a love story set in the distant past. Rydberg's book takes place in a fairy-tale version of the Middle Ages; the protagonist is a knight named Erland.

Over the course of the novel, the hero meets a fate that would have been familiar to the women: Erland divides into two people, each of whom loves a different woman, one by day and the other by night. The first is named Helena and is a Christian, while the other, Singoalla, comes "from afar," stays "not in any place," and possesses magical powers.[3] The knight is unaware that he's living a double life; he can no longer separate dream from reality, and the chaos of impressions drives him mad. The thoughts rove as shadows through his soul, Rydberg wrote, like "broken pictures."[4] What Erland retains are the "fragments of a more beautiful past."[5]

Such a fatalistic view would hardly have impressed af Klint. She had long since stopped believing that people could have only a single personality. In her view, Erland needed to understand that Singoalla, his beloved with magical powers from the East, was not "other" but part of him, his other half and alter ego. Af Klint told Rydberg's spirit about her discovery; a friend recorded her words:

> Does it not bring you great joy to know that Singoalla received Erland's blue etheric body, and Erland that of Singoalla? Would it be so dangerous to explain that Erland's being is the truth and Singoalla's is love, that their powers double each other through this great miracle?[6]

Reading *Singoalla* stimulated af Klint and her circle to reach bold conclusions. According to the notebook, Erland was being guided by Singoalla toward "the goal." Man is led "through the woman," an insight that needed to be widely disseminated:

> Feel free to sing this sentence out on the squares and in the streets, it does not hurt; the woman is the one who leads, the man the one who accompanies . . . this is progress in evolution. Christianity has poorly explained the position of man & woman to each other.[7]

In a word, gender roles were turned upside down and the church was severely admonished, nothing less.

When Hilma and her friends declared Singoalla to be the guide of Erland and the prototype of a female hero, in Lancén's eyes Hilma herself transformed into a knight. "You are the female counterpart to Saint George," Lancén said to Hilma in September, when their love was just beginning, and recorded it in the notebook.[8]

[18]

The Baltic Exhibition

On May 15, 1914, the Baltic Exhibition opened in the Swedish city of Malmö, with splendid new buildings, a majestic palace in the Moorish style, and the largest art show that had ever been seen on Swedish soil: 56 halls with 3,500 paintings and sculptures, attracting 850,000 visitors.

The exhibition was meant to symbolize international understanding; its purpose was to solidify Sweden's alliances with its neighbors in the Baltic region: Germany, Denmark, Finland, and Russia. But at the end of June, news came from the city of Sarajevo that Archduke Franz Ferdinand, heir to the Austro-Hungarian throne, and his wife, Sophie, had been assassinated, with the result that the exhibitors suddenly found themselves enemies. On August 1, Germany declared war on Russia.

Af Klint was represented at the Baltic Exhibition. The Association of Swedish Women Artists was invited to take part in the show, but what had first seemed good news turned out to be anything but. The great halls were reserved for men, especially the poster boys of the Swedish art scene, from Larsson and Zorn to Bruno Liljefors and Prince Eugen. The female artists were tucked away in the back corner of the exhibition's labyrinth, in two little rooms near a stairwell and emergency exit.[1] To include every member of the association, the walls had to be plastered with paintings: two hundred in all. Though officially af Klint was no longer a member, one of her paintings was shown: *Träget Arbete* (Hard Work).[2] Like her previous submissions to the association's exhibitions, the painting was representational. Its appearance marked a farewell: never again would af Klint take part in an association show.

While the public flooded the grand halls of the Baltic Exhibition, only a predictably small trickle of visitors found their way to the female artists, whose work was summarily adjudged "second-rate" by a prominent critic.[3] Crowds poured into the Russian section to marvel at the large historical landscapes of Nicolas Roerich, a painter, set designer, and Theosophist.[4]

Viewers also gathered before five paintings that were harder to comprehend. The fact that they bore such titles as *Composition VI* only increased the confusion. One reviewer suggested the canvases might show cholera bacteria, greatly magnified and running amok (fig. 35).[5] Others, however, eschewed such irony and revered the paintings as the newest creations of a promising innovator, Wassily Kandinsky. They knew they were viewing the kind of spiritual painting the artist had described in his treatise *Concerning the Spiritual in Art*, published in 1910. It ends, prophetically, "this spirit in painting stands organically in direct relation to the new construction of the spiritual realm, which has already begun, for this spirit is the soul of the epoch of great spirituality."[6] Like af Klint, Kandinsky considered nonrepresentational abstraction to be the natural manifestation of the spirit—and its opposite, representational naturalism, to testify to a materialist view.

But Kandinsky had bigger problems in 1914 than wondering about the reception of his work in Malmö. He had registered for the Baltic Exhibition using a Munich address, having lived in Germany for nearly twenty years. But because he had been born in Moscow, he was deported as an enemy alien by the Germans when war was declared.[7]

The alleged price for his *Composition VI* was leaked to the press. According to one article, Kandinsky was asking 30,000 marks for

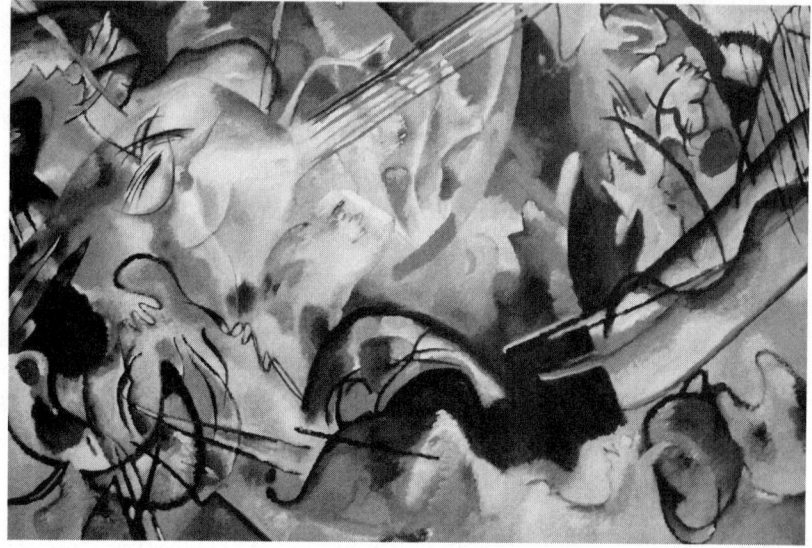

35. Wassily Kandinsky, *Composition VI*, 1913, oil on canvas, 195 x 300 cm.

it—or 120,000 Swedish crowns.[8] The Nationalmuseum in Stockholm paid 16,500 crowns for a self-portrait by Anders Zorn from
the Baltic Exhibition and 80,000 for *The Chemist* by Wilhelm Leibl.
When, at the end of the show, the city of Malmö was offered Kandinsky's paintings for significantly less than the original prices, the
offer was rejected. The paintings couldn't really be considered art,
Kandinsky was told by way of explanation.[9]

It is unlikely that Hilma traveled to Malmö in support of her
single painting. She probably heard about the exhibition from
friends; perhaps she read a few reviews. In any case, she had more
important things on her mind, including the dream of founding
a school where children could learn from an early age to cultivate
their spiritual capacities.[10]

War

Two swans collide on a canvas, one white, one black. Af Klint started a new cycle called *The Swan* in September 1914, while throughout much of Europe war was exploding (see plate 32). The two birds face off like mirror images; blood drips from their wings. In the next painting of the cycle the animals pierce each other's breasts with their beaks, bending their necks to the other's wounds to drink the liquid that flows from their bodies like streams of light. Fire shoots up in violent flames, as if triggered by a chemical reaction.

Looking out the window of her new studio at Eriksbergsgatan, not far from her apartment, af Klint could see the formations of birds flying south for the winter.[1] Migrating birds had come to epitomize Sweden since the publication in 1906 of Nobel Prize–winner Selma Lagerlöf's book *The Wonderful Adventures of Nils*, in which the young protagonist is led on a journey through Sweden by wild geese.

Now, though, deadly battles were being fought on the ground below any geese careless enough to stray from Swedish airspace. In the east, the front stretched from the Baltic to the Dead Sea. In the west, German troops occupied Belgium and Luxemburg and were advancing toward northern France. Only Sweden, Norway, Denmark, the Netherlands, and Switzerland remained neutral. When the women's magazine *Idun* published an article on the Malmö Exhibition, highlighting the contribution of the Women's Association, it was dwarfed by coverage of the expanding war, including a photograph of a German Zeppelin bombing the cathedral in Antwerp and depictions of the German cavalry and the ruins of the town hall in Leuven, Belgium.[2]

In October Hilma celebrated her fifty-second birthday. The year 1914 ended with four more paintings in the *Swan* series, the darkest of her oeuvre.

The artist worked on the series until March 1915. With each painting the birds progressively shed their fixed forms; they multiply and rearrange themselves in new configurations. What had looked in the previous year like turmoil and struggle transformed into tidy geometry. Divided circles appear; yellow and blue meet in their centers. In the innermost ring of the seventeenth painting, the texture of the paint changes, becoming uneven, pigmented, like skin (see plate 33). A tiny triangle appears in the center. It is black and skin-colored, like death and life, like the pierced breast of the black swan.

Af Klint's work was undergoing a transformation. The letter forms had disappeared, and with them the spirals, loops, and sinuous lines, as well as the eyelet and hook. The bright orange was gone, and the prevalence of green. The forms became more geometric, the compositions more symmetrical. The circle dominates, inciting a trend that extends through the next two series, *The Dove* and *Altarpieces*.

Something else changed as well. The new series were increasingly informed by works in the artist's library. In the *Tree of Knowledge* she had referenced Steiner's cosmic tree with "roots going upward" and "branches going downward." In *The Swan*, she explores one of the most popular occult symbols, treated extensively by Blavatsky in *The Secret Doctrine*. The white swan was called Hansa, Blavatsky explained, and the black swan Kali Hansa. Hansa-Vahana was "he who uses the Hansa as his vehicle." "Hansa, as every Hindu knows," the founder of Theosophy continues, "is a fabulous bird, which, when given milk mixed with water for its food (in the allegory) separated the two, drinking the milk and leaving the water; thus showing inherent wisdom—milk standing symbolically for spirit, and water for matter."[3]

But as the artist also learned from Blavatsky, the swan was not just the animal form of Brahma for the Hindus: the swan connects the elements, living both in the water and in the air, and it was important to the ancient Greeks, as in the myth of Leda and the Swan.[4] The swan in Hilma's paintings perfectly maps the descriptions in *The Secret Doctrine*. It is black and white; it pierces its own breast and drinks the liquid until matter becomes spirit. The paintings also pursue a formal logic: the animal transforms into geometric figuration; what was representational becomes abstract.

Blavatsky's writings range from ancient India to classical Greece and on to contemporary Europe. She moves from religion to science, from mysticism to modern chemistry. Ashvattha, the tree of being and life described in the Bhagavad Gita and painted by af Klint as the *Tree of Knowledge*, sprouts from the wings of Hansa, the swan. According to Blavatsky, two snakes entwine up the trunk of the tree, turning Ashvattha to Caduceus, the Greek Hermes' winged staff. From here, Blavatsky leaps through time to Birmingham in England and the meeting of the Chemical Section of the British Association in 1887. Blavatsky refers to a lecture by Sir William Crookes, a physicist, chemist, Theosophist, and member of the Royal Society. Crookes's lecture deals with the formation of elements, from "knots and voids in a primitive, formless fluid." If this figure were to be projected in space, it would form a figure eight, called a "lemniscate" by mathematicians. Blavatsky translates: "A lemniscate [stands] for the evolutions downward, from Spirit into matter."[5] Following modern chemistry, Blavatsky explains, the snakes that wind around Ashvattha and Caduceus become the lemniscate.

Af Klint's geometric approach, which emerges in the *Swan* series, heralds a new phase. Until the start of the war, her series had always included biographical elements, such as the dual being she formed with her friends. For that, the artist had broken with old systems of order and transformed matter into spirit. But now the challenge was greater. Every day the newspapers were filled with reports of violence and destruction. Could the swan and *The Secret Doctrine* help explain the war? What did Blavatsky have to say on the matter?

Though Blavatsky died in 1891, her books were still widely read. Fierce criticism from scientists and intellectuals had hardly made a dent in their popularity. At the same time, scandal had periodically shaken the Theosophical Society. There was much gloating when

Blavatsky's alleged magical abilities were proven to be based on simple tricks. Her oracular style and the ambiguity of her writings were coopted by political movements, on both the left and the right. Under the banner of Theosophy people fought for Indian independence and the rights of workers and women, but also for supremacy of the so-called "Aryan race."

Af Klint did not believe in supermen or Aryans, as did many who cited Blavatsky.[6] She did, however, share with the founder of Theosophy the view that materialism was the root of all evil, the denial of spirituality and spiritual values. Materialism, Blavatsky wrote in a prescient passage, always leads to strife and to "the division of races, nations, tribes, societies and individuals into Cains and Abels, wolves and lambs."[7] Nationalism was a poison that followed from materialism, setting the welfare of the many above the welfare of all. Blavatsky advised the study of mystical texts as an antidote, for they showed the significance of unity, of old symbols and wisdom that endured through the eras: Ashvattha, Caduceus, lemniscate. No destruction was accidental or innocent.

Thus the higher meaning of the swan is not difficult to understand. For af Klint, it is the bringer of light, the messenger that turns matter back into spirit, that travels between cultures and connects old beliefs with the newest research. It is the source of meaning and unity when the world sinks into chaos.

[20]

Saint George

In 1915 the mysterious, robed women returned to af Klint's paintings in a new series. Each of the seven small paintings shows a simple room with a chair and a curtain. The pictorial space is filled by a dark figure whose head covering and hem touch the upper and lower edges of the painting. Unlike the nuns in flowing white tunics and glistening light painted by Hilma three years earlier, this figure is cloaked in dark blue. The bright series of praying women from 1912 had been titled *A Female Series*, while this new one was called *A Male Series*.[1] Yet the figure portrayed in *A Male Series* is not a man but a woman praying in various positions: seated, standing, walking. Sometimes the hands are folded. Other times the palms are placed flat together, as in Dürer's *Praying Hands*. In still other paintings the arms are open and the palms turned upward to the sky, as in the Muslim tradition. As if in answer to the supplicant, light falls onto the praying figure at a different angle in each work.

The paintings of *A Male Series* are a reminder that the women around Hilma had not stopped holding rituals for the purpose of communicating with higher beings. They continued to use the old altar of The Five with its steps, cross, and rose (see fig. 15). The Thirteen also prayed and wore robes at their sessions. In the Rosicrucian tradition, worship sometimes took the form of theater, with role play and multiple speakers. But the project of nurturing one's masculine side can only be traced to insights the women had cultivated themselves, without clear precedent.

When Hilma began the next series, *The Dove*, she took on the male alter ego of Saint George, with whom she was already associated in the notebooks, most recently by Sigrid Lancén.[2] In *The Dove*, Hilma stretched the knight's battle across four canvases without his sword's ever touching the dragon (see plates 34 and 35). Instead of attacking the enemy with his weapon, George raises it to the heavens and pierces an oval, above which floats a cross with a rose. As if this completed a magical circuit, the dragon dematerializes to become as transparent as a puff of air. The knight looks down at his former enemy, the monster he has transformed rather than killed. Hilma explained the series several years later, after its fourteen images were done: "The harder Saint George fights against the great dragon, the stronger it becomes; the beast is defeated only with thoughts directed inward, toward celestial aid."[3]

As Hilma was painting the series, World War I raged on. Italy declared war on Austria-Hungary. German Zeppelins dropped bombs on London. The artist spent the summer at her lake house on Munsö, where she finished the *Tree of Knowledge* series, but to continue painting into the fall, she needed to find a new studio. After Eriksbergsgatan she located a new space on Ynglingagatan in the north of Stockholm, which she moved into with her paintbrushes, paint, and several sheets of gold leaf.[4]

The three large paintings that came next constitute her *Altarpieces* series. They each contain the Buddhist Wheel of Dharma that appears in Charles Leadbeater's *Man Visible and Invisible* (see fig. 21). In the first painting, wheels connect the planes of perception, and af Klint piles them into a great tower, its tip pushing into a golden circle and sparking a radiant fire (see plate 36). In the second painting the circle rotates like a planet, and in the third it nearly fills the canvas. At almost 2.4 meters, these works were so large they had to be painted on the floor. Little shoe prints can be seen on them a few centimeters from the gold leaf that fills the circles.[5] The *Altarpieces* conclude the great cycle *Paintings for the Temple*, which includes 193 works and was begun in 1906. When the commission was finished, the calendar showed December 1915.

On the Western Front, in Flanders, the German army was using poison gas against British troops. Sweden remained neutral. On December 23, just before Christmas, Wassily Kandinsky arrived in Stockholm to spend the winter. An article on his paintings from the Baltic Exhibition had appeared in the Swedish magazine *Ord och Bild*. The author, Bror Gadelius, professor at the Karolinska Institute and one of the country's leading psychiatrists, had declared *Composition VI* (see fig. 35)—the largest nonrepresentational work in the show—to be an expression of mental illness. In this kind of art, said Gadelius, "we encounter an autistic tendency, a sinking into the Ego, which seeks to give art new content consisting of the formless abysses of the life of the soul. The fact that this tendency is rooted in unfathomable darkness, in something 'subhuman,' infinitely close to pathological breakdown, surely need not be further developed here."[6]

Gadelius was writing in the name of a science that had become quick to designate as "pathological" or "sick" anything it could not explain. For Gadelius and his cohort, art influenced by the spiritual world was beyond comprehension. The number of mental asylums in Sweden continued to rise.[7]

[21]
Kandinsky in Stockholm

World War I had an unexpected impact on Stockholm. Art flourished, and the capital became more international. Artists who didn't want to fight in the war fled their homelands for the few islands of neutrality in Europe, above all Switzerland and Sweden. Zurich became the capital of Dada, with Cabaret Voltaire as its headquarters, while Stockholm turned into a miniature Berlin, centering on "Karl Gummeson, Konsthandel," a new gallery at Strandvägen 17, a chic address by the harbor.[1] The painter Isaac Grünewald connected the art dealer Karl Gummeson with Herwarth Walden, the founder of the magazine *Der Sturm* and the Berlin gallery of the same name.[2] Walden's second wife, Nell Roslund, was Swedish, and she too had recently begun to make nonrepresentational work. During the war, Gummeson mounted one avant-garde exhibition after another in his gallery, showing the work of Franz Marc, Kandinsky, and Gabriele Münter. All three had previously exhibited at Walden's gallery in Berlin.

Marc had been drafted into the German army and was killed in the 1916 Battle of Verdun. Kandinsky, on the other hand, abhorred the war and had made plans in Switzerland to meet his longtime lover and fellow Blaue Reiter member Gabriele Münter in Stockholm where, he promised—and not for the first time—he would marry her.

When Münter (1877–1962) arrived that summer she moved into a pension on Stureplan, a grand square in downtown Stockholm.

She was not yet forty. On her first evening in the city, she wrote: "I feel I have never seen anything as beautiful, excellent, and pleasant as Stockholm. As if from a better planet."[3] Urban life in Stockholm suited her as it had not in Munich, which she had fled with Kandinsky and other members of the Blaue Reiter to take refuge in the town of Murnau south of Bavaria's capital. Münter's Stockholm paintings are full of ladies with large hats walking tiny dogs. She began painting squares and building facades; the red wooden Dala horses named for Sweden's densely wooded Dalarna province start showing up in her interiors.

The collegiality of Sweden's artists, who welcomed Münter warmly, must indeed have struck her as "from a better planet." In December 1915 she showed her paintings in a group exhibition at the Gummeson Gallery, then again in March 1916 in a solo show. That same month Liljevalchs Konsthall opened in the Djurgården neighborhood, and Münter was invited to participate in a show there organized by the Association of Swedish Women Artists. The infighting that af Klint had experienced a few years earlier had passed. The German Expressionist got along just as well with the once-conservative women's association as with Sigrid Hjertén and her husband, Isaac Grünewald, whose group the Young Ones had once excluded women. When Kandinsky arrived in Stockholm, he and Münter were invited to dine with Prince Eugen at the Waldemarsudde. There is a single surviving photograph of Münter and Kandinsky during their time together in Stockholm. Kandinsky sports a hat and bow tie and Münter a gleaming white hat and matching fox fur muff. Kandinsky often complained to Münter about his money troubles. She, too, had financial difficulties, but she did what she could to support them both and helped organize a show for him at the Gummeson Gallery in February 1916.

During his months in Stockholm, Kandinsky rarely painted in oil. Instead, he worked in watercolor, in pencil, and in ink. His works on paper show wonderlands with delicate boats, mountains, towers, lakes, and rainbows that hearken back to his early works inspired by Russian fairytales. At the same time, the slender figures walking or riding horseback are reminiscent of Saint George in a blue cloak and headdress riding a horse, the coat of arms of the Blaue Reiter, which Kandinsky had painted in 1911 and used again on the cover of the group's *Almanac* in 1912. With that figure as their symbol, Marc and Kandinsky advocated for a new kind of painting, for "the proliferation of the spiritual movement" and a creative expression beyond "aimless, materialist art."[4] Like af Klint, Kandinsky identified with the delicate Saint George who fought so unflinchingly against evil despite the superior size and strength of his enemy. Kandinsky had brought a 1911 painting of the saint with him to Stockholm. The canvas shows only a great lance—*pars pro toto*—stabbing diagonally through a tumult of forms.[5]

One of Kandinsky's Stockholm works on view in the Gummeson Gallery shows a little old man with a long white beard who bore a striking resemblance to Nicolas Roerich, the Russian painter whose works had also been shown in Malmö.[6] The figure rides through the painting on a Viking boat like the ones Roerich had received such praise for painting at the Baltic Exhibition. Did the two artists know each other? Had they met in Russia? Roerich was connected to avant-garde circles in France and his homeland and was also a member of the Theosophical Society, which Kandinsky had admiringly called "a tremendous spiritual movement."[7]

There is a direct connection between the 1914 exhibition in Malmö and Kandinsky's show at Karl Gummeson's two years later. The five nonrepresentational paintings he had shown in Malmö had to remain there after the Baltic Exhibition, since the war made it impossible to transport them out of Sweden. The group included *Composition VI*, the painting that Gadelius had used to "diagnose" an "autistic tendency" (see fig. 35). Gummeson included several other abstract works in the show that an American collector had commissioned from Kandinsky. These too could not be shipped during the war—and were stored by a Dutch collector in Amsterdam.[8]

Gummeson's customers strongly preferred Kandinsky's fairy-tale landscapes with their exotic figures, and these works sold well. The large nonrepresentational paintings, on the other hand, found no takers, and Stockholm's collectors were to retain this reticence for decades. When Kandinsky once again showed abstract watercolors at Gummeson's, in the 1930s, he wrote to a sympathetic critic: "In Stockholm my watercolor exhibition was quite successful— 'morally,' but there were no sales. Sometimes one has had it up to here with morality. The only comfort is that this is the only kind of morality to be found on earth today."[9] Reviews of Kandinsky's 1916 show concentrated mainly on the works that collectors ignored, that, according to popular opinion, showed nothing. An editor from the daily newspaper *Dagens Nyheter* met with Kandinsky to decipher the work. Kandinsky was only too happy to oblige: he explained that he first had to free himself from nature to find a mode of expression. He believed that depictions of houses, trees, and people contributed as little to the understanding of art as birds twittering, plates clattering, or thunder rumbling did to music. Instead, one needed to push toward the "core of the soul . . . and must learn something about the language of color before one understands it, that is all."[10]

The journalist was impressed by Kandinsky's explanation as well as by the "cool gaze of his gray eyes." Even the visitors to Gummeson's Gallery who stared at the walls in confusion didn't fluster the artist, he wrote.

Another critic was less sympathetic. His article appeared on the same day, in the same newspaper, right next to the interview. Tinged with irony, it described the societal to-do at the opening and predicted that the works would be much discussed, as people in Stockholm loved to talk about things they didn't understand.

The word "abstraction" did not appear in either article. There is no suggestion that Kandinsky saw himself as the inventor of abstraction or that he had painted "the world's first abstract painting," as would later be claimed. Instead, he expressed his distaste for Paris with its constant pursuit of the latest craze. He had no time for "novelty," he said; he wished only for "peace and quiet."

At the end of March 1916, Kandinsky left Sweden for Russia. He did not keep his promise to Gabriele Münter. In Russia, he met the twenty-year-old Nina Andreevskaya and married her instead.

Parsifal and Atom

Not for the first time, af Klint's life ran counter to the zeitgeist. More international artists were coming to Stockholm; the number of galleries and exhibitions was growing. But the artist had become less interested in the city; plus, it was becoming harder to find staples owing to the war, so she decided to move permanently to Munsö. In August she sketched out her idea for a studio. It was to stand next to Furuheim, her lake house, and would be eight by twelve meters, and twelve meters tall. The drawing shows a box with a roof, a fireplace, and a large window. On the second floor there would be an apartment. The studio would be on the ground floor, and the ceilings high enough to hang *The Ten Largest*. There would also be a separate prayer room.

She drew an oval on the floor plan: ideally, the studio would have curved walls, as if one were inside an egg. The whole thing was her plan for a "shared workspace."[1]

Whose workspace was explained in another notebook, in late summer of 1916. Hilma imagined a research and residential community on Munsö for her friends and herself. Their first project would entail eight years of research into the realms of plants, animals, and minerals. This endeavor, so the promise went, would bring the group closer together. In Hilma's words: "henceforth our work is not separated from each other."[2]

Her body of work grew with incredible speed. The temple cycle, finished in 1915, comprised nearly two hundred paintings, and another 144 works were created in fall 1916 on Munsö: small watercolors painted over ten weeks from early October to mid-December.[3] The artist named the series *Parsifal*, after the medieval epic poem on which Richard Wagner also based an opera. Wagner's *Parsifal* was popular in Stockholm, in whole or in part: "Karfreitagszauber" from act 3, for instance, was performed in April 1916.[4]

The artist began her series with a motif suitable for a stage design. A dark spiral is tightly wound around a small hole in the middle of a sheet where the paper has been scratched away (fig. 36). It was only a sketch, Hilma noted in the margin; the actual work was to be much larger: 1 by 1.4 meters.[5] On that scale the viewer would confront a dark opening large enough to create the sensation she was being sucked into a vortex, head over heels, toward a new start, a birth, a plunge into the world. One of the following sheets shows an embryo that matures first into a boy, then into a girl. Parsifal too changes sex: he is male and female, a dual being. From the artist's point of view, Parsifal is undergoing the evolution of the soul. As in the historical epic, which describes the hero's ascent from knight to Grail King, the victory is ultimately a spiritual one. Parsifal's adventures teach him not only strength, honor, and courage, but also humility, mercy, and loyalty. The bisexuality is af Klint's addition. Wagner would not have approved of this change any more than most of his contemporaries.

As she produced the series, Hilma varied her approach. Some sequences are nonrepresentational, intensely reduced: there are paintings of nothing more than a point surrounded by a circle. Others have a narrative inference, such as the boy who grows into a girl. Some paintings seem to foretell much later works in modern painting—for example, Hilma's colored squares anticipate those painted by Josef Albers decades later in New York.[6] Other works seem to recall earlier traditions, such as Jacob Boehme's gnostic productions from the early seventeenth century. The artist drew upon the whole of art history, including what was to come: *Framåt*, a monochrome painting, consists of a single word below a brilliant red square (see plate 37). The word means "forward" and refers to the movement of force that helped her, as she wrote, to "go forward."[7]

The series also suggests that the artist was not alone. Parsifal, the main character, is repeatedly surrounded by twelve figures. Together they form the group of The Thirteen, which had replaced The Five.[8]

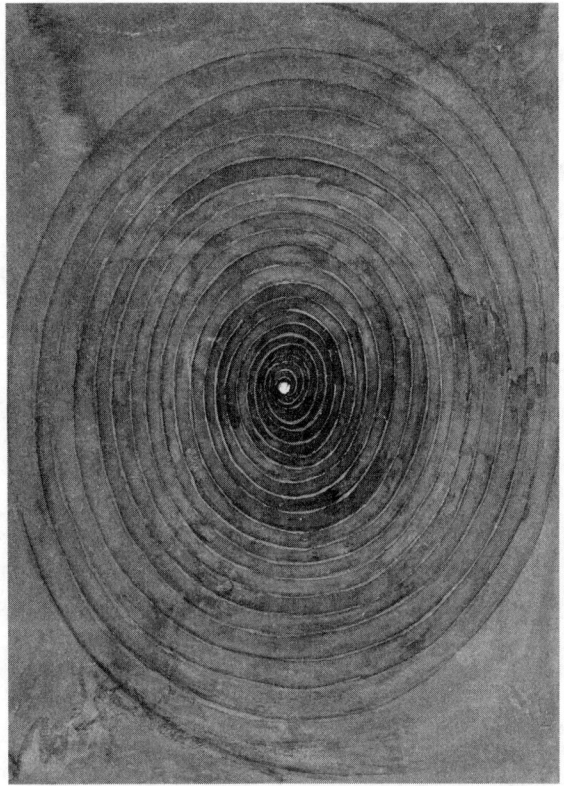

36. *No. 1, Group I, The Parsifal Series,* 1916, watercolor and pencil on paper, 24.8 cm x 26.1 cm, Stiftelsen Hilma af Klints Verk, HaK 202.

Was Hilma aware of the recent fuss that had been made over Kandinsky? Had she seen the catalogue from Gummeson's? The simple answer is we don't know, but she may well have been too busy to pay close attention. She was painting so much that she was running out of space, both in the studio and in her apartment, even when she rolled the paintings, stacked them, leaned them against the walls, and shoved them under the bed. Paintings seemed to be everywhere, getting in the way of new pieces that were in progress. At the same time, in the past she had taken pains to seek out kindred spirits—for example in the Women's Association or when she exhibited with the Theosophical Society in 1913—suggesting that she might have pricked up her ears when an artist who shared her interests in a "spiritual art" exhibited in Stockholm. Plus, the Gummeson Gallery was centrally located on the harbor promenade. The artist and her friends would have had to cover their eyes to miss the arrival of the newest avant-gardes from Berlin and Munich.

She would have agreed with much that Kandinsky had to say about art. "According to us," he wrote, "only those artists who have within themselves the calling to create new spiritual values are necessary for art." Such works "have no practical use and are therefore of no material value."[9] But viewers could travel through them to a "world previously unknown," to "the land of new spirit."[10] Hilma held the same opinion.

And then? Would she have wished for her own exhibition at Gummeson's? The similarities between her work and Kandinsky's did not alter the fact that the gallery wasn't an option for her—for several reasons. For one, only a fraction of her paintings would have fit in the cramped storefront. *The Ten Largest* would immediately have been excluded because of the low ceilings.[11] For another, she had no interest in selling the works she produced. It would have been paradoxical to create paintings for a temple, including the recent altarpieces, and at the same time hope they would hang in a living room above a collector's sofa.

Kandinsky would have understood. Working in exile, he felt the show at Gummeson's did not contribute to his long-term goals: he wanted more than to sell paintings. Like Hilma, he dreamed of a permanent home for his work so that it could remain together and be shown together, in a space of his own design. This was "my old dream," Kandinsky wrote sorrowfully in a later letter from Weimar, when once again he had failed to realize his dream at the Bauhaus. Kandinsky expected "of <u>every</u> art a further, more powerful, not yet present <u>inner</u> development, a deepening of the human spirit— which is only beginning to approach the world spirit—<u>completely and utterly</u> freed from external purpose."[12] But when he exhibited at Gummeson's in Stockholm, such absolutist goals were distant. The challenge was to create a balance between the need to earn money with art and the hope of initiating a spiritual turn with these very same paintings. Perhaps Kandinsky recalled the optimistic sentences he had written in the Blaue Reiter's *Almanac* two years before the war broke out. "In practical life," he had written, "one will hardly find a person who gets off the train in Regensburg when he wants to travel to Berlin. In spiritual life, disembarking in Regensburg is a fairly common occurrence."[13] Many were too quick to give up, to lower their expectations, to compromise in form and content, it had seemed to him at the time. Since then, though, he had learned the hard way that one doesn't always have the freedom to make idealistic choices.

But for af Klint, matters were clear. Exhibiting with Gummeson would have meant getting off the train in Regensburg instead of continuing to Berlin. She wrote nothing about this in her notebooks, and the name Kandinsky does not appear until the late twenties.[14]

In January 1917 the artist began a new series in watercolor and gave it the title *Atom*. She knew that the atom was actually divisible, despite the Greek word from which the term derived. Atoms decayed and could be split—the Curies had proven it. In *Atom*, two squares appear on the paper, one large and one small, each divided into four cells (see plate 38). The configuration within the squares changes with each painting. These changes are related but occur on two distinct levels: the "physical" and the "etheric." As in *Tree of Knowledge*, the goal is to escape the limits of the physical body to reach the etheric. "The body is capable of rising above its earthly ties by listening to the supernatural energies," af Klint writes directly on the fifth painting of the series.[15] In her notebook she adds: "I am an atom in the universe that has access to infinite possibilities of development, and it is these possibilities I want, gradually, to reveal."[16] Microcosm and macrocosm mirror each other, everything has a counterpart, nothing stands alone.

She was also writing at a feverish pace. Between 1917 and 1918 she wrote a work of 2,058 pages, which she called "Studies of the Life of the Soul." Here again she discusses the division of humanity into men and women and the necessity of overcoming this dichotomy on a higher, spiritual level. She writes about "womanman" and "man-woman" and the misleading external appearances of the sexes:

> I will begin with a side note of great importance. Many who fight in this drama are dressed in the wrong clothing. Many female costumes conceal a man. Many male costumes conceal the woman.[17]

The artist calls this a "side note," but in fact she was demanding a complete reversal of social expectations. Her female contemporaries were reviled as "mannish" if they claimed freedoms that were thought to be the privilege of men. She does not dwell on the narrow-mindedness of the society in which she lived. For her, the blurring of the boundaries between the sexes was the freest state of the soul. Not only that: she argued that the spirit strives toward such a state, following the law of completion, the longing for union that is characteristic of all living beings.

In her paintings, she had already portrayed the Manwoman and Womanman dozens of times as Asket and Vestal, eyelet and hook, blue and yellow, as Saint George or Parsifal with sword and shimmering armor, as girl and boy. As early as 1906's *Primordial Chaos* she had painted man and woman emerging from the shell of a snail, the hermaphroditic animal that unites the sexes. The artist called her work "the fifth gospel." Modesty wasn't her strong suit.

[23]

The Studio on Munsö

In the meantime, someone else must have tended to practicalities. The studio house on Munsö was built over the course of 1917. Following Hilma's plan, there was a great hall with a high ceiling, making it possible to show *The Ten Largest*. They were rolled around large vertical pillars and displayed in this curved form. The paintings of

Primordial Chaos, *Eros*, *The Large Figure Paintings*, and *Evolution* were hung on the walls. *The Swan* and *The Dove* were presented on easels. The second-floor apartment had two rooms and a kitchen and housed *A Female Series* and *A Male Series*, as well as paintings from Hilma's Academy days. The two stories were connected by a spiral staircase, and an exterior staircase also gave access to the upper floor. The façade was designed in the gothic style, with arched windows and a pointed double portal. The building was painted red, as was customary in Sweden for wooden houses, and the cornices were painted black.[1]

To build it, Hilma borrowed 3,000 crowns from Anna Cassel. Emilia Giertta is said to have taken care of the building permit, since the land belonged to her family. The high cost of building the studio house also forced Hilma to sell shares of Furuheim, which she had purchased in 1913, to Cassel, Gusten Andersson, and Sigrid Henström.[2] She also chased commissions to earn money. In a 1916 letter, she offered to paint a portrait for the prestigious Kungliga Patriotiska Sällskapet, a patriotic society founded by Gustav III in the eighteenth century. Her offer was declined.[3]

For the rest of her life, Hilma bore a grudge against Cassel for offering a loan instead of paying for the studio outright. More than two decades later, in February 1944, she revisited her resentment during an exchange with the soul of her deceased friend: "Do you remember how we decided to build a shared studio together. As we made the plan together, you said nothing. Was it not indecision, Anna? You had the means and I didn't, who was to set the plan in motion if not you. If you didn't want to build with me, you could have said so, but you were silent. So I took the step without you. Friends helped me, not you."[4] Another time, Hilma recalled that Anna had finally torn up the promissory note for the borrowed money but not until Hilma asked her to forgive the debt. "Due to the money issue," Hilma wrote, they parted ways around 1916, at least for a while: "She no longer maintained her position as longtime friend."[5]

In 1917 several hundred paintings were transported from Stockholm to Munsö, and tensions rose once again among Hilma's friends.

Like stowaways, old conflicts from the city accompanied them to the island.[6] In April and May 1917, there was a clash between Hilma and Gusten Andersson, moderated by Sigrid Henström (1866–1947), another member of The Thirteen, who recorded all the conversations. The disagreement erupted in the summer house and involved Gusten's old 1909 accusation that Hilma had thrown her "out of paradise." Back then, Gusten had written her allegations as "Sister Magdalena" and claimed that it was she who had fueled Hilma's painting process with her love and prayers. Now, seven years later, Gusten had not stopped wanting Hilma's love, but in vain.

Why, Hilma wanted to know now, had Gusten tried to enter the Garden of Eden "from the wrong side"? The artist called this "the greatest crime" of mankind and accused her friend of having "the nature of a vampire."[7] This aspect of Gusten's character had made it necessary for Hilma to distance herself. Though Henström's notes also include some conciliatory passages, Hilma and Gusten seem not to have resolved their problem.[8]

Looking back, Hilma would describe Emilia Giertta as Cassel's "dual soul."[9] The artist now turned more and more to another friend—Thomasine Anderson—the "thirteenth" in the group. Hilma had already written that Thomasine would be a great help "because of her trust and her belief in me."[10]

[24]

Thomasine Anderson

World War I was entering its fourth year when Hilma decided to move to Munsö with her mother and Thomasine Anderson.

It was becoming more difficult to get food in the city. Staples such as potatoes and grains were rationed. For certain products only substitutes were available: instead of coffee, citizens had to make do with beets, rye, or dandelion root, and with carbide instead of petroleum. Sweden managed to remain neutral in the war, but the government was forced to enter into complicated trade agreements—primarily with Germany and England—in order to stave off an economic crisis. In April 1917 hungry workers marched on Gustav Adolfs torg, a square bordered by government buildings and the opera, to draw attention to their plight and to demand universal suffrage and an eight-hour workday. The demonstrations were peaceful until mounted police were brought in, leading to riots.

In Russia, uprisings had led to revolution, forcing the czar to abdicate. Finland had broken from Russian protection and declared independence. But the upheaval led to shortages, and Finland was soon engulfed in civil war.

On Munsö there was little evidence of the events shaking the rest of Europe. The family estate on Adelsö was only a short row away. The summer had been too dry to bring in a good harvest; even so, it was easier to make ends meet on the islands of Mälaren than in the city. Hilma still hadn't found a way to make money, but there was no rent to pay on Munsö, which alleviated the situation considerably. Hilma's mother continued to receive a widow's pension, and Gustaf and Ida also provided some assistance.[1]

The few photos of Thomasine Anderson that survive show her in a nurse's uniform (fig. 37): a pinafore, nurse's cap above a high forehead, wavy hair pinned up. Anderson had met the af Klints years before, when she had helped care for Hilma's mother. She first appears in the notebooks in 1914 as number 13 in the group of The Thirteen.[2]

During the war, Thomasine Anderson worked for the Red Cross and helped with the exchange of prisoners between Russia and Germany and Austria-Hungary.[3] The belligerents had agreed to allow gravely wounded soldiers to travel home from the front. The number of men who had to be transported was in the tens of thousands: soldiers without arms, legs, or hands, with facial injuries, serious organ damage, or psychological trauma. The Red Cross had campaigned for the release of the wounded soldiers and had convinced the Swedish government to open a transport route through

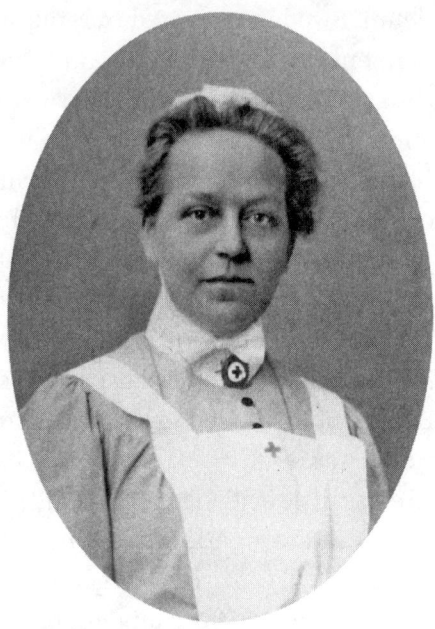

37. Thomasine Anderson,
undated, Stiftelsen Hilma af Klints Verk.

the country. Soldiers returning to Germany from the eastern front would board a ferry in the harbor city of Trelleborg, in southern Sweden, and cross the Baltic to Sassnitz on the German island of Rügen. A photograph from this crossing shows Anderson on deck in her nurse's uniform, next to a doctor and surrounded by other nurses. Her title was "Head Nurse."[4]

The wounded men in her care often began the journey in pitiable condition. The field hospitals lacked painkillers and anesthetics, so surgeries were performed under intense pressure, often with disastrous results. "War cripples" could not return to their former lives, and few succeeded in making a fresh start. One exception was Paul Wittgenstein, the Viennese concert pianist and brother of the philosopher Ludwig Wittgenstein, who lost his right arm in Russia but continued performing with his left hand after he returned to Austria. Maurice Ravel composed his famous Piano Concerto for the Left Hand for Wittgenstein, who could have been among the men Anderson accompanied to Germany.

Anderson's skills and knowledge helped turn Hilma's art in a new direction. She spoke fluent German, the language of Steiner and his Anthroposophical Society, and she translated many of Hilma's writings from Swedish. She was trained in the biological sciences and in medicine, fields that interested the artist. Under Anderson's tutelage Hilma began to focus on botany. Instead of common names like "rose" and "lily" she began to use the Latin names of plants, listing their active substances and curative powers. Her studies were aided by specialized dictionaries, which can be found in her library.[5]

Life with Anderson seems to have brought the harmony she craved. She found in her down-to-earth friend her other half, her complement and dual soul, without having to experience the conflicts and disappointments that had always arisen in her relationships with Anna Cassel and Gusten Andersson. As in those relationships, Hilma took on the male role, this time under the name of Gidro. "You yourself are Gidro," she would write later, in the forties. "We can call the force Thomasine."[6]

The Armistice of November 11, 1918, officially ended the war, but neither Hilma nor Thomasine believed there would be a lasting peace. Thomasine recorded a grim prognosis in the first of a series of notebooks written in German:

> A new doctrine will arise, with selection as its core: everything which is physically weak must be disposed of, only those with normal physical abilities and intelligence will be helped forward. Strength, beauty, intelligence, and spiritual flexibility must prevail on earth. Animals will be seen as tools and mercilessly discarded when they are no longer useful. Behind these concepts are dark powers that want to convince people that the goal of a single lonely individual can be achieved.[7]

On a personal level, Hilma's move to Munsö caused such bad feelings among The Thirteen that the group dissolved. Sigrid Henström, who had recorded the debate between Hilma and Gusten Andersson two years before, sent a typewritten letter to the island from Stockholm on May 13, airing her grievances. It took her six pages to recount the many injuries Hilma had caused. Henström accused her of sticking her head in the sand and acting as if nothing had changed with her move to the lake house. "How is it supposed to work if we all want to be in the house together, as we used to?" she demanded. Hilma, she continued, was blind to her own selfishness and could see flaws only in others. The letter ended with a clean break. "For this reason we cannot see ourselves as your 'pupils.'"[8]

There was no answer from Hilma that we know of and no further notes that mention a conflict around the move. Much later the artist would admit that she had been the one who "tore [the group] apart." She had many "missteps" to make up for, she wrote in 1943, though without specifying what those might be.[9]

———

Thomasine, Hilma, and her mother, Mathilda, spent only one year together on Munsö; a last photograph from this period shows Mathilda and her daughter together (fig. 38). The artist puts a hand on the shoulder of the older woman with snow-white hair. Sunlight filters through the trees, making bright spots against the dark ground, the bench, the wooden house, and the women's clothing. The picture does not betray the nearly ninety-year-old woman's final decline. In November 1919, when it grew too cold for her in Furuheim, Mathilda moved in with her elder daughter, Ida Haverman, in the Stockholm suburb of Djursholm. She died there two months later, in January.[10]

Hilma and Thomasine continued to live on Munsö. Their friendship was like a boat sailing out to the open sea, the anchor chain severed. They did not meet with the other women, whose names disappear from the notes for several years. The artist wrote her next texts in German, with Anderson's help.

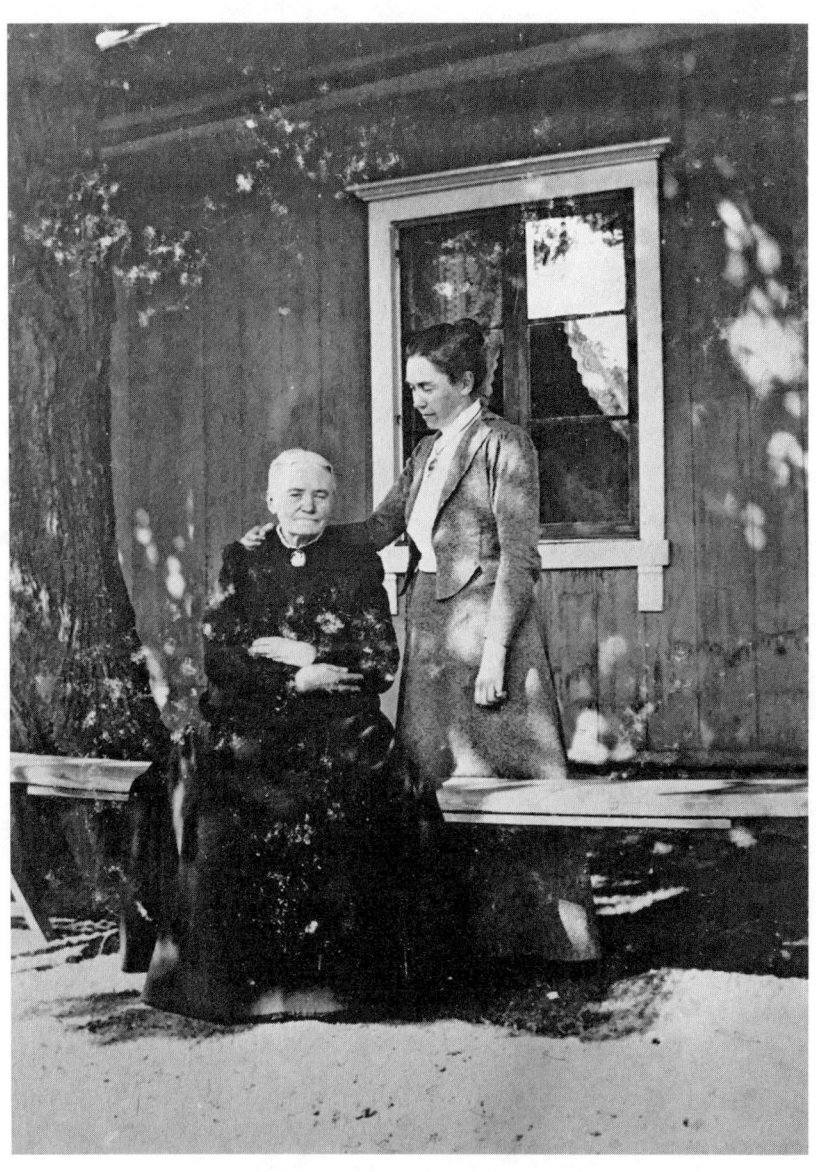

38. Hilma and her mother, Mathilda af Klint, on Adelsö, 1918,
Stiftelsen Hilma af Klints Verk.

PART FOUR

Dornach, Amsterdam, and London

The Suitcase Museum

From their base on the tiny island of Munsö, af Klint and Anderson began to direct their energies toward the wider world. This time the goal was not to broaden their own spiritual horizons, which already encompassed multiple universes and knowledge of previous lives, avatars, and the etheric body, but rather to focus on their immediate environment and to expand the reach of years of spiritual work.

Starting in 1919, a series of texts written in German testify to a great burst of optimism, which is reflected in their clarity. The previous texts by af Klint and her friends had mainly been spontaneous notes, many not converted into legible versions until the 1930s. Now, however, the artist began to write more deliberately. Her first German text is clean, with a title on the first page—"Thoughts of Hilma af Klint"—and a note: "Accompanied by a folder of drawings." It is dated "1.3 to 4.19.1919."[1]

There was a simple reason for the title page, the clear writing, the binding, the German language. The new writings were addressed to an audience that was German-speaking. Af Klint and Anderson had in mind the community that had settled in the Swiss town of Dornach, where the headquarters of the Anthroposophical Society—the Goetheanum, named by Rudolf Steiner after the German poet and scholar—was shortly to open. Af Klint followed the developments in Dornach from Sweden. Her archive contains two postcards from 1919. The first shows the wooden building of the Goetheanum in winter, along with the heating tower, a concrete building designed to look like a great flame. The second postcard shows the same buildings in summer: the trees are leafed out, the meadows are lush, and the domes gleam in the sunlight (fig. 39). A long row of workshops is also visible. Over several years, many volunteers had made their way to Dornach: sawing, sanding, carving, and hammering to help erect the building and outfit its interior.[2]

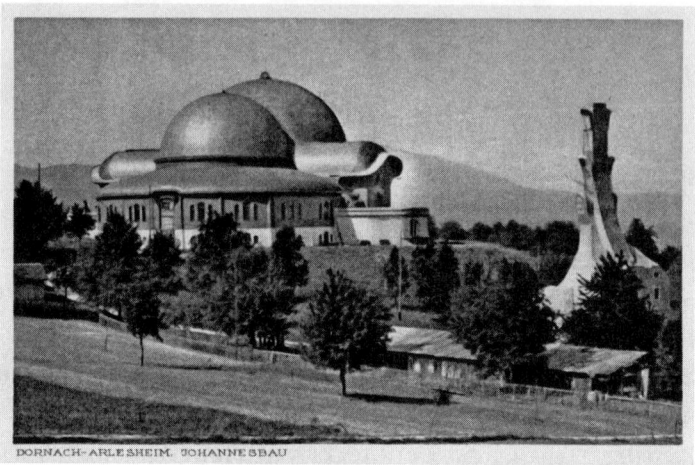

DORNACH-ARLESHEIM. JOHANNESBAU

39. Postcard from the Goetheanum.

In just a few years, Steiner had realized Hilma's long-standing dream. The vision of a spiritual center featured early in her notes, and the idea had been discussed among The Five as early as the 1890s; members of the Edelweiss Society also made plans for a stand-alone building early in their history.[3] Sometimes the word "temple" in Hilma's notes and those of The Five was a metaphor for the fixed place faith assumed in the heart or soul. Other times, the description in a notebook was concrete, with sketches and floor plans. The islands of Munsö and Adelsö are mentioned by the spiritual messengers as potential sites, and the first German notebook features a list of building materials: granite for the façade, alabaster for the interior. In another note Hilma wrote that the temple, "which keeps the pictures one day, should be built out of alabaster, this means be all white." On the front side of that paper she sketched the "studio building in the future": a large main house and two side wings, in the midst of meadows and trees. Using curved lines she drew a spiral facing the studio, marking the site as a force field.[4]

But over the course of 1919, she developed a new plan.[5] She made an appointment to meet with a photographer on Munsö. There on a dry early summer day, a camera was set up and paintings were

carried out of the studio and positioned on the north wall one by
one, out of direct sunlight. More than two hundred photographs
were made to document them, beginning with the series *Primordial Chaos*, through *The Ten Largest* and finally the *Altarpieces*.
The black-and-white images were then used to paint miniatures in
watercolor. After months of work, the desk in the studio supported
two towering stacks: photographs on one side, watercolors on the
other. The artist pasted them all into albums, on facing pages:
watercolors on the left and photographs on the right (see plates
3–5). Sometimes she enlarged details of the paintings, for example Saint George, who appears in a fluttering cape at the margin of
the page that features the seventh painting of the 1916 series *The
Dove*. The images are numbered consecutively from 1 to 189.[6] The
title page includes the dimensions and dates of the original works
as well as the attribution "by Hilma af Klint." These specifications
were written by Thomasine Anderson in red pen.

Together, the reproductions fill ten landscape-format albums
with dark blue bindings. Three more volumes contain reproductions of Anna Cassel's series from 1913.[7] Photographing. Copying.
Pasting. Labeling. Dating. Soon the *Paintings for the Temple* and
Anna Cassel's painted tale of the rose were available in miniature,
in a transportable and presentable format. The suitcase museum
could be packed in a car or carried on a train or ship. It was ready
for the journey to Dornach. Hilma could not have prepared better.
She had high hopes of winning Steiner's approval.

[2]

Flowers, Mosses, and Lichens

In addition to the suitcase museum, Hilma was working on some
other texts composed in German and accompanied by drawings and
watercolors. The war and its consequences had inspired the artist

to try to counter the destruction in some way. She felt it necessary to help life gain a foothold again. She writes: "where war has torn up plants and killed animals there are empty spaces which could be filled with new figures, if there were sufficient faith in human imagination and the human capacity to develop higher forms."[1] The title pages of the German notebooks reference the drawings that accompany the text, images that often resemble the charts used to illustrate science textbooks. Perhaps the fact that the works resemble scientific illustrations can be traced to Thomasine Anderson's influence. In any case, she is responsible for the captions and explanations written in pencil in a fine script. All of these works testify to the same impulse that produced the suitcase museum. Af Klint was ready to show her work in public and to explain it as far as she could. With Anderson's help, she felt ready to take this step.

What did the artist wish to tell the public? The message was the same as in previous years, but there was now a new portal to the insights. Instead of séances or spiritual gatherings, nature was key—immersion in nature was the first step in freeing oneself from a merely physical existence, the first step in transforming matter into spirit. The image of the rose returned; this time it was said to radiate golden particles that could fall upon people, who could then engage the original form of the plant and absorb its power. Af Klint writes: "The original form can be illustrated as a spiral that goes upward to search for new thoughts, and as a spiral that goes downward to search for new feelings."[2] The artist continued to work with the colors and forms she had used since 1906. But now the circles, squares, spirals, lines, and dots on the paper were more strongly interrelated; the connections ran clearly, step by step, through the images and texts. A spherical shape is labeled "hermaphrodite." The caption explains that "in the occult language," green, the color of the outermost ring in this image, is called "joy in life."[3] In the next image, the sphere is surrounded by a gold ring, resembling a coat of arms, and af Klint explains: "The realization of life is concealed in the realization of human dichotomy, in the law of completion."[4]

During the war, the artist had planned to systematically explore the interconnections in nature. "First I will attempt to understand the flowers of the earth," she wrote in a note from January 1917, ending the passage with "finally I will penetrate the forest, exploring the silent mosses, the trees, and the many animals that inhabit the cool, dark undergrowth."[5]

She recorded the results of these endeavors in April 1919, in a notebook titled "Flowers, Mosses, and Lichens." The first entry deals with liverwort, which grows in the shadows of trees on the forest floor. "Joy" is the feeling she associates with the plant. On the following pages, she describes and draws the force fields that she saw emanating from roses and sunflowers, from waved forkmoss and sac fungi. Love, submission, modesty, and despotism: everything human had a counterpart in the vegetal world. The "resistance of the flesh" could be overcome through thought, she wrote. Consideration of the plant world would give us insight into the composition of our own beings. "The characteristic of the flower soul is the speed within the emotional life and the freedom of the body." Since the soul of a flower was bound to no body, humans could absorb it into themselves.[6]

Colors gleam on the paper: gold and silver as well as red, yellow, blue, violet, and green (see plates 39 and 40). The drawings seem to hover over the pages, so fine are the pencil lines that outline the forms, with arrows, dots, squares, and circles. "Flowers, Mosses, and Lichens" brings together two traditions: it is a nature handbook illustrated with diagrams, like a scientific work, and the beauty of the images invites the viewer to dwell on them with quiet devotion, like a book of hours.

By studying nature, af Klint said, her readers could "rise to the heights of thought without fear of former fallacies," to turn inward and sense "the force within oneself."[7] Microcosm and macrocosm were connected, and in constant interaction. The artist writes: "Behind the effervescent force of the plant is concealed the warmth of feeling, behind the mobility of the animal lies the force of thought. Thought and feeling are united in the gravity of the stone."[8] Af Klint and Thomasine Anderson began to pack for their journey to Dor-

nach. The miniature museum in the blue albums was laid in suitcases with the German writings. The artist would bequeath three
notebooks to the Goetheanum, including the manuscript "Flowers,
Mosses, and Lichens." For months, the two women had been exuberant. "Joy in life" comes up regularly in the writings, a concept that
seems to have been shaping Hilma's thinking. She compared her
images to cells: they were "evidence of human liveliness" and were
driven by the same force that promoted growth in nature.[9]

Considering "Flowers, Mosses, and Lichens," who could doubt
her view? Insight was a positive experience: anyone could learn to
take joy in their position in the universe. From this beginning, anything was possible. "The livelier the vibration of the thoughts," af
Klint writes, "the more flexible life on earth becomes, anyone will
be able to work on matter with their imagination."[10]

The two Swedish women could hardly wait to go to work on
Dornach.

[3]

First Visit to the Goetheanum

In September 1920, Hilma and Thomasine set off on their first trip
to Switzerland.[1] Hilma's mother had died at the beginning of the
year, leaving her children a small inheritance, issued in equal shares
to Hilma, Ida, and Gustaf. Each received nearly 8,000 crowns. For
Hilma, the money was more than welcome, both for daily living
expenses and for the trip to Switzerland.[2] Her mother's death meant
that her time was her own again for the first time in years. There
was nothing to prevent her leaving Sweden. On the other hand, losing her mother raised larger questions. What was the relationship
of life to death? What happens once a person departs this world?
As Mathilda lay dying, Hilma had painted a new series comparing the major world religions, from Buddhism through Judaism to
Christianity and Islam. The series, *The Current Standpoint of the*

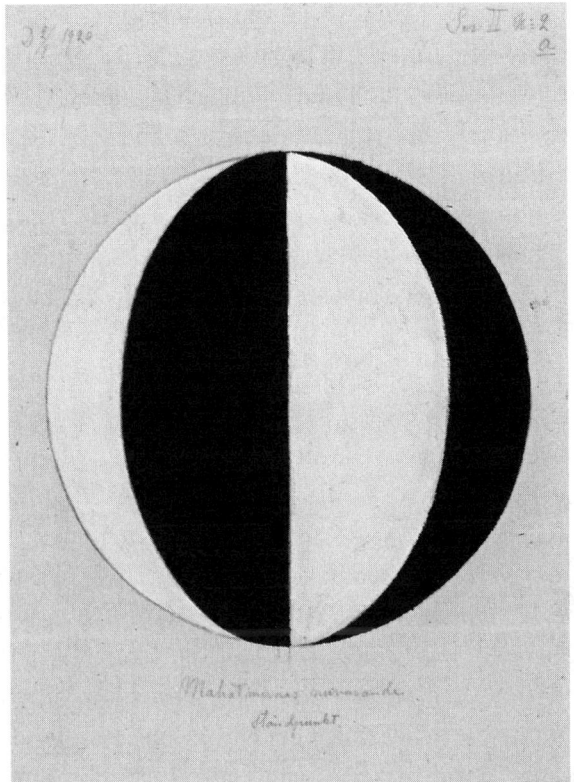

40. *The Current Standpoint of the Mahatmas, No. 2a*, 1920, oil on canvas, 36.5 x 27 cm, Stiftelsen Hilma af Klints Verk, HaK 469.

Mahatmas, consists of works that alternate white and black, as if to express death and life in consecutive incarnations (fig. 40).[3]

The two friends arrived in Dornach after the grape harvest, when the fall leaves were beginning to turn. They would come to know the town in all seasons: in spring, when the wisteria bloomed in the warm Upper Rhine; in summer, when it could be hot and humid, with everything covered in haze; in winter, when snow fell and Christmas trees were decorated in nearby Basel.

The friends rented a place in Arlesheim, a suburb of Basel that was close to Dornach and connected to it by train and tram lines. One of the first things they did was apply for membership in the

Anthroposophical Society, which was quickly granted.[4] They were hardly the only ones to come to Dornach to meet Steiner and see the unusual architecture. Much had been written about the buildings, and the plethora of reports and reviews made the Goetheanum a magnet, attracting visitors in droves. There were already plans to expand the train station, and the prices for guest rooms in town had risen. There were now several apartment buildings on the hill, designed in the style of the Goetheanum complex, but they were reserved for employees.

When the two women arrived, they may have asked where they could find Steiner. They likely would not have received an answer but instead information on when he would be lecturing and how to get tickets. They probably would have understood that it wasn't possible for the great scholar to welcome them in person. Anyway, there was no cause for hurry, not in a place like this, where everything they saw seemed to confirm their beliefs. Great meadows spread around the Goetheanum with beautiful grasses, flowers, and mosses. Hills and woods rose in the distance, with imposing rocks. The sky above displayed hundreds of stars; the artist drew them on a map along with the signs of the zodiac. (She herself was a Scorpio.)[5] Stars, animals, plants, and rocks mattered: they were the heart of everything. Nature was filled, as it were, with millions of tiny ladders to a higher, spiritual world, and it was af Klint's plan to bring what she saw as this news to Dornach. "Flowers, Mosses, and Lichens" records her insights in word and image. Immersing oneself in the natural world was the first step, the first rung of the ladder.

At the Goetheanum, she likely learned about another artist: Edith Maryon (1872–1924), an English sculptor. For the past several years, Maryon had worked with Rudolf Steiner, primarily on a group of large sculptures in his studio, mere steps from the Goetheanum. One story about Maryon attracted particular interest in Dornach: Steiner had nearly fallen from a three-story scaffolding in the studio, but Maryon had steadied him at the last moment, saving his life.

Since then, Steiner had considered their collaboration to be fated and described himself as "karmically connected" to Maryon. He put his complete trust in her, giving her free rein in artistic choices. "What she does, I do," he is quoted as having said of their working relationship.[6] In 1923, Steiner named Maryon director of the Fine Arts section of the Goetheanum, but she died of tuberculosis before she could step into the role.

Edith Maryon was not Steiner's only artist. "You are my hands," he told the painters commissioned to execute the ceiling in Dornach, including the Danish artist Baron Arild Rosenkrantz. Rosenkrantz was a confidant of Steiner and vividly described their collaboration in retrospect. Every elaboration, he recalled, was subject to Steiner's corrections; often everything was rejected outright and had to be started over. As to the paintings inside the small dome of the Goetheanum, Rosenkrantz remembers:

> The texture of the colours gave us painters great difficulties. No one quite understood what Rudolf Steiner desired. When half of the small cupola had been finished by the five painters, he had gradually to wash out everything that had been done and paint himself again to show how the colours had to be laid as a veil over each other. So here, as well, was a quite new technique, and a very difficult one. . . . Rudolf Steiner said that the technique is the initiation of the artist.[7]

Did af Klint know how many other artists there were in Dornach? Did she see them as competition? In her notebooks, she treats the art produced at the Goetheanum just as she treated most works by her contemporaries: without a word. There are no sketches or notes about *The Representative of Humanity*, the eight-meter-tall group of sculptures Maryon and Steiner were working on. Nor does she mention the ceiling paintings in the domed hall. She did sketch the Goetheanum's stained-glass windows,[8] but that's where she left it. She seems to have had no desire to join the ranks of artists who worked tirelessly on the Goetheanum. Each artist, it was later said, worked in the belief that "he was the only one who really understood the great Doctor and who worked according to his ideals."[9] Af Klint did not count herself among them.

The Swedish artist had a quite different view of her role in all this. She wished to work with Steiner as an equal. She was ready to make her life's work available to the Goetheanum as a complete cycle, all 193 *Paintings for the Temple*, which she had brought with her in miniature to show Steiner.

During her first visit, she never managed to speak to Steiner personally. His name does not appear in the notebook from October 1920, nor does Dornach or the Goetheanum. The notes close with a reference to a work of her own, a delicate-colored drawing of four snail shells, enclosed by circles, squares, triangles, and an oval. Globules rise like thought bubbles. It was unlike any kind of art being produced in Dornach.[10]

The two women departed on October 26, resolving to return soon.[11]

[4]

"Belongs to the Astral World According to Doctor Steiner"

It was another year before the women returned to Dornach. This time they arrived in December 1921, when the Munsö lake house was cold and uninviting. Furuheim had not been built for winter living, and the studio was even worse. During their second visit to Dornach, Hilma and Thomasine stayed six months, until June 1922, when the weather turned warm. On their first visit, they had worked on their notes and small drawings[1] and then, back in Sweden, had immersed themselves in Steiner's writings, even copying out several texts. One notebook features Anderson's transcription of a lecture on art. Naturalism was the wrong way, he argued, "no imitation of nature has ever achieved nature."[2] True art, he said, reveals the world of the spirit. People lose contact with the transcendental when they forget the time between death and rebirth, including previous incarnations. Thus most viewers understand spiritual art about as much as a dog understands human language. Just as a dog hears speech and understands it as barking, most people perceive only the material world in art. Af Klint must have felt understood by Steiner when she read those lines.

And perhaps the age of materialism was coming to an end. Signs were pointing to change not only in Dornach but in the wider world. Sweden was now led by a social democrat: Hjalmar Branting, a serious man roughly Hilma's age. Another social democrat had taken the reins in Germany. Friedrich Ebert would serve as the first president of the German Reich until his death in 1925. In Switzerland, women were still denied the vote, but this was of little significance at the Goetheanum, where the sexes were treated equally, with identical rights and responsibilities.

Af Klint's sympathies had been with the political left since 1906, when she had compared the beginning of her unusual artistic work to the upheavals in Russia. "It is easier for a Bolshevik to absorb the sunlight than it is for the average dominated person," she wrote shortly after World War I as the November Revolution raged in Germany.[3] Her library contained a copy of Jack London's *The People of the Abyss*, which had recently appeared in Swedish. The American writer's ambitious reportage on the slums of London was a passionate rebuttal of the capitalist system, for which af Klint also had no taste. The pursuit of riches and possessions was alien to her—another reason she felt at home in Dornach. The "noise of the world" fell silent in the face of calm, she wrote in 1919.[4]

The Anthroposophists valued an ascetic lifestyle; they prized moderation, calm, meditation. Nudism and unbridled sexuality did not figure into Steiner's experiment, in contrast to earlier Swiss reform colonies like Monte Verità on Lake Maggiore, on the border with Italy, where many Theosophists had settled around 1900.[5] In Monte Verità, voluptuous physicality was celebrated, but in Dornach, spiritualization was the goal. Dancers performed in flowing clothing with long sleeves in a form of movement art called Eurythmy, involving controlled physical release.

Hilma's long-awaited meeting with Steiner probably occurred in 1922. The artist had again brought all ten volumes of her suitcase museum (see plates 3–5) as well as photographs, which she was prepared to give Steiner should he wish to study her work further. The painter and her friend wanted to remember every word of the great scholar's reaction in order to record it later in the notebooks. In fact, Steiner limited his feedback to four comments. They are given here in full:

"No. 13, 14, 15, 16, 17, 18, and 19 are described by Doctor Steiner as the best symbolically," Hilma wrote of the *Primordial Chaos* series in the first of the blue albums.

"Book 6 belongs, according to Doctor Steiner, to one grouping," she wrote in the second volume.

"Belongs to the astral world according to Doctor Steiner" is the comment on *The Ten Largest* in the fourth volume.

"A figurative painting belongs to this work (it is in the studio). It is called *Human Chastity*. See the notes from 1920 according to Doctor Steiner p. 47." This note is found in the tenth and final volume of the blue albums.[6]

There were also the comments Steiner had made in 1910. Hilma kept every one of them, written on small scraps of paper no larger than candy wrappers. One has been glued into a notebook.[7] That is either all Steiner could say or all he wished to say. Af Klint mistakenly saw it as the beginning of a significant engagement with her work, the first provisional comments, which would be followed by more. But her hope for a deeper exchange was never fulfilled.

The notebooks in which the two women recorded the Dornach lectures include more than a hundred pages, densely written and frequently accompanied by drawings. The themes are wide-ranging. Anderson delved into Gregor Mendel's theory of genetics. Af Klint dedicated herself to Steiner's lectures on art, some of which she heard in Dornach, others she read. Steiner spoke of the ideal painter who guided the soul into outer space. "His work unites mankind with heaven," Hilma wrote on February 24, 1922. While in Dornach, she needed only to take a tram to visit works by the Old Masters, which were the primary subjects of Steiner's lectures. It took less than twenty minutes to reach the Kunstmuseum Basel with its collection of paintings by Cranach, Holbein, Breughel, Rubens, and Rembrandt. In Steiner's texts, af Klint also encountered the ideas of Johann Wolfgang von Goethe, in particular his work on color theory. "Goethe begins where physics ends," she wrote.[8]

In 1922 she painted more than seventy watercolors, creating the series *On the Viewing of Flowers and Trees*. The paintings are an attempt to capture the ancient image of plants, the original form and immanent color. This idea also owes much to Goethe, who assigned colors moods and human faculties, from reason to imagination. Red predominates in the works from this year (see plate 41).

Hilma used a different technique for these paintings and for most that followed. She prepared paper by wiping it with a moist sponge, so that when paint was applied, it would run and take on a life of its own. This wet-on-wet method was recommended by Steiner, and it suited her.[9] For years she had suffered from pain in her hands, and it was easier to paint in a way that left some things to chance.[10]

She may also have taken to heart one of Steiner's core principles: Steiner wanted to free painting from the tyranny of line; it was to be completely color. One must "be very careful to paint out of the color when painting," Thomasine noted from one of his lectures, "not out of line, because the line lies in painting." For the first time, lines disappear from af Klint's paintings.[11]

The Fire and the Letter

Hilma and Thomasine left Dornach in June and returned again in December. They wanted to spend that Christmas and New Year's enjoying the festivities at the Goetheanum. A dance performance was held on New Year's Eve, accompanied by a lecture by Steiner. When Steiner took the stage in his black suit that evening to talk about the tasks of humanity, every seat in the domed hall was filled. He called upon the audience to bring the euphoria of new beginnings into the coming year, as "the mood of the beginning of a new era, of the uprising of new life." If enough people were ready to participate, a cosmic New Year could begin.[1]

The event was over by ten o'clock, in keeping with the Anthroposophical ideal of moderation. The audience returned to their dwellings, and the lights slowly went out on the hill. A few people took the tram into Basel to take part in festivities there. When the bells chimed midnight in the city and fireworks were set off, it took several minutes before the crowd gathered in front of the cathedral realized why the outlines of the rooftops and towers of the city suddenly stood out against a "blood-red background," as a newspaper later reported. The night sky glowed to the south, from the direction of Dornach. The Goetheanum was burning.

We do not know where Hilma and Thomasine were as the flames raged on the hillside; they do not mention the fire in their notes.[2] The catastrophe lasted hours. The stained-glass windows shattered. The domes collapsed. The iron girders glowed and crumbled. Everything turned to ash. The stage, the chairs, the columns, the curtains, the carvings, the great ceiling paintings. A decade of work lay in ruins. Only the concrete foundation remained.

It took a few weeks to determine that the blaze may not have been an accident but the work of an arsonist. The fire seems to have

started between two walls in the center of the Goetheanum, allowing it to gain strength before the first smoke was observed. By the
time the alarm sounded and the firefighters arrived, the blaze was
raging and little could be done. In the aftermath, a man's charred
body was found who turned out to be a clockmaker from Arlesheim
who had recently joined the Anthroposophists. He was viewed as a
prime suspect, but, in truth, the actual circumstances surrounding
the fire could never be ascertained.

Hilma and Thomasine remained in Dornach until mid-January,
then departed for Sweden. They did not return for more than a year.
Just a few months after the fire, Steiner published plans for a new
building. The new Goetheanum was to be larger than the first, more
robust and stable, and built of concrete rather than wood.

Hilma took a break upon returning to Munsö. The archive contains no images from 1923, but at the start of the new year, she tried
to make up for lost time, creating over a hundred watercolors, some
in Sweden, some in Switzerland. The new work increasingly incorporated human organs and body parts: the kidneys, heart, navel,
and larynx.[3]

Since Steiner was preoccupied with plans for the new building,
Hilma adopted a new tactic for engaging him. Instead of hoping
their conversation would unfold naturally, she wrote him a letter
with her most pressing questions. She drafted the letter in German
without Thomasine's help:

1) First I must ask you: what should I do with all of my large paintings
    in Sweden?

    Can they be used by the Anthroposophical Society? I myself do
    not have the insight to explain the paintings. If you, Doctor, do not
    come to Sweden, perhaps it would be better to burn them?

    The first two parts you saw a long time ago, and you have pho-
    tographs of them, but afterward I made two large parts in addition
    which are a continuation of the first works.

    I was given these images by powers that I believe are good, but
    I think only you, Doctor, can decide whether it is appropriate to

entrust these paintings to the Anthroposophical Society in Sweden, or is it usable here.

2) For myself, I ask you to tell me whether it could be possible to overcome the great obstacle that my hardened muscles have provided
me with.

3) Perhaps I would also like to ask you whether it is right to use the
healing powers that are in my hands if I wish to help someone
physically.[4]

This version of the letter was never sent. By the time the women
boarded the train in Sweden, took the ferry and then another train
to arrive finally at the station in Arlesheim, the letter had shrunk to
a single sentence written in Thomasine's hand. A perforated piece
of grid paper served as a letterhead, dated April 24, 1924:

Doctor Steiner:

Should the paintings executed by me between 1906 and 1920, of
which you, Doctor, once saw several, be destroyed, or can they be
used somewhere?

Very respectfully yours,
Hilma af Klint[5]

Steiner did not write back, but he seems to have replied to Hilma
orally, with good news. When she and Thomasine packed their lug-
gage to travel back to Sweden, they were in an optimistic mood. At
the end of the year the artist gave a lecture at the Anthroposophical
Society in Stockholm and told the audience what Steiner had said:
"The answer was that it would be a shame to destroy it, and that
it could be used and is useful. As previously mentioned: the time
should now be right to communicate so much of the work's content
that individual members of the society may be able to take an interest in considering it in the place where it is located."[6] The answer
did not solve the most urgent problem of where and how her huge
body of work could be permanently accommodated. Nevertheless,

Steiner's reaction could be interpreted as a positive sign. He did not help her find a home for the paintings, but he did advise her to keep the work. He may have sensed that the friends would not actually destroy the paintings but rather had mentioned the possibility of doing so to pressure him to answer. Hilma later interpreted his statement to mean that her work should find its place in Scandinavia. According to Steiner, she wrote, it was "worth being kept in the North."[7]

Steiner never considered including the paintings in the new building. Still, Hilma received more encouragement than did many other great minds, who failed to elicit any response at all. Walter Gropius, director of the Bauhaus in Weimar, invited Steiner to teach at the

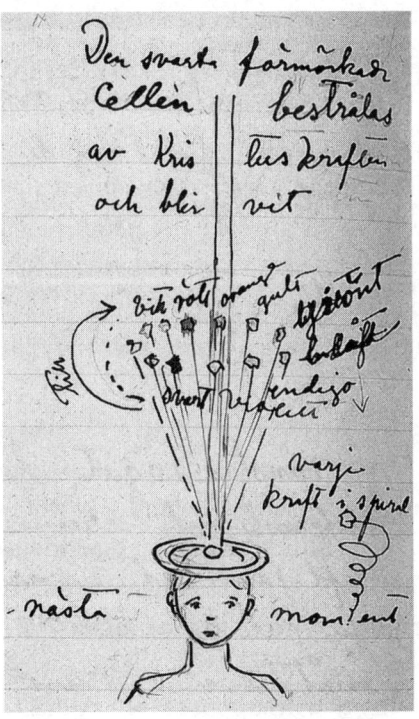

41. Notebook page from 1924, detail,
Stiftelsen Hilma af Klints Verk, HaK 1044.

school but never heard back. Piet Mondrian, the Dutch artist and co-founder of De Stijl, wrote a manifesto and sent it to Steiner. This too received no answer.[8]

In September 1924, af Klint and Anderson packed their suitcases and returned to Sweden. Back home in Munsö, the artist renewed contact with her spiritual guides, specifically Amaliel, who now called himself an "apprentice of the Boddhisatva." Af Klint's notebook from the period contains drawings that deal with the effect of colors on the soul and look like little comic strips (fig. 41).[9]

That same year, Steiner fell gravely ill. By the time the women returned to Dornach in April of 1925, Steiner had died.

[6]

Amsterdam

After years of waiting and hoping, Hilma suffered a crisis when Rudolf Steiner died. Nothing had been resolved: Steiner had offered vague encouragement but no real help. Hilma and Thomasine were still on their own with a large group of paintings that needed an audience and a permanent home.

They continued to visit Dornach, and they joined the Rudolf Steiner Society, which was organized soon after Steiner's death. It was led by Albert Steffen (1884–1963), who also became chair of the General Anthroposophical Society. The Swedish women were accepted into the society in 1926 when they were in Switzerland, this time staying at the Kölliker House, a guesthouse run by a house painter and his family. The address suggests that they had been relegated to the periphery of the Goetheanum and were not welcome in the inner circle.[1]

Hilma kept trying to win support for her work from the Anthroposophists. A notebook contains the names and addresses of painters at the Goetheanum, such as Maria Strakosch-Giesler and Louise van Blommestein,[2] suggesting she may have tried to make contact with them, hoping to gain acceptance. A copy of "Flowers, Mosses, and Lichens" was produced, probably by Thomasine; the women gave the original to the Goetheanum, where it went into the Dornach archive along with two other notebooks.[3] The *Tree of Knowledge* watercolor series of 1913 was also produced in duplicate in the same dimensions and media as the original; one set went to the Goetheanum, specifically to Albert Steffen, and af Klint kept the other.[4] She also donated some flower paintings, suggesting they be published in the *Goetheanum*. The answer was a long time coming. When it arrived, it was not from Steffen but from a member of his staff. The first sentence speaks volumes: "It has been a long time," the letter begins, "since you have not heard from me."[5] The phrasing is a slip, of course—the author meant to write "since you have heard from me"—but it confirms the vacuum in which Hilma found herself. No exchange. No answers. Nothing, for a long time. The letter declined the opportunity to publish the flower paintings but said they would be added to the library, where anyone interested could view them. Hilma was tilting at windmills.

Or was she? She was sixty-four years old but had not lost the ability to think in terms of beginnings rather than endings. Every rejection signaled a fresh start. One project invariably led to the next, and she was always ready to venture into new territory: in this she had not wavered since accepting the first painting assignment from the spirits many years before.

In 1927, it seemed her long-held dream just might come true. She met someone who was excited about her paintings, and just when the Goetheanum's doors had slammed shut for good. For once, she did not have to decide for herself how best to proceed. Someone else now offered to take charge, a Dutch woman named Peggy Kloppers-Moltzer (1881–1930), who wrote: Come visit me in Amsterdam, dear Miss af Klint![6]

In November the painter boarded a train to Holland. She had written essential Dutch words in her notebook. *Ontbijt* meant "breakfast," *boek* was "book," *Gracht*, "canal."[7] Hilma saw the slim figure of her new friend waiting on the platform as the train pulled in. Kloppers-Moltzer was a dancer and actress who performed under the stage name Else van Duyn. The two women had first met in Dornach. Kloppers-Moltzer had been there in connection with Eurythmy, an expressive art form developed by Steiner and his second wife. She was also on the board of the Anthroposophical Society in Amsterdam. During their time together in Dornach, she and Hilma had gone through the ten-volume suitcase museum with the *Paintings for the Temple*. Kloppers-Moltzer felt an immediate rapport. "The reproductions created a bond of friendship between us," she later wrote.[8] She understood that the images needed an audience. Moreover, Kloppers-Moltzer had a comrade in arms, another Dutch Anthroposophist, Adelyde Content. Together the women came up with a plan to borrow the museum in a suitcase to show to people in Holland. In April 1927 Content reported proudly in a letter that Album 5 had been passed around the audience in The Hague during one of her lectures.[9]

Kloppers-Moltzer approached the Anthroposophical Society in Amsterdam about sponsoring a show of Hilma's work. She concurrently contacted the editors of *Wendingen*, an art and architecture publication similar to *De Stijl*, the other Dutch avant-garde magazine.

Many contributors to *Wendingen* were sympathetic to Theosophy or Anthroposophy, and Kloppers-Moltzer had connections to the editors. The range of themes covered by *Wendingen* must have pleased af Klint: the magazine championed a holistic approach and published on the latest advances in design, science, and technology and even some spiritual content. The magazine juxtaposed the old and the new—a Remington typewriter alongside cult sites in Java, a modern thermos bottle and Russian icons. In 1925, the magazine devoted several consecutive issues to the visionary architect Frank Lloyd Wright.[10]

It was probably Kloppers-Moltzer who introduced af Klint to one of the magazine's most important contributors, Samuel Jessurun de Mesquita (1868–1944), an artist and graphic designer. When af Klint arrived in Amsterdam, he was working on the cover design for an issue devoted to Sweden.[11] It seemed likely that he could have some ideas on how to draw attention to Hilma's work. Hilma wrote down his name, with "exhibitor" next to it. On another page of the same notebook she made a little sketch that could be a portrait of de Mesquita[12] with dark curly hair and a beard; de Mesquita once drew a similar self-portrait. He taught at the art school in Haarlem, where M. C. Escher was one of his pupils. Escher would later try to help de Mesquita when Hitler's military took control of Amsterdam. De Mesquita was Jewish, like Peggy Kloppers-Moltzer's husband, an actor who also wrote for *Wendingen*.[13]

Hilma's time with the Klopperses was packed. She recorded the names and addresses of new acquaintances, along with tips on books to read and museums to visit. It is in the Amsterdam notebook that the name "Kandinsky" appears for the first time. "Kandinsky, pure colors, planes," she wrote. "In Russia there are several artists which live in color. Tatlin, Oswald."[14]

Kloppers-Moltzer had a flair for the dramatic and wore eccentric "rational" clothing so unusual that the Dutch queen was said to have once leaned out of her carriage to get a better look as the dancer walked past.[15]

The Klopperses lived a few minutes from the Rijksmuseum with its world-famous collection of Rembrandts.[16] Hilma spent hours there, sketching a Rembrandt painting of an old woman reading the Bible. The woman's hands touch the book tenderly. "First picture of his mother," she noted next to her sketch.[17] The motif fascinated her; she sketched another version of a Bible reader by Gerard Dou, a pupil of Rembrandt's. Perhaps the paintings reminded her of her own mother, or perhaps she saw herself in the religious devotion of the women.

She sketched other Old Masters at the Rijksmuseum: works by Anthony van Dyck, Gerard ter Borch, Bartolomeo Montagna, and Samuel van Hoogstraten. The notebook also has a sketch of a painting by El Greco, the Spanish mannerist so revered by Kandinsky and Franz Marc that they included him in the Blaue Reiter's *Almanac*. El Greco's stretched figures look like souls flying to heaven.[18]

The artist did not stay with the Klopperses, but at the Hotel Pomona in The Hague. The Pomona served vegetarian fare and enjoyed a fine reputation in reform circles since the philosophers Bertrand Russell and Ludwig Wittgenstein had met there to discuss the manuscript of Wittgenstein's *Tractatus logico-philosophicus*. The conversation had hinged on the limits of logic and philosophy, which Wittgenstein would later summarize in his famous sentence "Whereof one cannot speak, thereof one must be silent."[19] Hilma saw things differently. She knew from personal experience that there were phenomena that couldn't be put into words. But the place where philosophy and language fell silent was where art began. What could not be said could be painted—and the attempt to do so had been her task for many years.

When she left Amsterdam in mid-December, she and Kloppers-Moltzer had still not found an audience for the paintings. But even though talks with the Anthroposophists and the editors of *Wendingen* had not led to an exhibition, Hilma was anything but disappointed. The trip had encouraged her, and she began to look into the possibility of mounting a show in Sweden, in Malmö or Lund. She noted down rental prices, availability, and dimensions of exhibition spaces.[20]

The return trip from Amsterdam took her not to Munsö but to Uppsala, the old university town north of Stockholm, where Hilma and Thomasine now rented an apartment. The rheumatism in Hilma's hands was exacerbated by the cold, wet winter at Furuheim. The women would return to the island only when it grew warmer.[21]

[7]

London

Back in Amsterdam, Peggy Kloppers-Moltzer discovered it was not only the Dornach Anthroposophists who had reservations about af Klint's work, but the Dutch ones as well. The exploratory conversations did not go well, but before the proposal could be definitively rejected, Kloppers-Moltzer backed off and developed a new one. She was no more interested in endings than her Swedish friend was—she wanted progress. Her new idea was London. "As far as I understand," she wrote Hilma on January 2, 1928, "it should be no problem for you to exhibit whatever you want at the World Conference."[1] The women corresponded in German.

The World Conference on Spiritual Science was to be held in London that July, bringing together the national branches of the Anthroposophical movement for the first time. The event was organized by the Anthroposophical Society in England, which had taken such a long time to establish, it seemed as though Steiner's teachings would never catch on there. Edith Maryon, the sculptor who had saved Steiner's life, blamed the sluggishness on the fact that the English—English men in particular—had strong conformist tendencies. In a letter to Steiner, she had written: "Men in England are difficult to acquire without special effort. They will go to a lecture at the 'British Institution,' since everyone else does, or to a 'football match' or other sporting event. Aside from such events they are afraid of anything new, they worry they might be thought odd. . . . They do not wish to step outside of the flock of ordinary people."[2] The women were better, Maryon continued: they were more curious and open to new things.

By 1928, the Anthroposophical Society in England had a large enough following to host the international conference. Few members of the English branch had met Steiner, and they hoped that in hosting the event they could cultivate relationships with those who had known him personally and witnessed his work at the Goetheanum. Peggy Kloppers-Moltzer was on the organizing committee, responsible for the contribution of the Dutch branch. Since she spoke fluent English, she took the opportunity to lobby for af Klint. Photographs of the artist's work were sent to London.

Her prediction that there would be no problem arranging a show proved overly optimistic. The response from England was that, regrettably, it would *not* be possible to exhibit af Klint's works, whereupon the Dutch matron sat down at her desk and typed out the conference announcement word for word to remind the organizers of their original vision. She indicated she would have to "consider it a mistake" to exclude af Klint, and added that she had already made several prominent people aware that the London group was falling short of expectations. Dr. Zeylmans, the general secretary of the Anthroposophical Society in the Netherlands, had been informed, for instance. Her tone was even but determined. She left no room for doubt that she would make trouble, if necessary.[3]

An answer came quickly. A possibility had been found, the letter said in a conciliatory tone. But there were still concerns, which Kloppers-Moltzer parried effortlessly. The paintings weren't really Anthroposophical? That didn't matter; after all, Hilma's work was "begun in a time, that no Anthr. Society existed" and "ends in a full acknowledgment of the teachings of Dr. Steiner."[4] The paintings were too large and transport too difficult? Not a problem, transport and insurance would be taken care of.[5] Who would introduce the London audience to the paintings? This last objection came not from the organizers but from Hilma, who explained why she couldn't do it herself. First, she spoke no English. Second, "the works by me cannot be surveyed, they must be given to those persons who have striven" to draw a "line of connection from the inner world to the supernatural world."[6] Once again, Kloppers-Moltzer knew what to do. If the artist could not or would not interpret her paintings, she, Kloppers-Moltzer, would do it.

The artist had never received such support. More than two decades earlier, in February 1906, her spiritual guides had given her a few rules before she began the spiritual paintings. "One needs a friend at one's side," they had explained.[7] The painter had always had friends, she had never been alone. But Peggy Kloppers-Moltzer's dedication went beyond anything she had ever experienced.

The correspondence between the two women suggests they trusted each other implicitly. Once, when Kloppers-Moltzer didn't manage to write for several weeks, she excused herself with the words: "You must have thought: I was wrong about Frau Kloppers. She is not faithful!"[8] Af Klint answered: "I received your letter with the greatest pleasure. When Frau Kloppers has the chance—I thought—she will write. And I waited patiently. In general I feel when a person thinks of me and in what direction their thoughts go."[9]

To prepare for their joint appearance in London, Kloppers-Moltzer wished to come to Sweden. Hilma offered to pick her up at the train station in Uppsala, and together they would travel the hundred kilometers to the studio on Munsö. But fate intervened, and Kloppers-Moltzer had to cancel at the last minute; her mother was dying, and she would not be able to join Hilma in London, either. Hilma promptly sent condolences. The event had already gained so much momentum that it couldn't be canceled. On July 9, 1928, the paintings were loaded onto a steamship in Stockholm and taken to London. Shortly thereafter, the artist sent a postcard from London to Anna Cassel. Cassel had not been mentioned in the notebooks for years, yet the two seem to have still been friendly if not as close. Cassel was staying on Munsö at the time; the postcard was addressed to Furuheim. Hilma wrote ebulliently of her journey: "From Elm Lodge, Golders Green, London: Greetings to you and the Gierttas. We had a beautiful 4½ day crossing with the friendliest captain. He helped us with the automobile and now we are staying at a Dutch school, which I hope will be much cheaper than a hotel. Tomorrow we will be joined by Mrs. Merry, when we unpack the paintings, I assume."[10] Presumably "we" referred to herself and Thomasine. Kloppers-Moltzer had arranged lodging with a Dutch couple named de Vries who ran a school.

———

The program of the World Conference on Spiritual Science announced the opening of af Klint's exhibition on Wednesday, July 25, at four in the afternoon, which was to include an address by the artist (fig. 42).[11] She had requested a separate space because she did not want to participate in the large group exhibition organized by the Anthroposophists. She was granted "a room for from fifty to a hundred people."[12]

The conference lasted six days. Participants met in the Friends

Art

10.15 A.M. LARGE HALL. **Anthroposophy and the Artist.** BARON A. ROSENKRANTZ.

12 NOON. ART GALLERY.
Exhibitions of Goetheanum Paintings, by various Artists.

2.30 P.M. LARGE HALL. **The Artistic Use of Concrete.** M. WHEELER, M.A., F.R.I.B.A.

4 P.M. Exhibition of Paintings. MISS HILMA AF KLINT (Upsala). With an address.

5 P.M. LARGE HALL. **Music in East and West.** MR. ZAGWYN (Holland). At the piano :—Mr. JAN VAN DEN BERGH.

8.15 P.M. LARGE HALL. **The Evolution of Music in the light of Anthroposophy** (with musical examples). MISS JEANNE DE MARE.

8.15 P.M. RUDOLF STEINER HALL.
Demonstration of Eurhythmy by Artistes of the Goetheanum School of Eurhythmy, Dornach.

Thursday, July 26

Natural Science

10.15 A.M. LARGE HALL. **The Earth as an Organism.** DR. GÜNTHER WACHSMUTH, Secretary of the General Anthroposophical Society, Leader of the Science Section of the Goetheanum, Dornach.

12 NOON. LARGE HALL. **Spiritual Aspects of Astronomy.** FRL. DR. E. VREEDE, Leader of the Astronomical and Mathematical Section of the Goetheanum, Dornach.

3 P.M. LARGE HALL. **Experimental Researches into the Formative Forces of Nature** (illustrated by lantern slides). EHRENFRIED PFEIFFER. (In German. English translation by G. Kaufmann, M.A.)

5.30 P.M. RUDOLF STEINER HALL. Demonstration by the English students of the Rudolf Steiner School of Eurhythmy, London.

8.15 P.M. LARGE HALL. **Influences of the Stars on Earthly Substances** (Scientific experiments at the Biological Institute of the Goetheanum). Illustrated by Lantern Slides. L. KOLISKO.

42. Exhibition announcement for Hilma af Klint in the program of the World Conference on Spiritual Science, 1928.

House, a large, four-story brick building with an imposing columned façade. The building, owned by the Quakers, was centrally located on Euston Road, just a few steps from Euston Station. The British Library and British Museum were within walking distance. The leaders of the General Anthroposophical Society came from Dornach. Günther Wachsmuth, secretary and leader of the scientific section, gave a lecture on the earth as an organism. Elisabeth Vreede, leader of the astronomical and mathematical section, spoke on the spiritual aspects of astronomy. Albert Steffen, chair of the General Anthroposophical Society, had to back out at the last minute, so his welcoming address was read by a deputy.

During the conference, attendees were regaled with lectures on art, pedagogy, and medicine and introduced to innovations of all kinds. Eurythmic dances were performed to packed audiences, accompanied by instruments invented by the Anthroposophists. An exhibition of carvings and small sculptures by children deemed mentally and physically disabled by traditional doctors celebrated Steiner's method of curative education. By flying in the face of stereotypes and showing what the children could achieve, the show pointed out the narrowmindedness of conventional medicine. Anthroposophy could help society change for the better: this was the message of the exhibition.

The conference reportedly drew up to two thousand participants, with more than eight hundred crowding into the hall for some of the lectures. Daniel Nicol Dunlop (1868–1935), the Scottish Anthroposophist and chief organizer of the conference, was not fazed by the scale. International conferences were his specialty. A few years previously he had organized the World Power Conference in London, with experts from across the globe gathering to discuss sources of energy for the electricity on which industrialized nations now depended. The World Energy Council, which still exists, emerged from this conference.

Dunlop was a sober-looking man who parted his hair in the middle and wore glasses and a three-piece suit, avoiding any impression of spiritual remoteness. He was remarkably adept in fusing the spiritual and the practical; for him, energy was the key to all of it. He saw the power of energy working on many levels: in machines and people, flowing through wires and brains. His goal was to build an international union of nations based on new values. "The fact must be realized," he exhorted the participants, "that it does not pay in the long run to deal unfairly with any nation, and that the ultimate position of the victor may be worse than that of the vanquished."[13] Materialism and unbridled capitalism led to suffering, he explained. The time had come for a spiritual revolution.

———

The conference began on a Sunday. Three days later Hilma opened her exhibition. Addressing the guests, she explained the connections between her paintings and the Rosicrucians. We do not know precisely which paintings were shown, but the "enormous size: 2–3 m" mentioned in correspondence about the conference suggests they were from *Paintings for the Temple*. (One letter also mentions small works.)[14] Presumably, Hilma's lecture was translated as she spoke, but what she said we do not know. It must have been a challenge to explain what she had created—much of it was puzzling even to her.

The *Goetheanum* pronounced the conference a success, surmising that in view of the depth and breadth of the lectures, participants must have gone home satisfied.[15] There was not a word about af Klint.

The English magazine *Anthroposophy* reported the public enthusiasm for the conference and explicitly mentioned the "excellent little exhibition of Anthroposophical artists," organized by Baron Rosenkrantz, the Danish artist and disciple of Steiner who had helped paint the dome of the first Goetheanum. "In another room, Miss af Klint (Sweden) was showing her studies of Rosicrucian symbolism," the next sentence dutifully noted, but made no further comment.[16]

The day after af Klint's talk, *The Times* of London ran a review of the art exhibited at the conference. The anonymous critic referred to the color theory of Steiner and Goethe, specifically the idea that every color has a characteristic form. The works were based on this insight, the writer explained, then in the same paragraph found the paintings inconsistent: color and form were frequently in conflict, he said, as the naturalism avoided in the coloring often persisted in the representative forms. "We have a suspicion that . . . Steiner's principles are better adapted to non-representational art."[17]

Less representation, more abstraction—wasn't that precisely Hilma's approach? But the reviewer passed over her work just as others had done.

When the artist took down her paintings, packed them in crates, brought them to the harbor, and boarded the ship, nothing had changed. Despite her efforts and those of Peggy Kloppers-Moltzer, they had failed to create a buzz about the paintings, either in Amsterdam or in London. Many new ideas had been presented at the conference and enthusiastically received. But once more Hilma's work had been passed over, and she remained an outsider.

Perhaps it would have been different if Peggy Kloppers-Moltzer had been there. The sociable Dutch woman was used to dealing with artists and critics. She spoke English, and it would have been easy for her to cultivate new contacts. And in London there would have been plenty of like-minded people to meet beyond Anthroposophical circles: for even as Hilma was explaining to visitors that every person had both a masculine and a feminine side, just a few hundred meters away, at 52 Tavistock Place, the writer Virginia Woolf was wondering "whether there are two sexes in the mind corresponding to the two sexes in the body, and whether they also require to be united in order to get complete satisfaction and happiness." Like af Klint, Woolf believed in masculine and feminine aspects of the spirit, to be brought together. That text was published in her book *A Room of One's Own*. That same year, she would publish an unconventional novel, *Orlando*, the story of an English nobleman who could change his sex. Hilma certainly would have had something to say about that.[18]

She did not jot down any names or addresses in London, as she had in Amsterdam, and there are no surviving sketches from the trip. Such silence suggests she was acutely disappointed and wanted to forget the whole thing. On the other hand, she had at least one reason to celebrate: the month she was in London, the English parliament granted women the right to vote, despite the disapproval of Winston Churchill, then chancellor of the exchequer. The law gave the vote to more than five million English women.

Two years later, in April 1930, Hilma visited Dornach one last time. She was sixty-seven. The new, concrete Goetheanum building was finished; from a distance, it bore an uncanny resemblance to a human skull. It earned no mention in her notes from the trip, which amount to only a few comments on Anthroposophical artworks she saw in the studios. "Beautiful," or "Not beautiful," she noted, along with the names of the artists.[19] That was it. She was finished with Dornach. Debates on the direction of the society after Steiner's death had not calmed, and she was tired of it. "The fate of the Antr. Society is sealed," she wrote.[20]

She never saw Peggy Kloppers-Moltzer again. Her younger friend, admirer, and promoter had often mentioned in letters how exhausted she felt and now she was seriously ill. She died in April 1930 at the age of forty-eight. Marie Steiner, Rudolf's widow, wrote her obituary in the *Goetheanum*, ending mysteriously:

> Peggy Kloppers had to tame much in her life, repress much, transform much into the sustaining force of love. She will help us all on this path of breaking free.[21]

PART FIVE

Temple and Later Years

The Temple and the Spiral

Hilma and Thomasine spent the summer of 1930 on Munsö, and Hilma began to paint again. As far as we know, she had not produced a painting in four years. It may have been that her rheumatism had forced her to stop working, but she may also have been too busy. She had made several attempts to win a larger audience for her work: first in Dornach, then in Amsterdam, and finally in London. All had failed. The idea of renting an exhibition space in southern Sweden had also come to nothing. There is no further mention of any such plans in the notebooks; they seem to have been abandoned.

When the artist took up her paints and brushes again, her spiritual companions apparently rushed to her aid, as if they had been waiting for her hiatus to end. She painted waves and vibrations, the aura of flowers and the souls of plants, intertwining black and white snails, and historical figures. She painted primarily in watercolor, the colors bright and vibrant. Some works from this period are abstract, while others are representational. Early styles and themes returned. She began producing automatic drawings again in pencil, with the same jerky contours that typified those from twenty years before, when she had last undertaken such experiments. Then, she had sketched the long-legged man with the Phrygian cap (see fig. 25). Now Gustav V, the current king of Sweden, materialized on paper as an elongated figure, his heavy head bobbing on a thin neck. An accompanying note says that his wife, Victoria, had been the explorer Vasco da Gama in a previous incarnation. Notes about the automatic drawings also mention the king's personal physician, Axel Munthe.

These figures are joined by an uncanny-looking creature whose head resembles that of an embryo with an open fontanelle; its nose and mouth are flat. The ear, however, is fully developed, emerging from the head like a funnel. A winged creature blows a horn in the ear. Whatever comes from the horn—words, notes, or noises—penetrates to the oversized heart on the righthand side of the body, forming a connection like an umbilical cord. Does this reflect what af Klint felt? That she was fed and nourished from higher spheres, the way a placenta feeds a fetus? She dated the drawing August 7, 1930, but did not comment on the content.[1]

If af Klint had ever dreamed of uniting her two lives, she abandoned the hope in 1930. It was easy for her to switch between worlds, from the physical level to the astral. She was used to her abilities, even as their scope had broadened over the years. She heard voices, saw images with her inner eye, and was in contact with the souls of plants. She could look deep into herself or up to higher spheres; she remembered previous incarnations and possessed healing powers. It had all begun long ago when she had received a vision of two coffins just before her sister Hermina died. Contact with the spirit world continued while she was at the Academy, and 1891 brought her first experiences as a medium. Then came the Edelweiss Society, The Five, and the group of Thirteen. In hindsight, her development seems natural.

Yet she could never explain these experiences. That was the difficult part. Words failed to describe what seemed so natural. Her paintings offered insight into another world, but the source of revelation remained a mystery. Her spirit and hands created art, yet she did not understand the mechanism by which it all happened. When she had asked Rudolf Steiner what kind of beings she was in contact with, he had simply answered: "You don't ask that!"[2] She sometimes told this story as a placeholder for what she could not explain. Perhaps in such moments she wondered why people expected her to understand the process at all. In fact, what artist can truly understand how ideas develop in the mind and how they reach the canvas? Hilma was hardly the first one incapable of explaining their process.

Other than that, she had left no stone unturned in trying to find an audience. "We have a mission," she had written years before.[3] She had taken the mission seriously, understanding it as a logical extension of her primary task: making paintings. She sometimes recalled another prophecy, from 1906: that Anna would be "scorned," "but less than Hilma, who is called to lead the fight."[4]

Is it right to speak of the reactions to her works in terms of "scorn"? Artists who try new things or depart from the norm frequently meet with ridicule. Women have been particularly easy targets in the art world, especially when they were a minority. When the painter Sigrid Hjertén exhibited her work in Stockholm in 1918, the editor of the conservative art magazine *Strix* called her a "pure idiot." The models for her paintings came, he wrote, from the madhouse, and the paintings suggested their creator had a "perverse attraction to deformities."[5] The insults went unanswered, and soon a rumor circulated that Hjertén had gone insane.

The reactions to af Klint's paintings were hardly so fierce. No one had openly criticized her spiritual paintings at the first exhibition in Stockholm in 1913 or at the London show in 1928. In fact, she had received no attention at all. She and her works were ignored.

Af Klint had never expected to be understood by the art world per se. She had no ambition to exhibit at the Academy or in commercial galleries. She was not interested in buyers; she wanted an audience of seekers, people who would see in her paintings an alternative, a way out of materialism and toward "new thoughts" and "new feelings." She wanted to open people's eyes to the fact that life did not have to be merely quotidian, that the world was larger than what could be seen, that it was mutable and subject to transformation. Consciousness could determine being. Humankind could connect with the living spirit that she thought united all beings, from fauna to flora and even, as she pointed out several times, the mineral world. No one had to accept the cage of external reality. "The livelier the vibration of the thoughts," she had written in 1919, shortly before setting off for Switzerland the first time, "the more flexible life on earth becomes, anyone will be able to work on matter with their imagination."[6]

She did not know what would become of her large body of work, and over the years the question troubled her more and more. As the days grew shorter and fall turned to winter, the notebooks indicate that her spiritual companions turned in a different direction, as if they understood the loneliness of the task they had set for the artist and the heaviness of her burden. She was in crisis, but in December 1930 the spirits changed what felt like an ending into a beginning. The voices started coming to her again with new assignments; through the influence of her "inner sense organ," she wrote, she had drawn an image in the air that consisted of many small loops that came together in a circle. A message had followed the gesture in the form of a question: "Do you want to accept a task through your friends and guides, who are invisibly present?" In 1906 she had responded with an unequivocal "yes," but this time she was more cautious:

> If these guides are associated with Dr. Steiner and serve his beliefs and I am capable of accepting the task, I am willing to try.[7]

More notes came in rapid succession. Gregor, Amaliel, and Georg returned. Red circles, snails, spirals, and waves whirl through the black ink of the text. Asket and Vestal came back in plurality: there is mention of "thirty Askets" and "thirty Vestals." By January, the visual forms had stabilized. An octagon appeared, enclosed in rings of three geometric shapes, each with more sides. It was a floor plan. "Attempt at a building," af Klint noted beside the drawing, in pencil.[8] The new task seemed to be an architectural one.

A few weeks later she sketched the building again from a bird's eye view (fig. 43). The concentrically arranged cylinders were stacked on top of each other, their diameters decreasing with each layer, like a wedding cake.[9] The plans were clearly for a temple. By March the designs had developed further (fig. 44). The temple was now to be crowned by a lighthouse with a circular base. A "spiral staircase," the artist wrote, would lead to the observatory at the top of the temple. A three-meter-tall Egyptian-style door allowed entry to the tower. The doors were to be adorned with two "modern" figures, as past and present belonged together. One of the figures represents an astronomer, his right hand raised in greeting and his left resting on a globe. Next to him a woman holds the world globe in her hands.[10] Visitors to the temple would move through two spirals that led from the earth to the heavens, first in great curves through the cylindrical building, then in tight turns up the spiral staircase that led through the lighthouse to the observatory.

These images were not Hilma's first designs for a temple. But

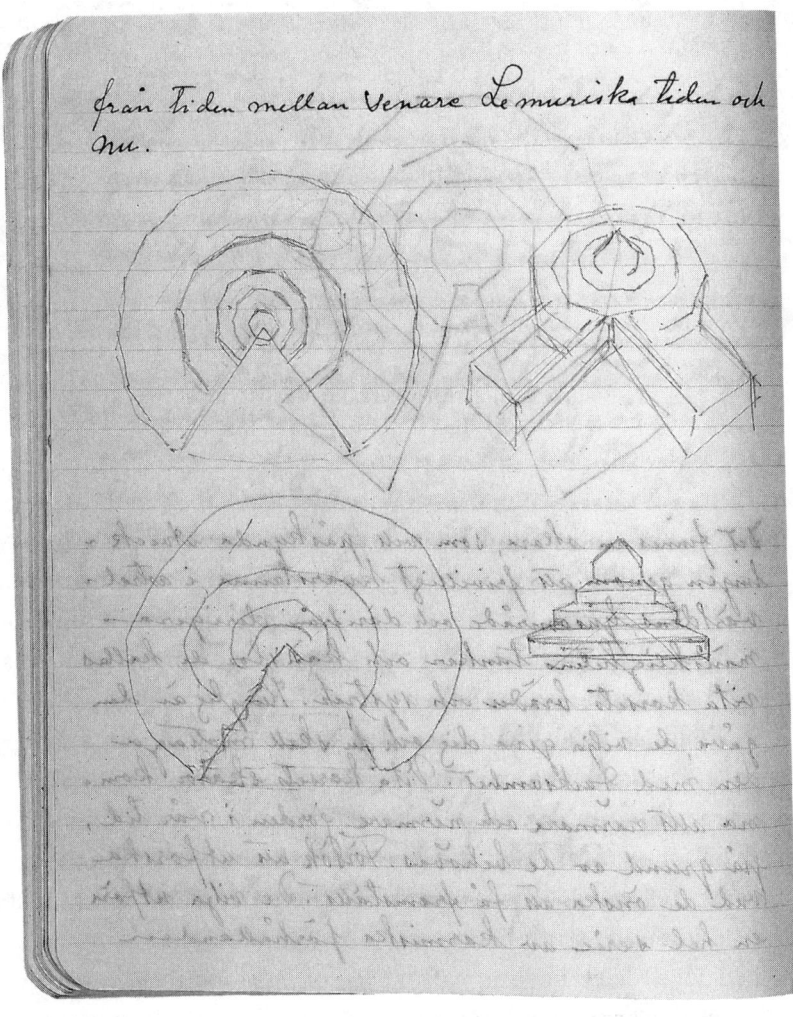

43. Temple design of 1931, notebook,
Stiftelsen Hilma af Klints Verk, HaK 1047.

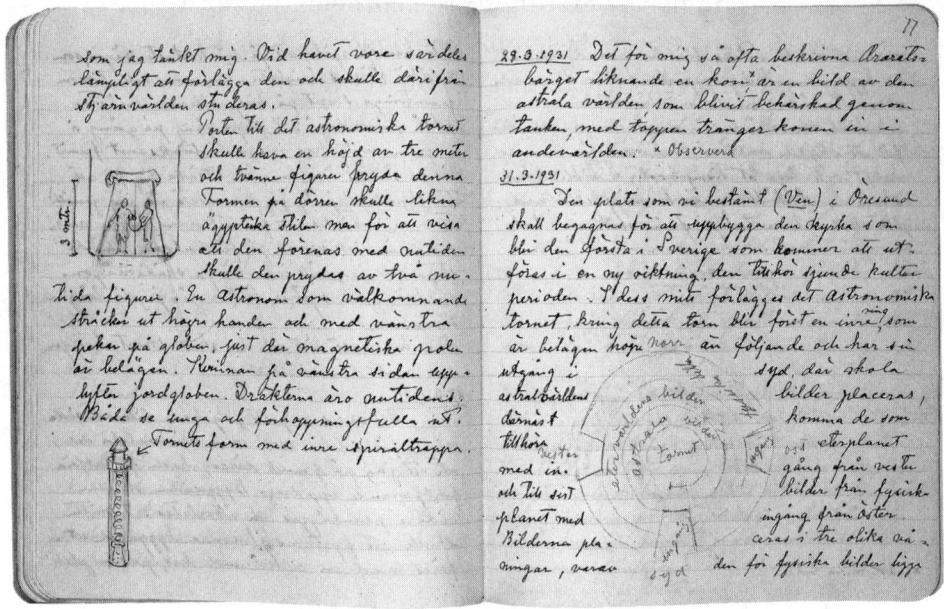

44. Temple design with observatory of 1931, notebook,
Stiftelsen Hilma af Klints Verk, HaK 1047.

none of the sketches from previous decades compared with the new ones. These drawings were precise and detailed; they transformed an idea into a plan. A garden would be planted, and there would be other buildings with study rooms and a large library. The artist wished to hang her cycle *The Ten Largest* there, among the books. In a previous design she had placed the series in the outer ring of the temple; the decisions about hanging her works were not final. The entire architectural ensemble was to be protected "from the wind" by a wall, she wrote. The site for the temple had already been chosen, and it was exposed. "(Ven) I Öresund," the artist noted, referring to the island in the strait between Denmark and Sweden.[11]

Nearly a quarter century after their execution, the *Paintings for the Temple* were given the architecture promised by their name—if only on paper. The design was the skin that would enclose the paintings, the body, the dual being, the astral hermaphrodite.

The location for the temple was not chosen at random. In the sixteenth century, Ven had been home to two world-famous observatories built by the Danish astronomer and alchemist Tycho Brahe. Hilma owned a book about his life and work, a historical novel by Vilhelm Østergaard.[12] Brahe used advanced instrumentation to survey the heavens from his observatory, while in the lab he investigated the effects of medicinal plants grown in his garden and harvested according to the phases of the moon. He built water reservoirs to power paper mills, and he had a printing press so he could publish his writings. He called his island domain Uraniborg, after Urania, the muse of astronomy. Brahe believed that the microcosm and the macrocosm were subject to the same laws and that everything was interdependent: the moon and the plants, the universe and the roots in the soil. Political upheaval in Denmark had forced him to leave Ven for the court of Rudolf II in Prague, where he died in 1601 at the age of fifty-four.

Af Klint's notes record train connections to Landskrona, the Swedish port city from which ferries departed to Ven. The ferry ride took a scant half hour, and upon alighting at the jetty in the island's harbor, she could have walked directly down the road to the site of Brahe's observatory. None of the historical buildings survived; the site was now occupied by fields and meadows, with scattered farmhouses. Brahe's castle and garden, mills and lakes, printing works and observatories were destroyed after he went in exile. As if he saw it coming, Brahe had a motto chiseled into the stone over the entrance to the main observatory: "Neither high offices nor power, only the scepter of science survives." Brahe was proven correct. Johannes Kepler, Brahe's student, continued his scientific legacy at the court of Rudolf II after the Danish scholar died. Brahe and Kepler are known today as pioneers of modern astronomy.

After a fifteen-minute walk, af Klint would have reached the empty plot of land where Brahe's castle and observatories had stood. Brahe had lived in a time that was not ready for him; the painter knew the feeling well. She featured Brahe in another notebook a couple of years later when she received the commission to "lay down

sketch after sketch Tycho Brahe's temple building."[13] More architectural drawings were the result.

The small island of Ven appears on her grandfather's maps,
marked by the fine lines of the *Sjöatlas*, in which land and sea looked
so tidy. Gustaf would surely have been pleased that her temple was
to have a lighthouse with an observatory.

[2]

+X

The notebook of 1931 contains not only designs for the temple but
other commissions from af Klint's spiritual companions: they
wanted more big paintings. Going through these notes later, the artist marked their suggestions with a star in the margin and wrote "I
could never do that."[1] That was true. In 1931 she was sixty-nine years
old, suffering from debilitating rheumatism. Her invisible friends
seemed not to appreciate the pains of earthly existence. Her last
large works had been painted more than fifteen years earlier. She
no longer had the strength to stretch canvases, mix paints, wield a
brush with a steady hand.

Af Klint closed the studio on Munsö at the end of the summer
of 1931. She and Thomasine Anderson did not return to Uppsala
but moved to Helsingborg, in the south. The friends rented a new
apartment in the center of Helsingborg at Kullagatan 58, in an art
nouveau building designed by a fellow student from the Academy,
Alfred Hellerström. Hellerström also designed the famous Helsingborg town hall, a playful brick building with battlements, towers, and a tall clocktower modeled after the campanile in St. Mark's
Square in Venice.

From the top story of the apartment building, one could see all
the way to Denmark. Helsingborg is located at the narrowest part
of Öresund, the strait between Sweden and Denmark that also con-

tains the island of Ven. From the window everything seemed within arm's reach: the harbor, the sea, the sailboats, the steamships, the shore on the far side. When ships sailed from Helsingborg, they did not disappear over the horizon into the majestic Baltic. They stayed in view, decorously crossing the blue strait to Denmark.

The weather in Helsingborg is mild; rhododendrons bloom in early summer. From Helsingborg, it is only a few kilometers to Landskrona, where ferries leave for Ven. Living in the south—even if only in the south of Sweden—made life easier for Hilma. The winters were less bitter, her pain decreased, and acute rheumatic episodes were rarer.

The move to southern Sweden was not a flight from the city to the country. Helsingborg was more populous than Uppsala and closer to the continent—to Denmark and Copenhagen, where Hilma found the art scene more interesting than in Sweden. She read Danish newspapers and in one of them came across an article about a Finnish painter named Ilona Harima (1911–86). Harima's paintings were influenced by Hinduism and Buddhism but, unlike Hilma's, were representational. Hilma wrote to Harima, describing the spiritual works she had begun to paint in 1906.[2]

Hilma's correspondence from this time includes another letter, this one addressed to her. The sender is unknown, as the last page is missing. The letter concerns the work of Martinus Thomsen (1890–1981), known professionally as Martinus. The Danish artist and writer believed, like Hilma, in the evolution of the soul in the spiritual world, and in multiple incarnations. His magnum opus, *Livets Bog* (*The Book of Life*), was published in 1932 and comprised seven volumes with elaborate illustrations. Martinus's images are nonrepresentational, colorful, and geometric. Hilma owned the first volume, and the author of the letter pointed out similarities between Martinus's work and hers. The person was "very pleased" that Hilma agreed with this assessment.[3]

Hilma began to find answers to questions that had long troubled her. Why, for example, should she struggle with the present, which would soon be history? What was the point of hoping for reactions from people who didn't understand her, the same sort who had razed Tycho Brahe's Uraniborg three hundred years ago? She was not the first person to face resistance from her contemporaries. But history shows that the present becomes the past at the very moment the future begins. Af Klint looked forward to this future. She did not doubt her work, but she doubted her contemporaries, and so she made a decision. The most important note she made in 1932 appears on the first page of a notebook. "+x" is written in pencil, followed by an explanation (see plate 42). "All works," she wrote, "which are to be opened twenty years after my death bear the above sign."[4]

The sign "+x" was added to most of the notebooks from 1905 onward. The blue books of the museum in a suitcase also feature it, thus extending the instruction to the *Paintings for the Temple*. She framed the sign with a square, so that it stands out like a control button. In a sense, it functioned like one. These were the works she wanted to preserve; everything else would be destroyed. With this notation, the artist locked her work in a time capsule and hurled it into the future.

[3]

A Temple in New York

While af Klint was planning her temple, art took a surprising turn on the other side of the Atlantic, thousands of kilometers away. One of the most important figures in the new movement was a painter named Hilla von Rebay (1890–1967), who wanted to establish a museum in New York City based on a concept many of her contemporaries would have found outlandish. But the painter did not have to convince them because she had an important supporter: Solomon R. Guggenheim (1861–1949), born into the Guggenheim family that had made a fortune in the mining industry.[1]

The two had met in 1928 in New York, when Rebay painted Guggenheim's portrait: in the painting the businessman is seated in an armchair; his crossed legs give him an elegant grace. His hair is short and white, his eyes icy blue and watchful. He wears a brown three-piece suit with knickerbockers. Rebay painted him in the academic style, though she had actually abandoned that approach years before. In Europe she had run in avant-garde circles, and she had been making nonrepresentational work ever since reading Kandinsky's *Concerning the Spiritual in Art*. Her paintings had been exhibited in Herwarth Walden's Galerie der Sturm in Berlin.[2] Rebay actually didn't think of herself as a portrait painter, but under the circumstances the pretense was worth it. By the time the sitting was finished, she had convinced Guggenheim that it was his mission to collect nonrepresentational art—exclusively.

The forty-year-old Rebay had big plans. In 1930, she wrote to the artist Rudolf Bauer: "It seems to me that a museum must be built in a fabulous style, with a quiet room, a large room, where the paintings will be nicely kept, so that only a few will be hung at a time, in rotation, and big names will be shown only occasionally." She called her dream "a temple of nonrepresentation and reverence." "Temple," she added, was a nicer term than "church."[3] Af Klint would have agreed, and this was hardly their only similarity.

Rebay called her building a temple because its mission was larger than that of a museum: it was to move visitors, enlighten and awaken them. Rebay was convinced that art shouldn't depict the external world but rather lead the way to a higher, spiritual reality. She was inspired by texts that af Klint knew well: the writings of Annie Besant, Helena P. Blavatsky, and Rudolf Steiner. Rebay had attended Steiner's lectures several times in 1904 and 1905, when she was not yet fourteen.

Her early engagement with esoterica was followed, like af Klint's, by classical art training. She studied in private painting academies in Paris and Munich. She referred to the style of painting she was drawn to—first as a painter, then as a collector, and finally as the founding director of the Guggenheim Museum—as "nonobjective." For her, this kind of art heralded a new era, a revolution, comparable to the discovery that the earth revolved around the sun. In the first book published by the Solomon R. Guggenheim Collection of Non-Objective Paintings, Rebay wrote: "For thousands of years astronomers, as well as laymen, believed that the earth was the center of the universe, around which all other planets revolved. . . . For an even longer period of time there was a belief that the object in painting was the center around which art must move. Artists of the Twentieth Century have discovered that the object is just as far from being the center of art as the earth is from being the focal point of the universe."[4] How Rebay's idea for a museum evolved is documented in photographs in the archive of the Guggenheim Museum. One of the earliest is from 1930, when Rebay visited the Bauhaus in Dessau.[5] Wearing a hat and a loose, modern suit with a silk scarf, she laughs. Her arm is linked with Guggenheim's on one side—he is in a three-piece suit, as always. On her other side stands Wassily Kandinsky, Bauhaus professor, beaming, perhaps thinking of the important sale he had just made—Rebay and Guggenheim purchased *Composition VIII*, from 1923, for the museum.[6]

Another photo, from 1937, offers a peek into Guggenheim's private suite at the Plaza Hotel in New York.[7] The décor is modern with art on the walls: works by Fernand Léger and Kandinsky, including *Composition VIII*. The collection did not yet have a permanent home. The next photographs document other temporary homes: a former car showroom in Manhattan in 1939 and Guggenheim's townhouse in 1948.

When Guggenheim and Rebay finally commissioned Frank Lloyd Wright (1867–1959), America's leading architect, to design a permanent home for the collection, the event was captured by a photographer. A 1945 photo shows Rebay with a scale model of the Guggenheim Museum (fig. 45), gleaming white, opened to show the visionary design of the interior. Instead of a stairwell connecting the floors, a single long ramp spirals upward. The upward-curving architecture embodies everything Rebay stood for—in particular, her conviction that nonobjective painting could free the viewer from the material plane and lead to higher forms of consciousness. Visitors were to go through a spiritual evolution, walking a kind of

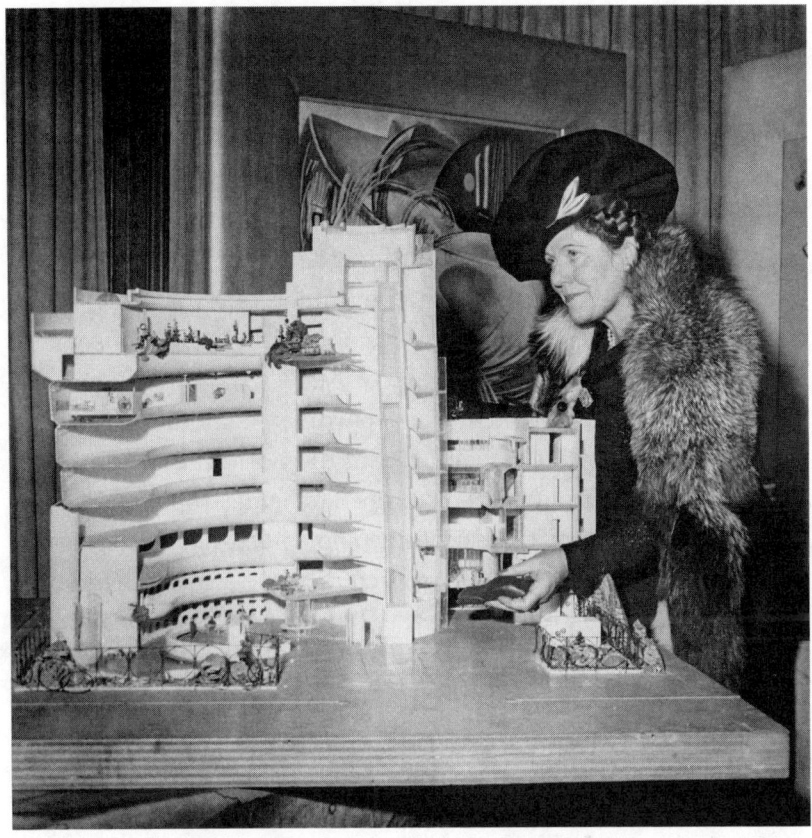

45. Hilla von Rebay with cross-section model of Guggenheim Museum,
designed by Frank Lloyd Wright, 1945.

metaphysical track that led upward, turn for turn, to the glass dome
at the top, opening the building to the heavens. In retrospect, Rebay
would say that she had always wanted her museum to be "a *spiral*
and have no *stairs*."[8]

For his part, Frank Lloyd Wright claimed to have gotten the idea
from nature. "I have found it hard to look a snail in the face," he once
said jokingly, "since I stole the idea of his house—from his back."[9]
When the Solomon R. Guggenheim Museum opened on New York's
Fifth Avenue in 1959, the temple of art that Rebay had envisioned
for nearly thirty years finally became a reality.

Af Klint knew nothing about the plan for the museum. Her note-books, as we know, also contained designs for a spiral-shaped temple for paintings that were primarily nonrepresentational; her build-ing also opened toward the stars. And she understood the spiral as a representation of spiritual evolution, the viewer's liberation from materialism and ascension to higher understanding. The temple with her paintings should be, as she noted in 1932, "a museum to show what lies behind the material forces."[10]

But the circumstances of the two women could not have been more different. Unlike Rebay, af Klint did not think the time was right to pursue her plans. In 1932 she had bequeathed her work to the future. Her reservations pertained not only to her own situation but to political developments, particularly in Germany, which she was following with growing unease. Dark times were coming, and she knew it. In Europe, an epoch of destruction was looming. The temple had to wait.

[4]

The London Blitz

In the early thirties, af Klint was regularly painting watercolors, fifty to sixty a year, some overtly political. On June 11, 1932, she painted the outline of England: the sea around the island is black, and from the lower righthand corner a figure breathes brown clouds to the west and a jet of fire shoots toward London (see plate 43). Eight years later, the English would refer to attacks by the German Luftwaffe on London and other British cities as "the Blitz."[1]

Directly following the watercolor of England, af Klint painted one depicting the Iberian peninsula. A column of purple smoke rises from the outlines of Spain, Portugal, Andorra, and Gibraltar, and a brown snake descends on Spain from above. "Predictions of war in Spain," the artist wrote in her notebook in June 1932, four years before Franco launched the coup that would precipitate the Spanish Civil War.[2]

Af Klint did not think in terms of military maneuvers, but she showed the watercolor to her nephew Erik af Klint. Erik, born in 1901, was in his early thirties. He had finished his studies at the military academy in Stockholm and had become an officer, following in the footsteps of his forefathers. Hilma and Erik sometimes spoke on the telephone; his number is framed by several thick pencil lines in her address book.[3] The young officer also stopped off to visit his aunt when fleet maneuvers took him along the west coast of Sweden, through the Öresund, past Malmö and Helsingborg. Of all the younger af Klints, Erik had the greatest appreciation for her art and worldview. "He understands," the spiritual messengers told Hilma, "that you have mysterious skills and that you know a lot which is unknown to him." Beyond Erik's acknowledgment of his aunt's gifts there was a personal bond: he understood, Hilma wrote in a notebook, "that you've had a wonderful life, and he likes staying with you." She was also fond of Erik's wife, Ulla, though the connection did not run as deep. "She understands some of it, and skips over the rest."[4]

Surely Hilma and her nephew talked not only about painting and spiritual development but also about politics. If there was to be another war, Sweden would have to devise a strategy for facing the conflict. The greatest danger seemed to come from two other countries bordering the Baltic Sea: Russia to the east and Germany to the south. Could Sweden remain neutral, as it had during World War I? What would happen with Finland and Norway? Erik was troubled by his aunt's watercolors; he did not yet know what to make of the outlines of the countries or what war was indicated in Spain. Looking back, he would say: "In 1932 she made two watercolors in the shape of maps—one of northern Europe, the other of the western Mediterranean. They clearly represent the bombings of London and the battles in the Mediterranean during the Second World War (1939–1945).... She showed me these works many years before the war began."[5] Erik would believe all his life that his aunt had the power to see into the future. And Hilma would make him the sole heir of her work.

Her talks with Erik revived old questions. What was the nature of the gift she possessed? How could it be explained? On the one hand, the artist was used to incursions by the supernatural into her daily life. On the other hand, she still could not explain it, and experience had taught her that it was generally easier to keep it to herself. Strategic silence made it simpler to deal with other people, for example, with Ulla, who remembered the painter as a good-natured family member who wore old-fashioned clothes. She was a "dignified older woman" who ate only fruit and vegetables, Ulla later recalled, but although her lifestyle was different she did not judge others and was "full of understanding."[6]

But even if Hilma did not exude missionary zeal and kept her questions private, they plagued her. Tirelessly, she searched for answers in her old notebooks, which she and Anna Cassel had been editing and revising together since the late twenties. The women lived in separate locations, yet sometimes Cassel would stay on Munsö, as when Hilma and Thomasine went to London in 1928. The word *genomgången*, meaning "reviewed," appears regularly on the first pages of the notebooks, often with a date. In some cases she and Cassel decided to make clean copies and destroy the originals. "Destroyed," she wrote in reference to the early notes from 1906 through 1908.[7] It is impossible to know what kind of liberties the women took in making the transcriptions. Their original task had been to record messages from on high, which probably meant they would go only so far in correcting the words of the divine.

Since quarreling about the studio building on Munsö, Hilma and Anna had grown more distant, though they never ended their friendship. To recall, Cassel had only been willing to loan money to build the studio rather than pay for it outright, and the dispute went on for years, as recorded in a notebook, until Cassel finally tore up the promissory note for 3,000 crowns.

In the meantime Cassel had found another "dual soul," Hilma believed: Emilia Giertta, the neighbor from Adelsö whose family owned the land where the studio stood on Munsö.[8] Hilma had found her own spiritual counterpart, her dual soul, in Thomasine Anderson. It was a deeper connection than she had felt with anyone else.

Throughout the thirties, Anna and Hilma worked on the early writings. Anna was living in Lidingö, near Stockholm, on the old family estate, a large property that Hilma had once painted.[9] Thomasine and Hilma now lived in Lund, in an apartment at Grönegatan 28, a quiet street in the old city, between the cathedral and the train station.[10] The street felt more like it belonged in a village, with trees towering over low buildings.

These moves may have been prompted by finances. Af Klint had sold all her shares in the lake house Furuheim to Cassel, presumably because she needed money.[11] Perhaps for this reason she moved during the winter to whatever apartment was available for the cheapest rent. Lund, a picturesque town with a historic cathedral and many brick buildings, offered certain advantages. It had a university and well-stocked libraries. Af Klint's appetite for books had not diminished; she continually acquired works on a wide range of subjects: Erich Maria Remarque's *All Quiet on the Western Front*, for example, as well as two volumes on "Mystics in Europe and India" by a Danish religious scholar, and a book on the "Understanding of the World According to the Rosicrucians" by Max Heindel, a Theosophist and Anthroposophist. Above all, there were more writings by Rudolf Steiner. Af Klint's faith in his worldview was untarnished, even if she had turned her back on Dornach. The list of publications by Steiner that she read or planned to read mushroomed, and in the next years it came to include nearly everything he wrote.[12] Later af Klint would bequeath most of her books to the institutions she frequented: Lund's public and university libraries. Her books are still available in the reading room of the university library, with penciled markings in the margins and passages underscored. "Renunciation is the power," for example, is underlined in her copy of Steiner's 1912 lecture "The Bhagavad Gita and the Epistles of Saint Paul."[13]

In the early thirties Hilma felt closer than ever to Steiner. The man who was so busy during his lifetime kept on teaching after his death, as she was informed: "at the university which is located in the astral world, where the high teacher Steiner works full-time." The "supernatural university" became a regular topic in the notebooks; Hilma was called its employee. She wrote that Steiner had promised to explain her first series, and he would now "perhaps" even help her organize her "last work." "He will answer you," she wrote, and things would turn out for the better. After all the battles she had endured, the time for a reward would come and the temple she longed for could be built. At times the connection between Steiner and the artist seemed downright symbiotic: she was his "tool," and he stood by her side.[14]

Even so Hilma continued to wonder about her premonitions and visions. Why, for instance, were maps of England and the Iberian Peninsula appearing in her watercolors? Steiner had always argued that mystical forms of knowledge could be learned through practice, just as one developed intellectual skills in school. "There slumber in every human being faculties by means of which he can acquire for himself a knowledge of higher worlds," he wrote. This esoteric knowledge, he held, was no more a secret than "writing is a secret for those who have never learned it."[15] But af Klint wasn't so sure.

[5]

Future Woman

The walls of the study where Hilma painted and wrote on Munsö were covered in watercolors, and books crowded a shelf next to the desk (fig. 46). Image and text were the flesh and bone of her thinking; without them it would have been impossible for her to break free of the system that most people, for simplicity's sake, refer to as "reality."[1]

Among the books she owned were two by Carl du Prel (1839–99), who had a lot to say about the varying states that enabled the

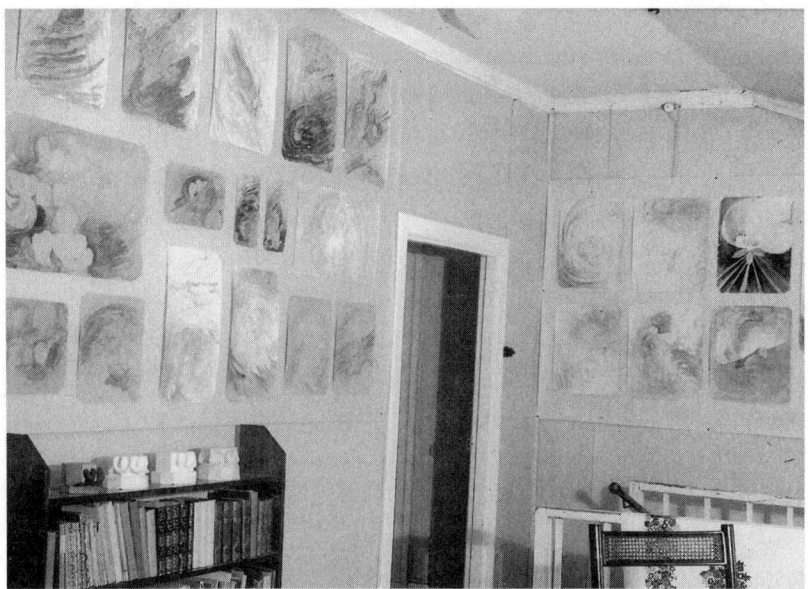

46. Study in Furuheim House on Lake Munsö, 1930s,
Stiftelsen Hilma af Klints Verk.

spirit to receive messages from other worlds.[2] In *The Philosophy of
Mysticism*, from 1890, du Prel called the capacity to receive messages and signals a "threshold of sensibility." He sometimes used
the term in combination with "future man."[3] His thesis was that
the "threshold of sensibility" would be further developed in "future
man." For du Prel, the refinement of perception was above all a biological process. If bodies could change, why couldn't sensory capacities? Fins became legs when animals had moved from sea to land
millions of years ago, and du Prel reasoned that similar processes
were true of the sense organs. He believed in a kind of migration to
land in human perception, an evolutionary leap. He was convinced
the senses have no absolute limits.

Du Prel mustered as evidence the vivid case of Friederike Hauffe
(1801–29), the "Seeress of Prevorst." In her hometown of Prevorst,
near Stuttgart, Hauffe experienced visions throughout her life. That
she could predict the future was confirmed by a reliable source: the

well-known writer, poet, and physician Justinus Kerner. Kerner cared for Hauffe during her last years and wrote two books about her, which were widely read in German.[4]

For du Prel, Hauffe represented a new evolutionary step: the future woman with a refined threshold of perception. "Her mystic capabilities were not limited to the subjective sphere," du Prel wrote, invoking Kerner; "rather, her feelers extended into an external world that was closed to normal consciousness."[5] She had been an extraordinary individual, the first herald of a possible type to come. Du Prel concluded: "One could almost say that in her, future man projected his shadow, since she exhibited as an individual what only a biological improvement can fully enfold: a shift in the threshold of perception. She lived in more intimate connection with nature than the rest of us. Metals and plants, animals and people had an effect on her in a way we cannot imagine."[6] Du Prel's description could in many ways also apply to af Klint. She too felt a close connection to nature, ranging from animals to metals, and she received signals that bypassed others. "Feelers" also aptly described the curious organs attached to the snails in her paintings, which looked like cast fishing lines.

"Friederike," af Klint wrote in a tiny notebook with a leather cover imprinted with forget-me-nots. The notebook lists other visionaries, male and female, including Bridget of Sweden.[7] The list offers a selective view of church history, beginning in the twelfth century with Hildegard von Bingen, the abbess, poet, and composer who was renowned for her beautifully illuminated manuscripts and who was granted permission by the pope to publish her visions. The sheer number of people who received the stigmata of Jesus was astounding. The history of the Catholic Church included "320 stigmatized," Hilma wrote; only 41 of them were men.[8]

Some of the visionaries on Hilma's list were not recognized by the Catholic Church, such as the Belgian Louise Lateau, who received visions of Jesus and Mary along with the stigmata and was examined before her death in 1883 by more than a hundred doctors and even more theologists, without conclusion.

One saint who figured often in Hilma's notebooks was Veronica, who allegedly lived in the time of Jesus. According to tradition, Veronica gave Christ her veil on the way to Calvary so he could wipe his face, which miraculously appeared on the fabric afterward. Hilma explored the legend in a drawing she made in one of her notebooks. She sketched Veronica in delicate pencil lines, in her hands the veil on which the face of Jesus is captured, the "Vera icon," translated as "true image." The portrait was more than a picture, Hilma wrote:

> Veronica saw on the canvas a picture that then appeared every time she looked at the canvas. She could also materialize the forces attached to the physical material and reveal it to other individuals.[9]

Veronica had received a magical sign with the veil, from which forces emanated. Did Hilma think the same of her paintings? Did they also release invisible forces? In any case, her spiritual companions advised the artist to stick to Veronica, saying, "she wants to give you a present."[10]

Af Klint did not see herself as a saint, but she could identify with lives marked by extreme highs and lows, by veneration and hostility. Neither governments nor church dignitaries were often pleased by miracles. Saints represented a rupture in the established order and threatened the structures of power. When a vision was recognized by the Catholic Church, the story often ended, particularly in the case of women, with the subject's being silenced, locked in a cloister, and the narrative coopted by the church for its own purposes.[11] A useful lesson for Hilma, perhaps.

There were differences of course. Hilma was privy to worlds never described in Christian canonical texts. Since 1906, she had been attuned to a broader cosmos described by spirals, snails, swans, letters, and abstract figures, with Askets and Vestals. She

47. "Notes on Letter and Words Pertaining to Works by Hilma af Klint," Stiftelsen Hilma af Klints Verk, HaK 1040.

had spiritual friends called Gregor and Ananda, names from disparate cultural contexts.

Around the same time that she was busy with the history of Christian visionaries, she started making entries in a notebook titled "Notes on Letters and Words Pertaining to Works by Hilma af Klint" (fig. 47). The notebook has many hundreds of entries, organized alphabetically, from A for "Akab," meaning "the search for the substance of love," to Y for "Ynglingasinnet," "the young man's nature," to which she added: "=WM."[12] Did she herself understand the meaning of the entries?

At first glance, the notebook resembles a dictionary. Esoteric symbols, words, and sequences of letters are written in red ink, with Swedish translations in black, all in Thomasine Anderson's handwriting. But at second glance, the clarity vanishes. There is no direct translation for what Hilma painted, and in the end, the letters become wayward, impossible to pin down. For "wu," which appears often in her paintings, there are more than a dozen entries. The meaning multiplies like a flock of birds that scatter in every direction when one tries to approach.

Was af Klint a future woman in du Prel's sense, a person with feelers and a shifted threshold of perception? She didn't know. Rudolf Steiner had a different theory. He distanced himself from phenomena like clairvoyance and visions. He once described the medial reception of messages as "atavistic." Steiner called visions the "legacy of an original, primitive state of human consciousness," and he warned of falling into "the same category as superstition, visionary dreaming, [and] mediumship (spiritism)," which were "degenerate practices."[13] Atavisms were characteristics that had outlived their usefulness but nonetheless persisted from prehistory as useless vestiges. Charles Darwin had given the pointed form of the human ear as an example, a reminder of our relationship to other animals. What if Steiner was right? Perhaps visions were nothing more than a phantom of evolutionary history, a kind of optical illusion, heat lightning from a past when the brain was not yet able to sort sensory impressions correctly. This was one of the many questions af Klint would return to through her life.

In the thirties, having visions became more dangerous than ever. Such inexplicable phenomena were given their ugliest name by modern medicine, specifically by psychiatry. Since the early twentieth century, professionals had described the state of hearing voices or hallucinating as a symptom of the dissociative disorder schizophrenia (among others). They began to treat the condition using insulin and electroshock therapies, and in the thirties the diagnosis became much more consequential when some doctors came to believe that symptoms of schizophrenia could be alleviated in patients by performing lobotomies, an operation in which nerve pathways in the brain were severed. Sigrid Hjertén, the artist and wife of Isaac Grünewald whose work was so lambasted by critics, was diagnosed with schizophrenia. She died in 1948 following a botched lobotomy.

6

National Socialism

Whenever Hilma opened the newspaper, she was confronted with reports from Germany. Every year the news grew more alarming. First there was the seizure of power by the National Socialists in 1933, then the emergency decrees, the Enabling Act, and the first concentration camps, where political opponents were imprisoned. In April 1933 it was reported that thousands of civil servants had been dismissed who were Jewish or held political views contrary to Hitler's regime. Books were burned, and Erich Maria Remarque's antiwar *All Quiet on the Western Front* was among the many that fell to the flames.

Ever since Hilma had painted England and Spain in 1932, she had stayed abreast of political conditions in Europe. In the 1930s and 1940s, Hitler's and Göring's names appear regularly in the notebooks. "Göring is a representative of rudeness, Hitler of a desire to rule over the masses,"[1] she is told by the voices that speak to her in August 1933. In January 1934 a message reads: "First, Hitler and Göring must be forced to resign. Stalin will overcome them, there will be a formal chaos in Germany, all this is happening fast enough. After that, the ground should be softened and new crowds appear with a real desire to achieve brotherly love on earth."[2] Tucked into her notebook of 1934–35 is an unusual find: a small newspaper photograph of Adolf Hitler shown in profile. Hilma was not in the habit of keeping images of politicians, and she probably used it to ask her spiritual guides about Hitler. "You shall receive knowledge of where Germany's men come from who are leaders," she recorded in July 1934, and the answer followed in the next line: "Hitler was born after 1600 in a harem." Göring, she was told, had been a eunuch, and Goebbels a slave. They all suffered from "megalomania," she added.[3]

These notes are hardly rigorous political analyses. Hilma had always seen the world from her own perspective, and this persisted into the 1930s, when her paintings and notes show an intensifying interest in the doctrine of reincarnation: she made portraits of friends in multiple incarnations, as both men and women.[4] She likewise assumed that Hitler, Göring, and Goebbels had changed sex over the course of their rebirths, but that they never understood the freedom associated with such transformations. Instead, the forces of destruction and hatred had multiplied within them, just as the "brown shirts with their swastikas" were an "expression of material desire and Luciferic self-love."[5] In 1933 she had dreamed that the female sex could intervene and change human destiny. "The woman," she had written, "will take control and save humanity."[6] This remained wishful thinking.

———

There were people in Hilma's circle who harbored sympathies for Germany's National Socialists, and some who openly supported them. She had acquaintances connected to Hitler's regime, particularly in the Edelweiss Society. She had not participated in the society for years, yet she still knew some of the members and would have been aware of major events in their lives.[7] One of Huldine Beamish's granddaughters, named Carin, had married Hermann Göring in 1923, the year of the Beer Hall Putsch, in which Göring had been implicated. When a warrant was issued for his arrest, the couple fled to Sweden, where Göring was treated for his morphine addiction at the Långbro mental hospital in Stockholm.

Meanwhile, Carin returned to Germany alone and visited Hitler in the Landsberg Prison. Following the meeting she gushed over his "goodness" and "selfless, natural heroism." Hitler, who wrote the first part of *Mein Kampf* in prison, gave her a photograph of himself inscribed "to the brave wife of my loyal comrade." Carin Göring put it up in her room.[8] When she died in 1931, she was buried in Sweden. But in 1934 Göring brought her body back to Germany, erected a mausoleum for her, and named his new country estate Carinhall in her honor.

Throughout the 1930s, Göring filled his estate with art from Jewish collections plundered first in Germany and Austria and then, after the war began, in France and the Low Countries. While Hilma was trying in her notes to fathom the phenomenon of National Socialism, a biography of Carin Göring was published by her sister, Countess Fanny von Wilamowitz-Moellendorff, who was likewise a loyal Nazi. Wilamowitz-Moellendorff praised Carin's alleged spiritual powers, explaining them in the context of the Edelweiss Society led by her mother and grandmother. Hundreds of thousands of copies of the book were printed in Germany, and it was widely read in Sweden as well. Hilma probably had not seen Carin since the latter was a teenager.

But Carin Göring was not an isolated case. There was another woman from the Edelweiss Society Hilma may have known personally, a close friend of Wilamowitz-Moellendorff. Mary Karadja, née Smith, was the youngest daughter of a Stockholm distiller. At nineteen, she married Prince Jean Constantin Karadja Pasha, an Ottoman diplomat. Widowed at a young age, Mary Karadja belonged to the Edelweiss Society and wrote books on spiritualism and astrology. In 1928 she moved to Locarno, Switzerland, where she founded the Christian Aryan Protection League with the goal of deporting European Jews to Madagascar. The state to be founded there would take care of the "territorial solution of the Jewish question," in the antisemitic jargon employed by Karadja and her comrades in arms. In 1934 Karadja pseudonymously published a text in France defending the authenticity of the *Protocols of the Elders of Zion*, a fabricated text claiming to prove there was a Jewish conspiracy bent on world dominion. Karadja's book was published the same year in Swedish.[9]

There were racist tendencies, too, among the Theosophists and Anthroposophists, whose founders remained important to Hilma. Blavatsky, who had died in 1891, inspired a movement that transformed her mythical "Root Race" into a biological origin theory. Nationalist occultists, proponents of so-called "Ariosophy," claimed there was a master race, the Aryo-Germans, who were destined to conquer all others.[10] Steiner also made statements that can only

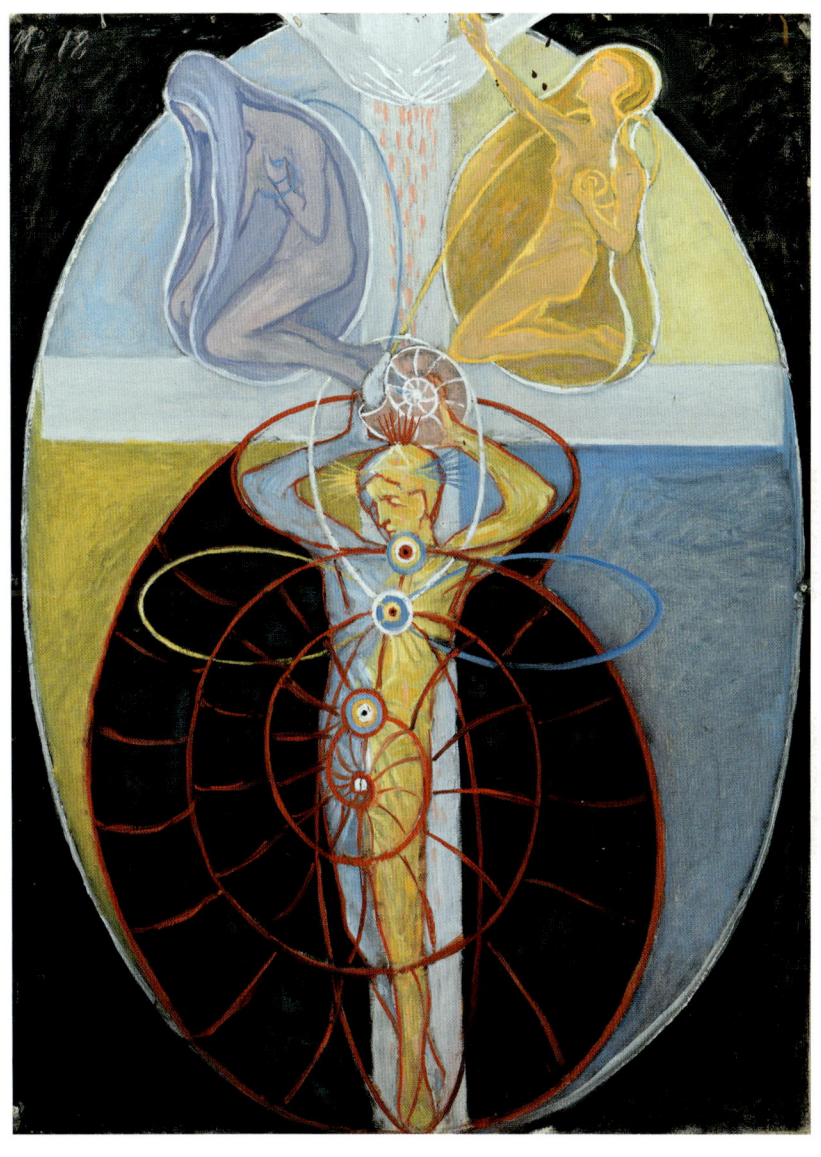

PLATE 31. *No. 1, Group VIII, Series US*, 1913, oil on canvas, 74 x 53 cm,
Stiftelsen Hilma af Klints Verk, HaK 126.

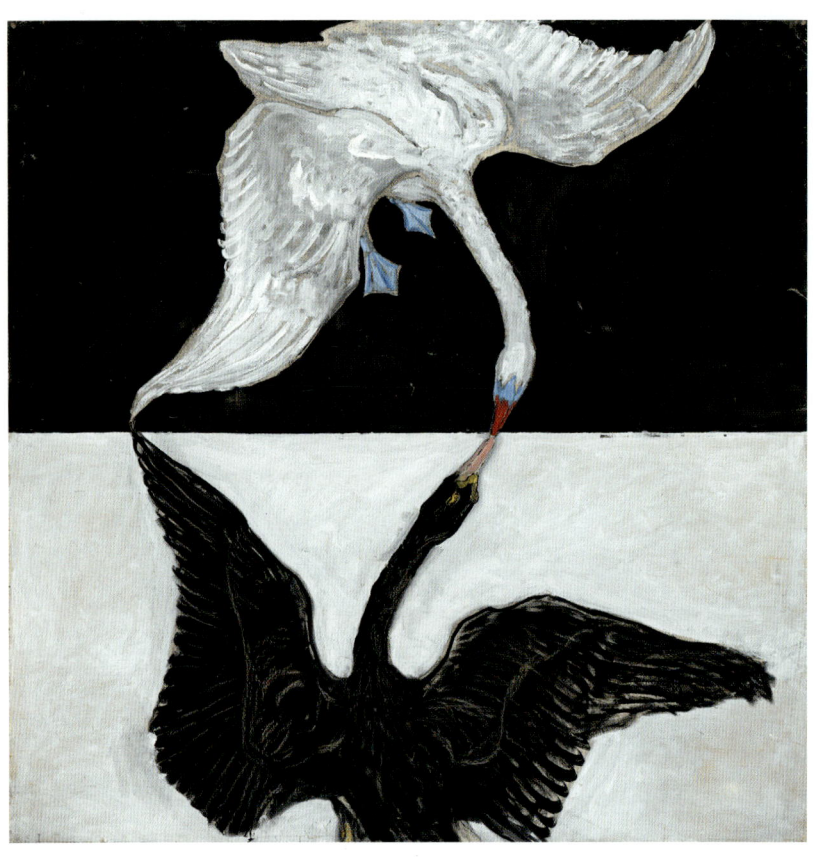

PLATE 32. *The Swan, No. 1, Group IX/SUW, Series SUW/UW*, 1915, oil and tempera on canvas, 150 x 150 cm, Stiftelsen Hilma af Klints Verk, HaK 149.

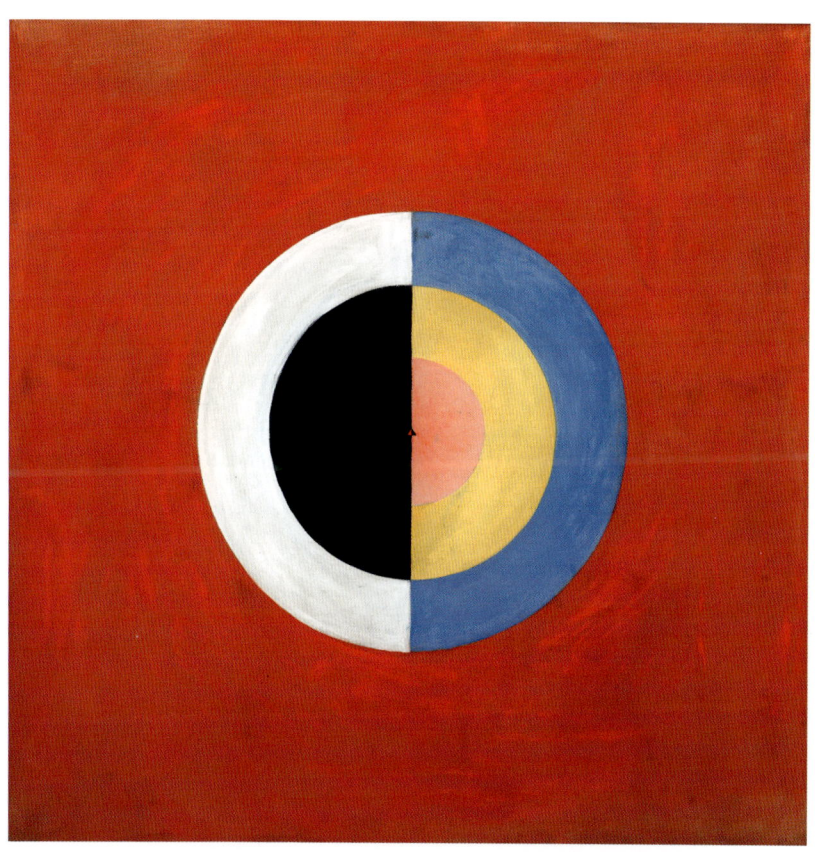

PLATE 33. *The Swan, No. 17, Group IX/SUW, Series SUW/UW*, 1915, oil and tempera on canvas, 150.5 x 151 cm, Stiftelsen Hilma af Klints Verk, HaK 165.

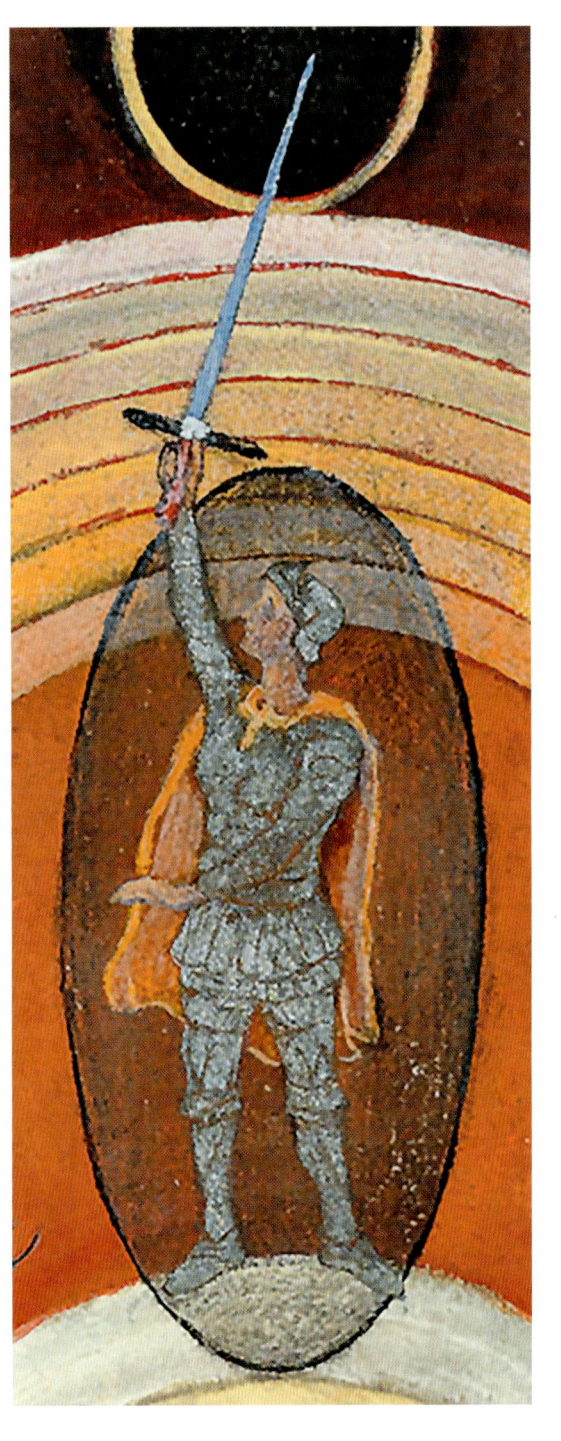

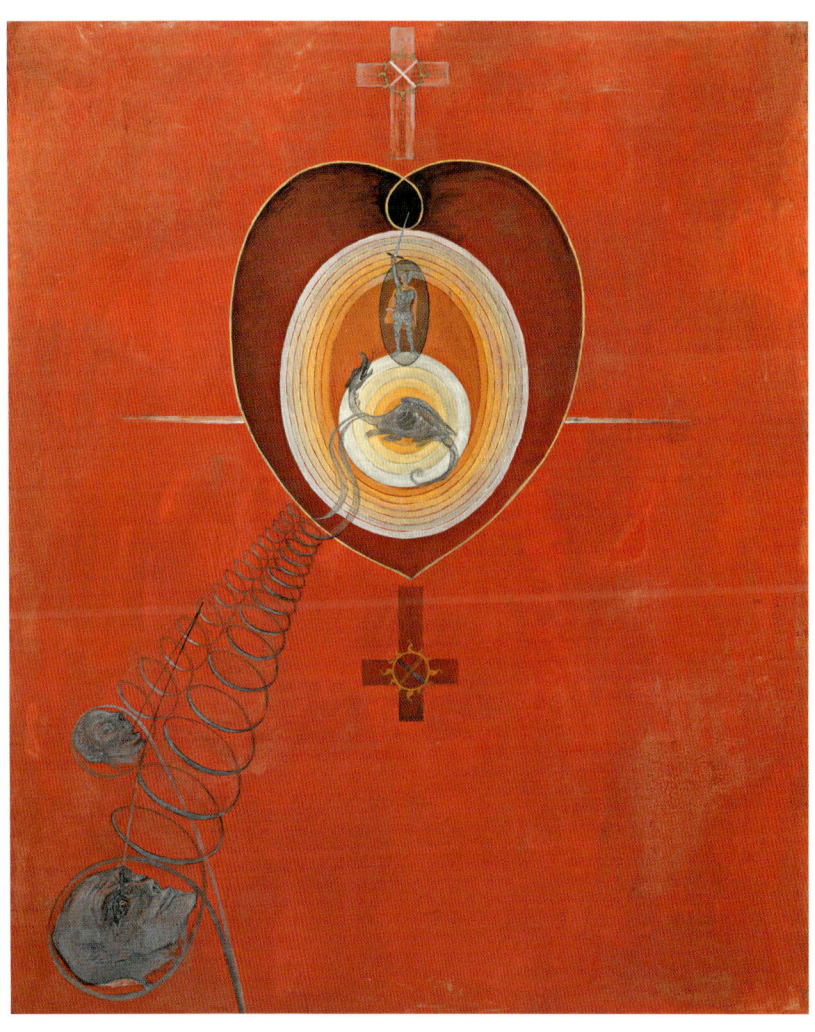

PLATES 34 AND 35. Opposite: Detail from *The Dove*; above: *The Dove, No. 8, Group IX/UW, Series SUW/UW*, 1915, oil and tempera on canvas, 158 x 130 cm, Stiftelsen Hilma af Klints Verk, HaK 180.

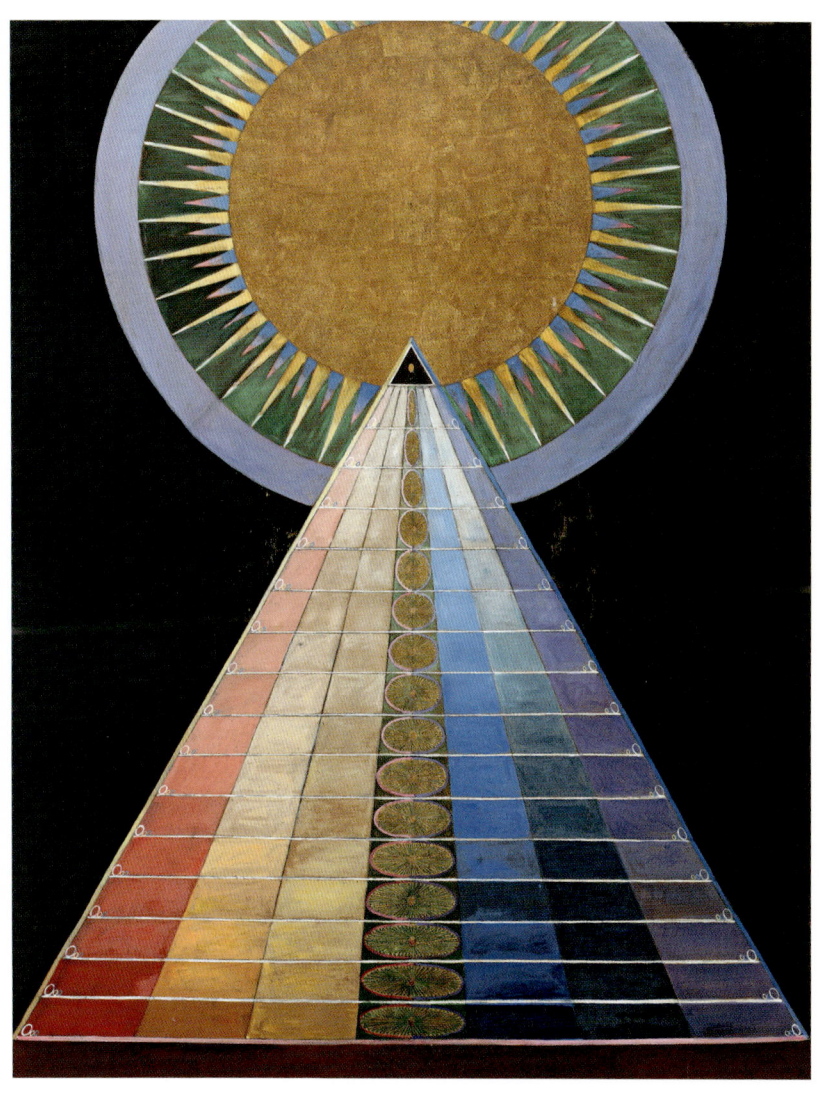

PLATE 36. *Altar Painting, No. 1, Group X, Altar Paintings*,
1915, oil and tempera and metal foil on canvas, 237.5 x 179.5 cm,
Stiftelsen Hilma af Klints Verk, HaK 187.

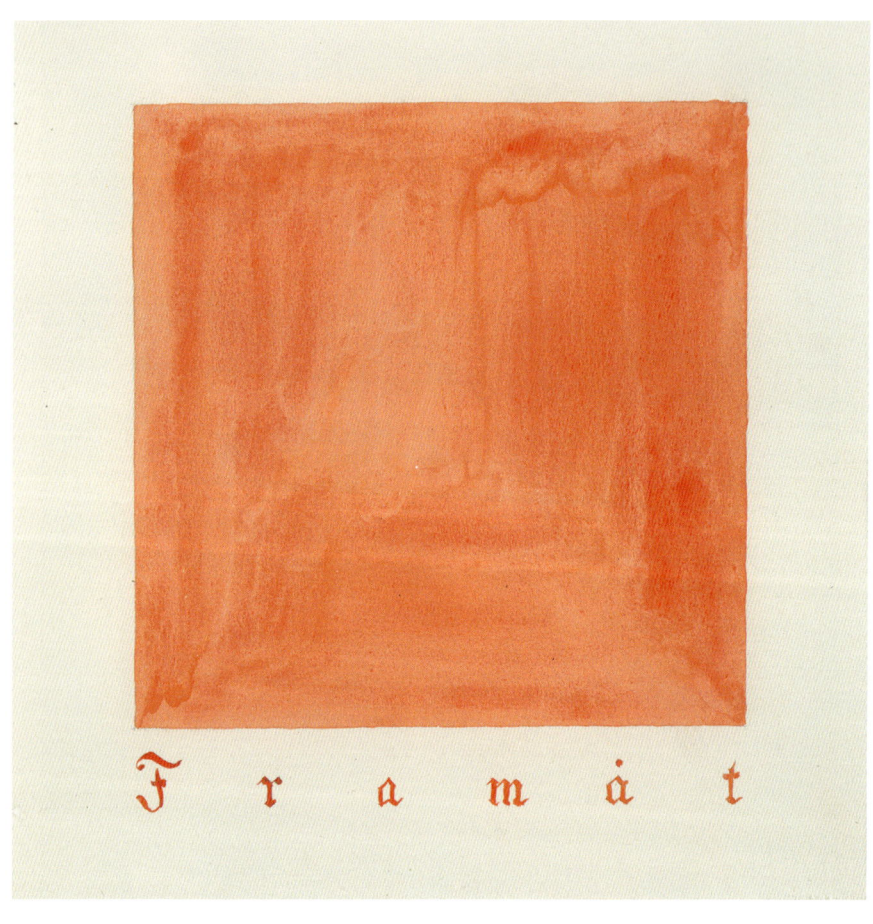

PLATE 37. *Parsifal Series, No. 90, Group I*, 1916,
watercolor and pencil on paper, 25 x 26.2 cm, Stiftelsen
Hilma af Klints Verk, HaK 244.

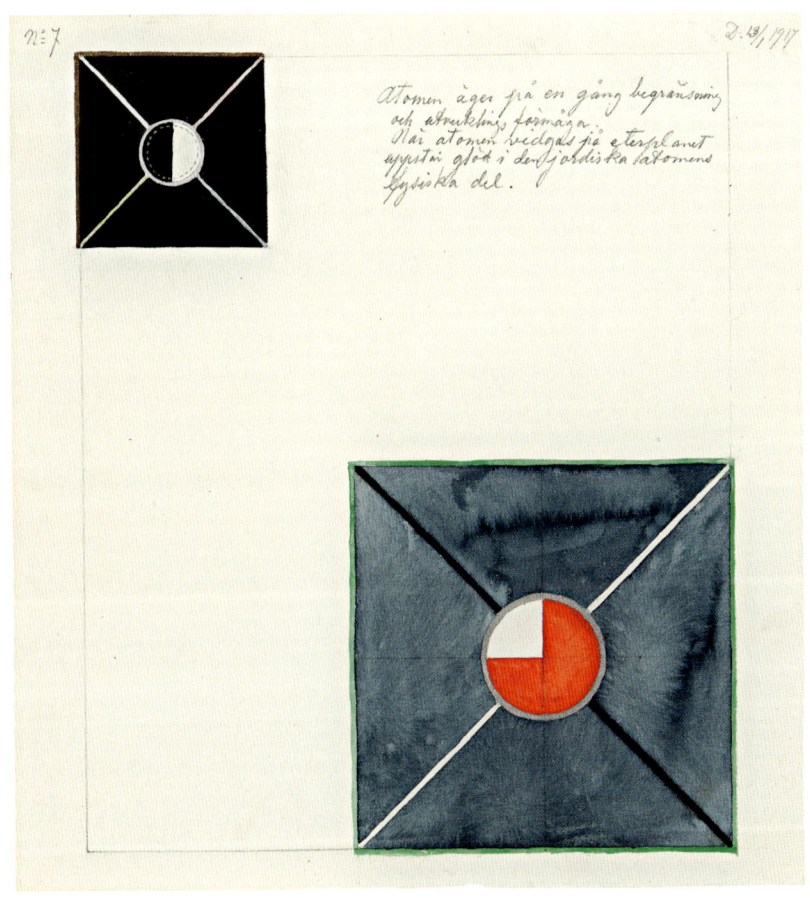

PLATE 38. *The Atom, No. 8*, 1917, watercolor, pencil, and metallic paint on paper, 26.9 x 25 cm, Stiftelsen Hilma af Klints Verk, HaK 360.

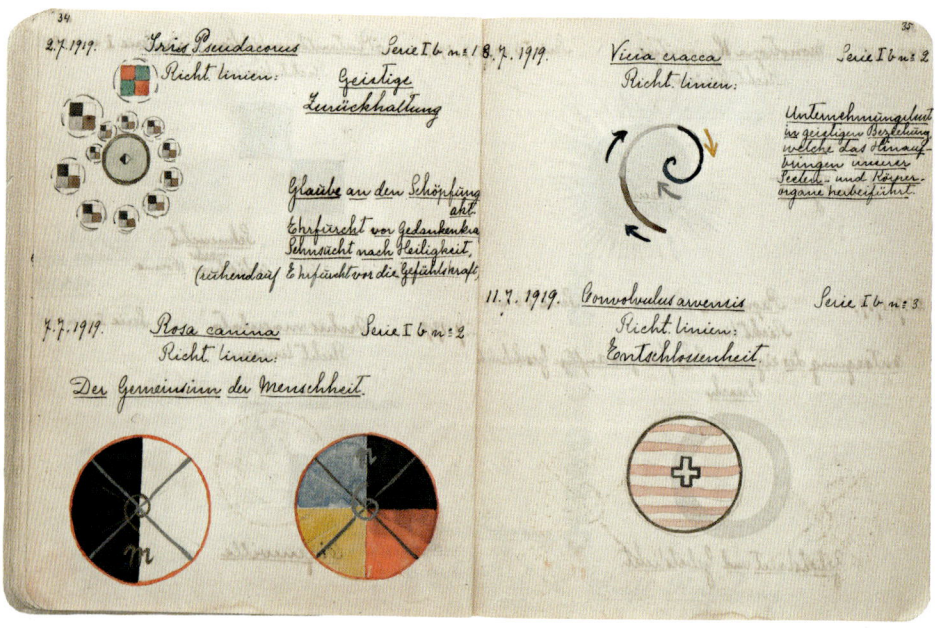

PLATES 39 AND 40. Notebook pages from "Flowers, Mosses, and Lichens," 1919, mixed media on paper, 20.5 x 16.5 cm, Stiftelsen Hilma af Klints Verk, HaK 588.

28

17.6.1919.   *Potentilla Tormentilla*   Serie I a nᵒ 5

Richt. linien:

Unschuld

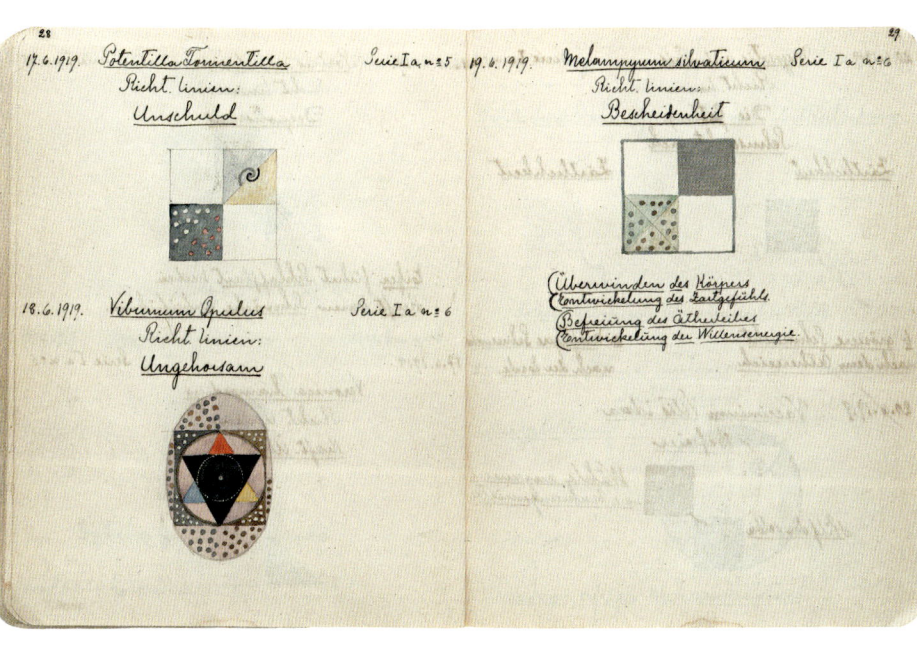

18.6.1919.   *Viburnum Opulus*   Serie I a nᵒ 6

Richt. linien:

Ungehorsam

19.6.1919.   *Melampyrum silvaticum*   Serie I a nᵒ 6

Richt. linien:

Bescheidenheit

Überwinden des Körpers
Entwickelung des Tastgefühls.
Befreiung des Ätherleibes
Entwickelung der Willensenergie.

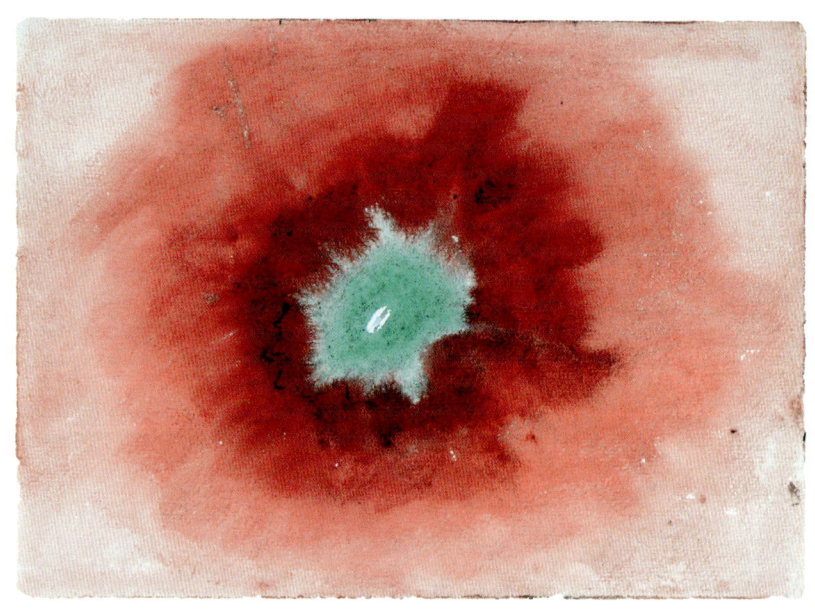

PLATE 41. From the series *On the Viewing of Flowers and Trees*,
July–October 1922, untitled, watercolor on paper, 17.9 x 25 cm,
Stiftelsen Hilma af Klints Verk, HaK 615.

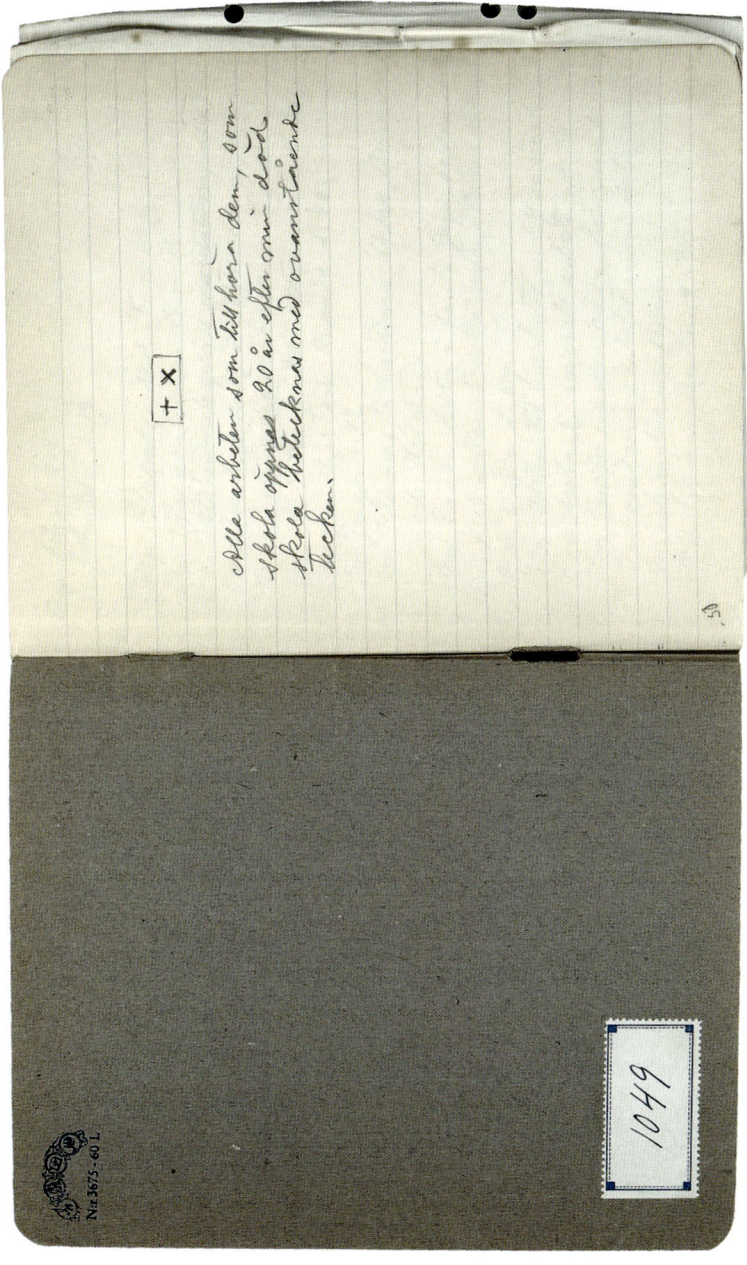

PLATE 42. In 1932 the artist bequeathed her work to the future with this notebook entry: "All works . . . which are to be opened twenty years after my death bear the above sign." Stiftelsen Hilma af Klints Verk, HaK 1049.

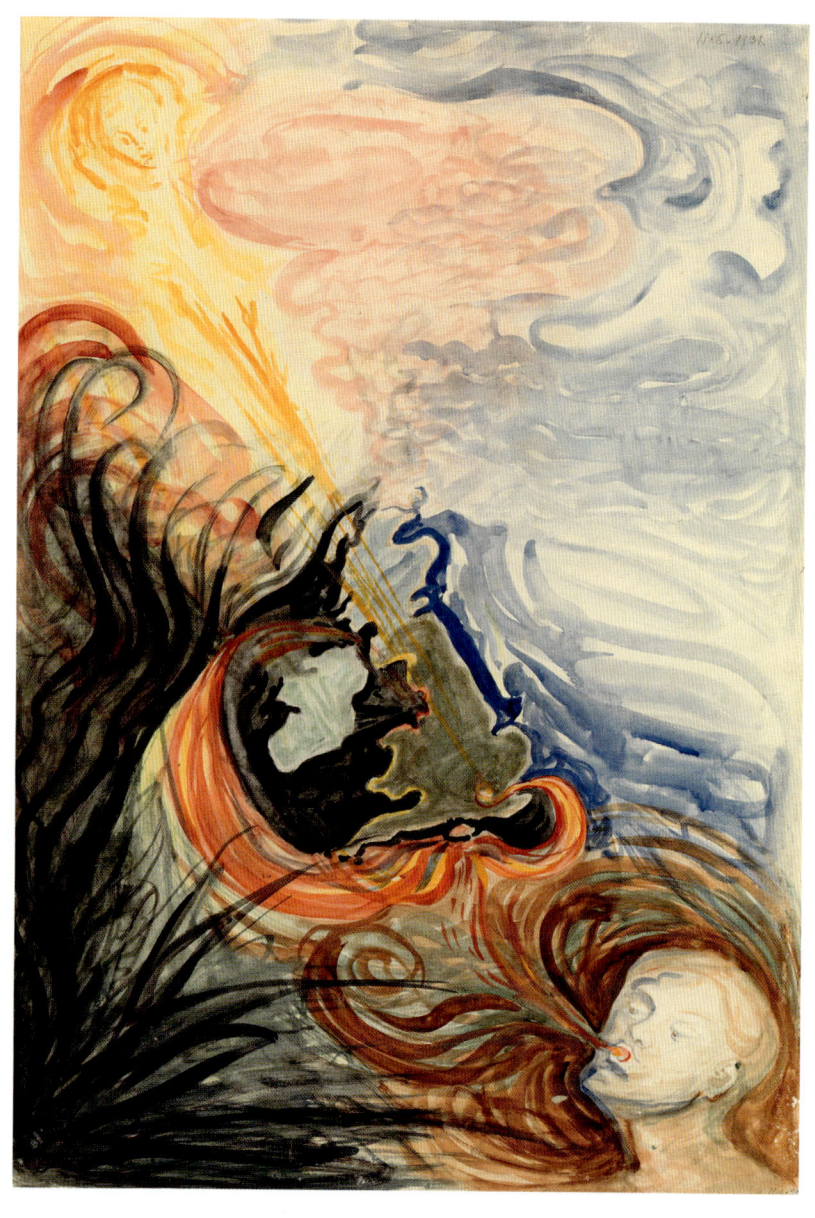

PLATE 43. *A Map—Great Britain/The Blitz*, 1932, watercolor and pencil on paper, 70.2 x 48.5 cm, Stiftelsen Hilma af Klints Verk, HaK 883.

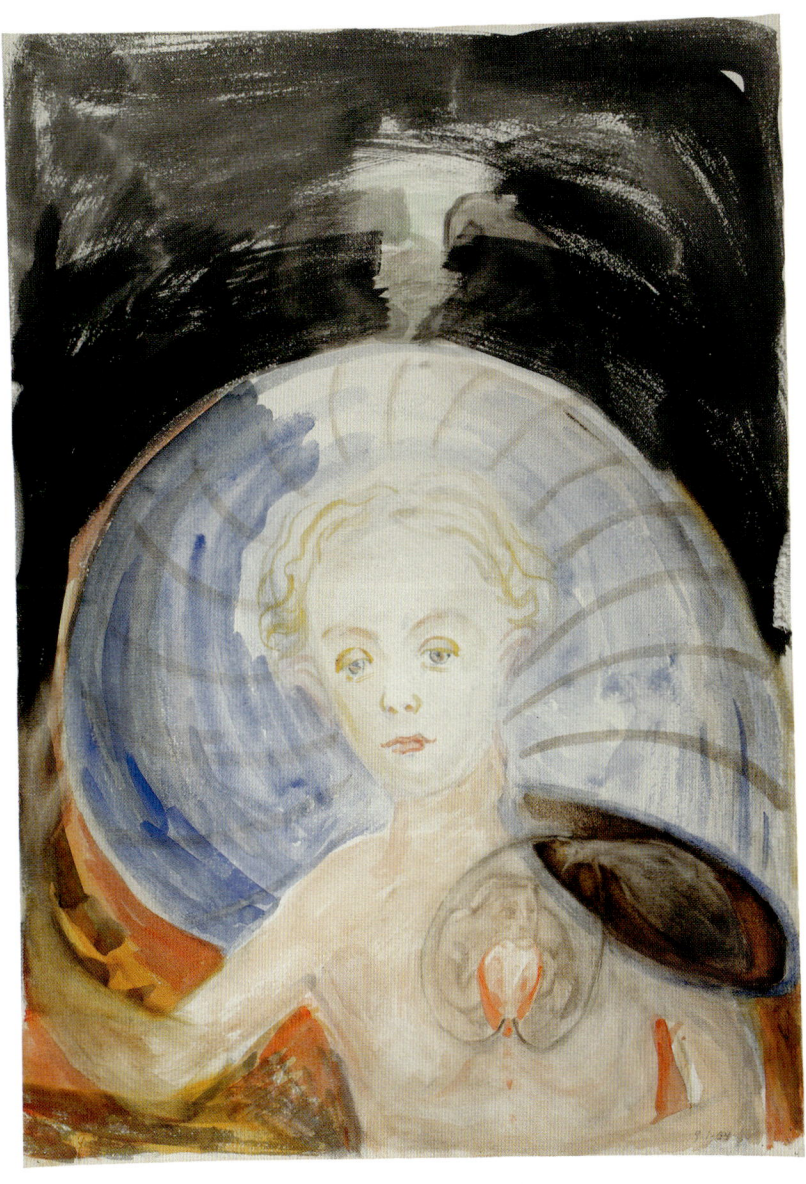

PLATE 44. *Untitled*, 1934, watercolor and pencil on paper,
Stiftelsen Hilma af Klints Verk, HaK 958.

properly be termed racist. In a 1923 lecture, he referred to the "white race" as the "future one," the "race creating in the Spirit," and described black people and the indigenous cultures of the Americas as "degenerated."[11]

The National Socialists, however, put little store in the opinions of the Theosophists and Anthroposophists. Both groups were viewed with suspicion and closely watched: they were accused of being internationalist and supporting "freemasons, Jews, and pacificists." Both had been banned in Germany—the Anthroposophists in 1935, and the Theosophists in 1937.[12] Even so, this did not stop some of them from cozying up to the Germans, who would eventually appropriate several of their technical innovations. Heinrich Himmler, Reichsführer of the SS, would employ Steiner's methods of biodynamic agriculture on SS farms, even as he dissolved the association of Anthroposophical farmers.[13] In the Dachau concentration camp, where prisoners were forced to do farm labor, a garden of medicinal plants was cultivated according to Steiner's biodynamic principles.

Did Hilma discuss these developments with her fellow Anthroposophists? Did she ever think about the 1919 entry she had made shortly after World War I that predicted a "new doctrine" would arise and attempt to destroy "everything which is physically weak"? To counter the destructive force she had developed her own spiritual botany, studying the powers of plants in "Flowers, Mosses, and Lichens," a project she took up again in 1933. She called the forces behind the coming ideology "dark powers," and she placed the virtue of the weak in opposition to the cult of the strong. She had also written of "distant days" when there would be people who were neither indifferent nor arrogant, "upon whose weak shoulders" spiritual development would go forward.[14] In 1934 she painted a delicate woman balancing a snail shell on her head, the painter's heraldic symbol. The snail shines like a halo in the black masses that surround the woman, seemingly protection and burden at once (see plate 44).

Throughout her life, Hilma held a dialectical worldview with evil and goodness being mutually generative, for without darkness, light was "unthinkable."[15] In walking a false path, humans could find the right one, she wrote.[16] But the news from Germany went far beyond the negative forces she recognized as intrinsic to the natural course of things. In her notes she considered who might be able to stem the tide of National Socialism. She began to interpret the colors in her watercolors politically: brown for National Socialists, red for Socialists and Communists. Red would have to keep brown at bay, she thought; "perhaps a war would be necessary."[17]

Hilma saw it as her task to give form to new ideas and to ensure that others knew about them. But many of her fellow human beings were uninterested in a transformation of the spirit. The current against which she swam had grown not weaker over time, but stronger. In April 1934 she drew her guardians for the first time. Ananda, Gregor, Amaliel, and Georg materialize on the page as "thought forms" (fig. 48). They shimmer in shades of green and whiz across the page like shooting stars on their way to the spiritual spheres.[18]

But the real world looked different. Wherever Hilma turned, ideas of superiority, privilege, and control were gaining ground. In Sweden as well as in Germany, right-wing thinking was taking hold. Fantasies of a "master race" were popular, and institutions were founded for the purpose of its "perfection." The Swedish State Institute for Racial Biology had been established in 1922 to consider how the "Swedish race" could be kept pure of "harmful" influences. In 1933 Germany instituted a Law for the Prevention of Hereditarily Diseased Offspring. In 1934 the Swedish parliament passed legislation allowing forced sterilization. Those deemed "insane" were the primary targets.

The highest levels of Swedish society continued to welcome German leaders. In 1939 King Gustaf V awarded Hermann Göring the Grand Cross of the Order of the Sword. That was the same year that Hitler instituted his notorious "euthanasia program" for the mentally impaired, including those who suffered from schizophrenia.

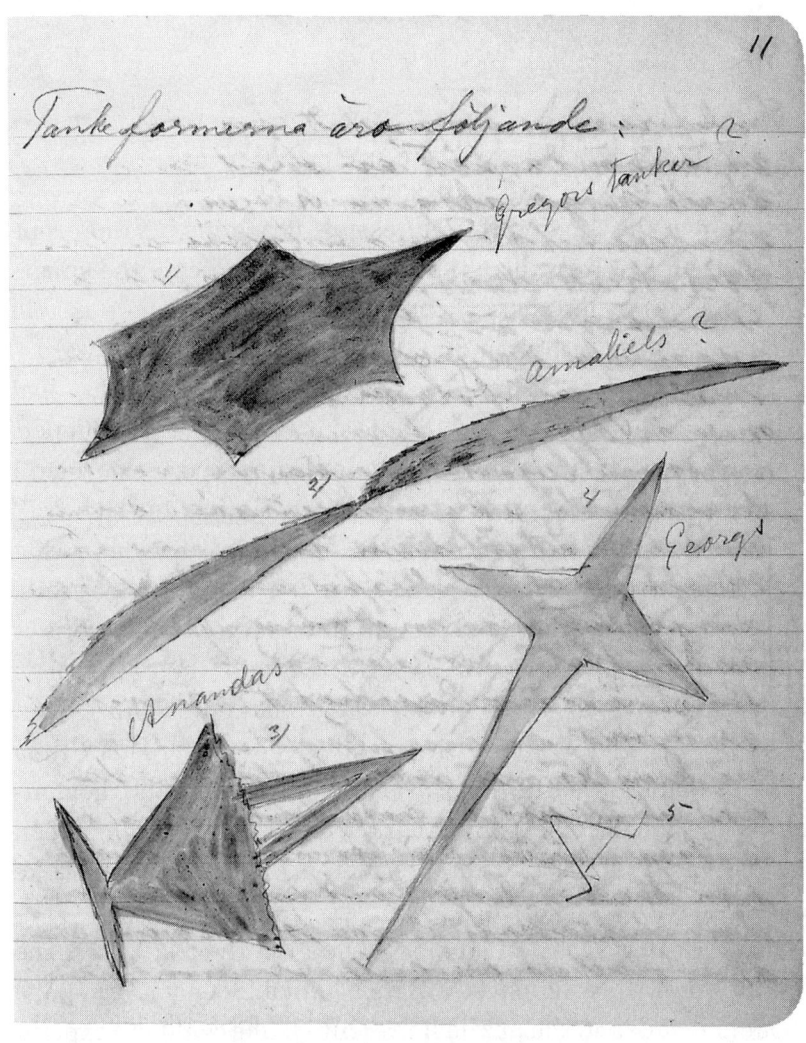

48. Sketch of thought-forms of Amaliel, Ananda, Georg,
and Gregor, 1934 notebook, Stiftelsen Hilma af Klints Verk, HaK 1072.

7

Lecture in Stockholm

Throughout the thirties, the depressing developments in Europe weighed on af Klint, though her notebooks indicate the spirits around her were optimistic: "Your time is coming soon," they told her in early 1937, "turn around and look back, but also look forward."[1] They treated her as if she were the same young woman they had first contacted decades before. While she valued their confidence, sometimes it frustrated her. "What am I supposed to do, when I have no strength?" Another time: "I am screaming: I need help."[2]

The most peculiar thing was that she still didn't know who or what these spirits were. "You wish to get to know us," the notebook says, then names her four most important interlocutors and describes them with colors. Georg was a "powerful red" and "shoots the whole color spectrum before you." Amaliel was a blue approaching violet, Ananda was gold turning to white, and Gregor was green.[3] Hilma had hoped for more: the descriptions diverged from the thought-forms she had sketched three years before in shimmering green (see fig. 48). This new piece of information only made her feel like she was starting over again.

In April 1937 she traveled to Stockholm to give a lecture at the invitation of the Swedish Anthroposophical Society. She spoke about her work and the puzzle it presented. She could not explain who the beings were who contacted her. Not even Steiner, she told the rapt audience, had been able to help her—his advice had been to find the answer herself. She felt some pressure to justify herself. "I hope that the listeners do not understand me as coming from an atavistic standpoint," she added, using Steiner's terminology.[4]

Af Klint explained that she had resigned herself to seeing things differently than Steiner. "Receiving knowledge and acquiring knowledge" were two different things, the artist stressed in the lecture. Steiner taught how to actively acquire knowledge "above one's own earthly abilities." Her experiences led her to insist that there was also another way—a passive way. "My life comprises the understanding of how to <u>receive help</u>, and the <u>struggle</u> to make my own what I have already received."[5]

Af Klint wrote out her lecture twice, with two different titles. At the top of one version she wrote, "Attempt to reach the astral plane through color experience"; the other was "Introduction to the presentation of my paintings."[6] The inclusion of "to the presentation" could mean that she had brought along slides to show her work to the audience. (A letter written several years later proves that she was interested in the newest projection technology.)

When she spoke in Stockholm, perhaps in a darkened room with slides of her work projected on a large screen, she was seventy-four years old. But as she talked about the paintings made so many years before, time faded and they seemed vividly present. To the members of the Anthroposophical Society who had come to hear her, she explained: "Every time I succeeded in executing one of my sketches, my understanding of man, animal, plant, mineral, yes, of creation in general, became clearer. I felt that I was freed, and raised above my more limited consciousness."[7] Painting was capable of transmitting this insight. She believed, she told the audience, "that the way of a painter or musician makes it easier for us to come into contact with other souls."[8]

It seemed she had struck a nerve that day, at least in some people. Her ideas had never been so well received. She was invited to give more lectures, and she began showing her works to anyone interested—at first just the watercolors, which were easy to transport. Soon, however, people were asking to visit her studio. She began to take visitors to Munsö, where her paintings still hung in the studio just as she had arranged them in 1917.

It may have been this encouragement that prompted her to start spending more time in Stockholm: Munsö was easier to reach from Stockholm than from Lund. Ulla af Klint would later report that Hilma often stayed overnight with them when she was on her way to the studio. The notebook from 1937 is labeled "Stockholmsboken," the "Stockholm book."[9] Erik af Klint later recalled that his aunt showed him all the paintings in her island studio in August 1938, adding, "We saw each other frequently after that."[10]

[8]

"Degenerate" Art in Germany and Abstract Art in New York

On October 26, 1937, af Klint celebrated her seventy-fifth birthday.[1] The situation in Germany was growing bleaker, while in Stockholm the art scene was becoming livelier and more cosmopolitan, just as it had during World War I. Again, the cause was flight and displacement, this time a result of the increasingly untenable policies imposed by Hitler's regime.

One of the artists forced to leave Germany was Lotte Laserstein (1898–1993), a Jewish painter. With her mother and her paintings, she arrived in Stockholm in December. The Galerie Moderne hosted an exhibition of her work created during the Weimar Republic when Germany was no longer a monarchy and not yet a dictatorship.[2] One 1928 work depicts a scene in Laserstein's Berlin studio. Laserstein sits at her easel in an industrial smock, looking more like an engineer than an artist, her dark hair cut short in the modern style. Before her reposes her friend Traute Rose, eyes closed. Her blond hair is also short; the head could be that of a man if the body were not so clearly a woman's.

The notebooks do not indicate that af Klint was aware of Laserstein even though the younger artist had been taken in by an aristocratic family, the Trolles, who traveled in some of the same circles as the af Klints.[3] If the two did meet, they would have discovered that they held several common views: Both believed that thinking beyond dualities would liberate humankind. Both saw the masculine and the feminine not as contradictions, but as possibilities open to both sexes without the need to choose. Laserstein painted women in male roles or with male attributes. Hilma's figures often had androgynous bodies, from the delicate Saint George to the abstract hermaphrodites who broke the boundaries of sexuality (see plates 27 and 28). "What is an angel?" af Klint would later write in a notebook. "You can call angels manwomen."[4]

But in Germany the days when ambiguity was tolerated were over. The freedom Laserstein had enjoyed during the Weimar Republic ended with National Socialism. As a Jew, Laserstein was prohibited from showing her work, and one of her paintings had been confiscated during the purges of "degenerate art."[5] She was not yet forty when she fled to Sweden, and she would never return to Germany. Her mother, on the other hand, decided not to stay in Sweden and was deported when she came home, dying in the Ravensbrück concentration camp in 1943.

In New York and other US cities, the German campaign against "degenerate art" induced a chain reaction that changed the course of both art and art history. Thousands of artworks were seized and removed from German museums and collections. Many were exhibited in the famous propaganda show organized by the German Reich in Munich, with the intent to defame them as products of "Jewish Bolshevism" or "mad incompetents." The more artists were persecuted in Europe, the more they found support across the Atlantic. Some German artists and intellectuals, like George Grosz, Erwin Panofsky, and Anni and Josef Albers, had already immigrated to the States. American newspapers were filled with stories about the totalitarian cultural policies of Hitler's regime. "Modernism Is Now Verboten," read a *New York Times* headline in July 1937.[6]

The reports alarmed collectors and new museums in New York that specialized in modern art from Europe. They saw that an important tradition was in danger, and they accorded abstract art an extraordinary status.[7] By then, many critics besides Hilla von Rebay believed that painting and sculpture liberated from the constraint of representation were the highest form of art. In March

1936, while Rebay was exhibiting more than one hundred nonrepresentational pieces of the Solomon R. Guggenheim collection for the first time, the Museum of Modern Art opened a major show, *From Cubism to Abstract Art*. But the proximity of the two institutions led to competition. The passionate admirers of abstraction couldn't agree on a critical understanding of "nonrepresentation."

As it turned out, Alfred H. Barr Jr. (1902–81), founding director of the Museum of Modern Art, held a very different view on the matter from Rebay's. He was not interested in the spiritual implications of abstraction or the evolution of the soul. For him, art was about form and the possibilities of a medium; he was interested in novelty and innovation. Barr perceived two trends in abstract art—one based on reason and logic, the other on feelings and the irrational. He termed the former "Apollonian," comparable to mathematics and architecture. The latter was "Dionysian," more closely associated with music.[8] Though he conceded that the "Dionysian" sometimes had mystical tendencies, he wished to stay clear of that conversation. In his view the history of abstraction was a surface phenomenon, the result of successive stylistic changes, from impressionism and postimpressionism to cubism and abstraction. Anything that distracted from that narrative of progress had no place in his modernist scheme: not Theosophy, Anthroposophy, politics, or reform movements; not antimaterialism, spirit, or women. In the "painting and sculpture" section of *From Cubism to Abstract Art*, there was not a single work by a female artist. Nor did Barr mention Rebay in the catalogue.[9]

Of the abstract artists still living in Europe, Kandinsky was among the first to understand how important the developments were in New York. Kandinsky was living in a suburb of Paris. The Bauhaus had been shut down by the Germans, first in Weimar and then in Dessau. Since then, sales of his work had been sluggish. In France, collectors favored cubism and surrealism. His work was spiritual, abstract, nonobjective—but none of this won him points in his new homeland.

Kandinsky had sent his New York gallerist, Israel Ber Neumann, to Moscow in 1935 to retrieve work from his old studio. For Kandinsky, a painting from 1911 that was "rolled up somewhere," without date or reference marks, was particularly important. He needed photographic proof of its existence for the following reason:

> It is truly the very first abstract painting in the world, as at that point not a single other painter was making abstract work.[10]

Not a single one? Did Kandinsky actually believe that? In fact, he knew better. In 1911, when he showed abstract work in the Blaue Reiter Exhibition in Munich, there was no talk of his being the only or the first. As an admirer of Theosophy, he had already read Besant and Leadbeater's groundbreaking 1905 book *Thought-Forms* (see plate 18), which included some nonrepresentational illustrations. He probably also knew about Katharine Schäffner's abstract images published in 1908 in *Der Kunstwart*, which Ferdinand Avenarius had called a "new language." Furthermore, he had witnessed mediums in Munich drawing and painting and even selling their antinaturalistic works as postcards.[11] The nonrepresentational field was therefore not exactly new when Kandinsky entered it. But the history of abstraction had not yet been written—that was just starting to happen in the mid-thirties, in New York.

Who would deny that times had changed? In 1911 in Munich, "spiritual" had been a key term in advanced art and "nonrepresentation" the result. The turn had been away from the material *appearance* of things, from the representation of nature. In New York, "abstraction" was a buzzword related to "nonrepresentation," but it was meant to refer to a preoccupation with visible form, at least according to Barr. Kandinsky knew it was no longer possible to start an artistic movement grounded in spiritual expression as he and Franz Marc had envisioned in 1912,[12] so now, twenty-five years later, he felt the need to assert his primacy in a movement that was being defined in New York. (The definition of modern art according to Barr would eventually have critical implications for the reception of af Klint's work as well.)

At the same moment in Munich, the National Socialists were determined to undermine his legacy. They included some of his work in the Degenerate Art Exhibition, bestowing upon it the caption "Crazy at All Costs."[13]

[9]

Tyra Kleen and the Plan for a Museum

Swedish newspapers were filled with stories about the Degenerate Art Exhibition, so we can assume that af Klint knew about it.[1] What she probably did not know was that on the other side of the Atlantic, doors were opening wide for nonrepresentational art. There were many points of connection between af Klint and Rebay, from their mutual enthusiasm for spiritual art to the plan for a spiral-shaped building to house it. But it was Barr's views and those of like-minded scholars that primarily shaped the canon. For the next several decades, abstraction was defined chiefly as a formalist experiment, and its founders were understood to be Kandinsky, Mondrian, Malevich, and Kupka.[2] Women had only a modest place in this version, and of course invisible beings and spiritual values had virtually none.

As af Klint aged, she was more frequently in contact with people who had already died. In 1936 Anna Cassel had stated in a letter that "you [Hilma] say that the dead interest you most." In the same letter Cassel confessed that she was unable to contact the dead herself and that it would require much more work than she could muster.[3]

In contrast Hilma's notebooks record conversations with the likes of Gusten Andersson, the friend to whom she had been so attracted while working on *Paintings for the Temple* in 1907, and with whom she had later quarreled so fiercely. Andersson had died in 1936. Now their disputes took a backseat as Hilma's notes describe peaceful scenes of them walking through a landscape, watching the dark recede as light came from the sky.[4]

Anna Cassel died in 1937, at the age of seventy-seven. Hilma continued to interact with her oldest friend and confidant, her Vestal, her accomplice in breaking from The Five. "Gusten and Anna still need you," Hilma's voices told her.[5] She was still in contact with Anna's surviving sisters, meeting up with them from time to time.

In February 1938, Hilma's sister Ida Haverman died, leaving her a significant inheritance. Ida's will mentions more than 100,000 crowns, of which Hilma was to receive half, the other half going to Ida's nephews Erik, Börje, and Victor af Klint.[6]

Hilma's greatest loss, however, was Thomasine Anderson, who died on April 14, 1940, and was buried in Malmö. Hilma drew the grave in her notebook.[7] The painter missed her friend so much that some entries sound like she herself longed to die. Once she wrote:

> I will come to you, as soon as you call me, I will be happy. I want, when I fall asleep, for my right side to touch your left, and thus we will walk together toward the summit of the light.[8]

Hilma wrote in her will that she wished to be buried next to Thomasine in the Malmö cemetery. When Thomasine died in 1940, Hilma had not painted for several years. Her eyes bothered her: internal bleeding in the right one had impaired her vision. She saw spots and had only peripheral vision.[9] Still, she continued to write every day in the notebooks, usually in pencil; the pages are covered with dense lines of writing.

But again, the notebooks offer an incomplete picture of what was happening in her life. Documents in the archive suggest she was secluded, having little contact with those around her. Her exchanges with higher worlds were what she wished to preserve and have us know about. She had never wasted time documenting events that she thought unimportant: for example, there is no mention of her work with the Association of Women Artists in 1910 and 1911, the exhibition with the Theosophists in 1913, or her trip to London in

1928. But another source tells a different story about the year 1940.

The diary of another artist, Tyra Kleen, suggests a much livelier side to Hilma: there were meetings and dates, excursions and picnics. On a hot August afternoon in 1940, for instance, Hilma sat in the garden of a villa in the Stockholm suburb of Lidingö. There was tea and cake, a walk through the garden, and salad in the evening.

Three days later, according to Kleen, they met again. This time, she and Hilma made an outing to Ekerö, across from Munsö. Four others came along: the surviving Cassel sisters, the artist Edith Knaffl-Granström, and an architect named Dal. Hilma had arrived at the arranged meeting point early and had waited half an hour for the others. Like many older people, she preferred to arrive too early rather than risk being late. The group spent part of the day at the Munsö studio. Three days later, there was a "long conversation" between af Klint and Kleen, presumably on the telephone.[10]

We have encountered Kleen before. She was the Symbolist artist who had been so dismissive of Joséphin Péladan and his Salon de la Rose + Croix in Paris. Kleen had traveled the world: she visited New York, and she lived in Java and Bali from 1919 to 1921, when Indonesia was still under Dutch rule. She returned to Sweden to live but didn't give up traveling. She went to Egypt and Greece, exhibited in London and Florence, and was in touch with curators and ethnologists throughout Europe. She wrote books and illustrated them, volumes with titles like *Mudras: The Ritual Hand Poses of the Buddha Priests and the Shiva Priests of Bali* or *The Temple Dances in Bali*. The books were translated into several languages.

Kleen also kept a diary, recording what she experienced not only in her waking life but also in her dreams. She favored dramatic presentation. She kept detailed records of what she wore and when, as well as noting her daily sunbath (when the weather allowed it). She had built a house in Lidingö and lived not far from the Cassel sisters.[11]

Kleen and af Klint had known each other for years. Though af Klint was twelve years older, they moved in the same circles. Kleen had visited the Edelweiss Society and was friends with several members. The two artists also knew each other through the Association of Women Artists, and in 1913 they both showed in the exhibition hosted by the Theosophists during the European Congress in Stockholm.[12]

But it wasn't until 1940 that the women developed more than a passing acquaintance. They knew they had mutual friends and sensed they might have similar interests, but neither had made a move to develop the relationship. In 1940 that changed. We do not know what prompted Kleen to contact af Klint. Perhaps her interest was fueled by what she had heard about her art.

The Second World War had been raging for a year. Supplies continued to be plentiful in Sweden; there were few of the shortages of the earlier war, let alone dire want. As before, the country managed to remain neutral. It was not unusual for tea and cake to be served, as they were in Kleen's garden in 1940. Still, the situation was distressing. The Russian army had marched into Finland and had bombed Helsinki. Norway was occupied by the Germans, and King Haakon had fled to London to govern in exile. The Germans now also controlled Denmark; thus Lund, where Hilma had her primary residence, was not far from a war zone. Parts of the Öresund, the narrow channel between Sweden and Denmark, were laced with mines, and even if Swedish territorial waters were not, there was still no chance of an excursion to Ven. Hilma's hoped-for temple seemed more remote than ever.

———

The Swedish military prepared for the worst. All males over the age of fifteen were called up. Stockholm was under a strict blackout order at night, and German troops regularly crossed into Swedish territory—on furlough, it was claimed, in order to preserve the appearance of neutrality.

But the exchange between Kleen and af Klint had nothing to do with war. Kleen was excited about af Klint's work and wanted to visit her studio. No one since Peggy Kloppers-Moltzer had shown such interest in her paintings.

"Dear Miss Kleen," Hilma wrote from Lund on August 1, 1940, prior to the studio visit, "thank you for all the interest that you have shown in my work, and for your care for me personally." She mentioned her eye problems and recommended some reading material including Steiner's *The Gospel of St. John,* which she sent to her younger admirer, and the *Goetheanum* published by the Anthroposophical Society.[13] Kleen, who had lived and studied in Dresden, Karlsruhe, and Munich as a young woman, spoke fluent German.

"Dear Miss af Klint," Kleen replied in the next letter, of September 1940, thanking Hilma for her letter and for the book. In the meantime, they had visited Munsö and Hilma's studio together. She was grateful, Kleen wrote, "to have made the acquaintance of both you & your art, & in particular the day out at your studio left an indelible impression on me. I only wish I could find the time to spend several days immersing myself on a fundamental level with your compositions. The impressions were too many and too strong for me to wish to absorb them in that short time."[14] Kleen also expressed a wish for reciprocal exchange. She would like to have Hilma's opinion of her work, too. She mentioned her illustrations of a cycle of poems by Viktor Rydberg, "The New Song of Grotte." She had made twenty-five pages of illustrations, she said. Hilma wrote the titles of several other works by Kleen in her notebook, including *Mudras.*[15] She owned Kleen's 1908 book, *Form*. Her notebook contains Kleen's address in Lidingö, along with a sketched map. The page also includes Kleen's telephone number: 656774.[16]

It seemed that the two had many common interests: Theosophy, Hinduism, renewal in art, mysticism, and enlightenment. But instead of building on mutual interests, the exchange went in a different direction and broke off, at least for a while. In the autumn of 1940, Hilma wrote another letter but never sent it. Kleen's suggestion of exchange or even collaboration seems to have unsettled her. The younger artist had proposed working together when she came to see the paintings on Munsö. After the studio visit Hilma tried to find words for her mixed feelings and quickly drafted a letter: "You wish to work together, or more accurately, to combine our work?

In what way and how? You are considerably younger and stronger than I, and like me, you are looking for an answer to the questions of life."[17] Hilma crossed out what she'd written, with an X through the entire page. Silence was also an answer. She did not contact Kleen again.

Three years passed—a long pause, during which Hilma began painting again in watercolor. In 1941 she made nearly two dozen paintings, containing typical motifs from her cosmos, including many snails. The animals stretch out their soft tentacles, their "feelers," as du Prel called the special organs that he believed future man would have. In other images, the dragon returns, and a weeping heart appears.

Another series of watercolors deals with the Goetheanum in Dornach. In the first image, the wooden building of the first Goetheanum is shown with a family of swans swimming toward it. In the next image, the building is engulfed in flames and the birds sink into the water. In the final work, the second Goetheanum is shown: angular, massive, and made of concrete, with the swans lying dead before it.[18] According to the series, the Anthroposophical Society in Dornach was destroyed when the first Goetheanum burned. The new building erected after Steiner's death failed to fulfill the task to carry on his legacy. The swan, the ancient symbol of the union of opposites, the bird that brings together the elements of water, earth, and air, was dead. From February onward Hilma took up her plan for a temple and made sketches in a notebook. Her spirits discussed her idea to install "Anna's pictures" together with hers in the same building and exhorted her to examine the purpose of her own paintings, which they called "paintings of the future." Hilma also produced four oil paintings in 1941, all of women dressed as nuns.[19] They are her last works in oil.

In March 1941 Hilma made an unusual series of watercolors that, for the first time, depict nature spirits. The spirits needed her help in connecting to the forces of the astral world, she was told and wrote it down. One spirit she had to keep from falling down, and she drew it landing in the safety of her own hands. The other spirit needed to be consoled, so she drew a slim figure with a face resembling that of a young Hilma and the body of a young man. Instead of hair, the figure's head is topped with a small snail shell which sends out rays that are received by a swan flying overhead (fig. 49). She noted that Steiner, long dead, had personally assisted with the coloring. He had advised her to use "Egyptian red" for the waves and a "very light" green for the face.[20]

When May 1943 arrived, Hilma wrote in a notebook that "fortunately" the English and Americans were going to attack Germany.[21] In July, British, American, and Canadian troops landed in Sicily, then in Normandy and the South of France. The hope that this signaled the beginning of the end proved correct. But for many, help came too late. Samuel Jessurun de Mesquita, the Jewish contributor to *Wendingen* whom af Klint had met in Amsterdam, was deported to Auschwitz in 1944 with his wife and murdered there. Their son died in Theresienstadt.

In September 1943, Kleen again got in touch with Hilma. She seems to have suspected no rancor as she started right in and asked the older woman to explain her worldview and the background of her work.[22] A grudging answer came from Lund; the letter is only a few lines, and the tone is cool. Hilma writes formally and curtly. Her outlook was Anthroposophic, she wrote. Her works, Rudolf Steiner had said, "should be kept and one day be used in the North and are worth protecting in their entirety." She believed in reincarnation. Hilma listed biographical information like bullet points. "It is my view of the work," she concluded, "that it must be preserved as a whole and not mixed with others."[23] The statement is unambiguous.

Hilma still seemed troubled by the idea of collaboration, but that wasn't why Kleen had written. Responding to Hilma's letter, she explained that money was available to her through a foundation set up by her father. She had made the sum over to the Sigtuna Foundation, an educational center run by the Lutheran Church in Sigtuna, one of the oldest towns in Sweden, about fifty kilometers northwest of Stockholm. Kleen wished to use her father's money, she wrote, to support a new building project there. The bishop in

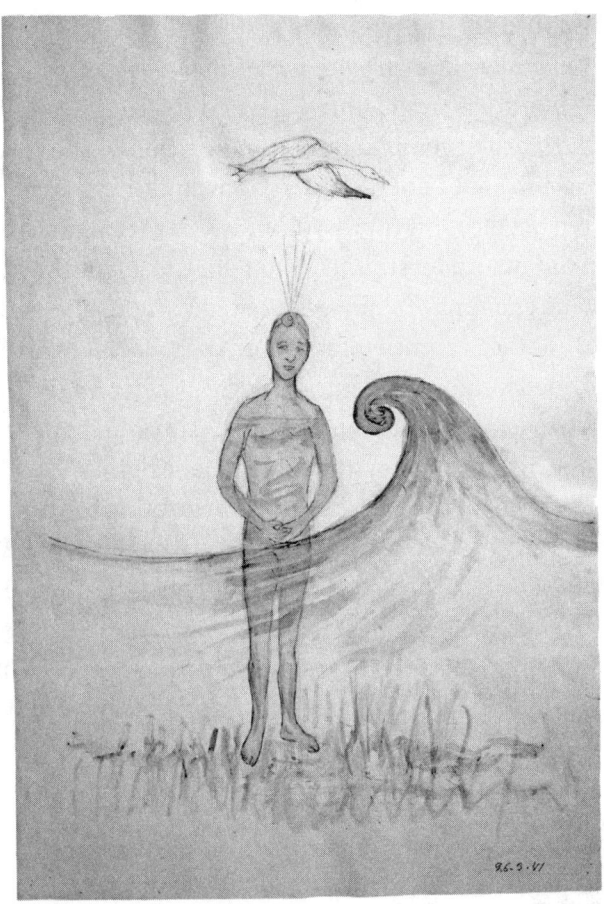

49. Watercolor drawing, March 26, 1941,
Stiftelsen Hilma af Klints Verk, HaK 1030.

charge of the foundation, Manfred Björkquist (1884–1985), wanted
the building to be a community education center, but Kleen had
bigger plans. She wanted it also to house Hilma's life's work—there,
it would be both protected and open to the public. If Hilma agreed,
the building would be designed with this in mind. "You wish your
work to be arranged as a museum," Kleen wrote, attempting to clear
up the misunderstanding: "There was never a question of other artworks occupying the same building."[24] There was some back and

forth. Hilma did not jump at Kleen's idea but instead made demands that she must have known were out of the question. She wished to design the building herself and to have control of the money. Kleen answered that the financial donation was tied to the foundation, and its mission could not be flouted. The building had to serve the educational needs of Sigtuna's youth; it was a legal requirement.

Hilma did not understand, or wish to. Kleen offered additional benefits. She could pay to move the artist's studio and assure her a place to live at the Sigtuna Foundation. Any medical care the elderly woman needed would be provided. For free. In her final letter Hilma wrote: "It was unfortunate that despite your interest in what I produced, you still didn't understand its higher origins. Yes, I'm speaking frankly now."[25] What seemed like a beginning for Kleen was an ending for af Klint. She couldn't have made it clearer how she felt about Kleen's spiritual opacity. In her notebook, she wrote that it was not she who needed help, but the other way around: Kleen needed her aid in spiritual matters.[26] Was this rejection tragic? What would history have looked like if af Klint's paintings had been moved to the Sigtuna Foundation and displayed in a building that exists today?

———

Af Klint was thinking ahead, well beyond the fear that her work might be shown alongside others'. Above all, she objected to the building's sponsors. "Putting the work one day in the hands of people who do not have an Anthroposophical outlook," Hilma wrote in the first letter in 1943, "might be problematic."[27] It was hard to argue with her on that point. Bishop Björkquist was a reformer who endorsed dialogue between religions and between science and faith, but he had limits. The voices that spoke to the painter were now calling her a "mystic" and urging her to accept and fulfill the role. According to the notebook they told her to "prepare yourself with great force for the opportunity to understand what is required of a mystic who wants to go forward."[28] A year before, they had counseled, "now is the time to gain greater knowledge of what is required of a mystic, as you are."[29] Would Bishop Björkquist be ready to recognize her as a mystic in the tradition of Bridget of Sweden or Hildegard von Bingen? It was unlikely. Her paintings would have been an alien presence in his institution, tolerated in good times but treated with hostility in bad. Viewers would not be given the opportunity to understand the works as a way to revelation. The Lutherans had their own principles. Sola scriptura. Sola fide. Sola gratia. Solus Christus.

Af Klint's mistrust of the official church ran deep. "My work may be more of a burden than a pleasure for the bishop," she wrote to Kleen.[30] The higher beings reinforced her unwillingness to compromise. They told her: "The children of the world will scorn your work. You will be derided by them, but that is better than becoming famous for earthly success."[31] Af Klint's rejection disappointed Tyra Kleen, particularly the suggestion that she didn't understand the work. In her first letter she had modestly asked for more time to immerse herself in it. Kleen wanted to facilitate the future af Klint dreamed of. But nothing came of it, and eventually she gave up trying.

By the time Kleen died in 1951 in Lidingö at the age of seventy-seven, her optimism seems to have dimmed. Like af Klint, she ordered that her work not be shown immediately after her death. Where af Klint foresaw twenty years between the present and the future, Kleen set the interval at fifty. Her works were seen for the first time in 2001.[32]

[10]

Last Months

In January 1944 Hilma traveled to Stockholm again. Her cousin Amelie had died, and Amelie's sister Hedvig needed her support. "Fulfill your duty to help," the notebook says.[1] Hedvig af Klint was only six years younger than the artist and an old woman herself. She lived in Djursholm, the wealthy suburb of Stockholm where Hilma's sister Ida had also resided. The neighborhood had an abundance of green spaces, and the streets were named after characters and places from the Nordic sagas.[2] Residents walked along "Eddavägen" or turned onto "Ragnarökvägen," named for a battle between the gods and the giants. Hilma's cousin's house was called Villa Klintegård.

Hilma wrote and wrote, filling four notebooks in 1944. It was as if she inhabited two bodies at once. In one she was preparing for death and crossing the threshold between worlds, back and forth. In the other she used every last moment to further her work. She knew she would die soon, and there were things to take care of first. "I am now left in my physical body," she wrote to her dearest, departed friends Anna Cassel and Thomasine Anderson. Before she left the earth, she continued, "I hope somehow to organize your and my work." She believed that Anna would help her.[3]

She had drawn up a will several years before, naming her nephew Erik af Klint the principal heir to her artistic and spiritual works. Erik was also to receive her writings and photographs. Hedvig, her cousin, would keep the furniture and other "effects"; she was to have the right "to choose first and to keep whatever of it she wanted."[4] The fate of her library was decided in a later amendment. The Lund University Library was to receive the Anthroposophical books published in German, while the Swedish books were to go to the Lund public library. In the same amendment, af Klint stressed that her legacy should go to the Anthroposophical Society—"if no other provisions are made."[5] "My desire for the work which began in 1907 and is still ongoing to come into good hands is what keeps me physically still alive," she had explained in her 1937 lecture at the Anthroposophical Society in Stockholm.[6]

Hilma's last paintings, of women dressed as nuns, were made the same year as her will, in 1941. Thereafter she made only small drawings to accompany her writings. This did not hinder her spiritual companions from suggesting more projects. In February 1944 she sketched a four-legged creature crouching like a dog that is begging its master to play. "This is to be the first image," the accompanying text says, as if a new series were about to commence.[7] Such plans were forged over and over, only to trail off. She had already done more than enough for a lifetime, but the spiritual companions seemed unwilling to let things end.

One of the highlights of her last months was a meeting with a new friend named Olof Sundström. Their relationship had grown deeper in 1943, the same year as the rift with Tyra Kleen. Perhaps Sundström had been a factor in her refusal to entrust her work to a church. Sundström was an Anthroposophist, artist, and sculptor, as he noted in a letter he sent the artist from Vallentuna, a small town near Stockholm. In a letter Hilma also referred to him as a "former photographer." Later, he would become a librarian at the Åbo Akademi in Finland.[8]

Af Klint had taken Sundström and his wife to her studio on Munsö. When she opened the wooden doors and invited the couple into her world of color and form, they were overwhelmed. Afterward, Sundström wrote her: "It became a 'major event' for me this summer, the visit to Munsö. When one experiences something like that . . . how close one is to the spiritual, that is something special, an experience of such power lets one discover the revelation of the transcendental. It gives one courage to keep striving, on the lonely path."[9] Revelations come with obligations, as Hilma herself had learned. Sundström had been profoundly affected by the studio visit, and he felt a growing sense of responsibility toward the artist and her work. He helped as much as he could. His wife shared his enthusiasm: she asked about the letters in the paintings and was told that Hilma shared her curiosity. Another time Hilma showed the couple the glossary of symbols she had devised.[10]

Sundström first took on small tasks: he helped Hilma with practical matters. In October that year she was to deliver another lecture in Stockholm. Ever since the 1937 talk, interest in her work had grown, attracting visitors to the studio such as Tyra Kleen and the Sundströms. Once, when she was showing her watercolors from the thirties, a visitor had felt "a sudden release," she noted.[11] She even reached out to the Theosophical Society and read Blavatsky again.[12]

Thinking about future speaking engagements, she asked Sundström to look into the newest projectors. A sciopticon turned out to be the best option, but slides would have to be made, and she worried about the cost. Money was tight; however, Hilma asked Sundström to arrange for a few slides. She always wanted to use state-of-the-art technology; she was never unsettled by progress or change—to the contrary, she thrived on it. After all, her spiritual friends never let her forget that she was "destined for the work of the future."[13] She was over eighty at this point.

In August Hilma moved in with her cousin Hedwig at Villa Klintegård. In October she stumbled and fell as she alighted from a streetcar, injuring her head and arm. She never recovered. The notes she had been making for nearly half a century break off with a last entry from October 9: "You have service to the mysteries before you and will soon understand what is required of you."[14]

On October 21 she closed her eyes. Forever, as the saying goes. Until the next incarnation, she would have said.

She did not foresee the storm of events that followed her death. According to her will, she wished for her remaining effects to be brought to Munsö and "kept with everything else there for as long as possible." But that was not to be. The prophecy in her notebook, that the "house will stay undestroyed" on Munsö, had been wrong.[15] As the will was being read, Erik af Klint learned that the studio was to be razed, along with the lake house Furuheim. The land still belonged to the Giertta family. Emilia had died in 1924, and her son apparently found what remained upon it to be a burden. He issued an ultimatum: the buildings had to be cleared out in three months.

There was no time for questions. Erik af Klint was in the military, he was occupied by the war, so it was left to Olof Sundström to do what had to be done. He moved to Munsö. In the three months allotted he organized, catalogued, and numbered everything. He created an index. The paintings were taken down, the canvases removed from their stretchers and rolled. Crates were built, filled, and transported off the island. The entire estate remained in the attic of the apartment building at Karlavägen 56, where Erik af Klint lived, until his retirement in 1966.[16]

Af Klint's other wish, to be buried next to her friend and partner Thomasine Anderson in Malmö, was not honored. Instead, an urn with her ashes was buried in the family plot in the Galärvarvskyrk-ogården naval cemetery in Stockholm, near her younger sister, Hermina, who had been dead more than sixty years.

It is not clear why her wishes were disregarded. Erik af Klint later wrote that his aunt had died during "the final phase of the Second World War" and that he'd had no time to attend to the business surrounding her death. He was a naval officer, absorbed in geopolitical events. Like Hermina's, Hilma's grave was not marked by an individual headstone. The *Svenska Dagbladet* reported on the funeral. Johann Sebastian Bach's cantata *Gottes Zeit ist die allerbeste Zeit* had been played on the organ. The article also mentioned the wreaths sent by the Theosophical and Anthroposophical Societies.[17]

Anyone who visits the cemetery today in search of Hilma af Klint's grave will find the names of many captains and officers. They trace the seafaring tradition that Hilma felt close to all her life. Her grandfather Gustaf had charted the depths of the Swedish waterways. She, as artist and mystic, those of the human soul. Her grandfather had been nineteen when he used his knowledge to help the Swedish fleet sail out of Vyborg Bay, escaping disaster. Her works would serve the same function, Hilma believed. They would show future generations the way.

[11]

Conclusion

Is that the end of the story? No, it is just the beginning. Af Klint's work survived unharmed in boxes in Erik's attic in a large Stockholm apartment building.

Olof's glowing obituary for the artist, in which he described her as a "visionary," was never published by the Anthroposophical Society. Instead, the *Goetheanum* in Dornach published its own obituary, six months late. It described af Klint as a failure—someone who wanted to cultivate "the ways of Anthroposophical research and art" but was unable to. "It was her great sorrow," the obituary said.[1]

When Erik af Klint retired in 1966, he brought the boxes of his aunt's works down from the attic with the help of his son, Johan af Klint. He had everything photographed and catalogued, and in the early seventies he asked two Stockholm museums if they might be interested in mounting an exhibition of the paintings. Both the Moderna Museet and the Nationalmuseum declined. Af Klint's paintings seemed to be derivative of Kandinsky's, he was told, even though they had been made well before Kandinsky had shifted to a nonobjective mode.[2]

The Swedish Anthroposophists proved more helpful, offering space to store the work. In 1972 Erik af Klint founded the Stiftelsen Hilma af Klints Verk. His son Gustav took over the foundation in 1979. Erik af Klint died in December 1981 and did not live to see the first exhibition featuring his aunt's paintings. The Los Angeles County Museum of Art opened the groundbreaking show *The Spiritual in Art: Abstract Painting, 1890–1985* in November 1986. A key figure who worked behind the scenes to make sure that the curator, Maurice Tuchman, knew about af Klint's paintings was Sixten Ringbom, an art historian who taught at the Åbo Akademie in Finland, where Olof Sundström worked as a librarian.[3] The more recent reception of af Klint's work is well-known, and is detailed in the introduction.

My aim with this book is to contribute to an understanding of the breadth and depth of af Klint's life and work. Her paintings, watercolors, drawings, and notebooks resemble a huge river system with countless twists, junctures, and branches, some flowing on the surface, others underground. As observed, af Klint led a much less secluded life than has been previously assumed. The greater the resistance she encountered, the more her ideas evolved on how to overcome it. She struggled for nearly two decades to find a public space for her paintings and showed her spiritual paintings for the first time when she exhibited with the Theosophists in Stockholm in 1913. Subsequently she developed her "museum in a suitcase," traveled to Dornach, Amsterdam, and London, and finally designed a spiral-shaped temple that was to be built on the island of Ven, complete with a lighthouse and observatory. Although she understood how difficult it would be to implement such a project, she rejected the offer by Tyra Kleen in 1943 to house her work at the Sigtuna Foundation. Af Klint found the place unsuitable, and any second-best solution was out of the question.

Much that this book contains is told here for the first time. Other things can only be touched on briefly and ought to be investigated more thoroughly. One of the particularities of af Klint's archive is that it contains not only her estate, but also those of two other artists. Several of Anna Cassel's works from 1913 have been discussed here, but there are countless other paintings, drawings, and notes that deserve to be researched. The af Klint archive also contains the large estate of Edith Knaffl-Granström, another Swedish artist and Anthroposophist who directed a painting school for children in Vienna, and many of the school's files. Knaffl-Granström is mentioned in Tyra Kleen's journal as one of the travelers who set out for Munsö in 1940 to visit Hilma's atelier, and two years later she is mentioned once in a notebook.[4] Nothing further is known about connections between the two women.

I have also attempted to map out a different history of abstraction. It begins in 1857, when the English writer Camilla Dufour Crosland recorded her experiences with spiritual apparitions and furnished her book with nonrepresentational illustrations and those by the artist Anna Mary Howitt. The thread continues through the artist Georgiana Houghton and her exhibition of nonrepresentational works in London in 1871, which she described as a "radical experiment." In Sweden, too, there was talk of a new kind of art in 1879 and 1896 in writings by Bertha Valerius. Early on af Klint got to know the stylistic diversity of The Five and the Edelweiss

Society by looking and drawing herself. The astonishing work she produced beginning in 1906 is at the center of this book. The tradition of a spiritual, nonrepresentational art continued, involving such advanced artists as Kandinsky, Mondrian, and Kupka. It was picked up in the United States by Hilla von Rebay, whose monument stands on Fifth Avenue in New York—the spiraling form of the Guggenheim Museum designed by the great American architect Frank Lloyd Wright.

The history of this spiritual abstract art has, from the beginning, been substantially shaped by women. "In the ages that are to come," Camilla Dufour Crosland wrote confidently in 1857, "Developed Woman will be the great artist."[5] In the end she was proven right, even if this recognition was a long time coming.

In this biography, it is not only people with names, birthdays, and addresses who get a chance to speak. Some of the supporting characters in af Klint's world were messengers from higher planes. Their names were Ananda, Gregor, Georg, and Amaliel, and not even af Klint could have said exactly who they were. The fact that they figured so importantly in the artist's life complicates the project of biographical writing and its registers.

I am aware that many of my colleagues in the humanities have drawn on sociological theories in an attempt to classify the supernatural occurrences that were anything but rare in the nineteenth century, both inside and outside the art world. The high proportion of women affiliated with spiritual movements such as Theosophy has been explained in relationship to the desire for autonomy. Women, so the theory goes, invoked higher authorities to demand rights that were denied them by society: by representatives of the state, the church, art, or science.[6] In addition, church historians have documented cases in the nineteenth century where divine authorities were invoked to justify homosexuality—for example, in the case of nuns in a particular Roman cloister.[7]

I do not employ such an interpretative schema in this biography.

In the case of af Klint, it seems to me presumptuous to ignore the artist's own experience of reality and to downgrade to the status of an expedient precisely the thing she regarded as key. She never questioned any of the transcendental phenomena and increasingly understood herself in later years to be a mystic. She also saw herself as an artist, healer, and visionary, and this judgment was shared by others close to her, for example Olof Sundström and her nephew Erik af Klint. She, who inhabited both female and male bodies, experienced the sexual encounters with her friends detailed here from a position beyond clear gender relationships. In this, I have relied on her descriptions of events whenever they exist. In cases when she passed over incidents without writing anything, I have attempted to close the gaps by consulting other archives.

The wonderful and the supernatural were part of af Klint's experience, but this did not make her discount the everyday. She was able to reconcile the two without feeling any contradiction or being thrown off course. In one moment she could speak to Ananda, her spiritual friend and companion, named after the Buddha's favorite student, and in the next catch the tram to the harbor in time to board the ferry across Lake Mälaren.

Today, when we perceive phenomena that we cannot explain or categorize, we often assume they must be illusions. We associate visions with drugs or psychic dysfunction. Af Klint would have seen this as a loss. Those who learn to look past the mysterious forget to pay attention to the extraordinary.

On the other hand, she had faith in future generations, who she believed would understand her work. Her wish was fulfilled in the sense that more people than ever before have seen and been excited by the art. Where that leads remains to be seen.

The painter and her friends Anna Cassel and Thomasine Anderson considered starting small to be the best strategy. In January 1917 Hilma explained how she wanted to proceed, and Thomasine wrote it down, in her calm, rhythmic handwriting:

First I will attempt to understand the flowers of the earth; I will take the plants that grow on land as my starting point. Then, with the same care, I will study what lives in the waters of the earth. Then the blue ether with its myriad creatures will be the subject of my study, and finally I will penetrate the forest, exploring the silent mosses, the trees, and the many animals that inhabit the cool, dark under-growth.[8]

That's how it could work, the friends imagined. That day they filled a dozen more pages in the notebook. Then they closed the book, went outside, and the cold winter air colored their cheeks red.

Afterword
by Johan af Klint

Hilma af Klint (1862–1944) began painting abstract works in 1906. She had excellent artistic training, having concluded her studies at the Royal Academy in Stockholm with top grades (1882–87). She was well versed in the natural sciences and followed the revolutionary scientific developments around the turn of the twentieth century. Her deep, lifelong interest in philosophy and religious questions began in 1879, when she was only seventeen years old. She was a careful observer of the world around her, and this is reflected in her work. The abstract paintings she made prior to 1920 are strongly influenced by the teachings of the Rosicrucians, the Theosophists, and esoteric Christianity. Her work can be described as an attempt to make the invisible visible.

Hilma af Klint was of small stature (just over five feet), but she was strong-willed, energetic, and resolute. This can be seen in the regularity of her stylistic development: she radically changed her way of painting three or four times over the course of her life. She was a tireless creator, rather than a devotee. She absorbed influences in order to transform and reshape them. This was true as much of her painting as of her religious convictions. It is therefore inaccurate to consider her a disciple of Rudolf Steiner. In 1930, she turned away in disappointment from the Anthroposophical Society in Dornach, where she had stayed many times, and she never went back.

For this book, Julia Voss took on the herculean task of going through Hilma af Klint's notebooks—all 26,000 pages of them, elegantly written by hand or typed in archaic Swedish. Julia Voss's work is invaluable for future researchers. Her book portrays Hilma af Klint as a balanced person with wide-ranging interests who worked for decades in the cultural center of Stockholm, gleaning inspiration from her artistic surroundings and positioning herself and engaging within them. Hilma af Klint engaged with the artistic movements of her time, as well as with art history and philosophy, and she traveled to many European cities.

I wish to thank Julia Voss in the name of the af Klint family for her methodical, revolutionary, and self-sacrificing study of Hilma af Klint. We are most grateful for the devotion to Hilma af Klint that shows throughout this book. These pages will long be an exceptional resource for research. Thank you, Julia.

JOHAN AF KLINT
Grandnephew of Hilma af Klint and former chair
of the Stiftelsen Hilma af Klints Verk

Afterword
by Ulrika af Klint

Hilma af Klint changed history.

It has been a great joy to see the growing interest in Hilma af Klint's (1862–1944) work, in particular in the last several years. She is a unique Swedish artist who is now gaining international attention. She is also a woman—the art world is changing, and society along with it. Her art is becoming an exceptional source of inspiration.

The year 2019 marked the seventy-fifth anniversary of Hilma af Klint's death. But the meaning of her legacy has only grown. She spent a lifetime engaging with the fundamental questions of existence. Hilma af Klint expanded the understanding of human consciousness and did not hesitate to leave the visible world behind her—along with the prejudices of her time.

The artist belonged to the second generation of women who were allowed to study at the Royal Academy of Art in Stockholm, and she graduated with excellent grades (1882–87). She was highly trained and hungry for knowledge. She was as interested in the spiritual movements of her time as in the latest scientific developments.

When she stopped painting representationally, she became both artist and researcher. Born into a family of naval officers and cartographers, she charted the spiritual dimensions of our existence. She received codes from the invisible world and made them visible. She turned these codes over to the future to decipher.

Happily, Julia Voss has now shed light on the enormous trove of more than 1,200 abstract works and 26,000 pages of writings that Hilma af Klint left behind. Her book shows exceptional dedication to both the person and her work. The work is based on comprehensive research, both in the artist's archive and in the many places where Hilma af Klint lived and worked. Our knowledge has thereby been greatly enriched—about Hilma af Klint as a person, and about the time and environment in which she lived.

I am sure that all of the members of the original board of the Stiftelsen Hilma af Klints Verk from 1972 would be extremely thankful to Julia Voss: my grandfather Erik af Klint, my father Gustaf af Klint, Arne Klingborg, Åke Fant, and Bert Vetterfalk.

In the name of the Stiftelsen Hilma af Klints Verk I wish to thank Julia Voss for the groundbreaking insights that her work brought to light—for the academic world and for all who wish to learn about Hilma af Klint.

ULRIKA AF KLINT
Chair of the Stiftelsen Hilma af Klints Verk since 2016

Hilma af Klint's Travels and Places of Residence

Johan af Klint and Julia Voss

1862-68. Karlberg Palace, Solna, Stockholm[1] (registered from October 26 to October 30)

1868-77. Norrtullsgatan 19, Adolf Fredrik Parish, Stockholm (registered from October 30)

1877-79. Norra Tullportsgatan 15, Adolf Fredrik Parish, Stockholm

1879-99. Stora Bastugatan 13, Adolf Fredrik Parish, Stockholm (registered until October 9)

1890s. Trips to Holland, Belgium, Germany, and Norway[2]

1899-1918. Brahegatan 54, Hedvig Eleonora Parish, Stockholm, with her mother and, beginning in 1904, the athletics instructor Sigrid Lancén, who moved in as a roommate (registered until October 10)

1903. Trips to the Wartburg in Thuringia, Germany, and then to Italy, including Verona, Venice, Florence, and Rome[3]

1918-26. Villa Furuheim, Munsö, with her mother and Thomasine Anderson[4] (registered October 10 through November 5)

1920. First trip to the Goetheanum in Dornach, Switzerland, with Thomasine Anderson[5] (September 20 to October 26)

1921-22. Second trip to the Goetheanum in Dornach, Switzerland, with Thomasine Anderson (December 9 to beginning of June)

1922-23. Third trip to the Goetheanum in Dornach, Switzerland, with Thomasine Anderson (building destroyed by fire on New Year's Eve; December 19 until mid-January, arrival perhaps as early as "October or November")

1923–24. Fourth trip to Dornach, Switzerland, with Thomasine
Anderson (beginning of April to beginning of September)

1925. Fifth trip to Dornach, Switzerland, with Thomasine Anderson (beginning of April to beginning of June)

1925. Sixth trip to Dornach, Switzerland, with Thomasine Anderson (September 20 to mid-October)

1926. Seventh trip to Dornach, Switzerland, with Thomasine
Anderson (end of March to beginning of June)

1927. Eighth trip to Dornach, Switzerland, with Thomasine
Anderson (April 12 to end of May or "maybe June")

1927. Trip to Amsterdam and The Hague, Holland[6] (fall)

1928. Trip to London, England (presumably with Thomasine
Anderson; June)[7]

1930. Ninth trip to Dornach, Switzerland, this time to the second
Goetheanum, with Thomasine Anderson (mid-April to beginning of May)

1926–31. Skolgatan 17, Uppsala, with Thomasine Anderson[8] (registered November 5 to September 14)

1931–32. Kullagatan 58, Helsingborg, St. Mary parish[9] (registered
September 14 to November 24)

1932–34. Karl X Gustafs gata 23, Helsingborg, with Thomasine
Anderson (registered November 24 to July 20)

1934–35. Karl XIs gata 11, Lund, with Thomasine Anderson (registered from July 20)[10]

1935–38. Grönegatan 28, Lund, with Thomasine Anderson

1938–44. Spolegatan 3A, Lund, with Thomasine Anderson, who
died on April 14, 1940 (registered until October 21)

1944. Villa Klintegård, Ösby, Djursholm, with cousin Hedvig af
Klint (from August; Hilma af Klint kept her official residence
in Lund)[11]

Hilma af Klint died on October 21, 1944, in Djursholm, following
an accident.

The Library of Hilma af Klint

Johan af Klint and Julia Voss

Where not otherwise noted, the books are held by the Stiftelsen Hilma af Klints Verk. The following abbreviations indicate other locations:

(*) = According to Åke Fant, the volume was part of Hilma af Klint's library, but it no longer exists in the archive of the Stiftelsen Hilma af Klints Verk.

(LS) = The volume was bequeathed by Hilma af Klint to the public library of Lund and listed in the 1945 inventory. Bibliographic details are taken from this list. According to the public library, all works have since been given to the university library.

(LU) = The volume was bequeathed by Hilma af Klint to the Lund University Library and listed in the 1945 inventory. Bibliographic details are taken from this list.

EDITIONS OF THE BIBLE

Bibeln. 1915. "Den Heliga Skrift i fullständig överennsstämmelse med Bibelkommissionens Normalupplago." C. W. K. Gleerups Förlag, Lund.

Biblia. 1869. "Det är All Den Heliga Skrift efter den uppå Konung Carl den Tolftes Befallning år 1703 utgifna edition med förändring i stafsättet." Tryckt uti Berlingsta Boktryckeriet på Fr. Berlings förlag, Lund.

NT. 1930. "Das Neue Testament Unseres Herrn und Heilandes Jesu Christi nach der Deutschen Übersetzung D. Martin Luthers." Privileg. Württ. Bibelanstalt, Stuttgart.

Personne, J., and W. Rudin. 1915. *Gamla Testamentet De Apokryfiska Böckerna.* Proföfversättning, P. A. Norstedt & Söners Förlag, Stockholm.

MAGAZINES AND PERIODICALS

Die Drei: Monatsschrift für Anthroposophie Dreigliederung und Goetheanismus (Stuttgart) 1 (1921); 2 (1922); 5 (1925): 2–12; 6 (1926); 7 (1927): 3–8. (LU)

Die Freie Waldorfschule (Stuttgart) 6 (1924). (LU)

Efteråt: Tidskrift för spiritism (1884–1901). (*)

Gäa-Sophia: Jahrbuch der naturwissenschaftlichen Sektion der Freien Hochschule für Geisteswissenschaft am Goetheanum Dornach (Dornach) 1 (1926)–2 (1927) (LU); 4 "Völkerkunde" (1929). (*)

Meddelanden från ledningen av antroposofiska sällskapet i Dornach 1924–25. (LS)

Natura. Eine Zeitschrift zur Erweiterung der Heilkunst nach geisteswissenschaftlicher Menschenkunde (Basel) 1 (1926), 11 (1928). (LU)

Österreichische Blätter für freies Geistesleben (Vienna) 3 (1926): 1.

Soziale Zukunft (Dornach) 5/7. (LU)

BOOKS

Adelborg, Ottilia. 1918. *Gråns—En by som varit*. Albert Bonniers Förlag, Stockholm.

Åman-Nilsson, G. 1932. *Abailard—Ett Medeltida Livsöde*. Albert Bonniers Förlag, Stockholm.

Andersson, N. J. 1871. *Elementar Flora*. Stockholm.

Arenson, A. 1921. *Die Kindheitsgeschichte Jesu*. Stuttgart. (LS)

———. 1922. *Jesu barndomshistoria, de båda Jesusbarnen*. Stockholm. (*)

Aubert, A. 1905. *En Renaissancekunstner Fra Giovanni da Fiesole med til- navnet Angelico 1387 til 1455*. Gyldendalske Boghandel, Nordisk Forlag, Trykt i Langkjærs Bogtrykkeri, Copenhagen and Christiania.

Bain, F. W. N.d. *Den moderna spiritism*. (*)

Bauer, M. N.d. *Rudolf Steiner och pedagogiken före 1905*. (*)

Beckh, H. 1921. *Der physische und der geistige Ursprung der Sprache*. Stuttgart. (2 copies, LS)

———. 1921. *Etymologie und Lautbedeutung im Lichte der Geisteswissenschaft*. Stuttgart. (LS)

———. 1930. *Der Kosmische Rhythmus*. Basel. (LS)

Besant, A. 1908. *Kristendomens inre lära eller Esoterisk kristendom*. Hugo Brusewitz Boktryckeri, Göteborg.

Besant, A., and C. W. Leadbeater. 1896. *Biblia. Det är All den Heliga Skrift*. (*)

———. 1915. *Bibeln*. (*)

Bierfreund, T. 1901. *Florens—Monumenter og Mennesker*. Gyldendalske Boghandel, Fr. Bagges Bogtrykkeri, Copenhagen.

Blavatsky, H. P. 1895. *Den Hemliga Läran—Sammanfattning av Vetenskap, Religion och Filosofi*. Översättning från tredje engelska upplagan (F. Kellberg), part 1, Världsdaningen. Svenska Teosofiska Samfundet, Stockholm.

————.1898. *Den Hemliga Läran—Sammanfattning av Vetenskap, Religion och Filosofi*. Översättning från tredje engelska upplagan (F. Kellberg), part 2, Människans Daning. Svenska Teosofiska Samfundet, Stockholm.

Blume, W. 1917. *Musikalische Betrachtungen in Geisteswissenschaftlichem Sinn*. Berlin. (LU)

Bock, E., and F. Rittelmeyer. 1922. *Zur religiösen Erneuerung*. Stuttgart. (LU)

————.1932. *Bühnenkunst am Goetheanum*. 2 vols. Dornach. (LU)

————.1935. *Denkschrift über Angelegenheiten der Anthroposophischen Gesellschaft . . . 1925–1935*. Dornach. (LU)

Briem, E. 1932. *Mysterier och Mysterieförbund*. Bokförlaget Natur och Kultur, Stockholm.

Charpentier, J. 1920. *Ur Indiens klassiska litteratur*. (*)

Cronstrand, S. A. 1823. *Om Astronomiens nyare Framsteg*. Ur K. Vet. Academiens Årsberättelser för 1822, J. P. Lindhs Enka, Stockholm.

Dele'n, C. 1814. *Fransyskt och Svenskt Lexikon*. Första delen, Tryckt hos C. Delén, Stockholm.

Doré, G. 1912. *Dante Alighieris Divina Commedia*. (*)

du Prel, Carl. 1890. *Det Dolda Själslifvet—eller Mystikens Filosofi*. Oscar L. Lamms Förlag, Stockholm.

————.1890. *Själsläran—framställd ur Synpunkten af Menniskoväsendets Enhet*. Looström & Komps Förlag, Stockholm.

Eckehart, Mester. 1917. *Predikener og Traktater*. Andr. Fred. Høst & Sons Forlag, Copenhagen.

Edgren & Jolin. 1894. *Läkemedlens användning och dosering*. Wilhelm Billes Bokförlag AB, Stockholm.

Ekholm, A. 1933. *Vildvin*. Seelig, Stockholm. (*)

Ervast, P. 1900. *Framtidens Religion—Några tankar och erfarenheter*. Wilhelm Billes Bokförlag AB, Stockholm.

————.1906. *Kortfattad Teosofisk Uppslagsbok*. Andra omarbetade upplagan, Teosofiska Bokförlaget, Stockholm.

Fogelklou, E. 1919. *Birgitta*. Albert Bonniers Förlag, Stockholm.

Fogelklou, E., A. Lindblom, and E. Wesse'n. 1917. *Legender från Sveriges Medeltid—illustrerade i svensk medeltidskonst*, parts 1 and 2. Bröderna Lagerström Boktryckare, Stockholm.

————.1917. *Legender om utländska Helgon*, part 2. Bröderna Lagerström Boktryckare, Stockholm.

Fränkl, O. 1930. *Die Anthroposophie R. Steiners*. Basel. (LU)

Goethe, J. W. von. N.d. *Faust—Der Tragödie erster Teil*. Verlag von Philipp Reclam jun., Leipzig.

Goetz, W. 1909. *Assisi*. Berühmte Kunststätten, vol. 44, Verlag E. A. See-mann, Leipzig.

Grönbech, V. 1932. *Mystikere i Europa og Indien*, 2–3, Copenhagen. (LS)

Hartman, F. 1889. *Magi—Hvit och Svart—eller Vetenskapen om det änd-liga och oändliga Lifvet*. Innehållande Praktiska Vinkar för dem som studera ockultism, Öfversättning från tredje engelska upplagan (Victor Pfeiff), Teosofiska Samfundets Svenska Afdelning, Stockholm.

Heinroth, J. C. A. 1835. *Tempelförgården*. Översättning från tyska, Stock-holm. (*)

Heydebrand, C. 1921. *Gegen Experimental-Psychologie* . . . Stuttgart. (LU)

———.1922. *Methodologisches zur Therapie* . . . Stuttgart. (LU)

Hohlenberg, J. E. 1918. *Kheopspyramiden och dess Hemlighet*. Magn. Bergvalls Förlag, Stockholm.

———.1918. *Nostradamus*. J. S. Jensens Forlag, Copenhagen.

Judge, W. N.d. *Bhagavad Gita*. (*)

Jung, Johan, H. 1812. *Andelära—framställd uti ett med Naturen, Förnuftet och Uppenbarelsen enligt svar på den frågan: Hwad bör man tro och icke tro om Aningar, Syner och Andars Uppenbarelse*. S. Norbergs Tryckeri, Göteborg.

Kalidasa. 1906. *Urvas och Hennes Hjälte*. Ett Skådespel, Berlingska Bok-tryckeriet, Lund.

Kallstenius, G. S. N. 1931. *Konsten—dess Väsen och Betydelse*. Bokförlaget Natur och Kultur, Stockholm.

Kleen, T. 1908. *Form*. A. B. Sandbergs Bokhandel, Stockholm.

Kornerup, E. 1918. *Khadía*. C. W. K. Gleerups Förlag, Lund.

Krok, Th. O.B.N., and S. Almquist. 1917. *Svensk Flora för skolor*, part 3: *Kryptogamer*. Albert Bonniers & Bokförlag, Stockholm.

Larsson, H. 1910. *Kunskapslivet—Uppfostringspsykologi*. Andra upplagan, C. W. K. Gleerups Förlag, Lund.

Levertin, O. 1911. *Samlade Skrifter—Utländsk Konst*. Albert Bonniers Förlag, Stockholm.

Lévy, E. 1915. *Rudolf Steiners världsåskådning*. Norrköping. (LS)

Liljendahl, E. 1922. *Swedenborg*. (*)

Ljungström, G. N.d. *Nostradamus*. (*)

London, J. 1919. *Avgrundens Folk*. Dahlbergs Förlag AB, Stockholm.

Maeterlinck, M. 1921. *Den Stora Hemligheten*. P. A. Norstedts & Söners Förlag, Stockholm.

Marcus, A. 1917. *Mester Eckhart*. Copenhagen. (*)

Martinus. 1930. *Das Neue Testament*. (*)

———.1932. *Livets Bog*. Vald. Pedersens Bogtrykkeri, Copenhagen.

Möller, H. 1909. *Anders Zorn*. Gleerupska Universitets-Bokhandeln, Lund.

Nietzsche, F. 1910. *Sålunda talade Zarathustra*.

Nizida. 1890. *Astralljuset—Försök till en framställning af vissa Ockulta Principer i Naturen jämte några anmärkningar öfver den Moderna Spiritism*. V. Härnkvists Förlag, Stockholm.

Norlind, E. 1939. *Borgeby-Minnen*. C. W. K. Gleerups Förlag, Lund.

Østergaard, V. 1907. *Tyge Brahe*. Gyldendalske Boghandel, Nordisk Forlag, Copenhagen and Christiania.

Oxon, M. A. 1892. *Från en Högre Verld—Meddelanden från Andeverlden i Religiösa Frågor*. Adolf Johnsons Förlag, Stockholm.

Petiscus, A. H. 1878. *Olympen eller Hellenernes och Romarnes Mytologi jämte Egypternes, Hinduernes och de fornnordiska Folkens Gudalära*. Hjalmar Linnströms Förlag, Stockholm.

Poulsen, F. 1925. *Den Delfiske Apollon och hans Helgedom*. AB Skoglunds Bokförlag, Stockholm.

Remarque, E. M. 1929. *Im Westen nichts Neues*. Im Propyläen-Verlag, Berlin.

Rittelmeyer, F. 1919. *Om Rudolf Steiners teosofi*. Norrköping. (LS)

Rittelmeyer, H. 1922. *Was will Dr. Rudolf Steiner?* 5th ed. Basel. (LU)

Römer, O. 1921. *Über den Zahnkaries . . .* Stuttgart. (LU)

Schiller, H. 1935. *Fallet Folkeson*. Åhlén & Åkerlunds Boktryckeri, Stockholm.

Schück, H. 1922. *Kulturhistoriska Skizzer*. Hugo Gebers Förlag, Stockholm.

Schuré, E. 1922. *Die grossen Eingeweihten*. Leipzig. (LS)

Seiling, M. 1913. *Teosofi och Kristendom*. Norrköping. (LS)

Singer, H. W. 1919. *Anselm Feuerbach—mit 61 Abbildungen, Briefen des Künstlers, gewählt und eingeleitet*. Hugo Schmidt Verlag, Munich.

Steffen, A. N.d. *Das Viergetier*. Zürich. (LS)

——.1922. *Die Krisis im Leben des Künstlers*. Bern. (LS)

——.1927. *Der Chef des Generalstabs*. Dornach. (LS)

Steiner, R. N.d. *Das Hereinragen . . . [mit anderen Schriften zu einem Buch gebunden]*. N.p. (LU)

——.N.d. *Die Bhagavad Gita und die Paulusbriefe*. Berlin. (LU)

——.N.d. *Die Geheimnisse der Schwelle*. Berlin. (LU)

——.N.d. *Die geistige Führung des Menschen . . .* N.p. (LU)

——.N.d. *Die geistigen Wesenheiten*. Berlin. (LU)

——.N.d. *Die Mysterien des Morgenlandes . . .* Berlin. (LU)

——.N.d. *Geistige Hierarchien . . .* Berlin. (LU)

——.N.d. *Kristendomnen som mystisk kjendsgjerning*. Christiania. (LS)

———.N.d. *Welche Bedeutung hat die okkulte Entwicklung des Menschen*... ? Berlin.

———.1905. *Schiller und unser Zeitalter.* Berlin. (LU)

———.1908. *Hvorledes erhverves kundskab om høiere verdener?* Christiania. (LS)

———.1909. *Das Vaterunser.* Berlin. (LU)

———.1909. *Die Erziehung des Kindes.* 2nd ed. Berlin. (LU)

———.1909. *Einweihung und Mysterien.* Berlin. (LU)

———.1909. *Haeckel, die Welträtsel*... 3rd ed. Berlin. (LU)

———.1909. *Jul.* Stockholm. (LS)

———.1909. *Teosofi.* Stockholm. (LS)

———.1909. *Unsere atlantischen Vorfahren.* 3rd ed. Berlin. (LU)

———.1910. *Das Wesen der Künste.* Berlin. (LU)

———.1910. *Die Pforte der Einweihung.* Berlin. (LU)

———.1910. *Lebensfragen der theosophischen Bewegung.* 2nd ed. Berlin. (LU)

———.1910. *Pfingsten.* N.p. (LU)

———.1910. *Theosophie und gegenwärtige Geistesströmungen.* Berlin. (LU)

———.1910. *Wie Karma wirkt.* Berlin. (LU)

———.1911. *Die geistige Führung des Menschen*... Berlin. (LU)

———.1911. *Die Prüfung der Seele.* Berlin. (LU)

———.1911. *Meddelelser af Akasha-Kroniken.* Copenhagen. (LS)

———.1912. *Der Hüter der Schwelle.* Berlin. (LU)

———.1913. *Die okkulten Grundlagen*... Berlin. (LU)

———.1913. *En väg till självkännedom för människan.* Norrköping. (LS)

———.1913. *Huru uppnås kunskap om högre världar.* Helsingfors. (LS)

———.1913. *Invigningens port.* Norrköping. (LS)

———.1913. *Vetenskapen om det fördola.* Stockholm. (LS)

———.1915. *Tankar under krigstiden.* Norrköping. (LS)

———.1915. *Über alte Weihnachtsspiele*... Berlin. (LU)

———.1916. *Den högre kunskapens grader.* Norrköping. (LS)

———.1916. *Vom Menschenrätsel.* Berlin. (LU)

———.1917. *Krist og Antikrist.* Dornach. (LS)

———.1917. *Pfingsten im Jahreslauf.* Berlin. (LU)

———.1917. *Von Seelenrätseln.* Berlin. (LU)

———.1918. *Blod är en mycket egen saft.* Norrköping. (LS)

———.1918. *Den andliga världens tröskel.* Norrköping. (LS)

———.1918. *Die Philosophie der Freiheit.* Berlin. (LU)

———.1918. *Det mänskliga livet.* Norrköping. (LS)

———.1918. *Der Seelen Erwachen.* Berlin. (LU)

———.1919. *Das Wiederscheinen des Christus . . .* Dornach. (LU)

———.1919. *Drei Vorträge über Volkspädagogik . . .* Stuttgart. (LU)

———.1919. *Entwicklungsgeschichtliche Unterlagen.* Berlin. (LU)

———.1919. *Goethe som fader till en ny estetik.* Norrköping. (LS)

———.1919. *Kärnpunkterna i den sociala frågan.* Stockholm. (LS)

———.192(illegible). *Vägen till översinnlig erfarenhet och kunskap.* Norrköping. (LS)

———.1920. *Die Aufgabe der Geisteswissenschaft . . .* Berlin. (LU)

———.1920. *Essenzen der Natur-Erkenntnis . . .* Stuttgart. (LU)

———.1920. *Goethes Geistesart . . .* Berlin. (LU)

———.1920. *Grenzen der Natur-Erkenntnis . . .* Stuttgart. (LU)

———.1920. *In Ausführung der Dreigliederung des sozialen Organismus.* Stuttgart. (LU)

———.1921. *Bausteine zu einer Erkenntnis des Mysteriums von Golgatha.* Berlin. (LU)

———.1921. *Der Christus-Impuls . . .* Berlin. (LU)

———.1921. *Die soziale Grundforderung . . .* Berlin. (LU)

———.1921. *Exkurse in das Gebiet des Markus-Evangeliums.* Berlin. (LU)

———.1921. *Goethes Weltanschauung.* Berlin. (LU)

———.1921. *Praktische Ausbildung des Denkens.* Stuttgart. (LU)

———.1921. *Vom Lebenswerk Rudolf Steiners.* Munich. (LU)

———.1922. *Anthroposophische Lebensgaben . . .* Berlin. (LU)

———.1922. *Das Karma des Materialismus.* Berlin. (LU)

———.1922. *Die Mission einzelner Volksseelen.* Berlin. (LU)

———.1922. *Erdensterben und Weltenleben . . .* Berlin. (LU)

———.1923. *Das Lukas-Evangelium.* 2nd ed. Berlin. (LU)

———.1923. *Das Mysterium von Golgatha.* Berlin. (LU)

———.1923. *Die Geisteswissenschaft . . .* Berlin. (LU)

———.1923. *Erbsünde und Gnade.* Berlin. (LU)

———.1924. *Die Mystik . . .* Stuttgart. (LU)

———.1924. *Grundlinien einer Erkenntnistheorie . . .* Stuttgart. (LU)

———.1925. *Anthroposophische Leitsätze . . .* Dornach. (LU)

———.1925. *Das Christentum als mystische Tatsache . . .* Dornach. (LU)

———.1925. *Die Kunst der Rezitation und Deklamation . . .* Dornach. (LU)

———.1925. *Einiges über das Rosenkreuzmysterium . . .* Dornach. (LU)

———.1925. *Wahrheit und Wissenschaft.* Dornach. (LU)

———.1925. *Wahrspruchworte.* Dornach. (LU)

———.1926. *Die karmischen Zusammenhänge der anthroposophischen Bewegung.* Dornach. (LU)

———.1926. *Goethes naturwissenschaftliche Schriften.* Dornach. (LU)

——.1926. *Pedagogischer Kurs für Schweizer Lehrer.* Stuttgart. (LU)

——.1926. *Sprachgestaltung . . .* Dornach. (LU)

——.1926. *Wege zu einem neuen Baustil.* Dornach. (LU)

——.1927. *Anthroposophie.* Dornach. (LU)

——.1927. *Das Initiaten-Bewusstsein . . .* Dornach. (LU)

——.1927. *Eine okkulte Physiologie.* Dornach. (LU)

——.1927. *Eurythmie als sichtbare Sprache.* Dornach. (LU)

——.1927. *Westliche und östliche Weltgegensätzlichkeit.* Dornach. (LU)

——.1928. *Das Hereinragen der geistigen Welt . . .* Berlin. (LU)

——.1928. *Das Johannes-Evangelium.* Dornach. (LU)

——.1928. *Die Apokalypse des Johannes.* Berlin. (LU)

——.1929. *Das Wesen der Farben.* Dornach. (LU)

——.1929. *Die Theosophie des Rosenkreuzers.* Berlin. (LU)

——.1929. *Neun Vorträge über das Wesen der Bienen.* Dornach and Basel. (LS, LU)

——.1930. *Das Markus-Evangelium . . .* Dornach. (LU)

——.1930. *Das Matthäus-Evangelium . . .* Dornach. (LU)

——.1930. *Kristus och den mänskliga själen.* Stockholm. (LS)

——.1930. *Vitaesophia: Der Ostergedanke . . . ; Der Christus-Impuls . . . ; Der Baldur-Mythos . . . ; Das Weihnachtsmysterium; Die Mysterien des Geistes . . . ; Geistige Osterglocken; Weihnachtsstimmung; Welten-Pfingsten . . .* 2 vols. Dornach. (LU)

——.1930. *Von der Initiation.* Berlin. (LU)

——.1931. *Ägyptische Mythen . . .* Dornach. (LU)

——.1931. *Der Mensch als Zusammenklang . . .* Dornach. (LU)

——.1931. *Der menschliche und der kosmische Gedanke . . .* Berlin. (LU)

——.1931. *Die okkulte Bewegung . . .* Dornach. (LU)

——.1931. *Geisteswissenschaftliche Erläuterungen zu Goethes Faust.* Vols. 1–2. Dornach. (LU)

——.1931. *Weltsylvester und Neujahrsgedanken.* Dornach. (LU)

——.1932. *Die Evolution vom Gesichtspunkte des Wahrhaftigen.* Dornach. (LU)

——.1933. *Et incarnatus est . . .* Dornach. (LU)

——.1933. *Kosmos und menschliche Geschichte.* Vols. 3–4. Dornach. (LU)

——.1933. *Von Jesus zu Christus.* Dornach. (LU)

——.1934. *Das Osterfest . . .* Dornach. (LU)

——.1934. *Die Sendung Michaels . . .* Dornach. (LU)

——.1934. *Joshu ben Pandira . . .* Dornach. (LU)

——.1934–37. *Esoterische Betrachtungen . . .* Vols. 2–4. Dornach. (LU)

———.1935. *Das pythische, das prophetische und das geisteswissenschaftliche Hellsehen*. Dornach. (LU)

———.1935. *Ein Weg zur Selbsterkenntnis* . . . Dornach. (LU)

———.1937. *Die drei Wege der Seele zu Christus* . . . Dornach. (LU)

———.1940. *Das Karma der anthroposophischen Gesellschaft* . . . Dornach. (LU)

———.1941. *Das erwartungsvolle Leben*. Dornach. (LU)

———.1941. *Die Geschichte des Spiritismus* . . . Basel. (LU)

———.1941. *Geschichte des Hypnotismus* . . . Dornach. (LU)

———.1944. *Mikaelimpulsen och mysteriet på Golgata*. Stockholm. (LS)

Steiner, R., and R. Boos. N.d. *Die Hetze gegen das Goetheanum*. Dornach. (LU)

Steiner, R., and G. Wachsmuth. 1941. *Die Geburt der Geisteswissenschaft*. Dornach. (LU)

Thedenius, K. Fr. 1871. *Flora öfver Uplands och Södermanlands Fanerogamer och Bräkenartade Växter*. Thedenius Förlag, Stockholm.

Uehli, B. 1921. *Rudolf Steiner als Künstler*. Stuttgart. (LU)

Usteri, A. N.d. *Die Pflanzenwelt* . . . N.p. (LU)

Vennerholm, J. 1901. *Grunddragen af hästens operativa speciella kirurgi*. Norstedts Förlag, Stockholm. (*)

Wachsmuth, G. 1942. *Bibliographie der Werke R. Steiners* . . . Dornach, 1942. (LU)

Wetter, G. P. 1926. *Innanför Herakles Stoder—En Resa i Nya Testamentets Värld*. Hugo Gebers Förlag, Stockholm.

Yeats, W. B. 1913. *Gitanjali (Sångoffer) av Rabindranath Tagore*. (*)

Zorn, A. 1909. *Små konstböcker*, no. 6: *Zorn*.

Acknowledgments

This book would not exist without the help and support of many people and institutions. First and foremost, I would like to thank the institution that enabled me to embark on such a large project in the first place: the Berlin Institute for Advanced Study. As a fellow in 2016–17, I was able to work in the archive of the Stiftelsen Hilma af Klints Verk for the first time, which got the ball rolling. I am deeply grateful to the institutions that granted me fellowships for further work: the Göttingen Institute for Advanced Study, the Max Planck Institute for the History of Science, the Center for Advanced Studies BildEvidenz at the Free University of Berlin, and the Center for Advanced Studies at the Ludwig Maximilian University of Munich. Each of these places gave me the opportunity to meet colleagues who furthered my work with suggestions, comments, and criticism. The seminars of these institutions were marvelous forums, and I therefore thank all the participants. For their special support, I thank Luca Giuliani, Anja Brockmann, Stefan Gellner, Kirsten Graupner, Menaka Guruswamy, Wiebke Güse, Sonja Grund, Gianna Pomata, Daniel Schönpflug, Katharina Wiedemann, Thorsten Wilhelmy, and Hubert Wolf from the Berlin Institute for Advanced Study; Martin van Gelderen, Paula Henrikson, Dominik Hünniger, and Nahed Samour from the Göttingen Institute for Advanced Study; Lorraine Daston, Cathy Gere, Lynn Nyhart, and Christine von Oertzen from the MPIWG in Berlin; Peter Geimer and Christopher S. Wood from BildEvidenz; and Annette Meyer and Burcu Dogramaci from the CAS in Munich.

In addition to the mentioned institutions my thanks go to the Axel och Margaret Ax:son Johnsons Stiftelsen, whose generous support allowed me among other things to travel to the important places of Hilma af Klint's life. The conferences organized by the foundation since 2013 on the artist's life and work have contributed to lasting change in the public perception of Hilma af Klint. I thank Kurt Almqvist, Viveca Ax:son Johnson, and Louise Belfrage for their expertise, helpfulness, and years of fruitful exchange.

This book would also not have been possible without the help of one individual. I am grateful above all to Johan af Klint, Hilma af Klint's grandnephew, who accompanied me on many research trips in Sweden. I owe so much to his knowledge, intellectual curiosity, generosity, and helpfulness. I gained a great deal from his critical and precise reading of the manuscript during the revision process, and the appendices are the product of our joint efforts. I am also grateful for the support of his sister Elisabeth Ersman and her daughter Hedvig Ersman.

Thanks also go to Ulrika af Klint, chair of the Stiftelsen Hilma af Klints Verk and daughter of Hilma af Klint's grandnephew Gustaf af Klint, for her trust and support of my research. I am also grateful to Ulf Wagner, member of the board of the Stiftelsen Hilma af Klints Verk.

I thank Monica von Rosen in Berlin for our lively exchange, valuable insights, and for generously making available to me documents from the archive of the Edelweissförbundet.

I am also deeply grateful to Tommy Lindqvist, who not only taught me Swedish but also tirelessly assisted my research by reading Hilma af Klint's writings and advising on historical questions. Many improvements of the manuscript are thanks to his critical reading.

My thanks also go to Daniel Birnbaum for years of exchange about Hilma af Klint in general, and in particular for reading the manuscript and giving valuable feedback.

I thank Hedvig Martin for the enlightening exchange and collaboration in archives. Her groundbreaking master's thesis redefines the relationship between Hilma af Klint and The Five; my description of the dynamics of the group rests on her research. The dissertation she is currently writing on the *Paintings for the Temple* will be another milestone.

I also thank Halina Dyrschka, director of the documentary *Beyond the Visible: Hilma af Klint*, for years of exchange and work in archives.

Marie Cassel has my gratitude for her spirit of contradiction and the wealth of information on Anna Cassel and Gusten Andersson that she made available to me.

All of the exhibitions on Hilma af Klint that have been mounted over the past several years led to new insights. For lively collaboration I thank Tracey Bashkoff, David Horowitz, and Ryan Newbanks of the Solomon R. Guggenheim Museum; Karin Althaus, Matthias Mühling, and Sebastian Schneider of the Lenbachhaus; Angelika Bartholl and Brigitte Martin of the Kunstraum Bogenhausen; and Iris Müller-Westermann, director of the Moderna Museet Malmö, who first showed me paintings by Hilma af Klint in Stockholm in 2008.

For the inspiring exchange and excellent support at the Rudolf Steiner archives in Dornach I thank Johannes Nilo and Stephan Widmer, as well as Walter Kugler, who also assisted me in word, deed, and archival research. Thank you to Christine Engels for her help and support at the archives of the Albert-Steffen-Stiftung in Dornach.

I am grateful to Göran Jönsson for his generous help in the archives of the Veterinary Institute in Skara—as well as expert explanations of the veterinary drawings of Anna Cassel and Hilma af Klint.

For the wonderful support and help in the archive of Tyra Kleens Samling in Valinge Gård I thank Kerstin Hermelin, as well as Karin Ström Lehander, who put us in touch.

For advice, notes, and information, I also thank Camilla Alriksson of the Sveriges Nationalbibliotek; Anna Maria Bernitz (née Svensson), a pioneer of research on Hilma af Klint; Andreas Bode, the former director of the International Youth Library in Munich; the journalist Anna Cnattingius; Albin Dahlström of the Moderna Museet; Caroline Edman of the Carl Larsson-gården; the journalist Yvonne Gröning; William Glassley from the Department of Earth and Planetary Sciences at the University of California; Ludwig Habighorst for his patient explanations of Indian miniature painting; Lotte Jaeger of the Collection Information Department of the Rijksmuseum; Nick Hopwood from the History and Philosophy of Science Department of Cambridge University; Jaishree Kannan, archivist at the Adyar Library and Research Centre, Adyar, Chennai; Janet Kerschner, archivist of the Theosophical Society in America; Dag Kronlund, archivist of the Royal Dramatic Theatre in Stockholm; Catrin Leo of the Tempelgården on Visingsö; Annie Lindberg of the Skissernas Museum in Lund; Monica Ostelius of the Teosofiska Samfundet in Stockholm; Tomas Östlund; Ulla-Karin Warberg of the Nordiska Museet; Ulrich Raulff, in his capacity as horse-loving historian; Anders Sahlén of the Adelsö Hembygdslags bildarchiv; Live Söderlund, grandmaster of the Swedish Rosicrucian Order Amorc; Matthias Sträßner of Deutschlandradio; and Rudolf Zwirner, in his capacity as book-loving conversation partner.

Finally, many thanks go to my German publisher, S. Fischer Verlag, for the generous mixture of enthusiasm and patience that accompanied the process of writing this book: Siv Bublitz, Yelenah Frahm, Alexander Roesler, and—at the beginning—Nina Sillem. I also thank my agent, Petra Eggers. Also a special thanks to Florian Illies for his early enthusiasm for Hilma af Klint and his support for this book.

The biggest thanks of all go to my family: for always having the best ideas, and no plan was too crazy for you, dear Philipp, Hans, Jim, and my dear parents!

One wonderful new contribution to the dynamic field of Hilma af Klint research is the seven-volume *Catalogue raisonnée*, published by Bokförlaget Stolpe and edited by Kurt Almqvist and Daniel Birnbaum. I thank the current board of the Hilma af Klint Foundation for access to many documents that have provided new insights in the English edition. In particular, I thank Kurt Almqvist, Daniel Birnbaum, Ulf Wagner, Jessica Höglund, and Ulrika af Klint from the foundation. My sincere thanks also to Anne Weise, editor of the Rudolf Steiner archives.

Thank you to the amazing team at the University of Chicago Press: to Dylan Montanari, Carrie Adams, and Elizabeth Ellingboe, and especially Susan Bielstein for her wonderful mix of rigor and enthusiasm. Thanks to Anne Posten for her beautiful translation.

Illustration Sources

Notes

In 1945 a system for organizing and numbering af Klint's artworks and notebooks was devised by Olof Sundström, who took care of her estate immediately after her death. His inventory is contained in the Stiftung Hilma af Klints Verk (Hilma af Klint Foundation) under the title "Förteckning över Frk. Hilma af Klints efterlämnade verk" (List of Miss Hilma af Klint's surviving works). Both the art and the notebooks were numbered in chronological order, beginning in 1906. Sundström used the abbreviation Lnr. for "löpnummer," meaning "ordering number," which was later replaced by HaK.

INTRODUCTION

1   HaK 1049, opening page. This reference refers to one of Hilma af Klint's private notebooks, the one that she numbered 1049. See author's note about nomenclature at the beginning of the notes.

2   Cf. HaK 556, 272. Unless otherwise noted, all quotations from Swedish have been translated into German by the author and then into English by the translator Anne Posten.

3   Cf. Tuchman, *Spiritual in Art*.

4   Cf. Kramer, "On 'The Spiritual in Art' in Los Angeles," 17f. Cf. also Birnbaum, Afterword, 125ff.

5   There have been many exhibitions of af Klint's work, but prior to 2013, monographic shows, with the exception of the one at the Albertina in Vienna, took place in smaller institutions and were primarily directed at specialist circles. Cf. Fant, *Hilma af Klints hemliga bilder*; Fant, *Hilma af Klint*; Liljevalchs Konsthall, *Hilma af Klint*; Hutchinson, *Hilma af Klint*; O'Reilly, *Hilma af Klint*. "The spiritual in art" was also repeatedly taken up as an exhibition theme and af Klint's work mobilized for this purpose. Cf. e.g. Loers, *Okkultismus und Avantgarde*; de Zegher, *3 x Abstraction*.

6   Müller-Westermann and Widoff, *Hilma af Klint*. (It is online here: http://www.nordstjernan.com/news/arts/5317/, cited from the *Wall Street Journal*.)

7   Cf. Extensive and enthusiastic coverage of the show in the *New York Times* and the *New Yorker*, https://www.newyorker.com/magazine /2018/10/22/hilma-af-klints-visionary-paintings, https://www.nytimes .com/2018/10/11/arts/design/hilma-af-klint-review-guggenheim.html.

8   The show was curated by Tracy Bashkoff. Cf. Bashkoff, *Hilma af Klint*, 49–63. Kurt Almqvist and Louise Belfrage of the Ax:son Johnson Foundation have organized conferences on af Klint's work since 2013 and published the proceedings. Cf. Almqvist and Belfrage, *Hilma af Klint: The Art of Seeing the Invisible* and *Hilma af Klint: Seeing Is Believing.*

9   On the reception history of af Klint's works after her death see also the conclusion of this book, pp. 303–4.

10   Iris Müller-Westermann had already begun to dispel the assumption that af Klint was a reclusive painter with no contacts in the art world. She also curated the exhibition at the Moderna Museet in Stockholm. Cf. Müller-Westermann, "Paintings for the Future: Hilma af Klint," 33–51.

11   The painting was purchased at auction and is held privately. Thanks to the Ax:son Johnson Foundation for the right to reproduce it.

12   Quaytman, "Five Paintings of 1907."

13   Cf. Fant, *Hilma af Klints hemliga bilder.*

14   The exhibition was organized by the Theosophists, cf. Teosofiska Samfundet, *Katalog konstutställning.*

15   An initial summary of the events appeared in the Guggenheim catalogue, though at the point of its publication I was not yet aware of the 1913 show. Cf. Voss, "Traveling Hilma af Klint."

16   The series acquired by Glenstone is published in Almqvist and Birnbaum, *Hilma af Klint: Catalogue raisonné*, 2:162–66. A catalogue of the exhibition at David Zwirner Gallery is forthcoming. Another forty-six watercolors turned up in 2021 and are privately owned in Switzerland. They, too, had been left by af Klint to the Goetheanum in Dornach to be exhibited or published there. Again, this never happened. These works show the flora and in some cases fauna of the artist's surroundings in double portraits: af Klint depicts each species in life-size detail while simultaneously charting its spiritual nature in abstract diagrams. Naturalism and abstraction are shown as two sides of creation. The carefully recorded dates and species names on the watercolors correspond to those of the notebook "Flowers, Mosses, and Lichens" from 1919 and 1920. At the time this biography went to press, the series was for sale. The watercolors will be published in the forthcoming volume

7 of *Hilma af Klint: Catalogue raisonné*. An index of the works can be found in af Klint's notebook HaK 589.

17 The previously mentioned publication by Iris Müller-Westermann in the catalogue of the Moderna Museet and Anna-Maria Svensson's work, which also presents af Klint's work in the context of the art of her time, are exceptions to this. Cf. Svensson, "Mellan abstraktion och esoterism."

18 The book by Burgin and Müller-Westermann is exemplary in emphasizing the independence of af Klint's spiritual understanding. Cf. Burgin, *Hilma af Klint: Notes and Methods*.

19 Cf. HaK 462, December 28, 1919, pg. 10.

PART 1, CHAPTER 1

1 Wollstonecraft, *Letters*, 17.

2 Wollstonecraft, *Letters*, 17.

3 Wollstonecraft, *Letters*, 15.

4 Nochlin, "Why Have There Been No Great Women Artists?," 147. See also Daniel Birnbaum, "Another Canon," 210–15.

5 Nochlin, "Why Have There Been No Great Women Artists?," 150.

6 Linda Nochlin published her essay more than a decade before the first posthumous exhibitions of Hilma af Klint's work.

PART 1, CHAPTER 2

1 Klint, introduction to *Beschreibung von den Küsten an der Ostsee*, n.p.

2 Fant, *Hilma af Klint*, 13. For a portrait of her father see HaK 1408.

3 The inventory of lighthouses can be found in HaK 555, 93–94; the painting in question is no. 6 of *The Ten Largest*.

PART 1, CHAPTER 3

1 From October 30, 1868, on, the af Klints lived at Norrtullsgatan 19. See appendix 1.

2 In Sweden, sculptures and religious imagery were often left in churches even after the Reformation. See Tångeberg, *Mittelalterliche Holzskulpturen und Altarschreine*, 1.

3 Erik af Klint refers to this quotation; see Fant, *Hilma af Klint*, 16. It also appears in a notebook from 1913; see HaK 564, 118.

4 See afterword by Johan af Klint.

5   The original painting no longer exists. The painting shown here is a copy from 1636.

6   On Sweden as a "Lutheran Superpower," see Stiftung Deutsches Historisches Museum, *Der Luthereffekt*, 76–77.

7   HaK 1349.

8   HaK 1350.

9   For debates over the education of girls in Sweden, see Linné, "Lutheranism and Democracy," 141. Erik af Klint writes of attendance at the "Normalskola för flickör" in "Hilma af Klint och hennes verk," 1.

10 Nauckhoff, *Ätten af Klint*, 159. Ida af Klint belonged to the Fredrika Bremer-förbundet from 1887 to 1902.

11 Whitlock, *Skolans Ställning till Religionsundervisningen*, section 23.

12 HaK 1092, 31. The note is from April 19, 1943.

PART 1, CHAPTER 4

1   On connections between spiritual and political movements see Owen, *Darkened Room*, as well as Larsen, "Infinite Redress."

2   Houghton, *Evenings at Home*, 70.

3   Houghton, *Evenings at Home*, 14 (fruit) and 20 (signals from dead sisters).

4   See Grand and Pasi, "Works of Art without Parallel," 9.

5   Grand and Pasi, "Works of Art without Parallel," 12.

6   She refers in the introduction to her exhibition catalogue to an artist named Henry Lenny who gave her early training. He is characterized as "deaf and dumb." See "Introductory Remarks" in Houghton, *Catalogue of the Spirit Drawings*.

7   Houghton, *Evenings at Home*, 57, 45.

8   Houghton, *Evenings at Home*, 30.

9   Houghton, *Evenings at Home*, 77–78.

10 Houghton, *Catalogue of the Spirit Drawings*, 7 (real objects) and 11 (sacred symbolism).

11 Houghton, *Catalogue of the Spirit Drawings*, 25 (spiritual cypher) and 8 (glorious hues).

12 Houghton, *Evenings at Home*, 76 (art without parallel) and 29 (new beauty), and *Catalogue of the Spirit Drawings*, "Introductory Remarks" (widely spreading oak).

13 Houghton, *Evenings at Home*, 71.

14 Houghton, *Evenings at Home*, 104.

15 Houghton, *Evenings at Home*, 104.

16 Yule, *Book of Ser Marco Polo*, 444, as quoted in Houghton, *Evenings at Home*, 129.

17 Blavatsky, *Isis Unveiled*, 601, as quoted in Houghton, *Evenings at Home*, 129.

18 Chaudhuri, *Western Women and Imperialism*. Annie Besant was particularly involved, joining the Indian National Congress in 1914.

19 Houghton, *Evenings at Home*, 132.

PART 1, CHAPTER 5

1 See portrait photo from the Hilma af Klint archive that appears in Bashkoff, *Hilma af Klint*, 230.

2 It is not known when Hilma af Klint and Bertha Valerius met. The af Klint archive contains early documents relating to Valerius, for example, a notebook containing the documentation of séances, titled "Ur Fröken Bertha Valerius efterlämnade papper, 26/7/1879–10/7/1882" (HaK 1152). Hilma also owned Valerius's printed text "Meddelanden från den osynliga verlden erhållna genom ett skrifvande medium" from 1886 (HaK 1165 / also 1154), marked with H. af Klint in pencil on the title page. Erik af Klint mentions that his aunt took part in "spiritistic séances in the years 1879–1882" without, however, providing names of the participants. These dates correspond with those on Valerius's notebook. See Erik af Klint, "Hilma af Klint och hennes verk," 3. These documents suggest early contact between the two painters.

3 The life of Bertha Valerius has not yet been thoroughly studied. See Rogh, "Bertha Valerius," 113–15, for an obituary, as well as Rhodin, "Edelweissförbundets historia." See also Dahlmann, "Kvinnliga pionjärer osynliga i fotohistorien," 47.

4 For more on the history of art education for women in Sweden, see Gynning, *Det ambivalenta perspektivet*.

5 The photograph is shown in Rogh, "Bertha Valerius," 114.

6 "Ur Fröken Valerius efterlämnade papper, 1879–1882," HaK 1152, 2.

7 HaK 1152, 4.

8 HaK 1152, 79.

9 Some of the entries are dated earlier than the label on the cover indicates. It is therefore possible that af Klint participated in the séances even earlier.

10 See Erik af Klint, "Hilma af Klint och hennes verk," 3.

11 On the importance of Swedenborg for spiritualism in the nineteenth century, see Webb, *Die Flucht vor der Vernunft*, 67–69, and Kracht,

"Vom Tischrücken zur ethischen Religion?" 153.

12   The famous American Fox sisters admitted to fraud in 1888. H. P. Blavatsky was also repeatedly accused of deception from 1884 on; see Zander, *Anthroposophie in Deutschland*, 1: 96–97.

13   HaK 1152, 3 and 6.

14   Oscar II's first letter to Huldine Beamish is dated January 10, 1882 and is signed with the pseudonym "Fingal." Copies of the correspondence between Oscar II and Huldine Fock are held in the private archive of Monica von Rosen/EWF. On the Theosophists, see Bogdan and Hammer, *Western Esotericism in Scandinavia*, 582.

15   The American Fox sisters, who practiced necromancy as part of stage shows, were seen as important members of the American spiritist movement, until they were found guilty of fraud. See Zander, *Anthroposophie in Deutschland*, 1: 82.

16   The entry is dated February 1879, but it is found on one of the later pages of the notebook, so the precise sequence of the séances is unclear.

17   "Ur Fröken Valerius efterlämnade papper, 1879–1882," HaK 1152, 51.

18   Henslow recounts the long creation process in *The Proofs of the Truth of Spiritualism*, 179. The painting was begun in 1856, according to Rhodin, "Edelweissförbundets historia," "Om Bertha Valerius Kristustavla."

19   Howitt's novella was published in 1852. See Alexandra Wettlaufer, "Politics and Poetics of Sisterhood." On Howitt in Munich, see Howitt, *Art-Student in Munich*.

20   The mother, also named Mary Howitt, lived from 1799 to 1888. On her daughter, the artist Anna Mary Howitt, see Althaus, Mühling, and Schneider, *Weltempfänger*, 33, and Wettlaufer, "Politics and Poetics of Sisterhood." Anna Mary Howitt's sister, Margaret Howitt, lived in Sweden in 1863 for a year and published her diary as *Twelve Months with Fredrika Bremer in Sweden*.

21   Howitt's book *Pioneers of the Spiritual Reformation* was published in 1883. On her mother's and sister's connections to Sweden, see Howitt Watts, *Pioneers*, 215. On Bremer and spiritualism, see Lindqvist, "Om Selma Lagerlöfs förhållande."

22   Houghton, *Evenings at Home*, 93–94.

23   Crosland, *Light in the Valley*, 148.

PART 1, CHAPTER 6

1   On the technical college, see Svensson, "Mellan abstraktion och esot-
    erism," 28. The training at Cardon's painting school is mentioned in
    Nauckhoff, *Ätten af Klint*, 159.

2   Little research has been devoted to the life of Kerstin Cardon. See
    Lundin, "Kerstin Cardon," 113–14, on the painting school. A. H. dates
    the founding of the school to the 1870s in "Svenska kvinnan inom de
    bildande konsterna," 312.

3   For a history of female artists, starting in the seventeenth century, see
    A. H., "Svenska kvinnan inom de bildande konsterna."

4   One of the first prepublication discussions of the text appeared in
    Dagens Nyheter on November 26, 1878. The publisher Jos. Seligmann
    & C:nis also printed large-format advertisements, for example in the
    Aftonbladet on November 30, 1878.

5   Lundin, *Oxygen och Aromasia*. Lundin notes in the foreword that
    he was inspired by the German writer Kurd Lasswitz and borrowed
    characters and plot points from the latter's 1878 novel *Bilder aus der
    Zukunft*.

6   Pietikainen, *Neurosis and Modernity*, 148.

7   Lundin, "Kerstin Cardon," 114.

8   *Palettskrap*, no. 15 (1879), as quoted in Cavalli-Björkman, *Eva Bonnier*,
    59.

PART 1, CHAPTER 7

1   Place and date of burial can be found at https://www.svenskagravar.se
    /gravsatt/46037895.

2   Nauckhoff, *Ätten af Klint*, 159. According to Johan af Klint, pneumo-
    nia was remembered in the family as the cause of death.

3   Wennberg-Hilger, "Das Seuchenhafte Auftreten von Lepra."

4   C. Larsson, *Ich*, 21.

5   Prinzing, "Die Entwicklung der Kindersterblichkeit," 577–635, 87–88.

6   On the deceased cousins, see death dates on the af Klint family tree in
    Nauckhoff, *Ätten af Klint*.

7   HaK 1073, 111.

8   As quoted in Fant, *Hilma af Klint*, 17. We do not know what years these
    were.

9   On the many connections between new discoveries and the arts, see
    Henderson, *Fourth Dimension*; in reference to Hilma af Klint see
    Almqvist and Belfrage, *Hilma af Klint: The Art of Seeing the Invisible*.

10 On Munch's spiritual interests, see Beyhan, "Science and Occultism in Edvard Munch's Painting."

PART 2, CHAPTER 1

1   The inclusion of life drawing in art curricula for women advanced unevenly across Europe. Private academies pioneered the practice of admitting women to the classes, while most of the state and royal academies prohibited it until after World War I. See Yvette Deseyve und Ralph Gleis, eds., *Kampf um die Sichtbarkeit. Künstlerinnen der Nationalgalerie vor 1919*, Exhibition Catalogue, Nationalgalerie, Berlin, 2019. On the debates in Sweden, see Gynning, *Det ambivalenta perspektivet*; for the situation in Germany see Krenzlin, "auf dem ernsten Gebiet der Kunst ernst arbeiten," 73–87, and Herber, "Frauen an deutschen Kunstakademien im 20. Jahrhundert."

2   HaK 1491, n.p.

3   HaK 1340.

4   HaK 1092, 31–32. The entry is dated April 19, 1943.

5   For the drawings, see HaK 1244 and 1235. On study at the academy see Kungl. Akademien för de fria konsterna, Elevkataloger, 1881–1969, Matrikel 805, Hilma af Klint, 9/4/1882–9/1/1887, Archive of the Royal Academy, Stockholm.

6   HaK 1488, 2.

7   HaK 1489, 16.

8   C. Larsson, *Ich*, 74. On the history of the women's department of the Stockholm Academy, see Gynning, *Det ambivalenta perspektivet*, 97–98.

9   For the mention see Erik af Klint, "Hilma af Klint och hennes verk," 1. A visit to Georg von Rosen is described in Lundin, "I museer," here 498–99.

10 Von Rosen's participation in the Cloverleaf group is first noted on November 13, 1886. See membership records in the private archive of Monika von Rosen/EWF.

11 She received the award in May 1884. See "Bildande konst," *Stockholms-dagblad*, no. 112, May 15, 1884, 5.

PART 2, CHAPTER 2

1   Erik af Klint, "Hilma af Klint och hennes verk," 3.

2   Hilma is a common Swedish name. When Bertha Valerius and her

friend Huldine Beamish established the "Edelweiss Society" in 1890 they counted a "Hilma Ahnström" among their early members. According to the member list Hilma Ahnström (1844–1920) joined in 1891. I thank Hedvig Martin for pointing this out to me. The fact that later minutes of the Edelweiss Society suggest a mentoring relationship between Valerius and af Klint speaks in favor of accepting the artist here as the one addressed. Notes on the June 22, 1886 séance in the private archive of Monica von Rosen/EWF.

3   Rhodin, "Edelweissförbundets historia," 10.

4   The brewery was called Beamish & Crawford. A book about the brewery mentions Huldine Beamish only in passing; see Drisceoil and Drisceoil, *Beamish & Crawford*. The best source of information is Rhodin, "Edelweissförbundets historia."

5   The photograph is held in the private archive of Monica von Rosen/EWF.

6   Notes on the June 22, 1886 séance in the private archive of Monica von Rosen/EWF.

7   Document in the private archive of Monica von Rosen/EWF.

8   Séance book titled "About Gustaf" in the private archive of Monica von Rosen/EWF. The book runs from 1882 to 1885. If Hilma Ahnström was addressed instead, there would have been no telepathy involved. Her mother had died in 1880. Usually Beamish contacted the dead directly, without going through a third person. Telepathy was nothing new to her. For years she had been in touch with spirits delivering messages about her son Gustaf, who was very much alive in England.

9   B. V., *Meddelanden från den osynliga*. The initials are found at the end of the foreword, on page 5. The document is sewn into HaK 1165.

10   B. V., *Meddelanden*, 50–51.

11   HaK 1094, 77.

PART 2, CHAPTER 3

1   Beuys, *Helene Schjerfbeck*, 149.

2   The painting measures 133 x 88 cm. Information from Stockholms Auktionsverk in an email from Johan af Klint, April 13, 2018.

3   Akademiens för de fria konsterna. Läroverkskatalog. Läroåret 1887–88, Stockholm 1888, Archive of the Royal Academy, Stockholm; also "Akademien för de fria konsterna," *Sydsvenska Dagbladet Snällposten*, no. 248, May 31, 1888.

4   The painting was auctioned through Stockholms Auktionsverk on May 30, 2020. Consignor and buyer are unknown.

5   Carl Larsson to Viktor Rydberg, 1889, as quoted in Sidén and Meister, *Ljusets magi*, 92–93.

6   "Bildande konst," *Stockholms Dagblad*, October 27, 1888.

PART 2, CHAPTER 4

1   Hedvig Martin, "Hilma af Klint och De fem," 58. This master's thesis is the most thorough piece of research into the history of "The Five" to date and clears up many misconceptions. I rely heavily on the results of Martin's research for details on The Five.

2   Anna Cassel to Hilma af Klint, November 1, 1930, February 19, 1931, June 26, 1936, and July 9, 1936, HaK 1103, archive of the Stiftelsen Hilma af Klints Verk. The notebooks are mentioned in the letter from 1930.

3   The postcard is in the possession of Cassel's descendants. A transcription was given to me by Johan af Klint.

4   Hedvig Martin, "Hilma af Klint och De fem," 57. On Anna Cassel see Bax, "Hilma af Klint Revisited, part 3: Anna Cassel."

5   The will is in the digital archive of the city of Stockholm; see Stockholms rådhusrätts bouppteckningsavd. E1: 184 (2102–2400), year 1937, no. 2262 (SSA). Information and value given in Martin, "Hilma af Klint och De fem," 58.

6   Both works are pictured in Sidén and Meister, *Ljusets magi*, 112–15.

7   Cassel's painting measures 94 x 53 cm, af Klint's is 148 x 88 cm. See Sidén and Meister, *Ljusets magi*, 255–56.

8   Meister, "Parisflickorna," 109–78.

9   Karl August Ehrensvärd, quoted in Nordensvan, *Schwedische Kunst des 19. Jahrhunderts*, 1.

10 HaK 555, 81.

11 See appendix 1.

12 Stamm, "Zwei Magische Orte der Moderne," 51.

13 Lundin, "I museer," 509–10. Blanch's Art Salon was located next to Blanch's Café, at Hamngatan 16. The rooms of the "Konstföreningen," were above the café; see ibid., 503 and 510.

14 Opponenternas utställning, *Illustrerad katalog*.

15 On the conflict with the academy see Facos, *Nationalism and the Nordic Imagination*, 15. The observation that this was the first illustrated catalogue is from Lundin, *I museer*. The catalogue listed participants alphabetically from "Andrén" through "Larsson" to "Zorn."

16 This led to the formation of the Konstnärsförbundet (Artists' Associa-

tion) by many of the artists involved with Opponenterna. The Konstnärsförbundet continued to lobby for reform of the Academy's organization, pedagogy, and exhibition programs until it ended in 1920.

17 Facos, "Controversy in Late Nineteenth Century Painting," 64.

18 The painting's title is *No. 64, Vid telefonen. (Porträttgenre), tillhör
grossh. O. Jacobsson*. See Opponenternas utställning, *Illustrerad katalog*, 10.

19 Rhodin, "Edelweissförbundets historia," 4–5. The first meeting of the
group took place on January 30, 1883.

20 On Theosophy in Sweden see Petander, "Theosophy in Sweden," 578.
For Lotten Cassel's admission on November 1, 1895, see Bax, "Hilma af
Klint Revisited." For an overview of spiritual movements in Sweden in
the late nineteenth century see Faxneld, *Det ockulta sekelskiftet*.

21 The society's name in Swedish is "Samfundet för psykisk forskning";
see Carleson and Levander, "Spiritualism in Sweden," 524.

22 Carleson and Levander, "Spiritualism in Sweden," 523. The founding
dates of the Spiritistiska Litteraturföreningen vary in the literature;
most likely it was started in the mid-1880s.

23 Busch's early books were titled *Genom dolda världen* (1888) and *Hvad
vill spiritism? En kort redogörelse för dess fenomen och etik* (1889).

24 Viktor Rydberg lived on Karlavägen in Stockholm until 1890, when he
moved to Djursholm, to the Villa Ekeliden.

25 On Rydberg and Theosophy see Lindqvist, "Om Selma Lagerlöfs
förhållande," 47.

PART 2, CHAPTER 5

1 HaK 1164, 92.

2 Rhodin mentions the use of the device without giving a source in
"Edelweissförbundets historia," 4.

3 HaK 1487, 25.

4 HaK 1164, 93–94.

PART 2, CHAPTER 6

1 The *Stockholm Dagblad* mentions a "still life" by Hilma af Klint in a
Konstföreningen exhibition: see *Stockholm Dagblad*, no. 276, October
30, 1886, 10. For information on the association's exhibition space, see
Lundin, "I museer," 503.

2 Åke Fant originally wrote that af Klint moved into a studio at Hamngatan 5 after her graduation; the 2013 catalogue of the Moderna
Museet in 2013 stated that this studio was granted to af Klint by the

Academy. Neither is correct. According to Eva-Lena Bengtsson at the archive of the Royal Academy of Fine Arts, the Academy did not grant studio space to its graduates. The location of af Klint's studio during the 1890s is unknown. Starting in 1902 she had a studio at Hamngatan 9, according to Erik af Klint, "Hilma af Klint och hennes verk," 1.

3 "Konst och literatur, I Theodor Blanchs Konstsalong," *Aftonbladet*, no. 123, June 1, 1891, 3. At this time Blanch ran a gallery at Drottninggatan 29C, where this exhibition took place.

4 *Aftonbladet*, April 29, 1893.

5 "Vid Nya Iduns," *Aftonbladet*, no. 27, February 3, 1890. The paintings were titled *Tidigt vår* and *Vinterlandskap*.

6 Ljungberger, *Blanch's Café*, date: 1918.

7 Zorn, *Små Konstböcker*. See appendix 2.

8 Bergh, "Målaren Ernst Josephson," 110–27.

9 On Josephson's late work and lifelong fascination with Rembrandt see Weinstein, *Northern Arts*. On the possible influence of Josephson's work on the avant-garde, see Schneede, *Vor der Zeit*.

10 On the exhibition see Lippincott, *Edvard Munch*, 53–54.

11 HaK 555, 43.

12 Undated document held by the Stiftelsen Hilma af Klints Verk. I am grateful to Monica von Rosen for information on Strindberg's participation in séances.

13 HaK 1613.

14 On the term and the history of the Symbolist movement in Europe see Facos, *Symbolist Art in Context*.

15 See appendix 2.

16 HaK 1450, n.d.

17 Levertin, *Samlade Skrifter*. See appendix 2.

18 In 1910, Kleen wrote a sarcastic retrospective on the salon for the newspaper *Aftonblandet*. See Franzén, "Tyra Kleen som symbolist," 68–69.

19 The Swedish press also reported on the exclusion of female artists from the Rose + Croix salons but withheld judgment. Greene, "Salon de la Rose + Croix," 16. For Swedish review see "Rose + croix," *Aftonbladet*, April 19, 1893.

20 Quoted in Franzén, "Tyra Kleen som symbolist," 72.

21 On Kleen's spiritual milieu, see Franzén, "Tyra Kleen som symbolist," 69–70. I owe information on Kleen's connection to the Edelweiss Society to Monica von Rosen.

22 The grant was 400 crowns; see "Stipendier för konstidkare," *Aftonbladet*, May 21, 1891.

23 HaK 1333 (Holland), HaK 1634 (Rhine), and Nauckhoff, *Ätten af Klint*, 159.

1 Erik af Klint, "Hilma af Klint och hennes verk," 1.
2 Nauckhoff, *Ätten af Klint*, 153.
3 In 1891 Hilma af Klint wrote of spending time with the daughter of her cousin Gustaf Helleday on Adelsö; see HaK 1164, 92.
4 The painting was enthusiastically reviewed, see "Konstutställningen. En första öfverblick," in *Dagens Nyheter*, no. 9844 (A), May 15, 1897, 3.
5 Quoted in Björk, "Det Besjälade Landskapet," 37.
6 On Bergh's national romanticism see Facos, *Nationalism and the Nordic Imagination*.
7 On *eques a penna rubra* see Karl af Geijerstam, *Modern vidskepelse*, 6.
8 Du Prel, *Philosophy of Mysticism*, 229. Hilma af Klint owned the 1890 Swedish translation of the book and a translation of *The Monistic Doctrine of the Soul: A Contribution to the Solution of the Riddle of Man* by the author from the same year. See appendix 2. On du Prel's importance see Pytlik, *Spiritismus und Moderne*. On the connection of his writings to af Klint's art see Linda Dalrymple Henderson, "Hilma af Klint and the Invisible in Her Occult/Scientific Context," in Almqvist and Belfrage, *Hilma af Klint. Visionary and the Spirit of Her Time*, 68–90.
9 Rhodin, "Edelweissförbundets historia," 18.
10 Rhodin, "Edelweissförbundets historia," 31.
11 For Beamish's biography see Rhodin, "Edelweissförbundets historia." On Tolstoy and Beamish, see Hellman, *Hemma hos Tolstoj*, 28.
12 Rhodin, "Edelweissförbundets historia," 10.
13 Von Bergen, "Huldine Beamish," 2. Von Bergen had visited Blavatsky in India in 1885, at the headquarters of the Theosophical Society.
14 Minutes from August 31, 1895, from the private archive of Monica von Rosen/EWF. June 8, 1896 is given in the membership list as the date of admission for Hilma af Klint and December 16, 1896 for Anna Cassel. The list is likewise in the private archive of Monica von Rosen/EWF. I thank Hedvig Martin for pointing out that there is another "Hilma" in the member list, Hilma Ahnström. Ahnström had joined the Edelweiss Society already on April 20, 1891, and thus cannot be the "Hilma" of the cited entry.
15 Obituary of Dr. Gustav Zander in *Der Theosophische Pfad*, 1920, 93–94. http://www.theosophie.de/images/stories/pdf/Theos_NR_1920_XIX _04-05-06-6.pdf.

16   See appendix 2.

17   Blavatsky, *Secret Doctrine*, vol. 2, part 1, stanza 6.

18   Ibid.

19   Pietikainen, *Neurosis and Modernity*, 48.

20   Krafft-Ebing, *Über gesunde und kranke Nerven*, 55.

21   HaK 1164, 92.

22   Séance of September 5, 1896, in minute book titled "Från den 5 September 1895," 2, private archive Monica von Rosen/EWF.

PART 2, CHAPTER 8

1   All nine notebooks are kept in af Klint's archive. So far no other notebooks from The Five have emerged. There is also a notebook (HaK 1155) that covers the period 1892–96. Neither The Five nor af Klint is mentioned in it. "Sigrid" is the common reference of the notebook. Thus it seems to belong to Sigrid Hedman, although kept in af Klint's archive. The first written mention of The Five occurs on Easter, April 24, 1896, in a notebook with the opening remark "messages received by Edelweiss Society or through its members 1896–1897." The entry is followed by a sketch with six initials, including those of The Five: A, C, M, S, H, G (see HaK 1153, 2). The notebook also contains séances from the Edelweiss Society with changing members; up to eight persons would join the meetings. Notebook HaK 1163 also contains some entries from 1918, but from a different context.

2   HaK 1156, 1. The notebook quoted here is marked with the Roman numeral I. The Five are mentioned as a group on page 37. The reason for the explicit mention seems to be that two other women attended the séance as guests.

3   HaK 1156, first page (unnumbered).

4   Hedvig Martin, "Hilma af Klint och De fem," 60.

5   HaK 1153. For the membership of the women see the membership records of the Edelweiss Society in the private archive of Monica von Rosen/EWF. Bertha Valerius spoke in winter 1897 and December 1906; see HaK 1159, 18, 19, 55; HaK 1162, 273 and 274; HaK 1163, 21.

6   Rhodin, "Edelweissförbundets historia," 14.

7   For Besant's books in af Klint's library, see appendix 2; a book with newspaper clippings about the visits to Stockholm is found in the archive of the bookstore of the Teosofiska Samfundet, Stockholm. On Nilsson and her magazine, see Sandal, "Gränslös mediering."

8   The couple were raising a niece. Hedvig Martin, "Hilma af Klint och De fem," 59.

9   Hedvig Martin, "Hilma af Klint och De fem," 63.

10 Hedvig Martin, "Hilma af Klint och De fem," 58–59.

11 Mathilda Nilsson's address, Kammakaregatan 6, appears most often in the records. It is mentioned in 1903 in HaK 1161, 265 and in 1905 in HaK 1162, 184. Her initials, M.N., are also frequently mentioned as location; see e.g. HaK 1159, 3, 7, 38, 132, 137, 149, 174, 178, 180, 185, 188, 252.

12 See "Studier av NT," list in the archive of the Stiftelsen Hilma af Klints Verk, no year, no catalogue number.

13 For example HaK 1153, June 8, 1897 (no page number), or HaK 1161, 13 and 191.

14 Leadbeater's book was published in 1896, and its English title is given in a notebook in 1904, HaK 1162, 98. The spirit "Ananda" starts talking to The Five in 1900. His name is of Indian origin, and he is also dealt with in Theosophical literature.

15 HaK 1161. The cover is labeled "Fredagsgruppen, d 9/11 1900 till d 14/3 1901." On Busch see part 2, chapter 4, note 22.

16 Oscar Busch and Selma Lagerlöf were in touch from 1891 to 1912. For this and his connection to Larsson and Zorn, see Lindqvist, "Om Selma Lagerlöfs förhållande," 52.

17 The author Karl af Geijerstam wrote two books (*Modern vidskepelse*, 1892, and *Den afslöjade Isis*, 1897) against Theosophy and reported in detail the fraud allegations.

18 On the Inferno crisis see Stockenström, "Crisis and Change," 79–92.

19 On Josephson's art in the late years of his illness, see Weinstein, *Northern Arts*, 352–53.

20 Pietikainen, *Neurosis and Modernity*, 15 and 35.

21 HaK 1162, 158. This message came on February 21, 1905.

22 On Blavatsky's Mahatmas see Zander, *Anthroposophie in Deutschland*, 1: 95–96.

23 The drawing books of The Five are numbers HaK S1 through HaK S15 (HaK 1514–HaK 1528) in the archive of the Stiftelsen Hilma af Klints Verk. The drawings of the Edelweiss Society are in the private archive of Monica von Rosen/EWF.

24 The photograph is reproduced in Müller-Westermann and Widoff, *Hilma af Klint*, 118.

25 HaK 1156, 38. For the associated image see HaK S2, 11. Thanks to Hedvig Martin for pointing this out.

26 Henslow, *Proofs of the Truth of Spiritualism*, 179.

27 HaK, S3, 4. The small sketch is glued on a larger paper, like another automatic drawing which is fixed on the back side, dated October 23, 1886. More drawings from the 1880s are kept in the same sketchbook.

28 *Teosofisk tidskrift* 3, no. 5 (May 1893), cover.

29 *Teosofisk tidskrift* 10, no. 8 (1897): 22–26. The foldout panel is included as an illustration in Besant and Leadbeater, *Occult Chemistry*. The relationship of the diagram to Hilma af Klint's works is perceptively illuminated in Fer, "Hilma af Klint: Diagrammer," 166.

PART 2, CHAPTER 9

1 Little was left of the grand frigate, since much of it had been turned into firewood. But the golden sun over the bow and the room with red velvet chairs had survived. The ship can be seen today at the Sjöhistoriska museet in Stockholm.

2 The film can be seen online at https://www.filmarkivet.se/movies /stockholmsutstallningen-1897. See also "Konstutställningen. En första öfverblick," *Dagens Nyheter*, no. 9844 (A), May 15, 1897, 3.

3 Ida was also the secretary of the Fredrika Bremer Association, the women's rights association fighting for universal suffrage. For five years she had been married to Knut Victor Haverman, an engineer and marshal in the fire department; Nauckhoff, *Ätten af Klint*, 159. The wedding announcement appeared on May 4, 1892, in "Bröllop," *Stockholms Dagblad*, no. 120, 3.

4 Greene, "Hilma af Klint and the Swedish Folk Art Revival," 102.

5 On the discovery of X-rays and their reception in Theosophy, see Morrisson, *Modern Alchemy*. See also part 3, chapter 2 of this book, "Revolution."

6 Martin, *Führer durch F. R. Martins Sammlungen*.

7 Forberg, *Die Rezeption indischer Miniaturen*.

8 Hagedorn, "Der Einfluss der Ausstellung *Meisterwerke muhammedanischer Kunst*," 297–98.

9 Quoted in Hagedorn, "Der Einfluss der Ausstellung *Meisterwerke muhammedanischer Kunst*," 301. On the epoch-defining importance of the show, see Lermer and Shalem, *After One Hundred Years*, 5–6.

10 Martin, *Sett, hört och kant*, 46–47.

11 Loosli, *Ferdinand Hodler*, 3: 187. The portrait was painted in 1916–17.

12 Martin, *Miniature Painting and Painters*, 1: 21. The volumes and the miniature, titled *Lutspelerskan*, are found in the library of the museum Carl Larsson-gården in Sundborn. I am grateful to Caroline Edman of the museum for a copy of the letter written by Harald Bildt to Carl Larsson in 1913. The communication took place via email on October 26, 2017. On the exhibition with works by af Klint in 1913, see part 3,

chapter 14 of this book, "First Exhibition with the Theosophists."
13 The studio photograph is undated. Yet in 1902 she illustrated Anna-
Maria Roos's children's story *Maria Ladybug* (Maria Nyckelpiga).
A variation or draft of the watercolor in the Hilma af Klint archive
(HaK1303) can be seen in the background of the photo. On the il-
lustration see "Julklappen," *Göteborgs Handels- och Sjöfartstidning*,
December 19, 1902. Already in 1901 *Maria Ladybug* was put onstage
in Stockholm. As the large drawings in the background resemble stage
designs, af Klint might have been involved already. See "Teater och
Musik," *Stockholms-Tidningen*, September 28, 1901.

PART 2, CHAPTER 10

1 HaK 1156, 114–15, and Hedvig Martin, "Hilma af Klint och De fem,"
68–69.
2 The Five built the altar in October 1900; see HaK 1160, 96. On Fludd's
rose see Rebisse, *Rosicrucian History and Mysteries*, 139. The symbols
of rose and cross were depicted in the very first drawing when The Five
were mentioned in April 1896, HaK 1153, 2.
3 For the sketch, see HaK 1149; for the painting, see HaK 47.
4 Today Luther is believed to have been born in 1483; according to tradition, Christian Rosenkreuz died in 1484. See Rebisse, *Rosicrucian
History and Mysteries*, 103.
5 See, e.g., "Rose + croix," *Aftonbladet*, April 19, 1893; "Occultismen i
Frankrike," *Göteborgs Handels- och Sjöfartstidning*, August 5, 1897.
6 Hartmann, *Magic, White and Black*, 19. For the translation that Hilma
af Klint owned, see appendix 2.
7 HaK 1159, 135.
8 HaK 1408. Another portrait is depicted in Fant, *Hilma af Klint*, 15.

PART 2, CHAPTER 11

1 Thanks to Göran Jönsson for the opportunity to look through the extensive photographic archives of the Veterinärmuseet in Skara.
2 Quoted in Kortüm, "Der schwedische Tierarzt John Vennerholm," 97.
3 Kortüm, "Der schwedische Tierarzt John Vennerholm," 48, 54. Veterinary students were granted the right to earn doctorates in 1935.
4 Kortüm, "Der schwedische Tierarzt John Vennerholm," 47–48.
5 The drawings are part of the estate of John Vennerholm in the archive
of the Veterinärmuseet in Skara, no archive number.

6 Photo from the archives of the Veterinärmuseet in Skara, no date. Thanks to Nick Hopwood for identifying the models as products of the Ziegler company in Freiburg.

7 Blavatsky, *Secret Doctrine*, vol. 1, part 3, section xvi.

8 Voss, *Darwins Bilder*, 151.

9 HaK 1298, 1299, 1300. They are printed in Vennerholm, *Grunddragen af hästens operativa*, as figs. 4, 41, and 118.

10 Vennerholm, *Grunddragen af hästens operativa*.

11 On the gradual replacement of horses, see Raulff, *Das letzte Jahrhundert der Pferde*.

12 Vennerholm's book does include some signed drawings, such as those by J. R. Dorff.

PART 2, CHAPTER 12

1 HaK 1159, 193–94. See also Hedvig Martin, "Hilma af Klint och De fem," 66.

2 HaK 1159, 101, and HaK 1158, 9.

3 HaK 1160, 75. For Georg's first appearance, see HaK 1159, 3; for Amaliel, HaK 1159, 261.

4 HaK 1160, 224.

5 For the telephone, see Müller-Westermann, "Paintings for the Future," 37.

6 "Julklappen," *Göteborgs Handels- och Sjöfartstidning*, December 19, 1902. On Anna Maria Roos, see Nordlinder, "Anna Maria Roos."

7 "Friskar vindar, jultidning VI," *Tidningen Kalmar*, no. 195, December 16, 1903.

8 The full title is *Lille Lapp-Natti och hans fostersystrar*; see Svensson, "Mellan abstraktion och esoterism," 32. The book was published in 1904. The children's book illustrations are catalogued in the archive as HaK 1301–5, as well as HaK 1396 and HaK 1397.

9 For example, HaK 1321–36, HaK 1346–48, and HaK 1367–78. The illustrations have been widely reproduced; see Müller-Westermann and Widoff, *Hilma af Klint*, 36. A report on the 1892 Sveriges allmänna konstförening exhibition mentions "blomsterstycken" (flower paintings) by af Klint; see "Sveriges allmänna konstförening," *Dagens Nyheter*, December 9, 1892.

10 On the grant see *Norrköpings tidningar*, May 21, 1891; for Ida af Klint and Gertrud Adelborg see *Stockholms Dagblad*, May 21, 1889. Roos also served as a secretary at the Fredrika Bremer Association.

11 Bergstrand, *En bilderboks-historia*, and Rådström, *Fröken Ottil*, 27–28, 53.

12　The design book was labeled "Tillhör artisten Hilma af Klint, Sthlm." It was purchased without accompanying documents at a flea market and incorporated into the collection of the Länsmuseet in Hudiksvall, where it was discovered in 2017 by Joel Bergroth. I received this information in an email from Johan af Klint on June 30, 2017.

13　Drawing of a horse's skull in the estate of John Vennerholm, archive of the Veterinärmuseet, Skara, unnumbered, undated.

14　For the works by Prince Eugen and Hilma af Klint see "Friska Vindar," in *Norrlandsposten*, December 23, 1902. On the purchase of the watercolor, see "Konst," in *Svenska Dagbladet*, December 21, 1903, 8.

15　Dam, "Visit to Professor Röntgen," 55.

16　HaK 1164. Af Klint recorded the messages on loose sheets of paper and later transferred them in ink to the pages of a notebook. Gidro also spoke to The Five starting on April 15, 1896, HaK 1153, 3.

17　HaK 1164, 70.

18　HaK 1164, 71. The message was received on August 29, 1901.

19　HaK 1164, 81.

20　HaK 1164, 81.

21　Power of attorney granted by Hilma af Klint to Robert Ludvig Haglund, 1903, Robert Haglunds autograf-samling (KB1/112), Robert Haglund Archiv, Kungliga biblioteket, Stockholm.

PART 2, CHAPTER 13

1　HaK 1151a, 9.

2　HaK 1151a. The sketchbook contains twenty unnumbered pages. If one counts the pages, the drawings are found on 5, 7, and 9.

3　Thanks to Marie Cassel for telling me about the chain, which is now owned by Bertil Sinander, one of the descendants of Magdalena Augusta Andersson. The accompanying note is from 1951.

4　Wolandt, *Selma Lagerlöf*, 139.

5　Carlsson, *Frihetslif!* 154.

6　HaK 1345.

7　HaK 1345.

8　The note says "Kedjan, en gåva antingen av Anna Cassel el Hilma af Klint från Rom där dessa båda låg och målade i början av 1900 talet" (The necklace, a gift by either Anna Cassel or Hilma af Klint from Rome, where they both stayed and painted in the early 1900s).

9　HaK 1159, 135.

10　"Meddelanden från den osynliga verlden erhållna genom ett skrifvande medium," Uppsala 1886, part of HaK 1165 (also 1154b).

11 Kandinsky even quoted the sentence in 1911; see Kandinsky, *Über das Geistige in der Kunst*, 37. On the origin and context of the sentence, see Vasold, *Rudolf Virchow*.

12 As quoted in Krüger, *Das Bild als Schleier des Unsichtbaren*, 13.

13 The dates of the trip to Italy are not known. The 1903 sojourn at the Wartburg and the execution of the power of attorney that same year suggest this as the time the journey took place.

14 HaK 1162, 8.

15 HaK 1162, 36. The date is December 8, 1903. In the records that af Klint made outside of the group and later copied into HaK 1156, there are automatic drawings beginning at the end of 1901; see HaK 1156, 73–74.

16 HaK 1162, 41.

PART 2, CHAPTER 14

1 Weininger, *Sex and Character*, 297; for the formulas, see ibid., 29.

2 Weininger, *Sex and Character*, 69.

3 "Nobelpristagarne," in *Dagens Nyheter*, December 11, 1903, 2.

4 Kemlein and Dieckmann, *Strindberg im Zeugnis der Zeitgenossen*, 201. Parentheses in original.

5 "Aug. Strindberg om kvinnodyrkan," in *Högenäs Tidning*, no. 127, October 24, 1903. The article refers to Strindberg's obituary of Weininger in the Austrian magazine *Die Fakel*.

6 On Ångström's defense of Marie Curie see Brian, *The Curies*, 79–80.

PART 3, CHAPTER 1

1 Martin, "Hilma af Klint och De fem," 74.

2 Erik af Klint, "Hilma af Klint och hennes verk," 3.

3 HaK 1162, 96.

4 Martin, "Hilma af Klint och De fem," 77.

5 HaK 418, 125. The undated notebook is labeled "Symboliska Teckningar och Ord av Hilma af Klint."

6 Of the 1908 series *US* and *WUS*, the notebook remarks, "This series was actually to have been made by Cornelia Cederberg, but since she did not dare to undertake it, Hilma had to," HaK 1177, first page (unnumbered), no date. See also Burgin, *Hilma af Klint*, 101, where this translation appears.

7 Membership register of the Stockholm lodge, Förteckning öfver Teosofiska Samfundets skandinaviska sektions medlemmar (Stock-

holmslogen), 1907, 5, Archive of the bookstore of the Teosofiska Samfundet Stockholm. Af Klint became a member on May 23, 1904, and
was assigned number 25919 in the register of the Theosophical Society
Adyar. Cornelia Cederberg joined later, in 1913.

8   Leadbeater, *Man Visible and Invisible*, chap. 2, para. 18.
9   Olcott, *Buddhist Catechism*, 63.
10   HaK 1522 (S9), 18. The drawing was produced on November 29,
     1904.

PART 3, CHAPTER 2

1   Nauckhoff, *Ätten af Klint*, 159. Ida still lived near her mother and sis-
     ter; she and her husband had moved to Djursholm, a suburb of Stock-
     holm.
2   Many newspapers reported on the talk; see in particular *Smålands-
     posten*, June 7, 1905.
3   Pierre Curie, "Radioactive Substances, Especially Radium." Nobel lec-
     ture, June 6, 1905. https://www.nobelprize.org/uploads/2018/06/pierre
     -curie-lecture.pdf.
4   Leadbeater, *Man Visible and Invisible*, chap. 2, para. 16.
5   Besant and Leadbeater, *Thought-Forms*, 11. The publication date for
     this book is often falsely given as 1901; see Crow, "Bibliographical Er-
     ror," 126–27.
6   Besant and Leadbeater, *Thought-Forms*, 73.
7   HaK 1072, 11, and HaK 558, 14, or HaK 577, 35. The Swedish word is
     tankeformer.
8   HaK 555, 2.
9   HaK 1526 (S13), 12.
10   HaK 1162, 173.
11   HaK 555, 5.
12   HaK 555, 4, December 1905. Emphasis in the original.
13   The album "Bilder från Skansen" with the illustration after af
     Klint's painting was published by Artur Hazelius in 1898; see https://
     digitaltmuseum.se/021016901117/hallestadstapeln-pa-skansen-i
     -stockholm-malad-av-hilma-af-klint-1895-illustration/media?slide=0.
14   HaK 1076, 11. The entry is from November 11, 1935. Adelborg died a
     few months later, on March 19, 1936. For the second entry see HaK
     1094, 3, dated November 25, 1943.
15   On Adelborg's lifelong interest in folk art and non-European art, see
     Öberg and Smolicki, *Ottilia Adelborg*.

PART 3, CHAPTER 3

1   HaK 555, 88. The series consists of 26 paintings whose full title is *Primordial Chaos, No. 1, Group I, Series WU/The Rose*, 1906–1907. The entire series is pictured in Burgin, *Hilma af Klint*, 36–53. A helpful overview chart of the *Paintings for the Temple* and their various titles has been compiled by Caroline Levander, in Müller-Westermann and Høgsberg, *Hilma af Klint*, 256 and 257.

2   HaK 555, 91. For *Snäckan* see Nauckhoff, *Ätten af Klint*, 156.

3   HaK 556, 112.

4   HaK 555, 10–11.

5   HaK 555, 62.

6   The doctrine of reincarnation was a frequent subject, often represented by the nautilus; see HaK 556, 341.

7   HaK 556, 257. The abbreviation "L" is explained two pages earlier.

8   HaK 555, 3, 4, 31, 42, 60, and 75.

9   For "Engelsberg," see HaK 555, 39, 41, 63, and 89; for "skogen på Adelsö," see HaK 555, 43.

10 The "Engelsbergmålarna" included Olof Arborelius, Mauritz Lindström, and Axel Fahlcrantz. According to the journalist and writer Yvonne Gröning, who has researched the cultural life of the region for decades, Hilma af Klint's name does not appear in the archives there. This information was received by email on September 15, 2017. On the Theosophists in Engelsberg, see Gröning, "Älskad Florrie Hamilton."

PART 3, CHAPTER 4

1   The series of eight paintings bears the full title *Eros Series, Group II, Series WU/The Rose*, 1907. The entire series is pictured in Burgin, *Hilma af Klint*, 54–60.

2   HaK 556, 267.

3   Email from Dag Kronlund, archivist of the Royal Dramatic Theatre, October 28, 2019.

4   Blavatsky, *Secret Doctrine*, vol. 2, stanza 2, 10.a.

5   HaK 556, 230.

PART 3, CHAPTER 5

1   HaK 556, 343. For the two later entries see HaK 1050, 6 (September 4, 1932) and HaK 1060, 13 (April 15, 1933).

2   Hilma af Klint to Olof Sundström, July 29, 1943, archives of the Stiftelsen Hilma af Klints Verk.

3 The roles only occasionally switched, indicated for example by "A is to paint, H sketch." HaK 556, 198.

4 HaK 1160, 187.

5 "Akasha" is mentioned early on in the notebooks, in HaK 555, before the page numbered 1. On the concept of the "Akasha" chronicle, see Zander, *Anthroposophie in Deutschland*, 620–21.

6 HaK 556, 266.

7 The paintings bear the titles *Sunrise* (HaK 37), *Evening Calm* (HaK 36), and *The Inner Domain* (HaK 35).

8 HaK 556, 274.

9 The full title is *The Large Figure Paintings, Group III, Series WU/The Rose*, 1907. The entire series is pictured in Burgin, *Hilma af Klint*, 61–66.

10 HaK 556, 274. Since 1902 her regular studio had been in Hamngatan 9; see Erik af Klint, "Hilma af Klint och hennes verk," 1.

11 HaK 556, 275.

12 Executed in May 1907, the painting is HaK 41. It is in *The Large Paintings* series.

13 For "unseen," see HaK 556, 274.

14 HaK 556, 272.

15 HaK 556, 340.

16 HaK 556, 274.

17 HaK 555, 8. Emphasis in the original.

18 HaK 556, 557.

19 HaK 416a, books 1 and 2.

20 HaK 556, 400.

21 HaK 555, 93–94.

PART 3, CHAPTER 6

1 Theodor Bierfreund, *Florens—Monumenter og mennesker*, 79–80; see appendix 2.

2 HaK 556, 354.

3 Af Klint writes of "arkitektpapper." The small, brown bound notebook in which this is found has no number and has not been scanned. The cover contains the label "Ur Hilma af Klints Anteckningar, Innehållet i kistorna på Spolegatan." The pages are not numbered: the quote can be found on the page that begins "De 10 bilderna utfördes . . ."

4 The notes in pencil can be seen, for example, on *No. 4* of *The Ten Largest*.

5   This anecdote was passed down in the af Klint family. I am grateful to Johan af Klint for bringing it to my attention.

6   The full title of the series is *The Ten Largest, Group IV, The Ararat Work*, 1907. See Levander in Müller-Westermann and Høgsberg, *Hilma af Klint*.

7   HaK 559, 164.

8   HaK 556, 366.

9   HaK 556, 353, 355 or 394. On Blavatsky's "Mahatmas," see Zander, *Anthroposophie in Deutschland*, 95–96.

10 On occult combinations of Hebrew letters see Nizida, *Astralljuset*, 19. The book is found in Hilma af Klints library; see appendix 2.

11 The resemblance has been pointed out by Bax, *Anna Cassel and Hilma af Klint*, 70.

12 HaK 556, 399 ("wu"), 281 ("mwu"), 192 ("ws"). For the glossaries, see HaK 418 and HaK 1040. See also an af Klint glossary in English translation, in Burgin, *Hilma af Klint*, 240–85.

13 HaK 556, 390.

14 HaK 556, 542.

15 HaK 555, 86.

16 HaK 556, 120.

17 HaK 556, 362.

18 For "Hilma i half trans," see HaK 1162, 291; for "omorganisiera," see HaK 1162, 294–95; for "alla de, som Hilma tänkt," see HaK 1162, 294.

19 HaK 1162, 295.

20 The first request to include Gusten came on May 31, 1907; see HaK 1162, 293. The request was repeated in August 1907, leading to prompt resistance; see HaK 556, 362. On "hostian," see HaK 556, 362.

21 HaK 556, 400.

22 HaK 556, 358–59, 373, and 376.

23 HaK 556, 365.

24 For "dualsmärtans övervinnande," see HaK 556, 389.

25 For "fullkomlighet" see HaK 556, 383; for "urbildspråk" see HaK 556, 383; for "utarbeta liljan inom sig" see HaK 556, 394.

26 HaK 102.

27 HaK 556, 394.

PART 3, CHAPTER 7

1   HaK 1525 (S12), 9, February 5, 1907, and HaK 1527 (S14), 4, January 22, 1907. Some of the women found the erotic images disruptive.

2   HaK 416b, n.p., image no. 3.

3   HaK 556, 380.

4   Blavatsky, *Index to the Secret Doctrine*, 89, 170.

5   HaK 556, 409.

6   HaK 556, 409.

7   Zimmerman, *Lesbian Histories and Cultures*, 46.

8   For the quotes on "Mountain King," see HaK 1165, 3; for "The broken soul," see HaK 1165, 6.

9   HaK 556, 417, and 422–23.

10 For "övergåv i denna stund alla mig," see HaK 556, 422; for "4 emot mig," see HaK 556, 427.

11 HaK 556, 459.

12 On representation of "conjunctio" and "androgyny," see Roob, *Hermetic Museum*, 358–59 and 372–73. On "conjunctio," cf. Pfisterer, *Kunst-Geburten*, 147–48.

13 HaK 555, 11.

14 HaK 556, 409. Emphasis in original.

15 For quote see HaK 556, 460. On the exhibitions, see Müller-Westermann, "Paintings for the Future," 278.

PART 3, CHAPTER 8

1   On Steiner in Weimar, see Gebhardt, *Rudolf Steiner*, 102–3.

2   See his 1907 designs for the European Theosophical Congress in Munich in Lierl and Roder, *Anthroposophie wird Kunst*.

3   HaK 556, 263–64, and 416. The entries that deal with Steiner that are recorded as being from 1907 were actually added later; the cross with which they are marked indicates this.

4   Steiner's lectures were announced in Swedish daily newspapers; see, e.g., *Stockholms-Tidningen*, March 27, 1908.

5   HaK 556, 527, from March 28, 1908.

6   Steiner gave the lectures in Munich between May 22 and June 6, 1907. The Stockholm lecture "The Rosicrucians" was held on March 30, 1908, for the Theosophical Society. I thank Anne Weise from the Rudolf Steiner Archive for the information.

7   HaK 556, 528. Hilma writes that she met Steiner "for the first time" on March 30. This cannot be the date of the studio visit, since the letters were exchanged in June.

8   Hilma af Klint to Rudolf Steiner, June 26, 1908, Rudolf Steiner Archive at the Goetheanum, Dornach. Af Klint also mentions a previous letter

that had gone unanswered, so it is likely this letter was the second one she sent.

9   Ibid.

10 Rudolf Steiner to Hilma af Klint, July 18, 1908, Rudolf Steiner Archive at the Goetheanum, Dornach. A typescript of the letter is held by the Stiftelsen Hilma af Klints Verk. A facsimile appears in Bartholl and Martin, *Between the Worlds*, 63.

11 Ibid.

12 The only documents dealing with the exchange in the Rudolf Steiner Archive in Dornach are the letters of June 26, 1908 (af Klint to Steiner), and July 18, 1908 (Steiner to af Klint). For "Doctor Steiner's notes" see HaK 1103, 136–44. I thank Kurt Almqvist for bringing these documents to my attention.

13 See HaK 1101, 35–36. The date of the lecture was December 9, 1924; see Sundström, "Förteckning över Frk. Hilma af Klints efterlämnade verk," 98. In the literature on af Klint, Steiner's possible studio visit has been dated in various ways: Her nephew Erik af Klint suggests that Steiner might have visited the studio on Munsö but does not give a year; see Erik af Klint, "Hilma af Klint och hennes verk," 8. Åke Fant believes the visit took place in 1908; see Fant, *Hilma af Klint*, 23.

14 "Teosofiska föreläsningar," *Aftonbladet*, January 3, 1910.

15 The anecdote, which has been passed along and elaborated on from publication to publication, can be traced to Åke Fant. See Fant, *Hilma af Klint*, 23 and 179.

16 Very brief comments by Steiner on paintings of the series "Evolution" are also noted in HaK 556, 501, 506, and 528. They were added in retrospect.

17 Rev. 1:8 (King James Version).

18 On Heyman's biography see Westholm, *Frank Heyman*; for the meeting with Steiner, see ibid., 3; see also Wahlström, *Sanningen om Filip*.

19 Quoted in Kugler, Halfen, and Wendtland, *Rudolf Steiner*, 34–35.

20 Frank Heyman, "Den ursprungliga bilden," Göteborg, October 25, 1906, in the archive of the Skissernas museum, bild- och klippsamling, Lund. The museum houses Heyman's estate. Heyman ordered in his will that all diaries and other notes were to be burned after his death; see Wahlström, *Sanningen om Filip*, 324.

21 Quoted in Kugler, Halfen, and Wendtland, *Rudolf Steiner*, 32.

22 Avenarius, "Eine Neue Sprache?," 186.

23 Voit, *Ab nach München!*

PART 3, CHAPTER 9

1   Matisse, "Notes of a Painter" (1908), 35.
2   Kollnitz, "Promoting the Young," 277.
3   Hodin, *Isaac Grünewald*, and Holmberg, "Reception of the Early European Avant-Gardes in Sweden," 424–25.

PART 3, CHAPTER 10

1   See Levander, in Müller-Westermann and Høgsberg, *Hilma af Klint*.
2   The date is noted on the drawings, and they are signed "The Five." HaK 556, 462. On the drawings of the Five, see Volz, *Hilma af Klint*, 81–95.
3   HaK 556, 512.
4   The students at the training institute were listed in the papers. On Sigrid Lancén see *Svenska Dagbladet*, no. 164, July 18, 1895, 2.
5   For the telephone book entry, see https://stockholmskallan.stockholm .se/PostFiles/SMF/SD/SSMB_0023983_1915_25.pdf. For the address, see https://sok.riksarkivet.se/?postid=Folk_126248723.
6   The *Svenska Dagbladet* reports her participation in the exhibitions of the Sveriges Allmänna Konstförening on December 17, 1906; on May 23 and June 1, 1907, an exhibition in Lund is mentioned.
7   HaK 556, 414. Sigrid Lancén had already been mentioned in 1901 and 1902; see HaK 1164, 71, 73, 77, 79–81.
8   HaK 557, 4 and 27.
9   HaK 557, 6.
10 HaK 1166, 20.
11 HaK 1166, 20.
12 HaK 1166, 8–9.
13 HaK 1166, 18.
14 HaK 557, 1.
15 HaK 557, 8–9.
16 The other members were Hélène Westmark, Emilia Giertta, Inga Jehander, Sigrid Henström, Siri Torgny, Emma Cassel, Lotten Rönquist, and Alma Arnell. See HaK 568, 97. When Thomasine Anderson joined in 1914, she was the thirteenth member. See HaK 557, 33 and HaK 1093, 36.
17 HaK 557, 8 and 15.

PART 3, CHAPTER 11

1   Quoted in Hodin, *Isaac Grünewald*, 48. The critic was August Brunius.
2   For the history of the organization's founding, see "Föreningen Sven-

ska Konstnärinnor," in *Idun, Illustrerad tidning för kvinnan och hemmet* 24, no. 3 (January 22, 1911): 38.

3 On the understanding of epilepsy in Sweden, see Pietikainen, *Neurosis and Modernity*, 61.

4 The men depicted are Sigfrid Ullmann, Knut Janson, and Birger Simonsson.

5 Protokollet vid sammanträde med styrelsen för föreningen Svenska Konstnärinnor i Stockholm, April 13, 1910, §3, p. 1. Archives of the Föreningen Svenska Konstnärinnor, Riksarkivet, Stockholm.

6 Hilma af Klint was voted "sekretarere" on October 12; see Protokollet vid sammanträde med styrelsen för föreningen Svenska Konstnärinnor i Stockholm, October 12, 1910, §3, 1. Anna Cassel joined on December 6, 1910.

7 Brian, *The Curies*, 79–80. For the portrait, see https://de.wikipedia.org /wiki/Knut_%C3%85ngstr%C3%B6m.

8 *Dagens Nyheter*, December 5, 1910. Ångström's portrait was also covered by *Dagens Nyheter* on October 4, 1910.

9 See the exhibition catalogue, "Svenska konstnärinnors utställning I K. Akademien för de fria konsterna, 1–30 mars 1911," 25. For Anna Cassel see ibid., 20.

10 Roos, "Svenska konstnärinnors utställning I," 115.

11 On the third exhibition, see Werenskiold, "Concepts of Expressionism in Scandinavia," 21.

12 Hilma af Klint resigned on April 22, 1911; see §2 of the minutes from April 22, 1911. Though she was not included in the membership list from May 28, 1911 on, she is mentioned twice more as a functionary; see the heading "styrelse" in "Matrikel öfver Föreningen Svenska Konstnärinnors ledamöter," 1911 and 1914 (Gefle, 1911 and 1914).

13 HaK 558, unnumbered and first page of notebook, dated August 5, 1911.

14 *Konst* 1, no. 1 (November 15, 1911); on its establishment see http://www .ub.gu.se/kvinndata/digtid/03/1911/dagny1911_48.pdf.

15 C. Larsson, "En Eternell," 3–4.

16 Marc, "Geistige Güter," 23, and Kandinsky, *Concerning the Spiritual in Art*, 20.

PART 3, CHAPTER 12

1 *Svenska konstnärinnor utställning 1911*, 17 (Adelborg), 20 (Cardon), and 14 (Valerius).

2 HaK 559, 44.

3   Kugler, Halfen, and Wendtland, *Rudolf Steiner*, 34. See also part 3, chapter 8, pp. 158–59 of this book. For the manifesto, see Heyman, "Den ursprungliga bilden." See also part 3, chapter 8, note 20. For "stor profet," see HaK 558, 14.

4   HaK 558, 17–18.

5   HaK 558, 60–61.

6   Kugler, Halfen, and Wendtland, *Rudolf Steiner*, 35.

7   Heyman, "Den urspringliga bilden," Göteborg, October 25, 1906, Skissernas museum archives, bild- och klippsammling, Lund.

8   HaK 558, 118. Parentheses in original.

9   HaK 555, 36.

10 The term "ancient image" recurs in Hilma af Klint's notebooks see for example HaK 556, 383. Heyman's sketch *Själens evolution*, pen and ink, 30 x 44.8 cm, is held in the Skissernas museum archives.

11 HaK 420, 38/39.

12 London, *People of the Abyss*, 263. Hilma af Klint owned a Swedish translation of the work; see appendix 2. On Heyman's time in London, see Westholm, *Frank Heyman*, 3 and 6.

13 Quoted in Arvidson, "Ett monumentalt misslyckande," 17.

14 HaK 558, 67.

15 HaK 558, 121–22.

16 The small brown notebook that contains this comment has no number and has not been scanned. The cover bears the inscription "Ur Hilma af Klints Anteckningar, Innehållet i kistorna på Spolegatan." The pages are not numbered; the quote is found on the page that begins "De 10 bilderna utfördes . . ." If Heyman made notes about his exchanges with af Klint, they have been destroyed, in accordance with his will. See part 3, chapter 8, note 20.

17 The quote appears in HaK 558, 149, and HaK 559, 34. The former's date is May 1912, the latter's June 1912.

PART 3, CHAPTER 13

1   HaK 558, 104. The dates given in the notebook differ from those marked on the drawings (HaK 119–25): 3/28 versus 5/13.

2   HaK 558, 105.

3   Ulla af Klint, interview.

4   For the names of The Thirteen, see part 3, chapter 10, note 16.

5   Erik af Klint is the first to report on the acquisition; see Erik af Klint, "Hilma af Klint och hennes verk," 7. Admiral Gustaf af Klint acquired

sole ownership of the property on Adelsö in 1912 for 75,400 crowns. Hilma af Klint's purchase of Furuheim is recorded in the town register on March 11, 1913. On ownership rights pertaining to Furuheim, see the entry "Mantalslängd for Brahegatan 52," Stockholms Stadsarkiv, Liljeholmen; and "Mantalslängd for the Villa Furuheim," November 21, 1918, Munsö register, Häradsskrivaren i Svartsjö fögderi, Arkiv II, ref.kod SE/SSA/2896N7Fiaa/65f. Thanks to Tomas Östlund for this information. On the rental of Furuheim in 1912, see Fant, *Hilma af Klint*, 25.

6   HaK 558, 3, 48, and 56.
7   HaK 558, 134.
8   HaK 559, 8. The twenty pages with sessions at the Stora Hotellet Norrköping are dated May 28 to May 30, 1912. The tickets can be found in the archive of the Hilma af Klint Foundation. For newspaper coverage, see "Teosoferna på congress i pingsten," *Dagens Nyheter*, May 28, 1912.
9   HaK 559, 44.
10 For China, see HaK 558, 48; for Finland, see HaK 557, 73.
11 HaK 559, 62.
12 HaK 558, 108; the paintings are HaK 112–18.
13 HaK 562. The book is labeled with the penciled note: "Ursprungligen A. Cassels bok införlivad i H. af Klints samling anteckningar." The first entry is dated November 12, 1912 and the last February 3, 1913.
14 All series described in the following pages are unnumbered items in the archives of the Stiftelsen Hilma af Klints Verk. The pages are dated; the first series was begun in March 1913.
15 HaK 562, 6.
16 On Fludd's images, see Roob, *Hermetic Museum*, 97.
17 See manuscript (HaK 1101) titled "Föredrag hållet af Fröken Hilma af Klint vid S. L. F., den 7. April 1913 å Praktiska Hushållskolan i Stockholm," 3 ("powers and capacities") and 5 ("World Tree" and "elemental force").
18 For departure times, see HaK 564, 72 and 76. For Ansgar, see HaK 564, 76. On the series *Tree of Knowledge*, see HaK 564, 28, 78, and 115. The numbers 1, 2, 3, 4, 5, and 6 are mentioned at HaK 564, 72, standing for Gusten Andersson, af Klint, Anna Cassel, Hélène Westmark, Emilia Giertta, and Inga Jehander.

PART 3, CHAPTER 14

1   Carolus, "Professor Julius Kronberg," 70–71, and P. F., "Julius Kronberg," 420.

2   Internationella Teosofiska Fredskongressen, 4, no. 33. The painting
    was preceded by 112 preparatory drawings.

3   See for example the review in *Aftonbladet* on June 26, 1913.

4   On Larsson and Zorn, see Internationella Teosofiska Fredskongressen,
    6 and 9.

5   The paintings are HaK 35, 36, and 37. They retain the frames from the
    1913 exhibition.

6   On Fidus, see Hollein and Kort, *Künstler und Propheten*, 56–89.

7   Af Klint usually gave her series a single title that included combina-
    tions of letters, for example *Primordial Chaos, Group I, WU/The Rose
    Series*. It is possible that the series sold; the catalogue indicates that
    visitors could request a price list. The oil sketches and drawings in
    the catalogue have the same titles as some oil paintings in the archive.
    HaK 112–18, called *A Female Series* (1912), corresponds with *The Series
    of Instruction* in the catalogue of 1913; HaK 142–48, called *A Male
    Series* (1915), corresponds with *The Series of Ascent* in the catalogue.
    The works in the archive are oil paintings; the works in the catalogue
    are listed as "drawings" and "oil sketches," which explains the differ-
    ence in the dates given. See "Förteckning över Frk. Hilma af Klints
    efterlämnade verk, sammanställd av O Sundström," 1945, 17 and 20, in
    the archives of the Stiftelsen Hilma af Klints Verk.

8   HaK 564, 118; for the bilingual catalogue of the exhibition, see Teoso-
    fiska Samfundet, *Katalog konstutställning*, 15–16.

9   See Teosofiska Samfundet, *Katalog konstutställning*, 5, no. 1.

10 "En teosofisk kättare," in *Aftonbladet*, June 9, 1913, 7. Steiner and Siv-
    ers were in Stockholm June 8–10; see Steiner and Steiner-von Sivers,
    Correspondence and Documents, 292. The lecture held by Steiner the
    same day in Stockholm was titled "Recognizing and Experiencing
    Immortality from the Perspective of Theosophical Insight." For the
    announcement of the talk, see "Antroposofernas ledare i Stockholm,"
    in *Aftonbladet*, June 7, 1913, 7.

PART 3, CHAPTER 15

1   The "Tree of Knowledge" first appears in the notes in April 1913, HaK
    564, 28, then again on 115. The back of the second watercolor, num-
    bered HaK 134, contains a text with the dates 21.–23.6.1913. *Series W,
    Tree of Knowledge*, 1913–1915 is numbered HaK 133–30 and 141. An
    almost identical version of *Tree of Knowledge* belongs to Glenstone, a
    private museum in Potomac, Maryland. See introduction, p. 7.

2   On the schism, see Zander, *Anthroposophie in Deutschland*, 1: 822–23.

The tickets from 1912 are printed with the words "Theosophical Morality. 3 Lectures by Herr Dr. Steiner, May 28., 29., and 30. In Norrköping. Tickets for all 3 lectures = 3 crowns." Another lecture by Steiner in Norrköping on July 13 is mentioned; see HaK 419, 18.

3   Steiner, "Nature of the Bhagavad Gita." Hilma af Klint's copy is held by the library of Lund University and her name is written on the cover. See Rudolf Steiner, *Die Bhagavad Gita und die Paulusbriefe* in appendix 2.

4   Steiner, "Nature of the Bhagavad Gita." "Brain" is underlined in pencil in af Klint's copy.

5   Steiner, "Nature of the Bhagavad Gita." Af Klint mentions early on and frequently the "Upanishads," which are part of "Veda"; see, e.g., HaK 556, 259, 276, 464, 496; HaK 557, 33; HaK 558, 84, 120.

PART 3, CHAPTER 16

1   HaK 1164, 10–11.
2   HaK 1164, 7.
3   HaK 1164, 12–13.
4   HaK 1164, 11–12.
5   HaK 1164, 15.
6   HaK 1164, 37.
7   HaK 556, 415.
8   HaK 557, 6.
9   HaK 1164, 59.
10 Gen. 2:23 (King James Version).
11 HaK 557, 2. The start date for work on the series is given as September 30 in HaK 1178, 1.

PART 3, CHAPTER 17

1   HaK 562, 86.
2   Rydberg was already aware that his book was being received warmly in spiritual circles. See Lindqvist, "Om Selma Lagerlöfs förhållande," 44 and 47.
3   Rydberg, *Singoalla*, 18.
4   Rydberg, *Singoalla*, 177.
5   Rydberg, *Singoalla*, 97.
6   HaK 568, 154–55. The notebooks on Rydberg's *Singoalla* are numbered HaK 568 and HaK 569. The writer is not named, but it is not af Klint's handwriting.

7   HaK 568, 130–31.
8   HaK 1164, 47.

PART 3, CHAPTER 18

1   A plan of the exhibition can be found in the exhibition catalogue and also in Sundberg, "Konsthallen på Baltiska utställningen," 23.
2   *Baltiska Utställning I Malmö 1914*, 49.
3   Sundberg, "Konsthallen på Baltiska utställningen," 25 (Swedish) and 20 (English).
4   Tillberg, "Kandinsky in Sweden," 328.
5   Tillberg, "Kandinsky in Sweden," 328.
6   Kandinsky, *Über das Geistige in der Kunst*, 125. Here translated directly by Anne Posten to preserve the recurrence of "spirit."
7   Tillberg, "Kandinsky in Sweden," 329.
8   *Idun*, May 24, 1914, 328.
9   On the acquisitions by the Nationalmuseum, see Sundberg, "Konsthallen på Baltiska utställningen," 20 (Swedish) and 32 (English). On the rejection of Kandinsky, see Tillberg, "Kandinsky in Sweden," 329.
10 HaK 564, 149–50.

PART 3, CHAPTER 19

1   In fall 1914 and spring 1915, she wrote in the notebook of painting in a room of the building at Eriksbergsgatan; see HaK 581, first page (unnumbered), and HaK 577, third page from the beginning.
2   *Idun*, September 27, 1914, 628.
3   Blavatsky, *Secret Doctrine*, 280.
4   For the Rosicrucians, it was a pelican that pierced its own breast to feed its young. The self-sacrificing pelican, a Christian symbol for the sacrificial death of Jesus, was, according to Blavatsky, "a direct outcome from the Eastern Secret Doctrine." Blavatsky, *Secret Doctrine*, 136.
5   Blavatsky, *Secret Doctrine*, 1509.
6   On the connection between Theosophy and racist ideologies, see Doering-Manteuffel, *Das Okkulte*, 197.
7   Blavatsky, *Secret Doctrine*, 1775.

PART 3, CHAPTER 20

1   HaK 142–48. In 1913 af Klint exhibited "oil sketches" of this series under the title "The Series of Ascent" in the exhibition organized by the

Theosophists; see part 3, chapter 14, p. 185 and note 7 from the same chapter.

2   Gusten Andersson had also addressed Hilma af Klint as "Saint George" as early as 1909; see HaK 1166, 3. For Lancén's use of the name, see HaK 1164, 47. Af Klint referred to the paintings as *Snt Göransbilderna*; see HaK 557, 105.

3   HaK 431, 32–33. The lines are written in German.

4   She writes in a notebook that in fall 1915 and spring 1916 "3 large and one smaller painting" were completed in the workspace at "Ynglingagatan (lokal No 3)"; see HaK 581, first page (unnumbered). The smaller painting she refers to is *Human Chastity*, HaK 193.

5   The prints can be seen on *Altarpiece, No. 2, Group X* from 1915.

6   Gadelius, "Om sinnesjukdom," 358.

7   On the growing number of mental asylums in Sweden around the turn of the century, see Pietikainen, *Neurosis and Modernity*, 35. On Gadelius, see ibid., 119–20.

PART 3, CHAPTER 21

1   The Gummeson gallery opened in 1912. On Roslund, Gummeson, and Grünewald, see Hegelund, *Min Nell*, 94–95.

2   Barnett, *Kandinsky and Sweden*, 22.

3   Quoted in Hille, *Gabriele Münter*, 137.

4   Kandinsky and Marc, foreword to *Almanach "Der Blaue Reiter,"* n.p., and Kandinsky, *Concerning the Spiritual in Art*, 4. The painting *St. Georg II* (1911) is in the collection of the Städtische Galerie im Lenbachhaus, Munich. On Saint George and the cover of the Almanach, see Heinz, "Der Drachenkämpfer Wassily Kandinsky."

5   The painting is *St. George II*, from 1911. See Barnett, *Kandinsky and Sweden*, 132–33.

6   The 1916 watercolor is called *The Boatman*. See Barnett, *Kandinsky and Sweden*, 168–69.

7   Kandinsky, *Concerning the Spiritual in Art*, 13.

8   Tillberg, "Kandinsky in Sweden," 332, and Barnett, *Kandinsky and Sweden*, 36.

9   Wassily Kandinsky to Will Grohmann, October 9, 1932, in Wörwag, *Wassily Kandinsky*, 313.

10   "Kandinski—färgsymphoniker. Ett samtal med den ryska målaren på vernissagedagen," *Dagens Nyheter*, February 2, 1916.

PART 3, CHAPTER 22

1　HaK 580, 65–66 and 89–92.
2　HaK 1165. The notes are on loose sheets of paper titled "building" attached to Gusten's notebook. They are dated but not numbered. The date given is August 3, 1916.
3　Preparations had been made for the works on Munsö, in early 1916, the artist wrote; see HaK 581, first page (unnumbered).
4　*Aftonbladet*, April 19, 1916.
5　Label on HaK 202.
6　Cf., e.g., HaK 270.
7　HaK 294.
8　For the paintings with thirteen figures, see HaK 232, 234 and 235.
9　Quoted in Barnett, *Kandinsky and Sweden*, 58.
10　Barnett, *Kandinsky and Sweden*, 60.
11　An old postcard shows the space of the gallery; see Barnett, *Kandinsky and Sweden*, 22.
12　Wassily Kandinsky to Will Grohmann, October 5, 1924, in Wörwag, *Wassily Kandinsky*, 59–60. Emphasis in original.
13　Kandinsky, "Über die Formfrage," in Kandinsky and Marc, *Almanach "der Blaue Reiter,"* 78.
14　HaK 1151c, n.p.
15　For the labels of the series, see Burgin, *Hilma af Klint*, 152–53.
16　HaK 579, 38/39. English translation quoted after Almqvist and Daniel, *Hilma af Klint*, 7.
17　The manuscript (HaK 421–30) was typed and bound in 1941–42 and was then given the title "Studies of the Life of the Soul, by Hilma af Klint 1917–1918, dictated and recorded by Doctor Anna Ljungberg. Typewritten after the original." Af Klint wrote "Studies of the Life of the Soul" between February 3, 1917, and July 9, 1918. For the quote, see typescript "Själslivet," vol. 2, pp. 450–51, Hilma af Klint Foundation.

PART 3, CHAPTER 23

1　For eyewitness accounts of the building, see Fant, *Hilma af Klints hemliga bilder*, 25–26, and Erik af Klint, "Hilma af Klint och hennes verk," 8.
2　For the ownership status, see Mantalslängd, uppgift till 1913 (and 1914, 1915, 1916, 1917, 1918) års mantalsskrivning i Stockholms stad och Hedvig Eleonora församling, kvarteret renen, huset nr 12, med

adress n:r 52 vid Brahegatan, stadsarkivet i Stockholm; and Kyrkoböckerna för Munsö, Häradsskrivaren; Svartsjö fögderi II AB Flaa 1941 Bild 3 (and Bild 20, sida 8), arkiv digital. I thank Tomas Östlund for the information.

3   "Begäran från Hilma af Klint att event. för K. Sällskapets räkning få måla porträtt av framl. med. fil. kand. Björn," (January 13, 1916) and "protokollet från K. Patriotiska Sällskapets Förvaltningsutskott sammanträde den 26 januari 1916," Riksarkivet.

4   HaK 1096, 13–14. The note was written in February 1944.

5   For "money issue," see HaK 1093, 11; "longtime friend," see HaK 1093, 9–10. The notes were written in October 1943.

6   The only person whose help with the move is mentioned in a note is Frank Heyman, the sculptor. See part 3, chapter 12, note 16.

7   For "Edens lustgård" and "porten från orätt håll," see HaK 582, 22–23. For "vampyrnatur," see HaK 582, 15. For Gusten Andersson's accusation in 1909, see HaK 1166, 8–9.

8   HaK 582, 22–23.

9   HaK 1092, 83. The notes were made on May 20, 1943.

10   Thomasine Anderson appears as no. 13 on July 3 and 13, 1914. See HaK 419, 12. For "tillit och tro på mig," see HaK 577, 32.

PART 3, CHAPTER 24

1   Ida, for example, transferred her shares of the estate to her sister, presumably before the sale to Gustaf in 1913. Ida Haverman's last will is from 1909; she died on February 28, 1938. On the will, see also part 5, chapter 9, note 6. I am grateful to Johan af Klint for this information.

2   Thomasine Anderson appears as no. 13 on July 3 and 13, 1914; see HaK 419, 12.

3   Obituary for Thomasine Anderson in *Das Goetheanum*, 1940, 83.

4   Zwerdling, *Postcards of Nursing*, 69.

5   E.g., *Flora över Uplands och Södermanlands Fanerogamer och Bräkenartade Växter* and *Elementar Flora*; see appendix 2.

6   HaK 1092, 56.

7   HaK 431, 15–16.

8   Sigrid Henström to Hilma af Klint, May 13, 1919, Stiftelsen Hilma af Klints Verk, uncatalogued.

9   HaK 1092, 81.

10   I am grateful to Johan af Klint for this information.

PART 4, CHAPTER 1

1   HaK 431, first page (unnumbered).
2   The archive also contains a full-page article on Rudolf Steiner and the Goetheanum from the Sunday edition of *Dagens Nyheter*, November 14, 1920.
3   Sketches for a chapel for the Edelweiss Society are held in the private archive of Monica von Rosen, along with a document titled "Tecknings-lista för bidrag till byggandet af ett Tempel," dated November 1, 1908.
4   For notebook entry, see HaK 431, 19. Also this text describes the temple as both a metaphorical place within the heart and a built archi-tecture. For sketch and notes, see HaK 1101.
5   The dating is approximate. The blue albums in the archive are undated. Since they contain remarks by Steiner, they must have been written prior to his death in 1924. See also Burgin, *Hilma af Klint*, 30.
6   The albums do not contain the so-called *Preliminary Works* (HaK 35, 36, and 37) or the painting *Human Chastity* (HaK 193). The official numbering system includes these works, which explains the reference to 193 *Paintings for the Temple*.
7   Af Kint's blue albums are reproduced in their entirety in Burgin, *Hilma af Klint*. Anna Cassel's blue albums are held in the Stiftelsen Hilma af Klints Verk.

PART 4, CHAPTER 2

1   HaK 431, 60.
2   HaK 431, 46–47. The description refers to the colored drawing on HaK 447.
3   HaK 431, 14.
4   For "Hermaphrodite," see the drawing HaK 441; the quote is from HaK 431, 16.
5   January 7, 1917, in HaK 579, 84–85.
6   The original of "Flowers, Mosses, and Lichens" is held in the archives of the Goetheanum in Dornach. The book is reproduced in its entirety in Bartholl and Martin, *Between the Worlds*, 98–121. There are also two further notebooks in Dornach that are unnumbered, one with red binding, the other black. The beginning of the red notebook is dated April 21, 1919, like the German manuscript with the same content, HaK 590. "Resistance of the flesh" is found in HaK 590, 2; on flower soul, see note dated May 12, 1919, verso.

7   HaK 590, 3.
8   HaK 431, 64.
9   HaK 431, 65.
10 HaK 431, 58.

PART 4, CHAPTER 3

1   The duration of the stays in Dornach is recorded in HaK 1118, 121.
2   The total inheritance was 22,142 crowns. Hilma af Klint received 7,381 crowns. For Mathilda af Klint's 1920 will, see "Södra Roslags domsaga AB F2A:20 1920," Riksarkivet, Stockholm. I thank Johan af Klint and Tomas Östlund for the information.
3   The paintings are HaK 468–75.
4   Hilma af Klint received a certificate of membership; it is dated October 12, 1920, and held in the Stiftelsen Hilma af Klints Verk. Her notebook HaK 585 records the place where she stayed as "Arlesheim."
5   The star chart is found in the Stiftelsen Hilma af Klints Verk and is labeled "Dornach 1914." Presumably af Klint copied the chart from a model.
6   Quoted in Raab, *Edith Maryon*, 204.
7   Rosenkrantz, "Rudolf Steiner's Influence on My Life," n.p. On the collaboration of Steiner and Rosenkrantz, see Julia Voss, "At male det åndelige."
8   The drawings are contained in the archive, numbered HaK 1189a–h. Notes on the windows can be found at the end of HaK 1127, n.p.
9   Quoted in Kugler, Halfen, and Wendtland, *Rudolf Steiner*, 76.
10 HaK 585, 81; the drawing is HaK 544.
11 The artist saved a story about the Goetheanum that appeared in the Sunday edition of a Swedish newspaper, complete with photographic supplement, "Rudolf Steiner, en modern kulturreformator," *Dagens Nyheter*, appendix to the Sunday issue, November 14, 1920.

PART 4, CHAPTER 4

1   For example, *Dornach in September 1920*, HaK 544. The notebook HaK 585 was written in Arlesheim.
2   HaK 1131, 37.
3   HaK 462, 57.
4   HaK 462, 1. For London's book, see appendix 2.
5   On Monte Verità, see Michalzik, *1900*.

6 Steiner's writings on chastity in myth are found in HaK 1126, 47.

7 On the notes in the blue albums, see Burgin, *Hilma af Klint*, 36 (HaK 1171), 66, (HaK 1173), 74 (HaK 1174), and 146 (HaK 1180). On the note in Steiner's handwriting, see HaK 1040, 1, 69, and 70.

8 HaK 1125. The page is not numbered, but it is the sixteenth page. The notebooks dealing with Steiner's lectures on art are HaK 1122–25.

9 Fäth and Voda, *Aenigma*, 31.

10 Af Klint sometimes thought the pain in her hands might be due to tension. Rheumatism as a possible cause of the pain has already been mentioned; see HaK 1164, 82.

11 HaK 1131, 54. Steiner's lecture is dated September 12, 1920.

PART 4, CHAPTER 5

1 R. Steiner, "Spiritual Knowledge Is a True Communion," 75.

2 Hilma af Klint drew the Goetheanum burning in 1941, see HaK 1025–27.

3 The watercolors from 1924 are HaK 664b–761.

4 Undated document in the archive of the Stiftelsen Hilma af Klints Verk. Paragraph breaks, numbering, and punctuation are as in the original, HaK 1103, 167–68.

5 Hilma af Klint to Rudolf Steiner, April 24, 1924, Goetheanum archive; a facsimile also appears in Bartholl and Martin, *Between the Worlds*, 61.

6 HaK 1101, 35f. The date is December 9, 1924. See Sundström, Förteckning, 98.

7 HaK 1093, 10. The entry is dated October 8, 1943.

8 On Gropius, see Fäth and Voda, *Aenigma*, 41. On Mondrian, see Bax, "Piet Mondrian," 139.

9 HaK 1044, 1 and 12. Misspelling in the original.

PART 4, CHAPTER 6

1 The requests for admission are found among Albert Steffen's letters in the archive of the Goetheanum in Dornach. They are dated March 22, 1926.

2 HaK 1151c.

3 On the three notebooks see part 4, chapter 2, note 6. The copy of *Flowers, Mosses, and Lichens* contains the note "original in the archive of the Goetheanum in Dornach." See HaK 588, first page (unnumbered).

Reproduced in Birnbaum and Noring, *Legacy of Hilma af Klint*. See also HaK 584, 24.

4   The series *Tree of Knowledge* is found in the archive of the Albert Steffen Foundation in Dornach, and the paintings are reproduced in Bartholl and Martin, *Between the Worlds*. None of the pages is labeled as being original, so the question of original and copy must remain open.

5   M. L. Groos-Waß to Hilma af Klint, February 15, 1927, archive of the Albert Steffen Foundation in Dornach. The letter mentions flower paintings that were to be added to the library. A copy can be found in HaK 1103, 110f. In addition, the Dutch Anthroposophist Adelyde Content seems to have received flower paintings, which she left to the library in Dornach. See Peggy Kloppers-Moltzer to Hilma af Klint, January 2, 1928, HaK 1102, 44. The pictures were never returned to the artist and were later considered lost. They have only since resurfaced, privately owned, in Dornach in 2022. See introduction, note 16.

6   The correspondence between Kloppers-Moltzer and af Klint began on January 2, 1928, and mentions the artist's trip to Holland the previous year; see HaK 1102. Notebook HaK 1138 starts with the entry "notes done in Holland Nov. 1927."

7   HaK 1151d, n.p.

8   Kloppers-Moltzer to af Klint, January 30, 1928, HaK 1102, 46.

9   Adelyde Content to af Klint, April 20, 1927, HaK 1103, 101.

10 On *Wendingen*, see Le Coultre, *Wendingen*.

11 The Swedish issues of *Wendingen* appeared in November 1927 and February 1928.

12 HaK 1151d, n.p.

13 His name was Herman Kloppers; see Le Coultre, *Wendingen*, 268, for contributors to the magazine.

14 HaK 1151c, n.p. The quote is in German; the errors are in the original.

15 Hohé, "Reform Dress."

16 The Kloppers lived at Hoofstraat 55.

17 HaK 1151d. Both painting and drawing are reproduced for comparison in Voss, "Traveling Hilma af Klint," 63.

18 Email of December 2, 2017 from Lotte Jaeger, Information Specialist—Research Services, Collection Information Department, Rijksmuseum, Amsterdam. Af Klint copied the head of an apostle; the painting happened to be on loan to the museum.

19 Wittgenstein, *Tractatus Logico-Philosophicus*, 74.

20 HaK 1151c, n.p. About leaving in December, see Adelyde Content to Hilma af Klint, December 21, 1927, HaK 1103, 106.

21 On rheumatism, see HaK 1044, 31. The entry is from August 26, 1928. The two friends lived in Uppsala from November 5, 1926, to September 14, 1931; see appendix 1.

PART 4, CHAPTER 7

1   Peggy Kloppers-Moltzer to Hilma af Klint, January 2, 1928, HaK 1102, 42.
2   Raab, *Edith Maryon*, 228.
3   Peggy Kloppers-Moltzer to Eleanor Merry, May 7, 1928, HaK 1102, 53.
4   Ibid.
5   Peggy Kloppers-Moltzer to Hilma af Klint, May 11, 1928, HaK 1102, 41.
6   Hilma af Klint to Peggy Kloppers-Moltzer, May 27, 1928, HaK 1102, 8.
7   HaK 555, 13.
8   Peggy Kloppers-Moltzer to Hilma af Klint, April 15, 1928, HaK 1102, 48.
9   Hilma af Klint to Peggy Kloppers-Moltzer, April 20, 1928, HaK 1102, 27.
10 A transcript of the postcard from July 17, 1928 was given to the author by Johan af Klint.
11 "Programme of the World Conference on Spiritual Science," *Anthroposophy* 3, no. 3 (1928): 395.
12 Peggy Kloppers to Hilma af Klint, May 11, 1928, HaK 1102, 41. For af Klint's wish for a room of her own, see Hilma af Klint to Peggy Kloppers-Moltzer, May 19, 1928, HaK 1103, 97.
13 Dunlop, *Power Resources of the World*, viii.
14 Peggy Kloppers-Moltzer to Eleanor C. Merry, January 30, 1928, HaK 1102, 46. For small works see Peggy Kloppers-Moltzer to Hilma af Klint, May 21, 1928, HaK 1102, 6.
15 *Das Goetheanum*, 1928, 132. Estimates of the number of participants are also found here.
16 *Anthroposophy: A Quarterly Review of Spiritual Science* 3, no. 3 (1928): 385.
17 "Art Exhibitions: Form and Spirit," 12.
18 Woolf, *Room of One's Own*, 147. The book was based on a series of lectures Woolf gave at Cambridge in fall 1928. On Woolf's interest in Theosophy, see Kane, "Varieties of Mystical Experience," 328–49.
19 HaK 1147, n.p. The title page contains the note "Dornach 1930/Paintings 1930."
20 HaK 1047, 33.
21 Steiner-von Sivers, "In Memoriam P. Kloppers-Moltzer."

PART 5, CHAPTER 1

1 The automatic drawings are HaK 764 and HaK 765.
2 HaK 1039, 4. The quote is also found in the manuscript for the lecture given on April 16, 1937.
3 HaK 559, 62.
4 HaK 555, 36.
5 Quoted in Cavalli-Björkman, *Sigrid Hjertén*, 139.
6 HaK 431, 58.
7 HaK 1047, 1.
8 HaK 1047, 51.
9 HaK 1047, 53.
10 HaK 1047, 76.
11 HaK 1047, 77.
12 V. Østergaard, *Tyge Brahe*. See appendix 2.
13 HaK 1062, 24. The entry is from March 20, 1933.

PART 5, CHAPTER 2

1 HaK 1047, 79.
2 Hilma af Klint to Ilona Harima, September 6, 1934; see Anttonen, "Ilona Harima," 2.
3 Unknown writer to Hilma af Klint, February 16, 1935, archive of the Stiftelsen Hilma af Klints Verk.
4 HaK 1049 (dated July to September 1932), opening page. The note also appears in HaK 1048 (dating from June 1931 to July 1932). Since 1932 is the overlapping date of both notebooks, it seems the most likely entry date. The timespan of twenty years is also mentioned in other notebooks; see HaK 1059, 48 and HaK 1088, 149.

PART 5, CHAPTER 3

1 Tracey Bashkoff was the first to investigate the parallels between the two artists. See Bashkoff, "Temples for Paintings."
2 Pfeiffer and Hollein, *Sturm-Frauen*.
3 Hilla von Rebay to Rudolf Bauer, April 16, 1930, quoted in Faltin, *Die Baroness und das Guggenheim*, 15.
4 Quoted in Guggenheim Staff, "The First Five Books," *Checklist* (blog), The Guggenheim Museums and Foundation (website), January 15, 2015, https://www.guggenheim.org/blogs/checklist/the-first-five-books.

5 Danzker, "Art of Tomorrow," 182–83.

6 Wörwag, *Wassily Kandinsky*, 162.

7 On the photographs of the history of the Solomon R. Guggenheim Museum, see "Solomon R. Guggenheim," The Guggenheim Museums and Foundation (website), last accessed November 16, 2020, https://www.guggenheim.org/history/solomon-r-guggenheim.

8 Hilla von Rebay to Frank Lloyd Wright, September 11, 1946, as quoted in *Arts Magazine* 52 (1978).

9 Frank Lloyd Wright to Gordon Strong, October 20, 1925, Ficheid S011A06, Frank Lloyd Wright Archives, as quoted in Bashkoff, "Temples for Paintings," 29.

10 HaK 1050, 5. The date is September 4, 1932.

PART 5, CHAPTER 4

1 HaK 883.

2 The painting is HaK 884. The quote is in HaK 1039, 8. This notebook is numbered twice. The number given here refers to the system that starts from the end of the notebook.

3 HaK 1151h, n.p.

4 HaK 1092, 1, 58, and 59. Erik and Ulla were married in 1934. Ulla talks of the visits; see Ulla af Klint, interview.

5 Quoted in Fant, *Hilma af Klints hemliga bilder*, 141.

6 The interview with Ulla af Klint was conducted in 2001 by the journalists Anna Cnattingius and Mats Brolin for Swedish television, but it was never broadcast. Excerpts were included in Halina Dyrschka's 2018 documentary *Beyond the Visible: Hilma af Klint*. I am grateful to Halina Dyrschka for access to the typescript of the interview and to Anna Cnattingius for permission to quote from it.

7 In 1927, the artist had begun copying what had been notebooks 1–12 and 13–30 into the notebooks HaK 555 and 556. The destruction of the originals is noted, without a date, in HaK 556, 112. The word *genomgången*, meaning "reviewed," appears regularly throughout the thirties; see HaK1047, opening page.

8 HaK 1092, 83. The note is from May 20, 1943. About the promissory note see HaK 1093, 11.

9 HaK 1211.

10 Beginning in 1935, Hilma af Klint lived at Grönegatan 28; see appendix 1.

11 Af Klint is listed as a co-owner of Furuheim until 1932, after which

Anna Cassel was the sole owner; see part 3, chapter 23, note 2. Anna Cassel's will lists her as the owner of the property; see Stockholms rådhusrätts bouppteckningsavd, E1:184 (2102–2400), year 1937, no. 2262 (SSA). I thank Tomas Östlund for this information.

12 See appendix 2. On Steiner and the list of his works, see HaK 1119 from 1941.

13 Steiner, "Nature of the Bhagavad Gita." Af Klint's copy is in the Lund University Library. The archive of Lund's Universitetsbibliotek contains the inventory list of book donations from 1945 (148 books), and the archive of Lund's Stadsbibliotek contains a list from January 1945 (34 books).

14 For "Universität i Astralvärlden," see HaK 1059, 25; for "överfysiska Universitätet" and "medarbetare" (employee), see HaK 1059, 37; for Steiner explaining, organizing, answering and the building, see HaK 1059, 48; for "verktyg" (tool), see HaK 1059, 30.

15 Steiner, *Knowledge of the Higher Worlds and Its Attainment*, 1, 3.

PART 5, CHAPTER 5

1 Another photo of the study reveals a meaningful detail. The bookshelf was topped by four small models, miniature replicas of the pillar capitals designed by Rudolf Steiner that were included in the first Goetheanum building in Dornach. The photo is in the archive of the Hilma af Klint Foundation. For a picture, see Bashkoff, *Hilma af Klint*, 232. For Steiner's capitals of the "Planetensäulen," see "Planetensäulen," AnthroWiki, last modified January 6, 2020, 14:12, https://anthrowiki .at/Planetens%C3%A4ulen.

2 See Sommer, "From Astronomy to Transcendental Darwinism."

3 Du Prel, *Philosophy of Mysticism*. "Threshold of sensibility" occurs many times; see 4, 128, 133, 148, 277, etc. For "future man," see 144. Af Klint's copy is copiously underlined, but it is impossible to tell when she made these marks.

4 Gabriel von Max painted Hauffe several times. On du Prel and the influence of his works on art, see Treitel, *Science for the Soul*, 108–9.

5 Du Prel, *Justinus Kerner und die Seherin von Prevorst*, 16.

6 Du Prel, *Justinus Kerner und die Seherin von Prevorst*, 17.

7 The notebook (HaK 1114) is not dated. It includes mention of the death of Rosalie Put in 1919 and J. A. Hammerton's *Wonders of the Past*, which was first published in 1923. The notes were most likely made in the 1930s. The pages are not numbered. Af Klint also owned a biog-

raphy of Bridget of Sweden by Emilia Fogelklou, a religious historian who was the first Swedish woman to receive a degree in theology. See appendix 2.

8 HaK 1114, n.p.

9 HaK 1048, 107, dated March 11, 1932.

10 HaK 1063, 51, dated July 15, 1933.

11 On miracles, visionaries, and Marian apparitions, see Blackbourn, *Marpingen*, and Schneider, "Marienerscheinungen im 19. Jahrhundert."

12 HaK 1040. See Burgin, *Hilma af Klint*, 247–85, for transcription and complete English translation. When the notebook was begun is not known. The last entries are dated February 10, 1935.

13 Steiner, *Erfahrungen des Übersinnlichen*, 101; Steiner, appendix to *Knowledge of the Higher Worlds and Its Attainment*. See also Zumdick, "Finding the Inner Form," 245.

PART 5, CHAPTER 6

1 HaK 1065, 26.

2 HaK 1069, 101.

3 HaK 1073, 29.

4 HaK 896, for example.

5 HaK 1039, 11. This notebook is numbered twice. The number given here refers to the system that starts from the end of the notebook.

6 HaK 1039, 30, from December 14, 1933. See above for the numbering system.

7 The last time the name "Hilma" appears in the minutes of the Edelweiss Society is on October 27, 1901. I am grateful to Monica von Rosen for this information, from her private archive, EWF, Berlin.

8 Wilamowitz-Moellendorff, *Carin Göring*, 108–9.

9 Hagemeister, "Karadja, Fürstin Mary-Louise," 76–77.

10 On the Ariosophists see Doering-Manteuffel, *Das Okkulte*, 197–98.

11 R. Steiner, "Colour and the Human Races"; R. Steiner, "Spirits of Form," 89.

12 Zander, *Anthroposophie in Deutschland*, 1: 217. On the often extremely contradictory occult movements, see Fäth and Voda, *Aenigma*, 21.

13 The Imperial Association for Biodynamic Agriculture was forbidden in 1941. See Zander, *Anthroposophie in Deutschland*, 2: 1602.

14 HaK 462, 31, from January 3, 1920. For the notes referring to "Flowers, mosses, lichens," see HaK 1059, 1. The date is March 12, 1933.

15 HaK 559, 30.
16 HaK 462, 59, from February 1, 1920.
17 HaK 1039, 33, from March 4, 1937.
18 HaK 1072, 11.

PART 5, CHAPTER 7

1 HaK 1039, 41.
2 HaK 1039, 45 and 39. Emphasis in the original.
3 HaK 1039, 36.
4 HaK 1039, 4. Steiner had ruled out visions and mediumship as legitimate sources of knowledge and considered them relics of a lower evolutionary state. For atavism, see Steiner, *Erfahrungen des Übersinnlichen*, 101; for degeneration, see appendix to Steiner, *Knowledge of the Higher Worlds and Its Attainment*.
5 HaK 1039, 5. Emphasis in the original.
6 The lecture is logged twice; see HaK 1039, 1–6, "Försök att medelst färgupplevelse intränga på astralområdet" (Attempt to reach the astral plane through color experience), and manuscript in the archive of the Stiftelsen Hilma af Klints Verk, HaK 1101, 1–9, "Inledning vid förevisandet av mina målningar" (Introduction for the presentation of my paintings). Both documents are dated April 16, 1937.
7 HaK 1039, 3.
8 HaK 1039, 4.
9 Ulla af Klint, interview with Ulla Cnattingius and Mats Brolin, and HaK 1039.
10 Erik af Klint, "Hilma af Klint och hennes verk," 9.

PART 5, CHAPTER 8

1 The women's magazine *Idun* published af Klint's photograph, along with those of five other women whose birthdays fell in the same week. "Hilma af Klint. Lund. Painter. 75 years on October 26," the caption noted. "Iduns Porträtt," in *Idun*, 1937, 22.
2 *Dagens Nyheter*, December 18, 1937.
3 On the Trolles and Laserstein, see Atlan, Gross, and Voss, *Kunst, Künstler, Politik*, 34–35. On the family ties of Trolle and af Klint, see Nauckhoff, *Ätten af Klint*, 9.
4 HaK 1092, 166, September 15, 1943. The "manwoman" is a recurrent theme; see HaK 582, 139f; HaK 1043, 79; HaK 1056, 78; HaK 1063, 62; and HaK 1065, 89.

5   Krausse, *Lotte Laserstein*, 191–92.

6   As quoted in Langfeld, *Deutsche Kunst in New York*, 109.

7   On debates around abstract art in New York, see Guilbaut, *How New York Stole the Idea of Modern Art*.

8   Barr, *Cubism and Abstract Art*, 19.

9   Female abstract artists were, however, included in sections dedicated to the applied arts, for example Alexandra Alexandrovna Ekster and Natalia Goncharova as set designers in the theater section. See Barr, *Cubism and Abstract Art*, 231.

10 Wassily Kandinsky to Israel Ber Neumann, December 18, 1935, Getty Research Institute, Wassily Kandinsky Papers, digital collections, series IV A, Letters to J. B. Neumann, 1935–1940.

11 On Kandinsky and *Thought Forms*, see Treitel, *Science for the Soul*, 125–26; Bätschmann, "Form der Farbe." On the history of abstraction before 1911, see Rosenberg and Hollein, *Turner, Hugo, Moreau*.

12 Marc, *Schriften*, 26.

13 Quoted in Faltin, *Die Baroness und das Guggenheim*, 155.

PART 5, CHAPTER 9

1   See *Dagens Nyheter*, July 20, August 1, and August 4, 1937.

2   Raphael Rosenberg mounted an exhibition that commendably attempted to get to the bottom of the myth of the "first abstract painting"; see Rosenberg and Hollein, *Turner, Hugo, Moreau*.

3   Anna Cassel to Hilma af Klint, July 9, 1936, HaK 1103, 132.

4   HaK 1092, 19–20.

5   HaK 1039, 43.

6   Ida Haverman died on February 28, 1938. See Ida Havermans bouppteckning, södra roslags domsaga (AB), F2A: 52 (1938), Riksarkivet, Stockholm. I am grateful to Johan af Klint for this information.

7   HaK 1151h, n.p.

8   HaK 1092, 38, April 23, 1943.

9   Hilma af Klint to Tyra Kleen, August 1, 1940, Tyra Kleens Samling, Valinge Gård.

10 I am grateful to Kerstin Gullstrand Hermelin, director of the archive Tyra Kleens Samling in Valinge Gård, for transcribing and making available the diary entries of August 6, 9, 10, 13, and 25, 1940.

11 Franzén, *Tyra Kleen 1874–1951*, 134–35.

12 On Kleen's contribution, see Teosofiska Samfundet, *Katalog konstutställning*, 11–12.

13 Hilma af Klint to Tyra Kleen, August 1, 1940, Tyra Kleens Samling, Valinge Gård.

14 Tyra Kleen to Hilma af Klint, September 9, 1940, Tyra Kleens Samling, Valinge Gård.

15 HaK 1151h, 15 and 28. In Swedish, Viktor Rydberg's cycle is "Den nya Grottesången." Hilma af Klint's notebooks also contain mention of an article from 1927 in the magazine *Ord och Bild*; see HaK 1151c.

16 HaK 1151h, 23 (map) and 3 (telephone number).

17 HaK 1151h, 40–41. A similar draft, dated "autumn 1940," can be found in HaK 1092, 165. Hilma af Klint notes that she had written the lines "after Miss Kleen was in the studio."

18 HaK 1025, 1026, and 1027. A description can be found in HaK 1084, 43.

19 HaK 1035–38. For temple plans and sketches, see HaK 1083, 25, 45, 105, 108, 113, and HaK 1085, 45. For "Annas bilder" and "framtids-bilder," see HaK 1083, 113.

20 HaK 1030, and for description see HaK 1084, 68–72 and 95.

21 HaK 1092, 99.

22 Kleen's request has not been preserved, only af Klint's response. See the following note.

23 Hilma af Klint to Tyra Kleen, September 3, 1943, Tyra Kleens Samling, Valinge Gård.

24 Tyra Kleen to Hilma af Klint, September 8, 1943, Tyra Kleens Samling, Valinge Gård.

25 Hilma af Klint to Tyra Kleen, September 23, 1943, Tyra Kleens Samling, Valinge Gård.

26 HaK 1092, 172.

27 Hilma af Klint to Tyra Kleen, September 3, 1943, Tyra Kleens Samling, Valinge Gård.

28 HaK 1092, 108.

29 HaK 1089, 11. The date is March 30, 1942.

30 Hilma af Klint to Tyra Kleen, September 9, 1943, Tyra Kleens Samling, Valinge Gård.

31 HaK 1092, 185.

32 For a short biography and reference to the fifty-years clause, see https://skbl.se/en/article/TyraKleen (accessed June 6, 2021).

PART 5, CHAPTER 10

1 HaK 1095, 4. Amelie had died while Hilma af Klint was delivering a lecture at the Anthroposophical Society in Lund.

2 Barton, "The Conscience of the Rich."

3 HaK 1094, 1.

4 Hilma af Klint's will of January 27, 1941. Archive of the Stiftelsen Hilma af Klints Verk.

5 Amendment to Hilma af Klint's will from June 28, 1942. Today, the books are still part of the collection of the Lund University Library. This information comes from an email from Karin Bergendorff, director of the Lund public library. For more on the books, see appendix 2. I am grateful to Kurt Almqvist for bringing the transfer to the Anthroposophical Society to my attention.

6 Manuscript of 1937 lecture; see part 5, chapter 7, note 6.

7 HaK 1096, 1.

8 Erik af Klint, "Hilma af Klint och hennes verk," 10, and Fant, *Hilma af Klints hemliga Bilder*, 30.

9 Olof Sundström to Hilma af Klint, undated letter, archive of the Stiftelsen Hilma af Klints Verk.

10 Hilma af Klint to Olof Sundström, July 29, 1943, archive of the Stiftelsen Hilma af Klints Verk; HaK 1092, 180. For English-language translation of the glossary, see Burgin, *Hilma af Klint*, 246–85.

11 HaK 1092, 54.

12 HaK 1095, 4.

13 HaK 1097, 116.

14 HaK 1098, 126–27.

15 HaK 1088, 149.

16 Erik af Klint, "Hilma af Klint och hennes verk," 10.

17 *Svenska Dagbladet*, October 27, 1944.

PART 5, CHAPTER 11

1 Fant, *Hilma af Klints hemliga bilder*, 30.

2 Erik af Klint, "Hilma af Klint och hennes verk," 12.

3 In 1965, as a fellow of the Warburg Institute in London, Sixten Ringbom published his first essay on spiritual influences in the work of Wassily Kandinsky; see Ringbom, "Art in the 'Epoch of the Great Spiritual.'" His famous study "The Sounding Cosmos" followed four years later.

4 HaK 1090, 44.

5 See Crosland, *Light in the Valley*, 148.

6 The difficulties that supernatural phenomena present to the humanities is described in Schneider, "Marienerscheinungen im 19. Jahrhun-

dert," through the example of the proliferation of visions of the Virgin Mary in the nineteenth century.

7   Cf. Wolf, *Die Nonnen von Sant'Ambrogio*. This case differs in many ways, since the nuns deliberately forged religious documents and perpetrated much abuse.

8   HaK 579, 84–85.

APPENDIX 1

1   Information on the Stockholm addresses comes from the Stockholm Stadsarkiv, from the registry (Mantalslängd) of the parishes in question.

2   See travel sketches labeled "Bruges" (HaK 1613 and 1633), "The Rhine" (HaK 1634), and "Holland" (HaK 1617), as well as Nauckhoff, *Ätten af Klint*, 159.

3   See travel sketches labeled "Wartburg" (HaK 1626) and the notebook "Italian Journey" (HaK 1151a).

4   Information on the address in Munsö comes from the registry (Mantalslängd) of the parish of Munsö.

5   A list with dates of "Trips to Dornach" is found in the notebook HaK 1118, 121. The notes are in ink, with penciled notes for the years 1922 and 1927 added, given here in quotes.

6   Peggy Kloppers-Moltzer, a Dutch Anthroposophist and friend of Hilma af Klint, mentions af Klint's stay in Amsterdam in a letter of January 30, 1928. The precise timing is not given, only "she was in Holland some months ago." See Peggy Kloppers-Moltzer to Eleanor Charlotte Merry, archive of the Stiftelsen Hilma af Klints Verk, uncatalogued. Notes on a visit to Amsterdam are found in the notebook HaK 1151d.

7   On Hilma af Klint's speech and exhibition in London, see "Programme of the World Conference on Spiritual Science," *Anthroposophy* 3, no. 3 (1928): 395. On July 17, 1928, she also sent a postcard to Anna Cassel at Villa Furuheim, Munsö; a transcript was supplied by Johan af Klint.

8   Information on the address in Uppsala comes from the register of the Uppsala Cathedral parish.

9   Information on the addresses in Helsingborg comes from the regional archive (Landsarkivet) in Lund.

10 Information on the addresses in Lund comes from the regional archive (Landsarkivet).

11 Erik af Klint, "Hilma af Klint och hennes verk."

Bibliography

ARCHIVES

Archive of the Albert-Steffen-Stiftung, Dornach
Archive of the Föreningen Svenska Konstnärinnor, Riksarkivet, Stockholm
Archive of the Kungliga Akademien för de fria konsterna, Stockholm
Archive of the Stadsbiblioteket, Lund
Archive of the Stiftelsen Hilma af Klints Verk, Sweden
Archive of the Teosofiska samfundet/bokhandeln, Stockholm
Archive of the Universitetsbiblioteket, Lund
Collection Information Department of the Rijksmuseum, Amsterdam
Getty Institute, Wassily Kandinsky Papers
Haags Gemeentearchief, The Hague
Private archive of Marie Cassel, Stockholm
Private archive of Monica von Rosen/EWF (Edelweissförbundet), Berlin
Riksarkivet, Stockholm
Rudolf Steiner Archive at the Goetheanum, Dornach
Skissernas Museum, bild- och klippsammling, Frank Heyman estate,
    Lund Stadsarkivet, Stockholm
Tyra Kleens Samling, Valinge Gård
Veterinärmuseet i Skara, John Vennerholm estate, Skara

ONLINE DATABASES AND ARCHIVES

Arkiv digital, https://www.arkivdigital.net/
Digitalt arkiv över äldre svenska kvinnotidskrifter, Göteborg universitet,
    http://www2.ub.gu.se/kvinn/digtid/
Rötter-Sveriges Släktforskarförbund, https://www.rotter.se
Svenska dagstidningar, Sveriges Nationalbibliotek—Kungliga biblioteket,
    https://tidningar.kb.se/

UNPUBLISHED WORKS

Hermelin, Kerstin Gullstrand. Excerpts from Tyra Kleen's journals, August
    6–25, 1940, and September 1–17, 1943. Transcript. Valinge Gård, 2019.

Klint, Erik af. "Hilma af Klint och hennes verk." Manuscript. Stockholm, December 1, 1967. Stiftelsen Hilma af Klints Verk, Stockholm.

Klint, Ulla af. Interview with Ulla Cnattingius and Mats Brolin. Film recording and transcript. Stockholm, 1999.

Martin, Hedvig. "Hilma af Klint och De fem: förberedelsetiden, 1896–1907." Master's thesis, Södertörn College, 2018.

Rhodin, Hans. "Edelweissförbundets historia." Master's thesis, Uppsala University, 1985.

Sundström, Olof. "Förteckning över Frk. Hilma af Klints efterlämnade verk." Unpublished typescript, 1945. Held in the Stiftung Hilma af Klints Verk, Stockholm.

PUBLISHED WORKS

A. H. "Svenska kvinnan inom de bildande konsterna." *Dagny: Tidskrift för sociala och litterära intressen, utgifven af Fredrika-Bremer-förbundet* 8 (1895): 305–13.

Almqvist, Kurt, and Louise Belfrage, eds. *Hilma af Klint: The Art of Seeing the Invisible*. Stockholm: Axel and Margaret Ax:son Johnson Foundation, 2015.

———, eds. *Hilma af Klint: Seeing Is Believing*. Stockholm: Axel and Margaret Ax:son Johnson Foundation, 2017.

———, eds. *Hilma af Klint: Visionary and the Spirit of Her Time*. Stockholm: Bokförlaget Stolpe, 2019.

Almqvist, Kurt, and Daniel Birnbaum, eds. *Hilma af Klint: Catalogue raisonné*. Vol. 2, *The Paintings for the Temple, 1906–1915*. Stockholm: Bokförlaget Stolpe, 2020.

Almqvist, Kurt, and Matthias Hessérus, eds. *Images of Sweden*. Vol. 3. Stockholm: Axel and Margaret Ax:son Johnson Foundation, 2016.

Althaus, Karin, Matthias Mühling, and Sebastian Schneider, eds. *Weltempfänger: Georgiana Houghton, Hilma af Klint, Emma Kunz*. Munich: Hirmer, 2018. Catalogue for an exhibition at the Lenbachhaus.

Anttonen, Erkki. "Ilona Harima: On the Road to Enlightenment." *FNG Research*, no.3 (2017): 2–6, https://fngresearch.files.wordpress.com/2017/05/fngr_20173_anttonen_erkki_article1.pdf.

"Art Exhibitions: Form and Spirit." *The Times*, July 26, 1928, 12.

Arvidson, Jens. "Ett monumentalt misslyckande: Frank Heyman och tämplet." *Valör: Konstvetenskapliga studier* 3–4 (2010): 3–17.

Atlan, Eva, Raphael Gross, and Julia Voss. *Kunst, Künstler, Politik*. Göttingen: Wallstein, 2013. Catalogue for an exhibition at the Jüdisches Museum, Frankfurt.

Avenarius, Ferdinand. "Eine neue Sprache? Zu den Zeichnungen von Katharine Schäffner." *Der Kunstwart* 21, no. 2 (1908): 183–93.

B. V. *Meddelanden från den osynliga verlden erhållna genom ett skrifvande medium.* Uppsala: R. Almqvist & J. Wiksell, 1886.

Baltiska Utställningen i Malmö 1914. Malmö: Malmö Boktryckeri, 1914.

Barnett, Vivian Endicott. *Kandinsky and Sweden.* Malmö: Malmö Konsthall, 1989. Exhibition catalogue.

Barr, Alfred. *Cubism and Abstract Art.* New York: Museum of Modern Art, 1936. First paperbound ed., 1974.

Bartholl, Angelika, and Brigitte Martin, eds. *Between the Worlds: Hilma af Klint, Emma Kunz, Jan Albers, Angelika Bartholl, Hansjoerg Dobliar, Bernd Ribbeck, Claudia Wieser.* Munich: Offizin Scheufele, 2018. Catalogue for an exhibition at the Kunstraum Bogenhausen.

Barton, Arnold. "The Conscience of the Rich: Djursholm, Birkstaden, and Swedish Liberalism." *Scandinavian Studies* 80, no. 2 (2008): 167–84.

Bashkoff, Tracey, ed. *Hilma af Klint: Paintings for the Future.* New York: Solomon R. Guggenheim Foundation, 2018.

———. "Temples for Paintings." In Bashkoff, *Hilma af Klint,* 17–32.

Bätschmann, Oskar. "Form der Farbe: Wassily Kandinskys Kunstwende." In *Kandinsky, Marc und der Blaue Reiter,* ed. Ulf Küster, 8–17. Basel: Prestel, 2016. Catalogue for an exhibition at the Fondation Beyeler.

Bauduin, Tessel M. "Science and Occultism in Hilma af Klint's Time and Her Work." In Bashkoff, *Hilma af Klint,* 186–191.

———. "Seeing and Depicting the Invisible: On Hilma af Klint's Modern Art and Spiritual Painting." 2017. https://pure.uva.nl/ws/files /15573067/Tessel_M._Bauduin_Seeing_and_Depicting_the_Invisible _untranslated_original_draft_2017.pdf.

Bax, Marty. *Anna Cassel and Hilma af Klint: Childhood 1907, Vision of a New Swedish Christian Identity.* e-book, 2021.

———. "Hilma af Klint Revisited (Part 1. The Theosophical Society in Sweden; Part 2: The Edelweissförbundet and The Five; Part 3: Anna Cassel, Hilma's 'Other Half')." *Bax Art Concepts and Services* (blog), May 10, 2017, http://baxpress.blogspot.com/2017/05/hilma-af-klint -revisited-part-i.html.

———. "Piet Mondrian and the Legacy of Western Esotericism." In Almqvist and Belfrage, *Hilma af Klint: The Art of Seeing the Invisible,* 129–40.

Bergh, Richard. "Målaren Ernst Josephson." *Ord och Bild* 2 (1893): 110–27.

Bergstrand, Ulla. *En bilderboks-historia: Svenska bilderböcker, 1900–1930.* Stockholm: Bonniers juniorförlag, 1993.

Besant, Annie, and Charles W. Leadbeater. *Occult Chemistry: A Series of*

Clairvoyant Observations on Chemical Elements. London: Theosophical Publishing Society, 1908.

———. *Thought-Forms. With Fifty-Eight Illustrations*. London: Theosophical Publishing Society, 1905.

Beuys, Barbara. *Helene Schjerfbeck: Die Malerin aus Finnland*. Frankfurt am Main: Suhrkamp Insel, 2016.

Beyhan, Deniz. "Science and Occultism in Edvard Munch's Painting *Puberty* and *The Tree of Knowledge of Good and Evil Sketchbook*." MA thesis, University of Texas, Austin, 2016. https://repositories.lib.utexas.edu/handle/2152/39078.

Birnbaum, Daniel. Afterword to Almqvist and Belfrage, *Hilma af Klint: Seeing Is Believing*, 125–27.

———. "Another Canon, or Why Have There Been No Great Women Artists?" In Bashkoff, *Hilma af Klint*, 210–15.

Birnbaum, Daniel, and Emma Enderby. "Painting the Unseen." In *Hilma af Klint: Painting the Unseen*, ed. Julia Peyton-Jones und Hans Ulrich Obrist, 9–12. London: Koenig Books, 2016. Catalogue for an exhibition at the Serpentine Gallery.

Birnbaum, Daniel, and Ann-Sofi Noring, eds. *The Legacy of Hilma af Klint: Nine Contemporary Responses*. London: Walther König, 2013.

Björk, Tomas. "Det Besjälade Landskapet." In *Symbolismus och dekadens*, ed. Karin Sidén, 37–56. Stockholm: Nordens Grafiska, 2015. Catalogue for an exhibition at Prins Eugens Waldemarsudde.

Blackbourn, David. *Marpingen: Apparitions of the Virgin Mary in 19th Century Germany*. New York: Knopf, 1994.

Blavatsky, Helena P. *Index to the Secret Doctrine by H. P. Blavatsky*. Los Angeles: Theosophy Company, 1939.

———. *Isis Unveiled*. Vol. 1. New York: J. W. Bouton, 1877.

———. *The Secret Doctrine: The Synthesis of Science, Religion, and Philosophy*. London: Theosophical Publishing Company, 1888; Theosophy Trust, 2011. Apple Books EPUB.

Bogdan, Henrik, and Olav Hammer, eds. *Western Esotericism in Scandinavia*. Leiden: Brill, 2016.

Brian, Denis. *The Curies: A Biography of the Most Controversial Family in Science*. Hoboken, NJ: Wiley, 2015.

Browne, Janet. *The Power of Place*. Vol. 2 of *Charles Darwin*. Princeton: Princeton University Press, 2002.

Burgin, Christine, ed. *Hilma af Klint: Notes and Methods*. Introduction and commentary by Iris Müller-Westermann. Chicago: University of Chicago Press, 2018.

Carleson, Robert, and Caroline Levander. "Spiritualism in Sweden." In Bogdan and Hammer, *Western Esotericism in Scandinavia*, 521–33.

Carlsson, Lena. *Frihetslif! Selma Lagerlöf och Sophie Elkan: Två ensamma fruntimmer på resa med kamera*. Karlstad: Votum & Gullers, 2017.

Carolus. "Professor Julius Kronberg." *Theosophical Path* 7 (July–December 1914): 70–71.

Cavalli-Björkman, Görel. *Eva Bonnier: ett konstnärsliv*. Stockholm: Bonniers, 2013.

———. *Sigrid Hjertén. Kvinna I avantgardet*. Stockholm: Bonniers, 2017.

Chaudhuri, Nupur. *Western Women and Imperialism: Complicity and Resistance*. Bloomington: Indiana University Press, 1992.

Claerbergen, Ernst Vengelin van, and Barnaby Wright, eds. *Georgiana Houghton: Spirit Drawings*. London: Paul Holberton, 2016. Catalogue for an exhibition at the Courtauld Gallery.

Crosland, Camilla Newton. *Light in the Valley: My Experiences in Spiritualism*. London: G. Routledge, 1857.

Crow, John. "A Bibliographical Error." *Theosophical History* 16, nos. 3–4 (2012): 126–28.

Dahlmann, Eva. "Kvinnliga pionjärer osynliga i fotohistorien." *Tidskrift för genusvetenskap*, nos. 3–4 (1993): 44–54.

Dam, H. J. W. "A Visit to Professor Röntgen at His Laboratory in Würzburg." *McClure's Magazine*, no. 5 (1896).

Danzker, Jo-Anne Birnie. "The Art of Tomorrow." In *Art of Tomorrow: Hilla von Rebay and Solomon R. Guggenheim*, ed. Jo-Anne Birnie Danzker. New York: Solomon R. Guggenheim Foundation, 2005. Exhibition catalogue.

Dickerman, Leah, ed. *Inventing Abstraction, 1910–1925*. New York: Museum of Modern Art, 2012. Exhibition catalogue.

Dixon, Joy. *The Divine Feminine: Theosophy and Feminism in England*. Baltimore: Johns Hopkins University Press, 2001.

Doering-Manteuffel, Sabine. *Das Okkulte: Eine Erfolgsgeschichte im Schatten der Aufklärung: Von Gutenberg bis zum World Wide Web*. Munich: Siedler, 2008.

Drisceoil, Donal Ó, and Diarmuid Ó Drisceoil. *Beamish & Crawford: The History of an Irish Brewery*. Cork: Collins Press, 2015.

Dunlop, Daniel N. "Power Resources of the World Available and Utilised." In *The Transactions of the First World Power Conference in London, June 30th to July 12th 1924*, vol. 1. London: Percy Lund Humphries, 1925.

du Prel, Carl. *Justinus Kerner und die Seherin von Prevorst. Mit einer photographischen Aufnahme von Justinus Kerner und Zeichnungen aus dem Skizzenbuche von Gabriel Max.* 2nd ed. Leipzig: M. Altmann, 1913.

———. *The Philosophy of Mysticism.* Vol. 2. Trans. C. C. Massey. London: George Redway, 1889. https://www.google.com/books/edition/The _Philosophy_of_Mysticism/4Z2SAfdgoUcC?hl=en&gbpv=1.

Eilenberger, Wolfram. *Zeit der Zauberer: Das große Jahrzehnt der Philosophie, 1919–1929.* Stuttgart: Klett-Cotta, 2018.

Facos, Michelle. "A Controversy in Late Nineteenth Century Painting: Ernst Josephson's *The Water Sprite.*" *Zeitschrift für Kunstgeschichte* 56, no. 1 (1993): 61–78.

———. *Nationalism and the Nordic Imagination: Swedish Art of the 1890s.* Berkeley: University of California Press, 1998.

———. *Symbolist Art in Context.* Berkeley: University of California Press, 2009.

Faltin, Sigrid. *Die Baroness und das Guggenheim: Hilla von Rebay—eine deutsche Künstlerin in New York.* Regensburg: Libelle-Verlag, 2005.

Fant, Åke. *Hilma af Klint: Okkultismus und Abstraktion.* Vienna: Eigenverlag der Albertina, 1992. Exhibition catalogue.

———. *Hilma af Klints hemliga bilder.* Helsinki: Konstcentrum, 1988. Catalogue (No. 3/1988) for an exhibition at Nordiskt Konstcentrum.

Fäth, Reinhold J., and David Voda, eds. *Aenigma: Hundert Jahre anthroposophische Kunst.* Revenice: Arbor Vitae, 2015. Catalogue for an exhibition at the Kunstmuseum Moritzburg, Halle (Saale).

Faxneld, Per. *Det ockulta sekelskiftet: Esoteriska strömningar i Hilma af Klints tid.* Stockholm: Volante, 2020.

Fer, Briony. "Hilma af Klint and Abstraction." In Almqvist and Belfrage, *Hilma af Klint: The Art of Seeing the Invisible,* 15–24.

———. "Hilma af Klint: Diagrammer." In Bashkoff, *Hilma af Klint,* 164–70.

———. "Hilma af Klint: The Outsider Inside Herself." In Almqvist and Belfrage, *Hilma af Klint: Seeing Is Believing,* 95–104.

Forberg, Corinna. *Die Rezeption indischer Miniaturen in der europäischen Kunst des 17. und 18. Jahrhunderts.* Petersberg: Michael Imhof Verlag, 2015.

Franzén, Niclas. "Tyra Kleen som symbolist." In Franzen et al., *Tyra Kleen 1874–1951,* 56–89.

Franzén, Niclas, et al., eds. *Tyra Kleen 1874–1951.* Vingåcker: Linderoths Tryckeri, 2016.

Gadelius, Bror. "Om sinnesjukdom, diktning och skapande konst." *Ord och Bild* 24, no. 7 (1915): 337–58.

Gebhardt, Miriam. *Rudolf Steiner: Ein moderner Prophet.* Munich: Deutsche Verlags-Anstalt, 2011.

Geijerstam, Karl af. *Modern vidskepelse: Et inlägg mot teosofi och spiritism jämte ett svar till Herr Carl von Bergen*. Stockholm: Albert Bonniers Verlag, 1892.

Grand, Simon, und Marco Pasi. "'Works of Art without Parallel in the World.'" In Claerbergen and Wright, *Georgiana Houghton*, 8–23.

Greene, Vivien. "Hilma af Klint and the Swedish Folk Art Revival." In Bashkoff, *Hilma af Klint*, 98–103.

———. "The Salon de la Rose + Croix: The Religion of Art." In *Mystical Symbolism: The Salon de la Rose + Croix in Paris, 1892–1897*, ed. Vivien Greene, 14–35. New York: Solomon R. Guggenheim Foundation, 2017. Exhibition catalogue.

Gröning, Yvonne. "Älskad Florrie Hamilton: herrgårdsfröken på Högfors." *Årsbok/Västmanlands läns museum, Västmanlands hembygdsförbund* 84 (2014).

Guilbaut, Serge. *How New York Stole the Idea of Modern Art*. Chicago: University of Chicago Press, 1983.

Gynning, Margareta. *Det ambivalenta perspektivet: Eva Bonnier och Hanna Hirsch-Pauli 1880-talets konstliv*. Stockholm: Bonnier, 1999.

Hagedorn, Annette. "Der Einfluss der Ausstellung *Meisterwerke muhammedanischer Kunst* auf die zeitgenössische Kunst." In Lermer and Shalem, *After One Hundred Years*, 285–316.

Hagemeister, Michael. "Karadja, Fürstin Mary-Louise." In *Handbuch des Antisemitismus: Judenfeindschaft in Geschichte und Gegenwart*, vol. 8: *Nachträge und Register*, ed. Wolfgang Benz. Berlin: de Gruyter Saur, 2015.

Hartmann, Franz. *Magic, White and Black: or, The Science of Finite and Infinite Life, Containing Practical Hints for Students of Occultism*. 3rd ed. London: George Redway, 1888. https://www.google.com/books/edition/Magic_white_and_black_or_The_science_of/whgPAAAAQAAJ?hl=en&gbpv=0.

Hegelund, Margareta Alin. *Min Nell: En ung svenska i expressionismens Berlin*. Halmstad: Arx förlag, 2018.

Heinz, Kathrin. "Der Drachenkämpfer Wassily Kandinsky: Über Helden und ihre Verbindungen." In "Helden: Mythische Kämpferfiguren im 20. Jahrhundert und in der Gegenwart," ed. Kathrin Heinz and Irene Nierhaus. Special issue, *Frauen Kunst Wissenschaft* 41 (June 2006): 35–50.

Hellman, Ben. *Hemma hos Tolstoj: nordiska möten i liv och dikt*. Stockholm: Appell förlag, 2017.

Henderson, Lynda Dalrymple. *The Fourth Dimension and Non-Euclidean Geometry in Art*. Rev. ed. Cambridge, MA: MIT Press, 2013.

Henrikson, Alf. *Svensk historia*. 5th ed. Stockholm: Bonnier, 1994.

Henslow, George. *The Proofs of the Truth of Spiritualism*. 2nd ed. New York: E. P. Dutton, 1919.

Hentilä, Marjaliisa, and Irma Sulkunen, eds. *Von heute an für alle! Hundert Jahre Frauenwahlrecht*. Berlin: Berliner Wissenschafts-Verlag, 2006.

Herber, Anne-Kathrin. "Frauen an deutschen Kunstakademien im 20. Jahrhundert: Ausbildungsmöglichkeiten für Künstlerinnen ab 1919 unter besonderer Berücksichtigung der süddeutschen Kunstakademien." Dissertation, University of Heidelberg, 2009.

Higgie, Jennifer. "Longing for Light: The Art of Hilma af Klint." In *Hilma af Klint: Painting the Unseen*, ed. Julia Peyton-Jones und Hans Ulrich Obrist, 13–20. London: Koenig Books, 2016. Catalogue for an exhibition at the Serpentine Gallery.

Hille, Karoline. *Gabriele Münter: Die Künstlerin mit der Zauberhand*. Cologne: DuMont, 2012.

Hjern, Thorsten. *Stockholms populäraste restaurant firar 70-årsjubileum: Blanch's café—en pigg och livkraftig sjuttioåring*. Stockholms nöjeslivs historia. Stockholm, 1938.

Hodin, Joseph Paul. *Isaac Grünewald*. Stockholm: Ljus, 1949.

Hohé, Madelief. "Reform Dress in the Collection of the Gemeentemuseum Den Haag." 2011. https://www.kci.or.jp/research/dresstudy/pdf/G_D63_HOHE_Reform%20Dress%20in%20the%20Collction%20of%20the%20G.D.H._ENG.pdf.

Hollein, Max, and Pamela Kort. *Künstler und Propheten: Eine geheime Geschichte der Moderne, 1872–1972*. Cologne: Snoeck, 2015. Catalogue for an exhibition at the Kunsthalle Frankfurt.

Holm, Michael Juul, and Tine Colstrup, eds. *Hilma af Klint: Abstrakt Pioner*. Humlebæk: Louisiana Press, 2014. Catalogue for an exhibition at the Louisiana Museum of Modern Art.

Holmberg, Claes-Georg. "The Reception of the Early European Avant-Gardes in Sweden." In van den Berg, Hautamäki, and Hjärtason, *Cultural History of the Avant-Garde in the Nordic Countries*, 422–434.

Hopwood, Nick. *Embryos in Wax: Models from the Ziegler Studio*. Cambridge, UK: Whipple Museum of the History of Science, University of Cambridge, 2001.

Horowitz, David Max. "'The World Keeps You in Fetters; Cast Them Aside': Hilma af Klint, Spiritualism, and Agency." In Bashkoff, *Hilma af Klint*, 128–63.

Houghton, Georgiana. *Catalogue of the Spirit Drawings in Water Colours, Exhibited at the New British Gallery, Old Bond Street*. London: W.

Corby, 1871. http://digital.slv.vic.gov.au/view/action/singleViewer.do
?dvs=1599733169165~343&locale=en_US&metadata_object_ratio=10
&show_metadata=true&VIEWER_UL=/view/action/singleViewer.do?
&preferred_usage_type=VIEW_MAIN&DELIVERY_RULE_ID=10&
frameId=1&usePid1=true&usePid2=true.

———. *Evenings at Home in Spiritual Séance. Welded Together by a Species of Autobiography*. 2nd series. London: E. W. Allen, 1882. https://
archive.org/details/eveningsathomei00houggoog/page/n10/mode/2up.

Howitt, Anna Mary. *An Art-Student in Munich*. London: Longman, Brown, Greene and Longmans, 1853.

Hutchinson, John, ed. *Hilma af Klint*. Dublin: Douglas Hyde Gallery, 2005. Exhibition catalogue.

Internationella Teosofiska Fredskongressen. *Katalog över Konstutställningen på Visingsö på 22–29. Juni 1913*. Uppsala: Almqvist & Wiksells boktryckeri-A. B., 1913.

Introvigne, Massimo. "Theosophy and the Visual Arts: The Nordic Connection." Presented at the International Conference on Theosophical History, London, September 20, 2014. http://www.cesnur.org/2014
/Nordic%20Theosophy%20and%20the%20Arts%20London.pdf.

Joseph, Branden W. "Knowledge, Painting, Abstraction and Desire." In Almqvist and Belfrage, *Hilma af Klint: Seeing Is Believing*, 117–24.

Kandinsky, Wassily. *Concerning the Spiritual in Art*. Trans. Michael T. H. Sadler. New York: Dover Publications, 1977. https://archive.org/details
/concerningspiritooookand/mode/2up.

———. *Über das Geistige in der Kunst insbesondere in der Malerei*. 3rd ed . Munich: R. Piper & Co., 1912. https://monoskop.org/images/c/cc
/Kandinsky_Ueber_das_Geistige_in_der_Kunst_Dritte_Auflage_1912
.pdf.

———. "Über die Formfrage." In Kandinsky and Marc, *Almanach "Der Blaue Reiter."*

Kandinsky, Wassily, and Franz Marc, eds. *Almanach "Der Blaue Reiter."*
2nd ed. Munich: Piper, 1914.

Kane, Julie. "Varieties of Mystical Experience in Writings of Virginia Woolf." *Twentieth Century Literature* 41, no. 4 (1995): 328–349.

Kemlein, H. Georg, and Friedrich Dieckmann, eds. *Strindberg im Zeugnis der Zeitgenossen*. Trans. H. Georg Kemlein. Leipzig: Kiepenheuer, 1982.

Klint, Gustaf af. *Beschreibung von den Küsten an der Ostsee und dem finnischen Meerbusen, zum Schwedischen Seeatlas gehörend*. Stockholm: Marquardschen Buchdruckerei, 1816.

Kollnitz, Andrea. "Promoting the Young: Interactions between the

Avant-Garde and the Swedish Art Market, 1910–1925." In van den Berg, Hautamäki, and Hjärtason, *Cultural History of the Avant-Garde in the Nordic Countries*, 275–90.

Kortüm, Manfred. "Der schwedische Tierarzt John Vennerholm und sein Land—eine Studie über einen verdienstvollen Mann im Spiegel seiner Zeit." Dissertation, Tierärztliche Hochschule Hannover, 1973.

Kracht, Klaus Große. "Vom Tischrücken zur ethischen Religion? Zur Unterscheidung der Geister im Spiritismus im 19. Jahrhundert." In Wolf, *"Wahre" und "falsche" Heiligkeit*, 149–166.

Krafft-Ebing, R. v. *Über gesunde und kranke Nerven*. Tübingen: Verlag der H. Laupp'schen Buchhandlung, 1885.

Kramer, Hilton. "On 'The Spiritual in Art' in Los Angeles." *New Criterion* 5, no. 8 (1987): 3.

Krausse, Anna-Carola. *Lotte Laserstein: Leben und Werk*. Berlin: Reimer, 2006.

Krenzlin, Ulrike. "'auf dem ernsten Gebiet der Kunst ernst arbeiten': Zur Frauenausbildung im künstlerischen Beruf." In *Profession ohne Tradition: 125 Jahre Verein der Berliner Künstlerinnen*. Berlin: Kupfergraben, 1992. Catalogue for an exhibition at the Berlinische Galerie.

Krüger, Klaus. *Das Bild als Schleier des Unsichtbaren: Ästhetische Illusion in der Kunst der frühen Neuzeit in Italien*. Munich: Wilhelm Fink, 2001.

Kugler, Walter. Introduction to Bartholl and Martin, *Between the Worlds*, 8–13.

Kugler, Walter, Roland Halfen, and Dino Wendtland. *Rudolf Steiner: Das malerische Werk mit Erläuterungen und einem dokumentarischen Anhang*. Dornach: Rudolf Steiner Verlag, 2018.

Langfeld, Gregor. *Deutsche Kunst in New York. Vermittler, Kunstsammler, Ausstellungsmacher 1904–1957*. Berlin: Dietrich Reimer, 2011.

Larsen, Lars Bang. "Infinite Redress: Politics in Spiritualism and Medium Art." In *Not Without My Ghosts: The Artist as Medium*, ed. Lars Bang Larsen, Simon Grant, and Susan Aberth, 77–86. Exhibition catalogue. London: Howard Gallery Publishing, 2020.

Larsen, Lars Bang, and Marco Pasi. "Spectres of Art." In *Georgiana Houghton: Spirit Drawings*, ed. Ernst Vegelin van Claerbergen and Barnaby Wright, 24–33. London: Paul Holberton, 2016.

Larsson, Anna Laestadius. *Hilma—en roman om gåtan*. Stockholm: Pirat, 2017.

Larsson, Carl. "En Eternell." *Konst* 1, no. 1 (November 15, 1911): 2–5.

———. *Ich: ein Buch über das Gute und das Böse*. Trans. Hans-Günter Thimm. Königstein: Langewiesche, 1970.

Leadbeater, Charles. *Man Visible and Invisible*. Adyar, India: Theosophical Publishing House, 1902. https://www.anandgholap.net/Man_Visible_And_Invisible-CWL.htm.

Le Coultre, Martijn F. *Wendingen: a journal for the arts, 1918–1932*. New York: Princeton Architectural Press, 2001.

Lehander, Karin Ström. "Tyra Kleen och hennes bakgrund." In *Tyra Kleen 1874–1951*, ed. Niclas Franzén et al. Vingåcker: Linderoths Tryckeri, 2016.

Lermer, Andrea, and Avinoam Shalem, eds. *After One Hundred Years: The 1910 Exhibition "Meisterwerke muhammedanischer Kunst" reconsidered*. Leiden: Brill, 2010.

Lierl, Karl, and Florian Roder, eds. *Anthroposophie wird Kunst: Der Münchner Kongress 1907 und die Gegenwart*. Munich: Kooperative Dürnau, 2008.

Liljevalchs Konsthall. *Hilma af Klint: Målningarna till templet*. Värnamo: Fälth & Hässler, 2000. Catalogue for an exhibition at Liljevalchs Konsthall.

Lindén, Gurli. *Vägen till templet—Hilma af Klint: Förberedelsetiden, 1896–1906*. Stockholm: h:ström, 1996.

Lindén, Gurli, and Anna-Maria Svensson. *Enheten bortom mångfalden*. Stockholm: Rosengårdens förlag, 1999.

Lindgren, Astrid. *War Diaries, 1939–1945*. Trans. Sarah Death. New Haven: Yale University Press, 2016.

Lindqvist, Sigvard A. "Om Selma Lagerlöfs förhållande till spiritism an teosofi." *Tidskrift för svensk litteraturhistorisk forskning* 81 (1960): 36–74.

Linné, Agneta. "Lutheranism and Democracy: Scandinavia." In *Girls' Secondary Education in the Western World: From the 18th to 20th Century*, ed. James C. Albisetti, Joyce Goodman, and Rebecca Rogers, 133–48. New York: Palgrave Macmillan, 2010.

Lippincott, Louise. *Edvard Munch: Starry Night*. Malibu, CA: Getty Museum Studies on Art, 1988.

Ljungberger, J. Erik. *Blanch's Café, 1868–1918*. Stockholm: Hasse W. Tullberg, 1918.

Loers, Veit, ed. *Okkultismus und Avantgarde: Von Munch bis Mondrian, 1900–1915*. Frankfurt am Main: Edition Tertium GmbH + Co, 1995. Catalogue for an exhibition at Schirn Kunsthalle.

Lomas, David. "The Meaning of 'Life': Hilma af Klint's *The Ten Largest*."

In Almqvist and Belfrage, *Hilma af Klint: The Art of Seeing the Invisible*, 193–210.

———. "Routes/Roots to Abstraction," In Almqvist and Belfrage, *Hilma af Klint: Seeing Is Believing*, 105–16.

London, Jack. *The People of the Abyss*. New York: Grosset & Dunlap, 1907.

Loosli, Carl Albert. *Ferdinand Hodler: Leben, Werk und Nachlass*. Vol. 3. Bern: Suter, 1923.

Loreck, Hanne. "Spiritual Alphabetisation." In Almqvist and Belfrage, *Hilma af Klint: The Art of Seeing the Invisible*, 211–26.

Lundin, Claës. "I museer och bland konstnärer." In *Nya Stockholm*, 472–515. Stockholm: Hugo Gebers, 1890.

———. "Kerstin Cardon." *Idun* 7, no. 15 (1894): 113–14.

———. *Oxygen och Aromasia: Bilder från år 2378*. Stockholm: Jos. Seligmann, 1878.

Madariaga, Isabel de. *Russia in the Age of Catherine the Great*. London: Weidenfeld and Nicolson, 1981.

Marc, Franz. "Geistige Güter." In Kandinsky and Marc, *Almanach "Der Blaue Reiter,"* 21–24.

———. *Schriften*. Cologne: Dumont, 1978.

Martin, Fredrik Robert. *Führer durch F. R. Martins Sammlungen aus dem Orient in der Allgemeinen Kunst- und Industrie-Ausstellung zu Stockholm*. Stockholm: P. Norstedt & Söner, 1897.

———. *The Miniature Painting and Painters of Persia, India and Turkey, from the 8th to the 18th Century*. Vols. 1 and 2. London: B. Quaritch, 1912.

———. *Sett, hört och känt: Skisser från Turkiet, Ryssland, Italien och andra land*. Stockholm: Bonnier, 1933.

Matisse, Henri. "Kunst und Künstler." In *Kunst und Künstler: illustrierte Monatsschrift für bildende Kunst und Kunstgewerbe* 7, no. 8 (1909): 335–47.

———. "Notes of a Painter" (1908). In *Matisse on Art*, by Jack D. Flam. New York: E. P. Dutton, 1978.

Meister, Anna. "Parisflickorna." In Sidén and Meister, *Ljusets magi*, 109–78.

Michalzik, Peter. *1900: Vegetarier, Künstler und Visionäre suchen nach dem neuen Paradies*. Cologne: DuMont, 2018.

Moritzberger, Ludwig. *Das strahlende Metall: Leben und Werk von Marie und Pierre Curie*. Stuttgart: Urachhaus, 1992.

Morrisson, Mark S. *Modern Alchemy: Occultism and the Emergence of Atomic Theory*. New York: Oxford University Press, 2007.

Müller-Westermann, Iris. "Hilma af Klint in Her Time and Now." In Almqvist and Belfrage, *Hilma af Klint: The Art of Seeing the Invisible*, 179–92.

———. Introduction and commentary to Burgin, *Hilma af Klint*.

———. "Paintings for the Future: Hilma af Klint—A Pioneer of Abstraction in Seclusion." In Müller-Westermann and Widoff, *Hilma af Klint*.

Müller-Westermann, Iris, and Milena Høgsberg, eds. *Hilma af Klint: Artist, Researcher, Medium*. Ostfildern: Hatje Cantz, 2020. Catalogue for an exhibition at the Moderna Museet.

Müller-Westermann, Iris, and Jo Widoff, eds. *Hilma af Klint—A Pioneer of Abstraction*. Ostfildern: Hatje Cantz, 2013. Catalogue for an exhibition at the Moderna Museet.

Nauckhoff, Adelaïde. *Ätten af Klint: Anteckningar af skläktpappar*. Stockholm: Centraltryckeriet, 1905.

Nilo, Johannes. "Das Sehen vor und nach dem Kunstwerk." In Bartholl and Martin, *Between the Worlds*, 68–77.

Nochlin, Linda. "Why Have There Been No Great Women Artists?" In *Women, Art, and Power, and Other Essays*, ed. Nochlin, 145–78. Boulder, CO: Westview Press, 1988.

Nordensvan, Georg. *Schwedische Kunst des 19. Jahrhunderts*. Leipzig: Seemann, 1904.

Nordlinder, Eva. "Anna Maria Roos." Svenskt kvinnobiografiskt lexikon. March 8, 2018. https://skbl.se/en/article/AnnaMariaRoos.

Öberg, Malin Pettersson, and Jacek Smolicki, eds. *Ottilia Adelborg: Assembling the World*. Gagnef, Sweden: Gagnef Artist in Residence Program, 2018. http://malinpetterssonoberg.com/wp-content/uploads/2018/12/Ottilia-Adelborg-Assembling-the-World-Print-ready-LOWERRES.pdf.

Oberter, Rachel. "Esoteric Art Confronting the Public Eye: The Abstract Spirit Drawings of Georgiana Houghton." *Victorian Studies* 48 (2006): 221–32.

Olcott, Henry S. *The Buddhist Catechism*. 33rd ed. Adyar: Theosophical Society, 1897.

Opponenternas utställning. *Illustrerad katalog, September–oktober 1885*. Stockholm: Looström & K, 1885.

O'Reilly, Sally, ed. *Hilma af Klint: An Atom in the Universe*. London: Camden Arts Centre, 2006. Exhibition catalogue.

Owen, Alex. *The Darkened Room: Women, Power and Spiritualism in Late Victorian England*. Philadelphia: University of Pennsylvania Press, 1990.

P. F. "Julius Kronberg." *Theosophical Path* 9 (1915): 420.

Pasi, Marco. "Hilma af Klint, Western Esotericism and the Problem of Modern Artistic Creativity." In Almqvist and Belfrage, *Hilma af Klint: The Art of Seeing the Invisible*, 101–16.

Petander, Einar. "Theosophy in Sweden." In Bogdan and Hammer, *Western Esotericism in Scandinavia*, 578–86.

Pfeiffer, Ingrid, and Max Hollein. *Sturm-Frauen: Künstlerinnen der Avantgarde in Berlin, 1910–1932*. Cologne: Wienand, 2015. Catalogue for an exhibition at Schirn Kunsthalle.

Pfisterer, Ulrich. *Kunst-Geburten: Kreativität, Erotik, Körper in der Frühen Neuzeit*. Berlin: Wagenbach, 2014.

Pietikainen, Petteri. *Neurosis and Modernity: The Age of Nervousness in Sweden*. Leiden: Brill, 2007.

Pinheiro Ventre, Luciana. *As Cores da Alma: A Vida de Hilma af Klint*. São Paulo: 300 Editoria, 2018.

———. "Charting the Invisible." In *Hilma af Klint: mundos possíveis*, ed. Jochen Volz, 145–73. São Paulo: Pinacoteca de São Paulo, 2018. Exhibition catalogue.

Prinzing, Friedrich. "Die Entwicklung der Kindersterblichkeit in den europäischen Staaten." *Jahrbücher für Nationalökonomie und Statistik* 72 (1899): 577–635.

Pytlik, Priska. *Spiritismus und Moderne: Ein kulturhistorisches Phänomen und seine Bedeutung für die Literatur*. Paderborn: Schöningh, 2005.

Quaytman, Rebecca H. "Five Paintings of 1907: A Short History Lesson by R. H. Quaytman." In Birnbaum and Noring, *Legacy of Hilma af Klint*.

Raab, Rex. *Edith Maryon: Bildhauerin und Mitarbeiterin Rudolf Steiners*. Dornach: Philosophisch-Anthroposophischer Verlag am Goetheanum, 1993.

Rådström, Anne Marie. *Fröken Ottil: En bok om Ottilia Adelborg, barnens konstnär och en pionjär för folklig kultur*. Falun: Dalarnas museum, 1980.

Raulff, Ulrich. *Das letzte Jahrhundert der Pferde: Geschichte einer Trennung*. Munich: C. H. Beck, 2015.

Rebisse, Christian. *Rosicrucian History and Mysteries*. Crowborough: Rosicrucian Collection, 2003.

Ringbom, Sixten. "Art in the 'Epoch of the Great Spiritual': Occult Elements in the Early Theory of Abstract Painting." *Journal of the Warburg and Courtauld Institutes* 29 (1966): 386–418.

———. "The Sounding Cosmos: A Study in the Spiritualism of Kandinsky and the Genesis of Abstract Painting." *Acta academiae aboensis, ser. A, humaniora, humanistika vetenskaper, socialvetenskaper, teologi* 38, no. 2 (1970).

Rogh, John. "Bertha Valerius." *Idun: Praktisk veckotidning för kvinnan och hemmet* 15, no. 8 (1895): 113–15.

Roob, Alexander. *The Hermetic Museum: Alchemy und Mysticism.* Cologne: Taschen, 2018.

Roos, Anna Maria. "Svenska konstnärinnors utställning I." *Dagny, Tidning för svenska kvinnorörelse, utgifven genom Fredrika-Bremer-förbundet af föreningen Dagny* 4, no. 10 (1911): 123.

Rosenberg, Raphael. "Was There a First Abstract Painter? Af Klint's Amimetic Images and Kandinsky's Abstract Art." In Almqvist and Belfrage, *Hilma af Klint: The Art of Seeing the Invisible,* 87–100.

Rosenberg, Raphael, and Max Hollein, eds. *Turner, Hugo, Moreau: Entdeckung der Abstraktion.* Munich: Hirmer, 2007. Catalogue for an exhibition at Schirn Kunsthalle.

Rosenkrantz, Arild. "Rudolf Steiner's Influence on My Life." *Mercury Arts Journal,* no. 1 (1983).

Rydberg, Viktor. *Singoalla: A Medieval Legend.* Trans. Joseph Fredbärj. London: Walter Scott, 1904.

Sandal, Christine. "Gränslös mediering: Tidskriften *Efteråt* och andekommunikation, 1892–1920." *Mediehistorisk Årsbok* (2020): 123–37.

Schjeldahl, Peter. "Hilma af Klints Visionary Paintings." *New Yorker,* October 15, 2018. https://www.newyorker.com/magazine/2018/10/22/hilma-af-klints-visionary-paintings.

Schneede, Uwe M., ed. *Vor der Zeit: Carl Fredrik Hill, Ernst Josephson, zwei Künstler des späten 19. Jahrhunderts.* Berlin: Frölich und Kaufmann, 1984. Catalogue for an exhibition at the Kunstverein in Hamburg.

Schneider, Bernhard. "Marienerscheinungen im 19. Jahrhundert: Ein Phänomen und seine Charakteristika." In Wolf, *"Wahre" und "falsche" Heiligkeit,* 87–110.

Shalem, Avinoam. "The 1910 Exhibition 'Meisterwerke muhammedanischer Kunst' Revisited." In Lermer and Shalem, *After One Hundred Years,* 3–16.

Sidén, Karin, and Anna Meister, eds. *Ljusets magi: Friluftsmåleri från sent 1800-tal.* Stockholm: Prins Eugens Waldemarsudde, 2016. Exhibition catalogue.

Smith, Roberta. "'Hilma Who?' No More: A Landmark Exhibition Explores a Swedish Pioneer of Modernist Abstraction." *New York Times,* October 11, 2018, C 15/20.

Sommer, Andreas. "From Astronomy to Transcendental Darwinism: Carl du Prel (1839–1899)." *Journal of Scientific Exploration* 23, no. 1 (2009): 59–68.

Stamm, Rainer. "Zwei Magische Orte der Moderne: Ida Gerhardi an der Académie Colarossi und in der Rue de la Grande Chaumière." In *Ida Gerhardi—Deutsche Künstlerinnen in Paris um 1900*, ed. Susanne Conzen, 49–61. Munich: Hirmer, 2012. Catalogue for an exhibition at the Städtische Galerie Lüdenscheid.

Steiner, Rudolf. "Colour and the Human Races." Lecture given in Dornach, Switzerland, March 3, 1923. In *The Workmen Lectures*, trans. M. Cotterell. New York: Anthroposophic Press, 1969; Rudolf Steiner Archive & e.Lib, 2016. https://wn.rsarchive.org/Lectures/GA349/English /UNK1969/19230303v01.html.

———. *Erfahrungen des Übersinnlichen: Die drei Wege der Seele zu Christus*. Ed. Rudolf-Steiner-Nachlaßverwaltung. Rudolf Steiner Gesamtausgabe 143. 14th ed. 1912; Dornach: Rudolf Steiner Verlag, 1994.

———. *Knowledge of the Higher Worlds and Its Attainment*. Trans. George Metaxa, with revisions by Henry B. Monges and Lisa D. Monges. Hudson, NY: Anthroposophic Press, 1947. https://www.google.com /books/edition/Knowledge_of_Higher_Worlds_and_Its_Attai /MzjqDvsZEPIC?hl=en&gbpv=0.

———. "The Nature of the Bhagavad Gita and the Significance of the Epistles of St. Paul. How the Christ Impulse Surpasses the Krishna Impulse." Lecture given in Cologne, Germany, December 31, 1912. In *The Bhagavad Gita and the Epistles of St. Paul*, trans. Lisa D. Monges and Doris M. Bugbey. New York: Anthroposophic Press, 1971; Rudolf Steiner Archive & e.Lib, 2001. https://wn.rsarchive.org/Religion /GA142/English/AP1971/19121231p01.html.

———. "The Spirits of Form as Rulers of Earthly Existence." Lecture given in Stuttgart, August 10, 1908. In *Universe, Earth, and Man: In Their Relationship to Modern Myths and Egyptian Civilization: Eleven Lectures Given in Stuttgart between 4 and 16 August 1908*. London: Rudolf Steiner Press, 1987. https://www.google.com/books/edition/Universe _Earth_and_Man/oZr-X7BwOXQC?hl=en&gbpv=0.

———. "Spiritual Knowledge Is a True Communion: The Beginning of a Cosmic Ritual Suitable for the Present Age." Lecture given in Dornach, Switzerland, December 31, 1922. Trans. Eva Knausenberger. Ed. Marsha Post. In *Reverse Ritual: Spiritual Knowledge Is True Communion*, by Rudolf Steiner and Friedrich Benesch, 59–76. Great Barrington, MA: Anthroposophic Press, 2001. https://books.google.de/books?id=

RszJMsyFmKgC&pg=PR3&hl=de&source=gbs_selected_pages&cad=2 #v=onepage&q&f=false.

Steiner, Rudolf, and Marie Steiner-von Sivers. *Correspondence and Documents*. Trans. Christian von Arnim and Ingrid von Arnim. London: Rudolf Steiner Press, 1988.

Steiner-von Sivers, Marie. "In Memoriam P. Kloppers-Moltzer." *Goetheanum* 7, no. 17 (April 27, 1930).

Stiftung Deutsches Historisches Museum, ed. *Der Luthereffekt: 500 Jahre Protestantismus in der Welt*. Munich: Hirmer, 2017.

Stockenström, Göran. "Crisis and Change: Strindberg the Unconscious Modernist." In *The Cambridge Companion to August Strindberg*, ed. Michael Robinson, 79–92. Cambridge: Cambridge University Press, 2009.

Subskriptionsprospekt zum *Almanach "Der Blaue Reiter."* Munich: Piper, 1912. https://de.wikipedia.org/wiki/Der_Blaue_Reiter#/media/Datei: Subskriptionsprospekt_zum_Almanach_Der_Blaue_Reiter,_1912.jpg.

Sundberg, Martin. "Konsthallen på Baltiska utställningen." In *Baltiska speglingar: Malmö Kunstmuseums samling: Tiden kring Baltiska utställningen 1914*, ed. Cecilia Widenheim and Martin Sundberg, 16–38. Lund: Arena, 2014.

Svensson, Anna-Maria. "Mellan abstraktion och esoterism." In *Enheten bortom mångfalden: två perspektiv på Hilma af Klints verk*, ed. Anna-Maria Svensson and Gurli Lindén. Stockholm: Rosengårdens förlag, 1999.

Swedenborg, Emanuel. *Die Wonnen der Weisheit betreffend die eheliche Liebe, dann die Wollüste der Torheit betreffend die buhlerische Liebe*. Tübingen: Verlag Expedition,1845.

Tångeberg, Peter. *Mittelalterliche Holzskulpturen und Altarschreine in Schweden*. Stockholm: Almqvist & Wiksell, 1986.

Teosofiska Samfundet/Theosophical Society, ed. *Katalog konstutställning i samband med teosofiska samfundets europeiska sektioners 7: de kongress i Stockholm 1913/Catalogue Art Exhibition in Connection with the Seventh Congress of the Federated National Societies in Europe of the Theosophical Society*. Stockholm: Wilhelmssons boktryckeri, 1913. Exhibition catalogue.

Tillberg, Margareta. "Kandinsky in Sweden—Malmö 1914 and Stockholm 1916." In van den Berg, Hautamäki, and Hjärtason, *Cultural History of the Avant-Garde in the Nordic Countries*, 325–336.

Treitel, Corinna. *A Science for the Soul: Occultism and the Genesis of the German Modern*. Baltimore: Johns Hopkins University Press, 2000.

Tuchman, Maurice, ed. *The Spiritual in Art: Abstract Painting, 1890–1985*. New York: Abbeville, 1986. Catalogue for an exhibition at the Los Angeles County Museum of Art.

Tucholsky, Kurt. *Schloß Gripsholm: Eine Sommergeschichte*. 5th ed. Frankfurt am Main: S. Fischer Verlag, 2018.

Tuchtenhagen, Ralph. *Eine kleine Geschichte Schwedens*. Munich: C. H. Beck, 2008.

van den Berg, Hubert, Irmeli Hautamäki, and Benedikt Hjärtason, eds. *A Cultural History of the Avant-Garde in the Nordic Countries, 1900–1925*. Amsterdam: Rodopi, 2012.

Vasold, Manfred. *Rudolf Virchow, der große Arzt und Politiker*. Frankfurt am Main: S. Fischer Verlag, 2015.

Vennerholm, John. *Grunddragen af hästens operativa speciella kirurgi*. Stockholm: Norstedts, 1901.

Voit, Antonia, ed. *Ab nach München! Künstlerinnen um 1900*. Munich: Süddeutsche Zeitung Edition, 2014. Catalogue for an exhibition at the Münchner Stadtmuseum.

Volz, Jochen, ed. *Hilma af Klint: mundos possíveis*. São Paulo: Pinacoteca de São Paulo, 2018.

von Bergen, Carl. "Huldine Beamish." *Idun*, no. 3, 1893, 1–3, https://gupea .ub.gu.se/bitstream/2077/49346/1/gupea_2077_49346_1.pdf.

Voss, Julia. "At male det åndelige: Hvaf Arild Rosenkrantz laerte af Rudolf Steiner." In *Baron Rosenkrantz: Farvernes Mystik*, 59–70. Catalogue for an exhibition at the Arken Museum for Modern Art. Ishøj, Denmark: Arken, 2020.

———. *Darwins Bilder: Ansichten der Evolutionstheorie, 1837–1874*. Frankfurt am Main: S. Fischer Verlag, 2009.

———. "Hilma af Klint and the Evolution of Art." In *Hilma af Klint: Painting the Unseen*, ed. Julia Peyton-Jones and Hans Ulrich Obrist, 21–36. London: Koenig Books, 2016. Catalogue for an exhibition at the Serpentine Gallery.

———. "Die Kunstgeschichte muss umgeschrieben werden." *Frankfurter Allgemeine Zeitung*, February 24, 2013.

———. "Die Thronstürmerin." *Frankfurter Allgemeine Zeitung*, April 16, 2011.

———. "The Traveling Hilma af Klint." In Bashkoff, *Hilma af Klint*, 49–63.

———. "Was die Geschichte fast vergessen hätte. Endlich: Das Moderna Museet in Stockholm kauft systematisch Kunst von Frauen." *Frankfurter Allgemeine Zeitung*, April 8, 2008.

———. "Wellen, Vibrationen, Schwingungen: Die andere Geschichte der

Abstraktion." In *Blauer Reiter: Das Moment der Abstraktion*, edited for the Franz Marc Gesellschaft by Cathrin Klingsöhr-Leroy. Munich: Hirmer, 2019.

Wahlström, Filip. *Sanningen om Filip—minnesbilder av Filip Wahlström*. Göteborg: Rundqvists Bokförlag, 1965.

Watts, Anna Mary Howitt. *Pioneers of the Spiritual Reformation: Biographical Sketches*. London: Psychological Press, 1883.

Webb, James. *Die Flucht vor der Vernunft: Politik, Kultur und Okkultismus im 19. Jahrhundert*. Wiesbaden: Marixverlag, 2009.

Wegman, J. "Konferenz für Geisteswissenschaft Rudolf Steiners hat vom 20. Juli bis zum 1. August in London getagt." *Das Goetheanum* (1928): 131.

Weininger, Otto. *Sex and Character*. 6th ed. London: William Heinemann, 1906. https://www.google.com/books/edition/Sex_Character /XrysvMtsAVwC?hl=en&gbpv=0.

Weinstein, Arnold. *Northern Arts: The Breakthrough of Scandinavian Literature and Art, from Ibsen to Bergman*. Princeton: Princeton University Press, 2008.

Wennberg-Hilger, Kajsa Katharina. "Das seuchenhafte Auftreten von Lepra in einigen Küstenregionen Westnorwegens im 19. Jahrhundert mit einem ergänzenden Bericht über die entsprechende Situation in Schweden." Dissertation, Friedrich-Wilhelms-Universität Bonn, 2011. http://hss.ulb.uni-bonn.de/2011/2659/2659.

Werenskiold, Marit. "Concepts of Expressionism in Scandinavia." In *Expressionism Reassessed*, ed. Shulamith Behr, David Fanning, and Douglas Jarman, 20–29. Manchester: Manchester University Press, 1993.

Westholm, Alfred. *Frank Heyman*. Göteborg: Rundqvists boktryckeri, 1951. Catalogue for an exhibition at Göteborgs Konstmuseum.

Wettlaufer, Alexandra. "The Politics and Poetics of Sisterhood: Anna Mary Howitt's *The Sisters in Art*." *Victorian Review* 36, no. 1 (Spring 2010): 129–46.

Whitlock, Anna. *Skolans Ställning till Religionsundervisningen i Sverige och andra länder*. Stockholm: Albert Bonniers Förlag, 1888. https://sv.wikisource.org/wiki/Skolans_st%C3%A4llning_till _religionsundervisnin- gen/De_protestantiska_l%C3 %A4nderna. Last accessed November 18, 2019.

Widenheim, Cecilia, and Martin Sundberg, eds. *Baltiska speglingar. Malmö Kunstmuseums samling. Tiden kring Baltiska utställningen 1914*. Lund: Arena, 2014. Exhibition catalogue.

Wilamowitz-Moellendorff, Fanny, Gräfin von. *Carin Göring*. With an afterword by Martin H. Sommerfeldt. Berlin: Warneck, 1934.

Wittgenstein, Ludwig. *Tractatus Logico-Philosophicus*. Trans. C. K. Ogden. London: Routledge, 1997.

Wolandt, Holger, ed. *Selma Lagerlöf: Liebe Sophie, liebe Valborg—Eine Dreiecks-Geschichte in Briefen*. Trans. Lotta Rüegger und Holger Wolandt. Stuttgart: Urachhaus, 2016.

———. *Värmland und die Welt: eine Biografie*. Stuttgart: Urachhaus, 2015.

Wolf, Hubert. *Die Nonnen von Sant'Ambrogio: Eine wahre Geschichte*. Munich: C. H. Beck, 2013.

———. *"Wahre" und "falsche" Heiligkeit: Mystik, Macht und Geschlechterrollen im Katholizismus des 19. Jahrhunderts*. Munich: Oldenbourg, 2013.

Wollstonecraft, Mary. *Letters Written during a Short Residence in Sweden, Norway, and Denmark*. London: Cassel & Company, 1889. Reproduction of the original. Frankfurt am Main: Outlook Verlag, 2018. Page references are to the 2018 edition. https:// books.google.de/books?id=S5RDwAAQBAJ&pg=PP2&dq=mary +wollstonecraft+letters+written+sweden&hl=en&sa=X&ved= 2ahUKEwj4r8nmnNDtAhXTQkEAHTK1CAcQ6AEwAXoECAEQAg#v =onepage&q&f=false.

Woolf, Virginia. *Orlando: A Biography*. London: Hogarth Press, 1928.

———. *A Room of One's Own*. London: Hogarth Press, 1935.

"The World Conference of Spiritual Science." *Anthroposophy: A Quarterly Journal of Spiritual Science* 3, no. 3 (1928): 383–90.

Wörwag, Barbara, ed. *Wassily Kandinsky: Briefe an Will Grohmann*. With the assistance of Annegret Hoberg. Munich: Hirmer, 2015.

Yule, Henry. *The Book of Ser Marco Polo*. Vol. 1. London: Murray, 1875.

Zander, Helmut. *Anthroposophie in Deutschland: Theosophische Weltanschauung und gesellschaftliche Praxis*. Vols. 1 und 2. Göttingen: Vandenhoeck & Ruprecht, 2007.

———. "Theosophy, Anthroposophy, Rudolf Steiner and the Zeitgeist of Historicism around 1900." In Almqvist and Belfrage, *Hilma af Klint: The Art of Seeing the Invisible*, 73–86.

Zegher, Catherine de, ed. *3 x Abstraction: Hilma af Klint, Emma Kunz and Agnes Martin*. New Haven: Yale University Press, 2005. Catalogue for an exhibition at the Drawing Center.

Zimmerman, Bonnie. *Lesbian Histories and Cultures*. Vol. 1. New York: Routledge, 2000.

Zumdick, Wolfgang. "Finding the Inner Form: Pathways to Hilma af

Klint's Change from Outer to Inner Experience." In Almqvist and Belfrage, *Hilma af Klint: The Art of Seeing the Invisible*, 243–54.

Zwerdling, Michael. *Postcards of Nursing: A Worldwide Tribute*. Philadelphia: Lippincott, Williams, and Wilkins, 2003.

Index

Abbe, Ernst, 47
Adelborg, Ottilia, 110–11, 132–33, 171, 316, 349n14
Albers, Anni, 287
Albers, Josef, 208, 287
Anderson, Thomasine, xiii–xv, 9, 214–18, *216*, 223, 225–30, 232, 234–38, 240–41, 244, 247, 255, 262, 270–71, 276, 287, 291, 300, 303, 307, 313–14, 355n16
Andersson, Magdalena Augusta "Gusten," 115–16, 132, 145–47, 149–53, 163–66, 172, 178, 181, 213–14, 217–18, 290–91, 358n18, 362n2
Andreevskaya, Nina, 206
Ångström, Knut, xii, 120, 168
Apuleius, 137
Arnell, Alma, 140, 145, 355n16
Avenarius, Ferdinand, 160, 289

Bahr, Eva von, 168
Barr, Alfred H., Jr., 288–90
Baudelaire, Charles, 76
Bauer, Rudolf, 265
Beamish, Huldine, 38, 56–59, 68, 73, 80–82, 84, 87, 89, 100, 279, 336–37n2, 337n4, 337n8
Becquerel, Henri, 119
Behm, Carl, 52
Bell, Alexander Graham, 47
Bergen, Carl von, 81, 341n13
Bergh, Richard, 72, 78–80, *79*, 95
Besant, Annie, 86, 93, *94*, 129–30, 182, 184, 186, 188, 265, 289, 316, 333n18, 344n29, *plate 18*
Beskow, Elsa, 172
Beskow, Natanael, 172
Bierfreund, Theodor, 115, 142, 316

Bildt, Harald, 98
Bingen, Hildegard von, 274, 299
Björkquist, Manfred, 296–99
Blake, William, 31
Blanch, Theodor, xii, 66, 68, 71–73, 82, 88, 103, 111, 140, 338n13, 340n3
Blavatsky, Helena Petrovna, 32–33, 39, 83, 87–88, 93, 96, 107, 116, 123, 138, 144, 148, 173, 198–200, 265, 280, 301, 316, 334n12, 341n13, 361n4
Blommestein, Louise van, 240–41
Boberg, Anna, 184
Boberg, Ferdinand, 184
Böcklin, Arnold, 75
Böhme, Jakob, 153
Borch, Gerard ter, 243
Brahe, Tycho, 261–62, 264, 323
Branting, Hjalmar, 233
Bremer, Fredrika, 24, 40
Bridget of Sweden (saint), 274, 299, 372–73n7
Busch, Charlotte, 87
Busch, Oscar, 68, 87, 339n23, 343n16

Cardon, Kerstin, xi, 42–44, 51, 63, 78, 162, 171, 335n2
Carlson, Mina, 167
Carlsson, Greta, 179
Cassel, Anna Maria Augusta, xi–xv, 9, 58, 63–69, 71, 82, 84, 87–89, 91, 102–9, *106*, 113–18, 123–24, 130, 132, 134–35, 138–39, 143, 145–46, 153, 162, 165–66, 168–69, 171–72, 174, 179–81, *180*, 184–86, 192, 213–14, 217, 225, 247, 270–71, 290–92, 300, 305, 307, 356n6, 358n18, 371–72n11, *plate 11*
Cassel, Lotten, 68, 82, 162
Catherine II ("the Great"), 127

Cederberg, Cornelia, xi, 87–91, 109, 117, 125, 130, 145–46, 148, 166, 175, 348n6, 348–49n7
Churchill, Winston, 252
Crookes, William, 199
Crosland, Camilla Dufour, 40–41, 44, 305–6
Curie, Marie, 119–20, 128, 167, 168, 211
Curie, Pierre, 119–20, 128–29, 134, 211

da Gama, Vasco, 255
Darwin, Charles, 47, 83, 91–92, 107, 277
Dickerman, Leah, 3
Doré, Gustave, 75, 317
Dou, Gerard, 243
Dunlop, Daniel Nicol, 249
du Prel, Carl, 80, 116, 272–74, 277, 295, 317, 341n8, 372n3
Dürer, Albrecht, 201
Duyn, Else van. See Kloppers-Moltzer, Peggy
Dyck, Anthony van, 119, 243

Ebert, Friedrich, 233
Edison, Thomas Alva, 47
El Greco, 243
Elizabeth of Hungary (saint), 179
Escher, M. C., 243
Eugen, Prince, 72, 111, 184, 194, 204

Fant, Åke, 6
Fidus, 184
Fitinghoff, Laura, 110
Fludd, Robert, 100, 181
Fock, Huldine, 82, 84
Franco, Francisco, 269

Gadelius, Bror, 202–3, 205
Giertta, Emilia, 175–76, 181, 213, 214, 247, 270–71, 302, 355n16, 358n18
Giotto, 142
Goebbels, Joseph, 278–79
Goethe, Johann Wolfgang von, 154–55, 223, 235, 251, 317
Göring, Carin, 279–80
Göring, Hermann, 278–80, 282
Gounod, Charles, 130, plate 18
Gregory VII (pope), 85

Gropius, Walter, 239–40
Grosz, George, 287
Grünewald, Isaac, 161–62, 167–68, 170–71, 203–4, 277
Guggenheim, Solomon R., 264–66
Gummeson, Karl, 203–6, 209–11
Gustaf V (Crown Prince Gustaf), 95, 255, 282
Gustav II Adolf, 55
Gustav III, 16, 35, 73, 95, 127, 213

Haakon VII, 293
Haeckel, Ernst, 107, 131–32, 143
Haglund, Robert Ludvig, 113
Hällström, Valborg, 69–70
Harima, Ilona, 263
Hartmann, Franz, 102, 116
Hauffe, Friederike, 273–74, 372n4
Haverman, Ida. See Klint, Ida af (sister of Hilma)
Haverman, Knut Victor, 344n3
Hazelius, Artur, 349n13
Hedin, Sven, 44
Hedman, Sigrid, xi, 86–87, 90, 99–100, 109–10, 125, 145, 148, 152, 166, 175, 342n1
Heindel, Max, 271
Helleday, Dr., 77–78, 84
Hellerström, Alfred, 262
Henslow, George, 91–92, 334n18
Henslow, John Stevens, 91
Henström, Sigrid, 213–14, 218, 355n16
Heppe, B. C., 62
Heyman, Frank, 158–59, 159, 161, 172–75, 354n20, 364n6
Hildebrand, Adolf, 174
Himmler, Heinrich, 281
Hitler, Adolf, 243, 278–79, 282, 286–87
Hjertén, Sigrid, 162, 170–71, 204, 257, 277
Hodler, Ferdinand, 75, 97
Holbein, Hans, 72, 235
Hoogstraten, Samuel van, 243
Houghton, Georgiana, 27–34, 39–41, 47–48, 305, plate 8
Houghton, Zilla, 28
Howitt, Anna Mary, 40–41, 305, 334nn19–21, plate 9, plate 10

Hunt, William Holman, 28

Jolin, Ellen, 167
Josephson, Ernst, 66–68, *67*, 72, 79, 88, 161
Judge, William Quan, 32

Kandinsky, Wassily, xiii, 1, 2, 97, 130, 161, 171, 195–96, *196*, 202–6, 209–11, 243, 265–66, 288–90, 304, 306
Kant, Immanuel, 37
Karadja, Mary, 280
Karadja Pasha, Jean Constantin, 280
Kepler, Johannes, 261
Kerner, Justinus, 274
Key, Ellen, 43, 111
Khnopff, Fernand, 74–75
Kleen, Tyra, xv, 76–77, 184–85, 290, 292–99, 301, 305, 318, 340n18
Klint, Anna af (sister of Hilma), 15, 45
Klint, Erik af (great-grandfather of Hilma), 15–17, 95, 127
Klint, Erik Viktor Philip Gustafsson af (nephew of Hilma), xv, 4, 21, 36, 46–47, 55–56, 111–12, 269–70, 286, 291, 300, 302–4, 307, 333n2, 354n13, 371n4
Klint, Gustaf af (brother of Hilma), 15, 24, 45, 95, 112, 162, 176, 215, 228
Klint, Gustaf af (grandfather of Hilma), 15–17, *16*, 22, 95, 99, 127, 141, 262, 303
Klint, Gustaf af (grandnephew of Hilma), 4
Klint, Hedvig af (cousin of Hilma), xv, 299–300, 314
Klint, Hermina af (sister of Hilma), xvi, 15, 23, 45–47, 73, 102, 256, 303
Klint, Hilma af: in the Association of Swedish Women Artists, xii, 167–71, 194–95, 291, 293; childhood and youth, xi, 15–26, 33, 45–46; family history, 15–18, 99, 127, 141; first experience with mediumship, 21; and The Five, xi, xii, 84–93, 99–102, 109–10, 112, 117–18, 123–25, 130–32, 134, 138–39, 145–49, 152–53, 163–66, 201, 208, 224, 342n1; last years and

afterlife, 1–5, 62, 284–308; meetings with Rudolf Steiner, xii, 7, 154–58, 234, 238; photographs of, *17*, *25*, *54*, *98*, *176*; studies at painting school and Royal Academy, xi, 33, 41–42, 51–55, 60–63, 77; studio on Munsö, xv, 139, 207, 212–13, 232, 262, 285, 294, 301, 302; and The Thirteen, xii, 166, 175–78, 181, 201, 208, 214–15, 217–18; trip to Amsterdam, xiv, 240–44; trip to Italy, xii, 113–18, 142; trip to London, xiv, 247–52, 291; veterinary medicine, experience with, xi–xii, 102–9; visits to the Goetheanum, 228–37, 252; World War I, 194, 197, 199, 201–3, 214–17; World War II, 269, 293, 296, 303
Klint, Hilma af, series: *Atom*, xiii, 8, 211, *plate 38*; *The Dove*, xiii, 198, 201, 213, 225, *plate 34*, *plate 35*; *Eros*, xii, 137–38, 141, 157, 213, *plate 24*; *Evolution*, xii, 8, 154, 155, 157, 213, *plate 27*, *plate 28*; *Group VIII, Series US*, 191–92, *plate 31*; *The Large Figure Paintings*, xii, 140, 149–52, *150*, *151*, 157, 213; *A Male Series*, 200–201, 213; *Paintings for the Temple*, xii–xv, 18, 202, 207, 225, 232, 250, 260, 264, 290; *Parsifal*, xiii, 207–8, *209*, *plate 37*; *Preliminary Works*, 134, 365n6; *Preparatory Studies*, xii, 175, 177; *Primordial Chaos*, xii, 133–37, 141, 157, 163, 173, 212, 213, 225, 234, *plates 19–23*; *The Swan*, xiii, 197–200, 213, *plate 32*, *plate 33*; *The Ten Largest*, xii, 142–49, 163, 174, 207, 212, 225, 234, 260, *plates 2–5*, *plate 7*, *plate 26*; *Tree of Knowledge*, xiii, xiv, 6–7, 181, 187–89, 198–99, 202, 211, 241, 368n4, *plate 29*, *plate 30*
Klint, Ida af (sister of Hilma), 15, *17*, 23–24, 45, 95, 128, 162, 168, 215, 218, 228, 291, 300, 332n9, 344n3, 349n1, 364n1
Klint, Johan af (grandnephew of Hilma), 4, 304
Klint, Mathilda af (mother of Hilma), xi–xiii, 15, *17*, 26, 59, 60, 110, 127,

Klint, Mathilda af (cont.)
162–63, 169–70, 189, 214–15, 218, *219*, 228, 313
Klint, Ulla af (wife of Erik Viktor af Klint), 270, 285, 371n4
Klint, Ulrika af (great-grandniece of Hilma), 4
Klint, Victor af (father of Hilma), xi, 15, *16*, 17–18, 26, 46, 68, 95, 102, 110, 134
Kloppers-Moltzer, Peggy, 241–47, 251–52, 293
Knaffl-Granström, Edith, 292, 305
Koch, Robert, 104, 108
Krafft-Ebing, Richard von, 84
Kramer, Hilton, 2
Kraus, Karl, 119
Kronberg, Julius, 137–38, 182, *183*, 184
Kupka, František, 1, 2, 290, 306

Lagerlöf, Selma, 43, 87, 115, 167, 197, 343n16
Lancén, Sigrid, 112, 163–66, 189–92, 194, 201, 313
Larsson, Carl, 44–46, 52, 63, 66, 72, 87, 98, 161, 170–71, 184, 194
Laserstein, Lotte, 286–87
Lateau, Louise, 274
Leadbeater, Charles, 87, 123, 125–26, *126*, 129–30, 202, 289, 316, 343n14, 344n29, *plate 18*
Léger, Fernand, 266
Leibl, Wilhelm, 196
Leonardo da Vinci, 114
Liljefors, Bruno, 194
Linnaeus, Carl, 35–36
London, Jack, 173–74, 233, 318
Lumière, Auguste Marie Louis Nicolas, 95
Lumière, Louis Jean, 95
Lundell, Johan August, xii, 168–69
Lundin, Claës, 43–44, 335n5
Luther, Martin, 101, 115, 345n4

Mach, Ernst, 119
Malevich, Kazimir, 1, 2, 290
Manet, Édouard, 42
Marc, Franz, 97, 171, 203, 205, 243, 289
Martin, Fredrik Robert, 96–98, 144

Maryon, Edith, 230–31, 245
Matisse, Henri, 97, 161, 167, 170
Maxwell, James Clerk, 47
Mazzolino, Ludovico, 116, *plate 16, plate 17*
Medici, Giuliano di Lorenzo de', 113
Medici, Lorenzo di Piero de', 113
Mendel, Gregor, 234
Mesquita, Samuel Jessurun de, 242–43, 296
Michelangelo, 72, 74, 113
Mondrian, Piet, 1, 2, 240, 290, 306
Monet, Claude, 42
Montagna, Bartolomeo, 243
Moreau, Gustave, 75
Morssing, Ise, 170
Munch, Edvard, 48, 73, 97, 137–38, 167
Münter, Gabriele, 97, 171, 203–4, 206
Munthe, Axel, 255

Nauckhoff, Adelaïde, 45
Neumann, Israel Ber, 288–89
Nietzsche, Friedrich, 318
Nilsson, Mathilda, xi, 86–87, 90, 102, 125, 130, 145, 148, 166, 175, 343n11
Nochlin, Linda, 14
Nordenskiöld, Adolf Erik, 53
Nordlander, Anna, 44
Notke, Bernt, 19–20, *20*

Olander, Valborg, 115
Olcott, Henry Steel, 32, 126
Oscar II, 34, 38, 42, 80, 95, 111, 127, 334n14

Panofsky, Erwin, 287
Péladan, Joséphin, 75–76, 101, 292
Petri, Julius Richard, 108
Pfeiff, Victor, 102
Plato, 82–83

Quaytman, Rebecca H., 6

Raphael, 114, 137
Ravel, Maurice, 216–17
Rebay, Hilla von, 264–68, *267*, 287–88, 290, 306
Remarque, Erich Maria, 271, 278, 319

Rembrandt, 72, 97, 235, 243, 340n9
Ringbom, Sixten, 304, 377n3
Rodenbach, Georges, 74–75
Roerich, Nicolas, 195, 205
Rönquist, Lotten, 135, 140, 145, 192,
    355n16
Röntgen, Wilhelm Conrad, 112, 129
Rose, Traute, 286
Rosen, Georg von, 52–53, 68, 71, 336n10
Rosenkrantz, Arild, 231, 250
Rosenkreuz, Frater Christian, 101,
    345n4
Roslund, Nell, 203
Rubens, Peter Paul, 61, 235
Rudolf II, 261
Russell, Bertrand, 244
Rydberg, Viktor, 68–69, 192–93, 294,
    339n24, 360n2

Schäffner, Katharine, 160–61, *160*, 289
Schjerfbeck, Helene, 60
Scholander, Karin, 184
Schulzenheim, Ida von, 167, 170
Sivers, Marie von, 154, 186, 252
Steffen, Albert, 240–41, 249, 319
Steiner, Marie. *See* Sivers, Marie von
Steiner, Rudolf, xii–xv, 7, 154–59, 161,
    172–74, 178, 186–88, 198, 217, 223–25,
    230–40, 242, 245–46, 249–52, 256,
    258, 265, 271–72, 277, 280–81, 284,
    294–96, 316–23, 353n7, 354n13,
    372n1, 374n4
Strakosch-Giesler, Maria, 240
Strindberg, August, 73, 80, 88, 119–20
Sundström, Olof, 301–2, 304, 307, 329
Swedenborg, Emanuel, 37, 318

Thomsen, Martinus, 263
Tingley, Katherine, 182, 184, 186
Titian, 28, 61
Tolstoy, Leo, 80
Tuchman, Maurice, 304
Tucholsky, Kurt, 38

Valerius, Bertha, xi, 33–43, 53, 56–57,
    58, 59, 68–70, 78, 81, 84–86, 90–93,
    92, 116, 125, 171, 305, 333n2, 336–
    37n2

Vallotton, Félix, 75
Vasari, Giorgio, 61
Vennerholm, John, xii, 103–9, 112, 323
Verlaine, Paul, 76
Victoria, Queen, 27, 30
Victoria of Baden (queen of Sweden),
    255
Virchow, Rudolf, 104, 117
Voltaire, 35–36
Vreede, Elisabeth, 249

Wachsmuth, Günther, 249, 323
Wagner, Richard, 130, 207–8
Wahlström, Charlotte, 169–70, 184
Walden, Herwarth, 203, 265
Wallace, Alfred Russel, 107
Watts, Anna Mary Howitt. *See* Howitt,
    Anna Mary
Weininger, Otto, 118–20
Whitlock, Anna, 24–26, 71
Wilamowitz-Moellendorff, Fanny Grä-
    fin von, 280
Wittgenstein, Ludwig, 244
Wittgenstein, Paul, 216–17
Wollstonecraft, Mary, 13–14
Woolf, Virginia, 251
Wright, Frank Lloyd, 8, 242, 266–67,
    306

Yule, Henry, 32–33, 39

Zander, Gustav, 82
Zeylmans, Frederik Willem, 246
Zorn, Anders, 72, 87, 97, 161, 184, 194,
    196, 318, 323